THE ROU

London
Restaurants

2003 EDITION

There are more than two hundred Rough Guide
travel, phrasebook and music titles, covering
destinations from Amsterdam to Zimbabwe,
languages from Czech to Vietnamese, and musics
from World to Opera and Jazz

Rough Guides on the Internet

www.roughguides.com

Rough Guide Credits

Text editor: James McConnachie **Series editor**: Mark Ellingham
Production: Andy Turner, Ed Wright
Photography: Giles Stokoe, James McConnachie
Proofreader: John Sturges

Publishing Information

This fifth edition published October 2002 by
Rough Guides, 80 Strand, London WC2R ORL

Distributed by the Penguin Group

Penguin Books Ltd, 27 Wrights Lane, London W8 5TZ
Penguin Putnam, Inc., 375 Hudson Street, New York 10014, USA
Penguin Books Australia Ltd, 487 Maroondah Highway,
PO Box 257, Ringwood, Victoria 3134, Australia
Penguin Books Canada Ltd, 10 Alcorn Avenue,
Toronto, Ontario, Canada M4V 1E4
Penguin Books (NZ) Ltd, 182–190 Wairau Road,
Auckland 10, New Zealand

Typeset in Bembo and Helvetica to an original design by Henry Iles.
Printed in Spain by Graphy Cems.

©Charles Campion, 2002 544pp includes index
A catalogue record for this book is available from the British Library.
ISBN 1-85828-909-2

THE ROUGH GUIDE TO

London
Restaurants

2003 EDITION

Written and edited by

Charles Campion

Additional research and reviews

George Theo, Margaret Clancy, Jan Leary, John Edwards

About Rough Guides

Rough Guides have always set out to do something different. Our first book, published in 1982, was written by Mark Ellingham. Just out of university, travelling in Greece, he took along the popular guides of the day but found they were all lacking in some way. They were either strong on ruins and museums but went on for pages without mentioning a beach or taverna, or were so conscious of the need to save money that they lost sight of Greece's cultural and historical significance. Also, none of the books told him anything about Greece's contemporary life – its politics, its culture, its people and how they lived.

So, with no job in prospect, Mark decided to write his own guidebook, one which aimed to provide practical information that was second to none, detailing the best beaches and the hottest clubs and restaurants, alongside interesting accounts of sights both famous and obscure, and up-to-the-minute information on contemporary culture. It was a guide that encouraged independent travellers to find the best of Greece, and was an immediate success, getting shortlisted for the Thomas Cook travel guide award, and encouraging Mark and a few friends to expand the series.

The Rough Guide list grew rapidly and the letters flooded in, indicating a much broader readership than anticipated, but one which uniformly appreciated the Rough Guide mix of practical detail and humour, irreverence and enthusiasm. Things haven't changed. The same writers who began the series are still the caretakers of the Rough Guide mission today: to provide the most reliable, up-to-date and entertaining information to independent-minded travellers of all ages, on all budgets.

Rough Guides now publish more than two hundred titles, written and researched by a dedicated team based in Britain, Europe, the USA and Australia. We have also created a unique series of phrasebooks, along with an acclaimed series of music guides, and a best-selling pocket guide to the internet. We also publish comprehensive travel information on our Web site: www.roughguides.com

About the Author

Charles Campion is an award-winning food writer and restaurant reviewer. He writes a restaurant column for the *London Evening Standard*, which won him the Glenfiddich "Restaurant Writer of the Year" award, and contributes to radio and TV food programmes, as well as a variety of magazines including *Bon Appetit* in the USA. His most recent book publication was *Real Greek Food*, which he wrote with chef Theodore Kyriakou.

Before becoming a food writer, Charles worked in a succession of London ad agencies and had a spell as chef-proprietor of a hotel and restaurant in darkest Derbyshire.

Help Us Update

We've tried to ensure that this fifth edition of *The Rough Guide to London Restaurants* is as up-to-date and accurate as possible. However, London's restaurant scene is in constant flux: chefs change jobs; restaurants are bought and sold; menus change. There will probably be a few references in this guide that are out of date even as this book is printed – and standards, of course, go up and down. If you feel there are places we've underrated or overpraised, or others we've unjustly omitted, please let us know: comments or corrections are much appreciated, and we'll send a copy of the next edition (or any other *Rough Guide* if you prefer) for the best letters. Please address letters to Charles Campion at:

Rough Guides, 80 Strand, London WC2R ORL or
Rough Guides, 4th Floor, 375 Hudson St, New York, NY 10014.

Or send email to: mail@roughguides.co.uk

Contents

Central London

Contents

The City & East London

North London

Contents

South London

West London

Indexes

Introduction

Welcome to the fifth edition of the Rough Guide to London Restaurants. If you used the first four, you will have noticed that the number of restaurants has stabilized around the 350 mark, but it is surprising how many openings and closures there have been within the space of a year. This edition has been extensively revised and as well as reassessing all the previous entries we have added a wide selection of new establishments.

Anyone who has lived or worked in London knows that while it may seem like one big metropolis to the outsider, it is really a series of villages. If you live in Clapham, you know about Clapham and Battersea, and maybe Brixton or Chelsea, while Highgate or Shepherd's Bush are far-off lands. And vice versa. Yet almost every other restaurant guide is divided up by cuisine, which assumes that this is your first criterion when choosing a place to eat. It shouldn't be. If you're meeting friends in Chiswick your best options might be French or Modern British; in Wembley or Tooting they might be Indian. But you want to know about that oddball great restaurant, too: whether it's an interesting newcomer like Tsunami in Clapham, or a new gastro-pub like The Ealing Park Tavern in South Ealing. This book divides London into five geographic sections (Central; City & East; North; South; West) and then breaks these down into the neighbourhoods, with restaurants arranged alphabetically in each section. Keep this guide handy and it will tell you where to eat well from Soho to Southall.

Another important thing to note about the restaurants selected and reviewed in this book is that they are **all recommended** – none has been included simply to make up the numbers. There are some very cheap places and there are some potentially pretty expensive places, but they all represent good value. The only rule we have made for inclusion is that it must be possible to eat a meal for £35 a head or less. In some of the haute cuisine establishments, that will mean keeping to the set lunch, while in some of the bargain eateries £35 might cover a blow-out for four. This guide reviews restaurants for every possible occasion from quick lunches to celebratory dinners. It also covers many different kinds of food – some fifty cuisines in all. In reality, we cover even more, as for simplicity we have used "Indian" and "Chinese" as catch-all terms.

Prices and credit cards

Every review in this book has at the top of the page a spread of **prices** (eg £12–40). The first figure relates to what you could get away with – this is the minimum amount per person you are likely to spend on a meal here (assuming you are not a non-tipping, non-drinking skinflint). The second relates to what it would cost if you don't hold back. Wild diners with a taste for fine wines will leave our top estimates far behind, but the figures are there as a guide. For most people, the cost of a meal will lie somewhere within the spread.

For a more detailed picture, each review sets out the prices of various dishes. At some time in the guide's life these specific prices (and indeed the overall price spreads) will become out of date, but they were all accurate when the book left for the printer. And even in the giddy world of restaurants, when prices rise or prices fall, everyone tends to move together. If this book shows one restaurant as being twice as expensive as another, that situation is likely to remain.

The reviews also keep faith with original menu spellings of dishes, so you'll find satays, satehs and satés – all of which will probably taste much the same. Opening hours and days are given in every review, as are the credit cards accepted. Where reviews specify that restaurants accept "all major credit cards", that means at least AmEx, Diners, MasterCard and Visa. Acceptance of Visa and MasterCard usually means Switch and Delta, too; we've specified the odd exception, but if you're relying on one card it's always best to check when you book.

Getting off the fence: the best

Every restaurant reviewed in this book is wholeheartedly recommended, but it would be a very strange person who did not have favourites, so here are some "six of the bests".

Best newcomers

Best Chinese or Southeast Asian

Best buzz

Best for blowing a banker's bonus

Best vegetarian dishes

Best classic French

Introduction

Best Pakistani or Punjabi

Best sushi

Best post-theatre or cinema

Best real cheapies

Best modernist Indian

Best for fish

Best for a bargain lunch

Best modern gastro-pub

Introduction

Best to impress

Best for eating alfresco

Best for solo dining

Best Italian cooking

Best seafood

Best for business

Best for good, affordable wines

Best for an authentically foreign meal

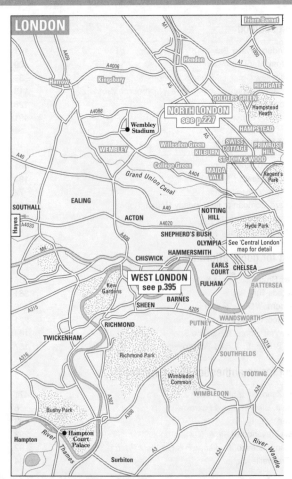

LONDON

Friern Barnet

M1

A406

A4006

A1000

A1

Hendon

Harrow

Kingsbury

A5

HIGHGATE

GOLDERS GREEN

A4088

Wembley Stadium

NORTH LONDON
see p.227

Hampstead Heath

HAMPSTEAD

Willesden Green

SWISS COTTAGE

PRIMROSE HILL

A40

WEMBLEY

KILBURN

ST JOHN'S WOOD

College Green

A404

MAIDA VALE

Grand Union Canal

Regent's Park

SOUTHALL

EALING

A40

Hayes

A4020

ACTON

A4020

NOTTING HILL

Hyde Park

SHEPHERD'S BUSH

M4

A406

OLYMPIA

See 'Central London' map for detail

CHISWICK

HAMMERSMITH

EARLS COURT

CHELSEA

WEST LONDON
see p.395

FULHAM

BATTERSEA

Kew Gardens

BARNES

A315

SHEEN

A205

WANDSWORTH

RICHMOND

PUTNEY

TWICKENHAM

A214

A316

Richmond Park

SOUTHFIELDS

TOOTING

Wimbledon Common

A24

A307

WIMBLEDON

Bushy Park

A308

Hampton

Hampton Court Palace

River Thames

A3

River Wandle

Subiton

A24

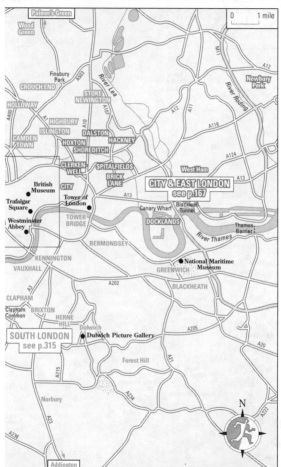

Central London

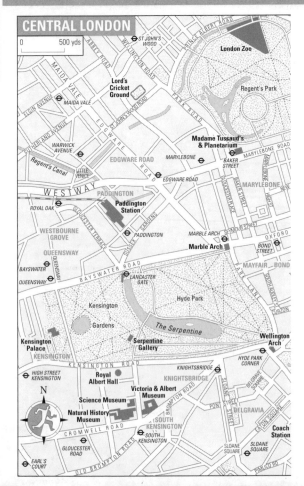

CENTRAL LONDON

0   500 yds

ST JOHN'S WOOD

London Zoo

Regent's Park

Lord's Cricket Ground

ABBEY ROAD

WELLINGTON ROAD

KING'S ALBERT ROAD

PARK ROAD

MAIDA VALE

ELGIN AVENUE

MAIDA VALE

SUTHERLAND AVENUE

WARWICK AVENUE

Regent's Canal

LITTLE VENICE

EDGWARE ROAD

ST JOHN'S WOOD ROAD

EDGWARE ROAD

MARYLEBONE

Madame Tussaud's & Planetarium

MARYLEBONE ROAD

BAKER STREET

MARYLEBONE

GLOUCESTER PLACE

BAKER STREET

W E S T W A Y

PADDINGTON

ROYAL OAK

GLOUCESTER TERRACE

Paddington Station

EDGWARE ROAD

PADDINGTON

SUSSEX GARDENS

GARDENS

SEYMOUR STREET

WESTBOURNE GROVE

QUEENSWAY

BAYSWATER

QUEENSWAY

QUEENSWAY

MARBLE ARCH

Marble Arch

OXFORD

BOND STREET

MAYFAIR — BOND

BAYSWATER ROAD

LANCASTER GATE

Hyde Park

PARK LANE

SOUTH AUDLEY STREET

CURZON

Kensington

Gardens

The Serpentine

Serpentine Gallery

Wellington Arch

Kensington Palace

KENSINGTON

KENSINGTON ROAD

HYDE PARK CORNER

HIGH STREET KENSINGTON

KNIGHTSBRIDGE

KNIGHTSBRIDGE

BELGRAVE SQUARE

Royal Albert Hall

Victoria & Albert Museum

BROMPTON ROAD

SLOANE STREET

BELGRAVIA

N

Science Museum

Natural History Museum

SOUTH KENSINGTON

PONT STREET

EATON SQUARE

Coach Station

CROMWELL ROAD

SOUTH KENSINGTON

SLOANE SQUARE

SLOANE SQUARE

GLOUCESTER ROAD

EARL'S COURT

OLD BROMPTON ROAD

PIMLICO ROAD

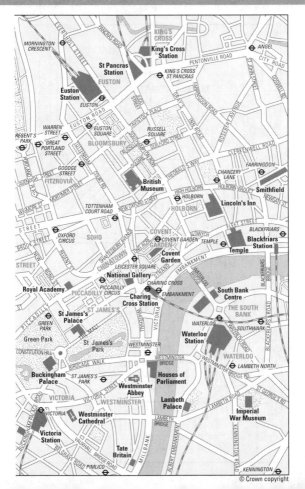

© Crown copyright

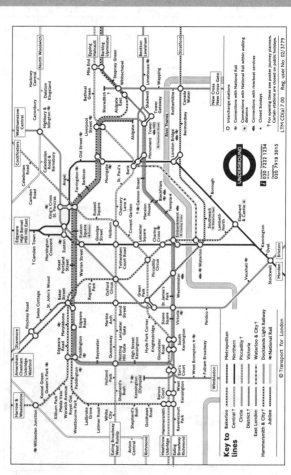

Central

Bloomsbury and Fitzrovia

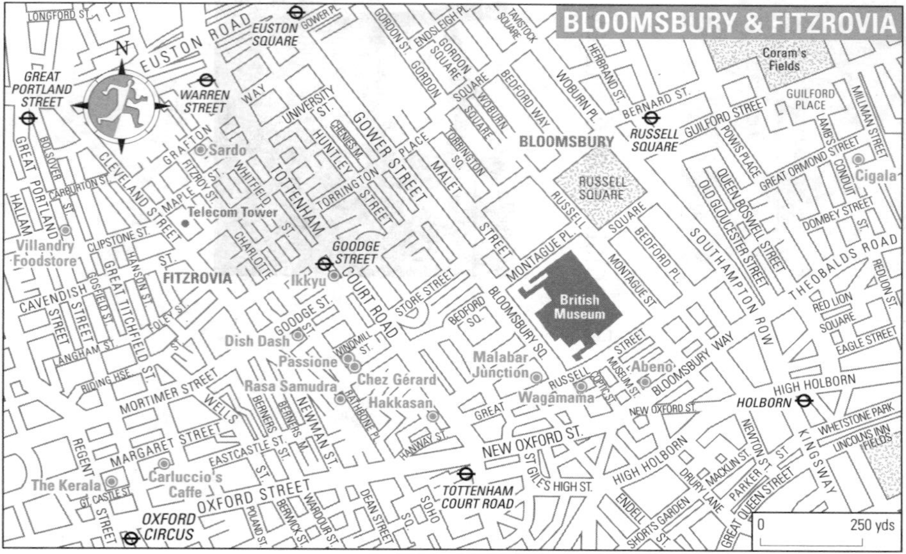

© Crown copyright

Abeno

Abeno claims to be Europe's only specialist okonomi-yaki restaurant, and it may well be. London has plenty of teppan-yaki restaurants – where the chef cooks gourmet morsels in front of you on the hotplate – but okonomi-yaki hasn't swept to popularity, perhaps because it is an altogether messier, more grass-roots sort of experience. Even the finest okonomi-yaki looks a bit like road-kill. Imagine a sloppy pizza crossed with a solid omelette then layered with all manner of odds and ends. Then imagine it being assembled and cooked on the table in front of you. Abeno is saved by the gentle and friendly service, the freshness of the ingredients, the charm of the cooks, and the low, low prices. And it's fun.

Cost	£9–35

Address 47 Museum St, WC1
℡ 020 7405 3211
Station Tottenham Court Road
Open Daily noon–10pm
Accepts All major credit cards except Diners

You could try yaki-soba (£6.95), a fried noodle dish with chicken, squid or pork. Or soba-rice, a natty combination of rice and noodles which is all the rage in Kansai – try it with pork and kimchi (£9.95). You could even try the upscale teppan-yaki fillet steak (£13.80). But you're here for the okonomi-yaki. The base is cabbage, egg and dough, with spring onions and tempura batter; all this is piled onto the hot plate. You specify whether you want deluxe or super deluxe, trad or wholemeal base, and off they go. Try tofu, corn and extra spring onion (£6.70/8.70); or Osaka mix – pork, kimchi and prawn (£6.95/9.95); or spicy Tsuruhasi – kimchi and an extra egg (£6.70/9.70); or Abeno special – pork, bacon, konnyaku, asparagus, squid, prawn and salmon, topped with an egg (£14.80); or London mix – pork, bacon, cheese and salmon (£8.80/11.80). These dishes are very tasty, and it's fun to watch the layering at work. And there are nice side dishes that will serve as starters, such as ika itame – squid with garlic and soy (£3.20), and miso soup (£2.20). Set menus take the angst out of ordering.

Don't visit this place in the height of summer, as the red-hot tabletop in front of you chucks out a fierce amount of heat. By the same token, keep your elbows and the menu well away from it – unless the smell of scorching stimulates your tastebuds.

Carluccio's Caffe

When Antonio Carluccio first ambled across our television screens, it was in his role as chef-proprietor of the upscale Neal Street Restaurant, and ultra-passionate mushroom hunter. Carluccio's Caffe is a much more mainstream concern than Neal Street, and it's also an extremely busy place, which makes for a great atmosphere. The downside is the likelihood of a queue at peak times. The front of the premises is a delicatessen-cum-shop; the mid-section is a bar; the rear is a café-restaurant. Commendable effort has been made to incorporate all that is admirable about Continental coffee shops and so often missing in London. Carluccio's is open throughout the day. Proper meals are available at all hours. The coffee is notably good. Children are welcome.

Cost	£8–24
Address	8 Market Place, W1; with branches
☎	020 7636 2228
Station	Oxford Circus
Open	Mon–Fri 8am–11pm, Sat & Sun 10am–10pm
Accepts	All major credit cards except Diners
⊕	www.carluccios.com

In the morning the temptations are croissants (from £1.20) and coffee: caffè ristretto (£1.15); cappuccino (£1.60); double espresso (£1.40) – pukka stuff. This segues into the main menu, on which there are always a couple of good soups to be had: zuppa di funghi (£3.90) or pasta e fagioli (£3.85) – note the fair prices. There's a good "bread tin" (£2.85) with sweet stuff at breakfast time and some moody Italian regional breads at meal times. There are sound antipasti, including Sicilian arancini di riso (£3.50), which are crisp, deep-fried rice balls filled with mozzarella or ragu. There are salads. Main courses range from calzone (£4.85) to a trad osso buco (£9.95), and from ravioli (£5.50) to fegato e patate (£8.95). Puds major in ice cream – gelati artiginali (£3.50). For a restaurant serving so many customers, the cooking is very good. Dishes are well seasoned, service is quick and the prices are fair.

Beware the shopping zone, lest you be tempted by the gleaming Piaggio Vespa ET2 50cc. You'll find it listed on the menu under "Transporti" and described as a "fully automatic scooter, carefully made and imported from Italy". It's priced at £1,650 – up £150 since 2001!

Chez Gérard

When the inner prompting shouts for steak frites, Chez Gérard is a very sound option. Though there are now a host of these popular brasseries spread throughout London, the Charlotte Street branch is the original and, some say, the best. When it opened, over twenty years ago, this type of French restaurant – where the steak is good and the frites are better – was a novelty; today, despite a recent lick of paint, Chez Gérard feels reassuringly old-fashioned. The latest development here has been to move the emphasis gently away from steak, and now there are more fish dishes, as well as chicken and even wild boar. But the approach is always Francophile, so you'll find salade de boudin noir au lard, French onion soup, loup de mer, snails and crème brûlée. The bread is crusty, the service Gallic, and the red wine decent. It's not cheap, but the food is generally reliable, and in summer you can eat al fresco at one of the pavement tables.

Cost	£20–50

Address 8 Charlotte St, W1; with branches
℡ 020 7636 4975
Station Goodge Street
Open Mon–Fri noon–11.30pm, Sat 6–11.30pm, Sun noon–10.30pm
Accepts All major credit cards
ⓦ www.sante-gcg.com

FRENCH

Start with rock oysters (£6.50 for six; £9.75 for nine; £13 for twelve), pâté de campagne (£4.85), or, for a real belt of nostalgia, a dozen snails in garlic butter (£5.45). The steaks come in all shapes and sizes – Châteaubriand is for two people (£31.50), while côte de boeuf rib-eye (£14.95) is now cooked "per person" rather than to share. There's a 9oz fillet steak (£16.55) and an entrecôte (£13.75). This is also one of the few places in London where you can get onglet (£9.95), a particularly tasty French cut. Everything from the grill comes with pommes frites and sauce Béarnaise. The new dishes include saucisse de poulet et champignons sauvages, choucroute au champagne (£9.95) and thon grillé sauce vierge (£13.50). But don't kid yourself – you're here for the steak frites. Salads, side orders of vegetables, desserts – including tarte Tatin (£4.75) – and a decent selection of regional French cheeses (£4.25) are all nicely in tune with the Gallic ambience. So too are the house wines (£9.50), which are so good that you can almost disregard the wine list.

There is also a very sound menu prix fixe available every evening and at Sunday lunch – just £15.95 for three courses. Gravadlax; onglet; pud makes pretty good reading.

Cigala

SPANISH

🍴 Cigala came through its first eighteen months with a hatful of glowing reviews. The chef-proprietor – Jake Hodges, one of the founders of Moro (see p.197) – has settled into a regime of blissfully straightforward Iberian dishes, and this is the place to try rabbit, ox tongue, patatas bravas and poached meats, as well as old favourites like the eponymous cigalas na brasa – langoustines with Romesco sauce.

Cost	£18–60

Address 54 Lamb's Conduit St, WC1
ⓣ 020 7405 1717
Station Russell Square
Open Mon–Fri 12.30–2.30pm & 6–10.45pm Sat & Sun noon–12.30pm
Accepts All major credit cards
ⓦ www.cigala.co.uk

Cigala is a very good restaurant. Look out for simple dishes. Strong flavours. Fresh ingredients. Real passion.

The menu changes daily. It is dependent on the markets and what the chef can find that looks good. This makes for seasonal dishes, and that is a huge plus. So a winter menu might start with caldo de perro (£5.50), a fish broth with chunks of cod spiked with Seville orange. Or revueltos de chorizo y pimentos (£6) – scrambled egg with chorizo and red peppers. Or lengua a la Aragonesa (£5.50) – ox tongue with pepper and sherry sauce. Or clams with garlic parsley and Manzanilla (£5). All these dishes are simple, well seasoned and have good combinations of flavour. Mains deliver in much the same fashion. Fabadas Asturianas (£15) is a rich, comforting bean stew with good, spicy chorizo, the Spanish blood sausage called morcilla and rashers of fat bacon. Delicious. Dorada a la plancha (£16.00) comes with judion beans, rocket and a Romesco sauce. Or there's tumbet (£13) which is an interesting vegetarian casserole made with aubergine, potatoes and tomatoes. Cocido Madrileno (£16.50) teams poached meats with chickpeas, cabbage and tomato sauce (£12.50). Puddings lie in wait: the walnut tart (£4) is actually a substantial walnut and chocolate pie. The wine list doffs its cap to a goodly selection of sherries, and features a good range of well-chosen Spanish wines. The cooking here is very adept and Mr Hodges has the sense to stick to simple, unpretentious dishes and simple, unpretentious presentation. This guarantees some very enjoyable meals.

There's a good set lunch here. Two courses cost £15 and three courses cost £18 (prices drop to £12 and £15 on Saturday and Sunday). And muster a party of between eight and forty and Cigala will open the tapas bar downstairs for your exclusive use.

Dish Dash

This modernist Persian restaurant has already evolved since it opened as a bar-led, high style, night-clubby sort of venue in 2000. As of 2002, a takeaway section has joined Goodge Street's host of lunchtime sand-wich operations, and there is also a remarkable "canteen lunch" offering simple set meals for people in a hurry. These start at £3.50 for the "Healthy" option, going on to £5.50 for "Hungry" and finally £7 for "Starving". Presumably anyone who is both healthy and hungry gets two lunches – they are certainly cheap enough.

Cost	£5–50
Address	57–59 Goodge St, W1
☎	020 7637 7474
Station	Goodge Street
Open	Mon–Wed noon–3.30pm & 6–10.30pm, Thurs & Fri noon–3.30pm & 6–10.45pm, Sat 6–10.30pm, Sun noon–3.30pm
Accepts	All major credit cards
⊕	www.dish-dash.com

The menu is a multi-sectioned affair, and is broken down into hot and cold mazzas, then breads, soups, grills, "mish mash", and side dishes. Though you can order just one or two mazzas (about £4 each), they are designed for sharing, with special plates to hold a selection of five (£12.50) or seven (£19). You'll find the classics, such as hummus, baba ghanoush and felafel, alongside less common offerings like omni houriya – a carrot dip with garlic and cumin; kuku subzumini – a thick herb omelette; habbar – pan-fried squid; or aroug shigar – courgette and haloumi fritters served with green chilli and mint. There's plenty of variety in texture and taste. Breads (all £1.50) are served and charged separately – choose from char-grilled Khobez, Persian village bread and barbari naan. In the grills section, alongside the ubiquitous kofta (£9) and shish taouk (£9.50), or chicken kebab, there is the Dish Dash seared steak (£13.50), which comes with sumac chips. The mish mash section is home to char-grilled lamb loin chops (£11) and seared swordfish (£13.50). Desserts are happily simple dishes such as date and walnut cake with fig jam and banana parfait (£4), and baklava with honey ice cream and toasted nuts (£4).

There's a short wine list, but the main bulk of the drinks is given over to cocktails, which are professionally made and agreeably strong. This means that Dish Dash is popular with a drinking crowd and tends to get loud and boisterous towards the end of the week.

Hakkasan

As you nod to the doorman and walk down the green slate tunnel that is the staircase, you could easily think that you were entering a super-plush theme park ride. Hakkasan opened in 2001 and is as impressively designed as only the judicious application of more than £3,000,000 can achieve. The double-smart cocktail bar has sprinted from empty to fashionably crammed in the twinkling of an eye. A large dining area sits inside an elegant and ornate carved wooden cage. Top-name designers from the worlds of film and fashion have given their all, and this is a smart and elegant place. The food is novel, well presented, fresh, delicious and, in strangely justifiable fashion, expensive.

Cost	£25–100

Address 8 Hanway Place, W1
℡ 020 7927 7000
Station Tottenham Court Road
Open Mon–Fri noon–2.30pm & 6–11.30pm, Sat & Sun noon–4.30pm & 6–11.30pm; Thurs–Sat bar open until 3am
Accepts All major credit cards

The starters are called "small eat" and do not shy away from expensive luxury ingredients. The three-style vegetarian roll (£6) teams a mooli spring roll with a bean curd puff and a yam roll. Good, but not great. Live native lobster noodles with ginger and spring onion (£38) cannot be many people's idea of a "small eat". Or there is grilled chicken Shanghai dumpling (£3.50). The main dishes are innovative and delicious: roast silver cod (£22) comes with champagne and Chinese honey. Abandon any lingering prejudices and try the stir-fry jellyfish, squid, beansprouts and Chinese chives (£8.50). Or there is steamed Morinaga tofu with prawn and black bean sauce (£9.50) – these are nests of the lightest, meltingest steamed tofu with the texture of fine panna cotta, each with a crunchy, large prawn. Memorable. There's also a dish of roast organic pork with red rice, ginger and Shao Hsing wine (£11.50), and a very good braised chicken with dried shitake and chestnuts (£11.50). By way of a staple, try the Hakka vermicelli (£8.50), which is a simple noodle dish that comes with a bowl of chive consommé to moisten the noodles down.

The dim sum (served only at lunchtime) have had a dramatic effect on the critics and for once the acclaim is unanimous. They are not cheap – har gau is £3.90, and a char sui bun £3 – but there are some very interesting dishes. Try spring onion cheung fun in XO sauce (£3.50), scallop shumai with tobika caviar (£5), or a baked venison puff (£3.90). Whisper it...these are better dim sum than you'll find in Chinatown!

Ikkyu

(🍴) Busy, basic and full of people
eating reliable Japanese food at
sensible prices – all in all, Ikkyu is a good
match for any popular neighbourhood
restaurant in Tokyo. What's more, it's
hard to find, which adds to the authenticity. Head down the steps and you'll
find that the restaurant has had a much-
needed lick of paint. It is still an engaging

Cost	£10–40

Address 67a Tottenham Court
Rd, W1
℡ 020 7636 9280
Station Goodge Street
Open Mon–Fri noon–2.30pm
& 6–10.30pm, Sun 6–10.30pm
Accepts All major credit cards

place, if quite obviously tailored to Japanese customers, but the strange-
ness comes over as politeness, and you won't feel completely stranded.
The first shock is how very busy the place is – you are not the first person
to discover what must be some of the best-value Japanese food in
London. If you cannot grapple with the lengthy menu, go for lunch and
turn to the "set" meals, such as mixed deep-fried croquette and prawns,
with rice and miso soup (£6.50).

Nigiri sushi is good here and is priced by the piece: tuna (£2); yellow
tail (£3); salmon (£1.70); mackerel (£1.40); cuttlefish (£1.70). Or
there's sashimi, which runs all the way from mackerel (£4.50) to sea
urchin eggs (£13), with an assortment for £13.50. Alternatively, start
with soba (£3.60) – delicious, cold, brown noodles. Then allow yourself
a selection of yakitori, either a portion of assorted (£5), or mix and
match from tongue, heart, liver, gizzard and chicken skin (all £1 a stick).
You will need a good many skewers of the grilled chicken skin, which is
implausibly delicious. Moving on to the main dishes, an order of fried
leeks with pork (£7.50) brings a bunch of long, onion-flavoured greens
strewn with morsels of grilled pork. Whatever the green element is, it is
certainly not leeks. Or there's grilled aubergine (£3.40), or rolled five
vegetables with shrimp (£8.20), which is like a Swiss roll made with egg
and vegetable with a core of prawn.

Ikkyu's menu has a good many delicious secrets, though the Japanese-
favoured drink, shouchu and soda (£3.50), is perhaps not among them –
shouchu is a clear spirit which tastes like clear spirit and the addition of
soda does little to improve it. Asahi and Kirin beers (both £2.70) are a
much better choice. Another doubtful order would be fermented soya
beans topped with a raw egg (£3.10), which in Japan is considered the
perfect start to the day, but is unlikely to woo you away from cornflakes.

The Kerala

In 1935, Gough Brothers opened Shirref's wine bar at 15 Great Castle Street at a time when such establishments were something of a novelty. Shirref's stood the test of time and became a favourite watering hole for musicians and actors working around the corner at the BBC in Portland Place. At the end of the 1980s it was taken over by

Cost	£6–22
Address	15 Great Castle St, W1
℗ 020 7580 2125	
Station	Oxford Circus
Open	Daily noon–3pm & 5.30–11pm
Accepts	All major credit cards

David Tharakan and continued to prosper – a good deal of wine was consumed and there was even a short menu of pub food favourites. The big changes came at the end of 1997, when David's wife Millie took over the kitchen and changed the menu. Shirref's started to offer Keralan home cooking, with well-judged, well-spiced dishes at bargain-basement prices. Since then The Kerala restaurant – which is what it has become – has gone from strength to strength.

To start with, you must order a platoon of simple things: cashew nut pakoda (£2.75), potato bonda (£2.50), lamb samosa (£2.75), chicken liver masala (£3.75), mussels ularthu (£3.75). These are honest dishes, simply presented and at a price which encourages experimentation. Thereafter the menu is divided into a number of sections: Syrian Christian specialties from Kerala; coastal seafood dishes; Malabar biryanis; vegetable curries; and special dosas. From the first, try erachi olathiathu (£4.95), a splendid dry curry of lamb with coconut. From the second, try meen and mango vevichathu (£4.95), which is kingfish cooked with the sharpness of green mango. From the biryanis, how about chemmin biryani (£5.95) – prawns cooked with basmati rice? Avial (£3.75) is a mixed vegetable curry with yoghurt and coconut. The breads are fascinating – try the lacy and delicate appams (two for £2.60) made from steamed rice-flour.

The people who run The Kerala are intensely proud of their country and its cuisine, and will be happy to help you discover glorious new dishes. The Kerala would be good value in the suburbs, but being hidden behind Oxford Circus makes it a contender for bargain of the age. Look out for the "lunch buffet" offers – a feast for under £5.

Malabar Junction

The cuisine at Malabar Junction is that of Kerala – the home province of the proprietor – and it is served up from two entirely separate kitchens and brigades of chefs, vegetarian and non-vegetarian, kept completely separate to comply with religious requirements. But however busy it may be down in the kitchens, inside the restaurant all is calm. This is a top-quality Indian restaurant, fully licensed, with a spacious dining room with comfortable chairs and a conservatory roof. None of which elegance is hinted at by the rather unprepossessing frontage at the Tottenham Court Road end of Great Russell Street.

Cost	£14–30
Address	107 Great Russell St, WC1
☎	020 7580 5230
Station	Tottenham Court Road
Open	Daily noon–3pm & 6–11.30pm
Accepts	All major credit cards except Diners
⊕	www.haridas.co.uk

Kerala is the spice centre of India, and all the Malabar dishes tend to be spicy and nutty. Curry leaves, cinnamon, coconut, chilli and cashew nuts prevail. There is also a good deal of fish. To start with, try the spinach vadia (£3.50) – small chickpea doughnuts made with spinach and ginger, deep-fried and served crunchy with two dipping sauces of yoghurt and tamarind. Or there's uppuma (£4), a kind of eastern polenta, which is semolina fried in ghee with onions, spices and cashew nuts. The special poori masala (£6.50) takes the form of two balloon-shaped puffed breads with a potato cake that's not a million miles from pricey bubble and squeak. For a main course, try some fish or seafood: the fish moilee (£8) runs the gamut of cinnamon, cloves, cardamom, green chillies, garlic, coconut and curry leaves, while the Cochin prawn curry (£9.50) is more tomatoey, and comes with huge prawns. Chicken Malabar (£8) applies much the same Keralan spice palate to chicken. From the array of vegetable dishes, try avial (£4.50), a combination of all sorts of vegetables with a host of woody and aromatic spices, or a plate of green bananas (£4.50), tangy and delicious.

You'll also find all the traditional Southern Indian vegetarian favourites listed on the menu here, including rava dosa (semolina pancake), uthappam (crisp lentil pancake) and iddly (rice and lentil cakes). This may well be the perfect restaurant for a mix of vegetarians and fish- or meat-eaters.

Bloomsbury & Fitzrovia

Passione

When Passione opened nobody had heard of Gennaro Contaldo, but just about everyone had heard of his protégé, Jamie Oliver, whose scooter-driving, drum-bashing antics keep a swath of middle England foodies firmly glued to their television screens. Gradually, however, Passione has built up a following on its own merits. Sure, the

Cost	£22–50

Address 10 Charlotte St, W1
① 020 7636 2833
Station Goodge Street
Open Mon–Fri 12.30–2.30pm
& 7–10.30pm, Sat 7–10.30pm
Accepts All major credit cards
⊕ www.passione.co.uk

food is in the same idiom as the stuff on the telly, but that's only to be expected, as Oliver spent his formative years in a kitchen run by Contaldo. Passione is a good restaurant. Simplicity, an unpretentious feel to the place, seasonal ingredients and talent in the kitchen – these are sure bets when it comes to eating. Be sure not to miss the splendid breads, including Contaldo's fabled foccacio – the one which the pukka chap is always banging on about.

You owe it to yourself to have four courses, and the portions are geared towards being able to manage such a splurge – how nice it is to have four delicious platefuls and not feel overstuffed. If you need any further encouragement, remind yourself that this is a restaurant where some dishes have actually come down in price! The menu changes daily, and there is a constant procession of specials. Among the antipasti, zuppa di lenticche (£6) is a rich lentil soup, while anguilla affumicata con salsa alle erbe (£6) combines the richness of smoked eel with a herb sauce. Then there is pasta and risotto: tagliatelle con tartufo (£9/11) is suffused with the heady scent of truffles, while risotto all'accetosella (£9/11) has the tasty tang of wild sorrel. Mains are rich and satisfying: pesce spada impanato con insalata di pomodoro (£16) is a simple dish of bread-crumbed swordfish topped with a tomato salad; while quaglie ripiene di frutta secca e castagne con radicchio al balsamico (£16.50) is quails stuffed with dried fruit and chestnuts. The service is slick here; this is a place where they understand the art of running a comfortable restaurant.

Puddings (all £5) are serious stuff, though it has to be said that the delicious gelato Passione, a swirl of zesty limoncello ice with a splash of wild strawberry folded into it, is for all the world a grown-up's raspberry ripple.

Rasa Samudra

(🍴) Rasa Samudra represents the "smart fishy" sector in Das Sreedharan's burgeoning portfolio of high quality South Indian restaurants (see the original Rasa, p.292; and the latest, Rasa Travancore, p.293). The food served is sophisticated fish cookery, the kind of stuff that would be more at home in Bombay than in London, consisting as it does of classy South Indian fish dishes – a million miles from familiar curry-house staples.

Cost	£18–40

Address 5 Charlotte St, W1
ⓣ 020 7637 0222
Station Goodge Street
Open Mon–Sat noon–3pm & 6–11pm, Sun 6–10.30pm
Accepts All major credit cards
ⓦ www.rasarestaurants.com

INDIAN/FISH & SEAFOOD

At first glance the menu may seem heart-stoppingly expensive, partly due to a strange and exclusively British prejudice that no curry should ever cost more than a fiver, even if made from the kind of top-quality ingredients that are worth £15 in a French restaurant. Note, however, that all the more expensive choices – which are often based on fish, usually the most pricey of ingredients – come complete with accompaniments. This makes them substantial enough to allow all but the greediest of diners to dispense with starters, except perhaps for the samudra rasam (£5.95), a stunning shellfish soup, or the array of pappadoms, papparvardi and achappam (£4). Plus wicked pickles (£3.50). And maybe the meen cutlets (£4.50), which are like fishcakes made with tuna and cassava. For main course, koonthal olathiathu (£9.95) – squid cooked with onion, curry leaves, ginger and fresh coconut – is well offset by pooris (£2.50) and spicy potatoes (£5.25) as side dishes. Other good choices include koyilandi konju masala (£12.95) – prawns cooked dry with ginger; fish moily (£10.50) – a curry of king fish cooked in coconut milk; and arachu vecha aavoli (£10.95) – tilapia cooked with shallots, red chillies and tamarind, a dish which is well complemented by beetroot curry (£6.25) and a chapati. The cooking is well judged and the spices well balanced.

If you are still nervous of the bill, don't be – the food is worth it. Serious gastronauts should opt for the Kerala feast (seafood £30; vegetarian £22.50). This takes the worry out of ordering.

Sardo

Following a refurb in the summer of 2001, Sardo has re-emerged as a self-proclaimed flagship for Sardinian food. The proprietor, Romolo Mudu, who also acts as front of house, comes from Caligari and is from the old school of pepper-mill wielding maître d's. Coupled with plain but fairly uninspired decor, this may make elderly diners feel that they have wandered into the Terrazza restaurant circa 1980. Take heart, the food is more interesting than you would expect and is particularly good when you concentrate on the specials.

Cost	£18–40

Address 45 Grafton St, W1
☏ 020 7387 2521
Station Warren Street
Open Mon–Fri noon–3pm & 6–11pm, Sat 6–11pm
Accepts All major credit cards
🖥 www.sardo-restaurant.com

Fregola is a Sardinian pasta that comes in small enough pieces to take over the role of rice or pearl barley as a soup thickener; at Sardo such soups crop up on the specials board, so look out for fregola ai cozze (£6.90), a rich, tomatoey gunk with enough fregola to give an almost risotto-like texture. The alici alla Sardo (£7.90) are also good – marinated anchovies served on rocket and tomatoes, with a few strips of grilled aubergine for good measure. Or there is mosciamo di tonno (£7.90), the prized central fillet of a tuna that is salted and wind-dried and, like its Iberian counterpart mohama, has a very concentrated flavour. Delicious. Move on to something simple, but impressive, like tonno alla griglia (£13.75) – a large chunk of tuna, raw inside, seared outside, spanking fresh and tender as butter. Or maybe salsiccia Sarda (£10.50) appeals? The proprietor will happily discuss his brother's recipe for these home-made sausages, which have a distinctive aniseed tang. For dessert, go trad Sardinian: sebada (£4.50) is a puff pastry filled with orange peel and cheese and topped with honey, a combo which works surprisingly well. Or there is a splendid array of five or six different pecorino cheeses (£4.50). The wine list includes a page of reasonably priced Sardinian specialities, and there are some distinctive, aromatic whites – note the Vermentinas.

Remember to check out the specials: it is rumoured that occasionally this restaurant gets a shipment of the justly famous mountain prosciutto made from mutton, though naturally this is set aside for favoured regulars. Thankfully, other Sardinian delicacies like donkey escalope and vinegared pig's ear have yet to be sighted.

Villandry Foodstore

As both foodstore and restaurant serving breakfast, elevenses, lunch, tea and dinner, Villandry began in more fashionable but cramped surroundings in Marylebone High Street. Its success brought the need for larger premises and, thus installed in Great Portland Street, a handsome foodstore gives onto a modern and rather stark dining room. Passing displays of some of Europe's most extravagant ingredients may jangle the nerves and alarm the wallet, but if you're serious about your food, and you have time to wait for careful preparation, Villandry won't disappoint.

Cost	£22–55

Address 170 Great Portland St, W1
℡ 020 7631 3131
Station Great Portland Street
Open Daily 8.30am–10.30pm
Accepts All major credit cards except Diners

The menu changes daily, so you won't necessarily find all – or indeed any – of the dishes mentioned here. But as you'd expect at the back of a foodstore that caters for the well-heeled sector of the foodie faithful, ingredients are scrupulously chosen and prepared with care. At its best, this kind of "informal" menu is surprisingly demanding on the cook – and exact cooking is crucial to ostensibly simple dishes. To start, you may be offered a cannellini bean, pancetta and Swiss chard soup (£6); smoked ricotta, toasted almonds, shaved fennel, pousse and tapenade (£7.75); marinated tiger prawns, sweet potato, sweet corn and piquillo pepper salsa (£9.50); or a plate of charcuterie (£6.75/11.75). Main courses are often hugely impressive: braised lamb shank with mash and roast carrots (£14.75); pan-fried fillet of turbot with Puy lentils, spinach and porcini cream (£17.25); roast pork, roast new potatoes, black pudding apple and sage (£15.50). Desserts include moist chocolate cake (£5.50) and, unsurprisingly, given the array in the shop, there's an extensive if expensive cheeseboard (£10.50), served with terrific walnut and sourdough breads.

Wine prices, like the food, are distinctly West End, though there are reasonably priced house selections. Overall, standards are high, and the balancing both of flavours and of the menu itself suggests that the kitchen brigade knows what it's doing and isn't afraid to buck the trends. Lunch prices are a tad easier on the wallet.

Wagamama

Wagamama has been trendy – and packed – since the day it opened, and its popularity shows no signs of falling off. Which is fair enough, because this is as good a canteen as you'll find, serving simple and generally rather good Japanese food at very reasonable prices. What it's not is a place for a relaxed or intimate meal. The basement interior is cavernous and minimalist, and diners are seated side by side on long benches. At regular eating times you'll find yourself in a queue lining the stairway – there are no reservations. When you reach the front, you're seated, your order is punched into a hand-held computer, then the code numbers for your dishes are written on the low-tech placemat in front of you – a legacy of the day when the radio-ordering system failed. There's beer and wine available, as well as free green tea.

Cost	£8–17

Address 4 Streatham St, WC1; with branches
℡ 020 7323 9223
Station Tottenham Court Road
Open Mon–Sat noon–11pm, Sun 12.30–10pm
Accepts All major credit cards
ⓦ www.wagamama.com

Dishes arrive when they're cooked, so a party of four will be served at different times. Generally that means ordering a main dish – noodles in soup, fried noodles or sauce-based noodles – or a rice dish. Side dishes can also be pressed into service as a sort of starter: yasai yakitori (£4.50) is char-grilled chicken with the ever-popular yakitori sauce, while gyoza (£3.95) are delicious, fried chicken dumplings. The mains include a splendid chilli beef ramen (£8.50) – slivers of sirloin steak in a vat of soup with vegetables and noodles (it's good etiquette to slurp these). Also good is the yasai katsu curry (£6), which is boiled rice with a light curry sauce and discs of deep-fried vegetables; and yasai chili men (£6.25), a vegetarian "everything-in" dish with courgette, ginger, mushroom, carrot, peas, tomato, tofu and so on, plus ramen noodles. If this all sounds confusing, that's because it is. To enjoy Wagamama you'll need to go with the flow.

It's not often that a restaurant offers a glossary that includes its own name. Wagamama is described as "Willfulness or selfishness: selfishness in terms of looking after oneself, looking after oneself in terms of positive eating and positive living". It seems to work here and at the numerous other branches scattered around town.

Chinatown

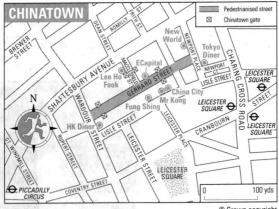

© Crown copyright

China City

White Bear Yard lies off Lisle Street to the north. There's a large gate and an archway; go through the arch, cross the courtyard, and you'll come to a large, glass-fronted Chinese restaurant which seats five hundred diners on three floors. Go early. You will see the restaurant change from cavernously empty to bustling and packed. The service is "Chinatown-brusque", but a combination of good flavours, large portions and sensible pricing has brought success. In 2002, however, the menu was simplified, and several of the moodiest dishes have disappeared. This is a trend to be deplored. China City stipulates a "minimum charge of £10 per person", but don't be put off – this is not an expensive restaurant and you will have to go some to spend a lot more.

Cost	£10–25
Address	White Bear Yard, WC2
☏	020 7734 3388
Station	Leicester Square
Open	Mon–Sat noon–midnight, Sun 11.30am–10.30pm
Accepts	All major credit cards

Both the old favourite and the home-style dishes are good here. Naturally, the menu includes sweet and sour pork, sesame prawn toast and crispy duck with attendant pancakes, but, for a change, why not start by trying the Peking hot and sour soup (£2)? Then perhaps the steamed fish with ginger and spring onion sauce (£13.50)? Or the fried prawns in spicy hot and sour sauce (£8.50)? Alternatively, look in the section on hot-pot dishes: mixed seafood with bean curd in hot pot (£8.50) is a casserole containing fresh scallops, huge prawns, crisp mangetout and bean curd, all in a terrific sauce. The simpler dishes are good too: try fried noodle with shredded chicken (£4.50). And just to see something green on the table and so appease your conscience, order choi sum in oyster sauce (£5).

"Seasonal price" is a caption to strike fear into the heart of even the most experienced diner. At China City you'll find them alongside all the lobster dishes. These include deep-fried lobster with garlic and chilli, and baked lobster with ginger and spring onion. Ask the price, you'll get a straightforward answer – and it may just prove surprisingly accessible.

Chinatown

ECapital

This restaurant, which opened in Spring 2002, is a welcome addition to the Chinese scene, as it showcases the somewhat neglected cuisine of Shanghai. The chef is David Tam, who won all manner of awards when at Aroma II. The interior is striking: the ceiling is painted deep fuschia, the walls are a nondescript cream, the lighting is soft – and that's it. For once less really is more. This is a comfortable, unpretentious place to eat and the food is both delicious and fascinating.

Cost	£14–50

Address 8 Gerrard St, W1
☏ 020 7434 3838
Station Leicester Square
Open Daily noon–midnight
Accepts All major credit cards except Diners

The menu's left page is a safety blanket of familiar favourites, from crispy seaweed to sweet and sour pork; turn to the right to find a host of good things from Shanghai. Starters include drunken chicken (£8), or cold chicken marinated in sweet wine, and paper-thin seasoned beef (£8), a stunning dish of slices of slow-cooked beef in a chilli-spiked, savoury marinade. The warm starters section includes the classic Shanghai pan-fried dumplings (£5), with good crispy bits, but the out and out star is the thousand layer pig's ear (£8). It's a slight exaggeration, as there are just 21 layers, but imagine small strips of agreeably chewy streaky bacon, cut thin, and tasting gelatinous and savoury. Pig's ear rarely tastes this good. The grandstand main course is beggar's chicken (£25). The chicken is seasoned with pickled cabbage and shredded pork, then wrapped in lotus leaves and given a casing of flour and water paste; the entire parcel is baked and, when the casing is smashed at table-side, the fragrant chicken is revealed within. You can also try sea bass West Lake style (£16), or Shanghai braised yellow eel (£12). Last, but not least, look out for the elite Chinese teas – floral and elegant.

The lunch menu at ECapital showcases all the famous Shanghai cold snacks (priced between £5 and £8 each), and fills in with some more substantial noodle dishes. Look out for a dish called "spring onion deep pan pizza" – it's more refined than the stuffed, flat onion breads you buy at the roadside in Shanghai, but just as tasty.

Fung Shing

Fung Shing was one of the first restaurants in Chinatown to take cooking seriously. Twenty or so years ago, when it was still a dowdy little place with a mural on the back wall, the kitchens were run by the man acknowledged to be Chinatown's number one fish cook, chef Wu. When he died, in 1996, his sous-chef took over. The restaurant itself has changed beyond recognition and now stretches all the way from Lisle Street to Gerrard Street, ever bigger and ever brassier. Even if there has been a slight decline in overall standards, the menu is littered with interesting dishes, the fish is still very fine and portions are large. Unfortunately, prices are creeping ever upwards, and you need to pick carefully to be sure of anything good.

Cost	£22–60

Address 15 Lisle St, WC2
℡ 020 7437 1539
Station Leicester Square
Open Daily noon–11.30pm
Accepts All major credit cards
🖰 www.fungshing.com

By Chinese restaurant standards, the menu is not huge, topping out at around 160 dishes, but the food has that earthy, robust quality which you only encounter when the chef is absolutely confident of his flavours and textures, whatever the cuisine. To start, ignore the crispy duck with pancakes (half for £20), which are good but too predictable, and the lobster with noodles (£19 a pound, with noodles £2 extra), which works out expensive. Turn instead to the steamed scallops with garlic and soya sauce (£2.75 each) – nowhere does them better. Or spare ribs, barbecued or with chilli and garlic (both £8). The prosaically named "mixed meat with lettuce" (£8.50) is also good, a wonderfully savoury dish of mince with lettuce-leaf wraps. You could also happily order mains solely from the chef's specials: stewed belly pork with yam in hot pot (£9.95); crispy spicy eel (£10.95); roast crispy pigeon (£14); or oysters with bean thread vermicelli in hot pot (£11.50). The other dishes are good too: perfect Singapore noodles (£6), crispy stuffed baby squids with chilli and garlic (£9.50), and steamed aubergine with garlic sauce (£7.50).

The Fung Shing has always been a class act, but what is unusual, certainly in Chinatown, is the gracious and patient service. This is a place where you can ask questions and take advice with confidence.

HK Diner

Opened in late 2001, HK Diner is a relatively new, light, bright, busy, modern sort of place, so if you like your Chinese restaurants seedy and "authentic" you will almost certainly walk past with a shudder. "It looks more like a burger bar, so how can it possibly..." Pre-judging this place would be a major mistake, however, as the food is very good, and there is no iron rule that slick-ness means rip-off. Prices are not cheap, but they are not over-the-top either, and the prospect of getting decent food very late at night (HK stays open until 5am at the weekend) is a beguiling one. Service is attentive, you don't wait long for food, and the tables turn over at a ferocious pace.

Cost	£8–35

Address 22 Wardour St, W1
☎ 020 7434 9544
Station Piccadilly
Circus/Leicester Square
Open Mon–Thurs & Sun
noon–4am, Fri & Sat noon–5am
Accepts All major credit
cards except Diners

The menu offers all the Cantonese favourites, from very good salt and pepper spare ribs (£5.50) to grilled dumplings (4 for £3.50) and steamed scallops on the half shell (£2.40 each). For main course, deep-fried squid with salt, pepper and garlic (£8) is as light, crisp and un-rubbery as you could wish, or there's fried mussels in spicy sauce (£8). Braised beef brisket (£7.50) is rich and filling, as is honey barbe-cued pork (£6.50). The Singapore noodles (£4.50) is a model of its kind. From the vegetable dishes, choose the fried snow pea shoots with minced garlic (£7) if you love garlic – this is the one to guarantee that even good friends will keep their distance for the next couple of days. The simple dishes, such as fried noodles with mixed meat (£4.50) and the congee (£5) – a glutinous rice porridge – will delight late-night revellers, whatever state they find themselves in.

The management has installed a patent Chinese milkshake machine from Hong Kong, and for £3 you can enjoy a tall glass of crushed ice with various flavourings and a secret spoonful of "pearls" – these are chewy, pea-sized balls of agar jelly. You drink your milkshake through a special large-gauge straw and, as you suck up the drink, the pearls shoot into your mouth and rattle around. It's as if you have become a living pinball machine. There are twenty different flavours: coffee is good, pas-sion fruit is OK.

Lee Ho Fook

Encouraged by the glowing reports in the guidebooks, lots of tourists set out to eat at Lee Ho Fook on Macclesfield Street but never actually manage to find it. This is a genuine Chinese barbecue house – small, spartan and cheap, with the food good of its kind. But the restaurant is not so helpful as to have a sign in English. Thus many potential non-Chinese diners find themselves at the larger, grander, more tourist-friendly Lee Ho Fook around the corner in Gerrard Street. These, then, are the directions: Macclesfield Street runs from Shaftesbury Avenue in the north to Gerrard Street in the south; on the west side is a backstreet called Dansey Place and, on the corner, with a red and gold sign in Chinese characters and a host of ducks hanging on a rack, is Lee Ho Fook. Inside there's a chef chopping things at a block in the window and four or five waiters. Sit down and you get tea, chopsticks and a big bottle of chilli sauce placed in front of you. Tables are shared and eating is a brisk business.

| Cost | £5–12 |

Address 4 Macclesfield St, W1; with branches
☎no phone
Station Leicester Square
Open Daily 11.30am–11pm
Accepts Cash only

The main focus of the short menu is an array of plated meals – a mound of rice with a splash of soy sauce "gravy" and a portion of chopped barbecued meat balanced on top. Choose from lean pork loin, crisp fatty belly pork, soya chicken or duck (all £4.10), or suckling pig (£6.50). You can also mix and match – half pork, half duck, say – or order a "combination" of mixed roast pork, soya chicken and duck with rice (£5). Some choose to order the meats without rice – perhaps a whole duck (£18) or a portion of suckling pig (£7). There's also a thriving takeaway trade.

Because of the specialized nature of this place, the other menu items are all too easily overlooked. Try adding a plate of crisp vegetables in oyster sauce (£3.80) to your order. And, before the main event, perhaps choose a bowl of won ton soup (£2.20), or the even more substantial won ton noodle soup (£2.80). The extension into the shop next door has doubled the number of seats but, aside from that, this establishment continues to do a simple thing very well, which is not as easy a trick to pull off as it sounds.

Mr Kong

You have to wonder whether the eponymous Mr Kong flirted with the idea of calling his restaurant King Kong – despite its marathon opening hours, at all regular mealtimes it's full of satisfied customers who would support such an accolade. Going with a party of six or more is the best plan when dining at Mr Kong, as that way you can order, taste and argue over a raft of dishes. You can share, and if there's something you really don't like, you can exile it to the other end of the table. If there's something wonderful, you can call up a second portion. It's a canny strategy, and means that you can never be caught out.

Cost	£8–22
Address 21 Lisle St, WC2	
☎ 020 7437 7341	
Station Leicester Square	
Open Daily noon–3am	
Accepts All major credit cards	

Sad to say, but several Chinatown stalwarts that have got smarter, busier and richer have lost some of their more obscure menu items along the way. Mr Kong is teetering on the brink. Where once there were three menus, there are now only two. But you can still get deep-fried stuffed pig's intestine (£8.50) – Oriental chitterlings! The main menu is rather safety-first, but sliced pork, salted egg and vegetable soup (minimum two people; £2.10 each), something of a house speciality, is worth a try. It's rich and very good, and the salted egg tastes pleasantly cheesy. Then try deep-fried crispy Mongolian lamb (£6.50), from the "Chef's specials", which is a very crisp breast of lamb with a lettuce-leaf wrap – avoid the accompanying hoi sin sauce, which is very sickly. The sautéed dragon whiskers with dried scallops (£11) are made with fresh pea shoots. Back to the main menu for a good, spicy Singapore noodle (£4.20); Kon Chin king prawn (£7.90) – an interesting prawn dish in a spicy toma-toey sauce; stewed beef flank Cantonese style in a pot (£5.90); and seasonal greens in oyster sauce (£4.60) – dark green, crunchy and deli-cious.

Portions are generous and, even when dishes contain exotic ingredi-ents, prices are reasonable. Just ignore the decor, which despite a refurb and new chairs in 2002 is still resolutely ordinary.

New World

When the 1990s saw the arrival of the mega-restaurants, giant two- and three-hundred-seater emporiums, the proprietors of this long-established Chinese restaurant were right to feel aggrieved and ask what all the fuss was about. The New World seats between four and six hundred people, depending on how many functions are going on at any one time. This is probably the largest single restaurant in Europe, but when you arrive you invariably have to wait in a sort of holding pen just inside the door until the intercom screeches with static and you are sent off to your table. The menu, leather-bound and nearly twenty pages long, features everything you have ever heard of and quite a lot you haven't. In any case, you don't need it – go for the dim sum, which are served every day from 11am until 6pm.

Cost	£6–18

Address 1 Gerrard Place, W1
☎ 020 7734 0396
Station Leicester Square
Open Daily 11am–midnight
Accepts All major credit cards

The dim sum come round on trolleys. First catch the eye of a waiter or waitress with a bow tie, to order drinks, and then you're at the mercy of the trolley pushers. Broadly speaking, the trolleys are themed: one has a lot of barbecued meat; another is packed with ho fun – broad noodles; another with steamed dumplings; another with soups; another with cheung fun – the long slippery rolls of pastry with different meats inside; and so on. A good mix would be to take siu mai (£1.70) and har kau (£1.70) from the "steamers" trolley. Then char sui cheung fun (£2.80) – a long roll with pork. Then some deep-fried won ton (£1.50) – little crispy parcels with sweet sauce. Or perhaps try something exotic like woo kwok (£1.70) – deep-fried taro dumplings stuffed with pork and yam. And something filling like char sui pow (£1.70) – steamed dough-nuts filled with pork; or nor mai gai (£2.80) – a lotus-leaf parcel of glutinous rice and meats.

If you arrive after 6pm, you're on your own: there are literally hundreds of dishes on the main menus. However, Chinese functions apart, New World is really best as an in-and-out dim sum joint. It's about eating and not, as the sticky carpet immediately declares, design and fripperies.

Chinatown

Tokyo Diner

Tokyo Diner offers conclusive proof that you needn't take out a second mortgage to enjoy Japanese food in London. Stacked up on three floors of a block that clings to Chinatown's silk skirts, this is a friendly eatery that shuns elaboration in favour of fast food, Tokyo-style. The place was actually set up by a Nipponophile Englishman, but the kitchen staff are all Japanese and its Far Eastern credentials bear scrutiny. The decor, crisp and minimalist, leaves the food to do the talking, which it does fluently – if the number of Japanese who walk through the doors are any indication. If you don't know your teppan-yaki from your kamikaze, or your sushi from your sumo, you'll be glad of the explanatory notes on the menu. When your food arrives, pick a set of chopsticks, snap them apart – the menu recommends that you rub them together to rid them of splinters – and get stuck in. Japanese style, the Tokyo Diner does not accept tips.

Cost	£8–25

Address 2 Newport Place, WC2
℡ 020 7287 8777
Station Leicester Square
Open Daily noon–midnight
Accepts MasterCard, Visa, no cheques

Top seller is the soba noodle soup (£5.10), thin brown buckwheat noodles in a soya broth. It's pleasant, filling and very popular with the drop-by lunchtime trade. Don't be afraid of slurping it – as the menu explains, slurping is OK. Or try the set lunch in a bento box of rice, noodles, sashimi and your choice of teriyaki, all for around £11.50. The bento will dispel once and for all the misconception that Japanese food is just for picking at, though watch out for the little green mound of wasabi, which will blow your head off if you're not careful – it should be mixed in a saucer with soy sauce, and used to dunk a morsel into. Other bento favourites include the ton katsu bento (£11.50), which is a kind of superior breadcrumbed pork escalope. If you don't have appetite enough for a full-on bento box, skip the curries – as the menu admits, they're a bit like school food – and head straight for the sushi and sashimi. They too come in "sets": try the nine-piece nigiri set (£8.90), which is very good value, or the hosi-maki set (£4.90), which comprises six pieces of salmon, three pieces of cucumber and three pieces of pickled radish.

To wash it all down, the Japanese beer Asahi (£1.99) is good, or there's complimentary Japanese tea. For a special treat, try the rich, sweet plum wine (£2.99 for 125ml), which is surprisingly moreish and quite delicious.

Covent Garden & Holborn

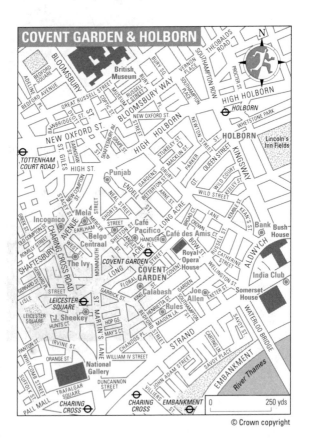

COVENT GARDEN & HOLBORN

© Crown copyright

0   250 yds

Bank

A good many foodists believe that this restaurant is the closest London gets to re-creating the all-day buzz and unfussy cuisine of the big Parisian brasseries. Bank opens for breakfast (Continental, Full English, or Caviar), lays on brunch at the weekend, does a good-value pre-theatre (5.30–7pm) and lunch prix fixe (both are £10 for two courses, £12.50 for three), and has a bustling bar. And then there's the other matter of lunch and dinner for several hundred. Whatever the time of day, the food is impressive, especially considering the large numbers of people fed, and if you like things lively you will have a great time. If you're leaving after 10pm, incidentally, and want a taxi, go for the cabs arranged by the doorman; black cabs are rare as hen's teeth around here after the Drury Lane theatres empty.

Cost	£16–60

Address 1 Kingsway, corner of Aldwych, WC2; with branches
☎ 020 7379 9797
Station Holborn
Open Mon–Fri 7–11.30am, noon–3pm & 5.30–11.30pm, Sat 11.30am–3.30pm & 5.30–11.30pm, Sun 11.30am–3.30pm & 5.30–10pm
Accepts All major credit cards
🌐 www.bankrestaurants.com

The menu changes seasonally, so dishes may come and go. Start with something simple – simple to get wrong, that is – a Caesar salad (£6.50), say, or a smoked haddock and ricotta tart (£6.50); or push the boat out with a well-made terrine of foie gras and plum chutney (£11). Or go for shellfish. A key role in Bank's history was played by one of London's leading catering fishmongers, so crustacea such as cold lobster in shell (half £15.50, whole £31) or dressed crab with ginger and wasabi dressing (£12.50) should be reliable. The fish dishes are equally good, from an ambitious sea bass chicory Tatin with watercress salad (£19.50), to a traditional Halibut fish and chips (£18.50), featuring mushy peas and tartare sauce. Meat dishes are well-prepared brasserie fare such as lamb shank, pea puree and creamed barley (£15.95), and glazed belly of pork with Chinese cabbage (£13.50). Puds include a chocolate fondant with mandarin sorbet (£6.25), and bread and butter pudding (£4.80).

Breakfast specialists may find themselves turning to the "Morning Glory" breakfast cocktail (£4.50). You have to view a drink that blends oats, tropical fruit milk and honey with some suspicion.

Belgo Centraal

The Belgians invented mussels, frites and mayonnaise, and Belgo has done all it can to help the Belgian national dish take over London. The Belgo group's flagship restaurant is a massive metal-minimalist cavern accessed by riding down in a scissor-powered lift. Turn left at the bottom and you enter the restaurant (where you can book seats); turn right and you get seated in the beerhall, where diners share tables. With 95 different beers, some at alcoholic strengths of 8–9%, it's difficult not to be sociable, or perhaps to while away a few minutes pondering the age-old question...name six famous Belgians.

Cost	£5–30

Address 50 Earlham St, WC2; with branches
℡ 020 7813 2233
Station Covent Garden
Open Mon noon–10.30pm, Tues–Thurs noon–11.30pm, Fri & Sat noon–midnight, Sun noon–10.30pm
Accepts All major credit cards
🌐 www.belgorestaurants.com

Belgo has cornered the London mussels market and no mistake. A kilo of classic moules marinières served with frites and mayonnaise (£10.95) has fresh mussels that have clearly been cooked then and there. Other options include classique (£11.95), with cream and garlic; and Provençale (£11.95), with tomato, herbs and garlic. And there are many alternatives for the non-mussel eater. Start with a salad Liègoise (£4.95) – a warm salad with green beans, egg, tomato and bacon lardons. Or the cheese croquettes (£5.95), made with Orval beer. Move on to carbonnade Flamande (£9.95) – beef braised in Geuze beer with apples and plums, and served with frites; or escalope de thon grillé (£10.95) – marinated tuna steak with gingered vegetables and a lemon butter sauce; or the famous Belgian speciality, chicken waterzooi (£9.75) – a rich chicken casserole. Desserts, as you might expect, are strong on Belgian chocolate. They include, among many others, traditional Belgian waffles with dark chocolate and hazelnut ice cream (£3.95). Belgo delights in special offers: there's a £5.75 lunch, and a more elaborate prix fixe at £12.95. Belgo delivers value, atmosphere and sound food, but it's the awesome beer list that makes it a must-visit.

In Belgo's mission to promote all things Belgian, no stone is left unturned. You'll even find Brussels sprouts with Ardennes ham (£2.75) – a brave but foolhardy attempt to popularize what is Britain's least favourite vegetable?

Café des Amis

This is the latest incarnation of an old-established restaurant just around the corner from the newly resurrected Opera House. Where once it was Gallic shabby, all is bleached, blond wood. All is modern, all is clean and bright. The resuscitated menu sits uneasily with its French section headings – "Les plats", "Les entrées" – as it darts from influence to influence: salmon terrine with guacamole meets confit of halibut and pumpkin gnocchi. The venerable clientele, many of whom used to have half a meal before the opera, and a dessert in the interval, are in shock. However, from a food point of view, there's only good to report. In the hands of a predominantly French team, the bistro menu has been shaken into the new millennium. Service is efficient and friendly, while the set menus, served pre- and post-theatre, are a real bargain: two courses £12.50, three courses £15.

The menu changes seasonally, but you might start with a dish like chilli crab millefeuille with fresh coriander (£7.50). Or prosciutto with buttered salsify and wild rocket (£8). Between starters and mains you'll find dishes that can be served as either – Caesar salad (£5.50/8.50); marinated artichoke risotto with smoked mozzarella, shaved truffle and wild rocket (£7.50/11.50); or pumpkin gnocchi with seared scallops, pancetta and sage butter sauce (£8.50/14.50). The "main" kind of main courses run the gamut, from roast rump of lamb, Provençal ravioli and black olive jus (£16.50); through char-grilled tuna, black bean and chorizo cassoulet (£14.50); to slow roast rib of beef with mash, preserved garlic, horseradish cream and red wine jus (£15). The off-peak prix-fixe menu features starters such as game rillettes with black olive focaccia; mains such as grilled salmon, Savoy cabbage and caviar beurre blanc; and desserts such as lemon tart with honey crème fraîche. The cooking is sound, the presentation on the plate is good, and the prices are reasonable.

The wine-bar under the restaurant is as dark and cavernous as the restaurant above is light and bright. And so it should be!

Cost	£12–35

Address **11–14 Hanover Place, off Long Acre, WC2**
℡ 020 7379 3444
Station Covent Garden
Open Mon–Sat 11.30am–11.30pm
Accepts All major credit cards
⊛ www.cafedesamis.co.uk

MODERN EUROPEAN

Café Pacifico

The salsa is hot at Café Pacifico – both types. As you are seated, a complimentary bowl of searing salsa dip with corn chips is put on your table. As you eat, hot salsa music gets your fingers tapping. The atmosphere is relaxed and you're soon in the mood for a cold Tecate (£2.90) or Negro Modelo (£2.90) beer. There are nine Mexican beers, a good selection of wines and dozens of cocktails. Parties can enjoy a pitcher of Margaritas (£27.95) to serve eight people. But Pacifico's tequila list is the highlight. There are more than sixty varieties, ranging from £2.60 to £100 a shot, and including some very old and rare brands.

Cost	£15–30
Address	5 Langley St, WC2
☎	020 7379 7728
Station	Covent Garden
Open	Mon–Sat noon–midnight, Sun noon–11pm
Accepts	All major credit cards except Diners
ⓦ	www.cafepacifico-laperla.co.uk

The menu is a lively mixture of old-style Californian Mexican and new Mexican, so while favourites like fajitas, flautas and tacos dominate, there are also some interesting and unusual dishes. Portions are generous and spicy, and many main courses come with refried beans and rice. Refried beans at Café Pacifico are smooth and comforting, and just the thing to balance the spicy heat. Try nachos rancheros (£7.95, £6.75 vegetarian) for starters and enjoy a huge plate of corn chips with beans, cheese, guacamole, onions, sour cream and olives. Excellent for sharing. Taquitos (£4.50) – filled fried baby tacos – are very tasty, too, as are smoked chicken quesadillas (£5.50) – flour tortillas with chicken, red peppers and avocado salsa. Main courses include degustación del Pacifico (£9.75), which includes a taste of almost everything. The burrito especial (£9.15) gives you a flour tortilla filled with cheese, refried beans and a choice of roast beef, chicken or ground beef, covered with ranchero sauce. Roast beef is slow-cooked and falling-apart tender. Look out for their modern Mexican dishes like spice-rubbed sirloin steak (£13.95) – these are available from 6pm.

Café Pacifico has been a place to party since 1978 and claims to be London's oldest Mexican restaurant. And, yes, they do have a bottle of mescal with a worm in it.

Calabash

The Calabash is a very cool place, in the old-fashioned, laid-back sense of the word. The restaurant, deep within the bowels of the Africa Centre, is at once worthy, comfortable and cheap. The same complex features a splendidly seedy bar, a live music hall, and African arts and crafts for sale. The food is genuine and somewhat unsophisticated, and the menu struggles bravely to give snapshots of the extraordinary diversity of African cuisine. They manage dishes from North, East and West Africa, as well as specialities from Nigeria, Ivory Coast, Senegal and Malawi. So if you're looking for a particular dish you may be out of luck. However, if you want a cheerful atmosphere, a small bill, and wholesome, often spicy and usually unfamiliar food, the Calabash is worth seeking out.

Cost	£10–25

Address The Africa Centre, 38 King St, WC2
℗ 020 7836 1976
Station Covent Garden
Open Mon–Fri noon–2.30pm & 6–10.30pm, Sat 6–10.30pm
Accepts All major credit cards except Diners

Starters include familiar dishes like avocado salad and hummus (both £2.20) along with interesting offerings such as aloco (£2.30), which is fried plantain in a hot tomato sauce, and sambusas (£2.95), a vegetarian cousin of the samosa. Those with an enquiring palate will pick the gizzards (£2.95), a splendid dish of chicken gizzards served in a rich, spiky pepper sauce. Grilled chicken wings (£2.60) are less exotic but very good nonetheless. Main courses are marked according to origin. From Nigeria comes egusi (£6.95), a rich soup/stew with spinach, meat and dried shrimps, thickened with melon seed. Yassa (£6.50) is grilled chicken from Senegal, while doro wot (£6.95) is a pungent chicken stew from Ethiopia, served with injera, the soft and thin sourdough bread. From Malawi there is nyamam yo phika (£7.75), a rich beef stew made with sweet peppers and potatoes. Drink whichever of the African beers is in stock at the time you visit.

One of the best dishes, simply called "chicken" (£6.25), takes the form of superb fried chicken served with a ferocious hot sauce. The chef who handles the frying is a master craftsman who manages to get the outside perfectly crisp and the inside perfectly tender. Order this to get an inkling of what the Colonel has been striving for all these years.

Incognico

On the rear of the menu is a picture of Michelin-bespangled chef Nico Ladenis (for he is the Nico in question), kitted out as Zorro. So there you have it, the name of this eatery is a play on words, and one so ponderous as to reveal its Gallic heritage – the French have never really grasped puns. Fortunately they are pretty good at dishing up sensible food, and when you are talking about classic French cooking they have few equals. The dining room is comfortable and done out in dark brown tones, the only cavil being that some of the tables are packed in a bit tightly, so that you could whisper in a loved one's ear and still share the billing and cooing with your neighbours.

Cost	£17–70

Address 117 Shaftesbury Ave, WC2
℡ 020 7836 8866
Station Covent Garden/ Tottenham Court Rd
Open Mon–Sat noon–3pm & 5.30pm–midnight
Accepts All major credit cards

The cooking is very sound here. The menu is a long one and, while not actually being old-fashioned per se, there are enough old favourites to please the stickiest stick in the mud. Starters such as salmon and potato salad (£11.50), open ravioli of goat's cheese (£9.50), and terrine of foie gras (£17) all strike a chord. As do mains like ossobuco (£15.50), which is delightfully rich and served with a Parmesan risotto. And veal kidneys in mustard sauce (£12.50). Or wing of skate with capers (£14.50). Or grilled baby Dover sole with tartare sauce (£14.50). Puddings (all £5.50) carry on the theme successfully: rice pudding; crème brûlée; lemon tart. Be warned: your wallet may hate the wine list.

The set menu (available at lunch and 5.30–7pm) changes daily and is an outstandingly good deal. For £12.50 you get three courses and, joy of joys, there is an equally priced pichet of vin rouge (£7.50 for 50cl). There are two choices per course and the dishes are appealing. The choice may be between smoked salmon and horseradish cream, or ravioli of goat's cheese with red peppers and basil oil; followed by breast of guineafowl with lentils, or grilled sea bass with basil purée and red pepper oil; culminating in crème brûlée with soft Italian cheese and red fruit, or vanilla bavarois with blackcurrant coulis. This is a very good deal indeed.

India Club

When the India Club opened in 1950, the linoleum flooring was probably quite chic; today it has a faded period charm. Situated up two flights of stairs, sandwiched between floors of the grandly named Strand Continental Hotel (one of London's less prominent establishments), the Club is an institution, generally full, and mostly with regulars, as you can tell by the stares of appraisal given to newcomers. The regulars, in love with the strangely old-fashioned combination of runny curry and low, low prices, don't mind traipsing downstairs to the hotel reception to buy a bottle of Cobra beer – they quite understand the inflexibility of English licensing arrangements. These stalwart customers can be split into two categories: suave Indians from the nearby High Commission, and a miscellany of folk from the BBC World Service down the road in Bush House.

Cost	£6–12
Address	143 Strand, WC2
☎	020 7836 0650
Station	Charing Cross
Open	Mon–Sat noon–2.30pm & 6–10.50pm
Accepts	Cash or cheque only

The food at the India Club predates any London consciousness of the different spicings of Bengal, Kerala, Rajasthan or Goa. It is Anglo-Indian, essentially, and well cooked of its kind, although to palates accustomed to more modern Indian dishes it is something of a symphony to runny sauce. Mughlay chicken (£5.20) is a wing and a drumstick in a rich, brown, oniony gravy, garnished with two half hard-boiled eggs; while scampi curry (£6) is runny and brown, with fearless prawns swimming through it. Masala dosai (£3.60) is a well-made crispy pancake with a pleasantly sharp-tasting potato filling. Dhal (£3.30) is yellow and ... runny. The mango chutney (40p) is a revelation: thick parings of mango, each three inches long, are chewy and delicious. Breads – paratha (£1.60), puris (two for £1.80) – are good, while the rice is white and comes in clumps (£2).

You should heed the kindly warning of your waiter about the chilli bhajis (£2.60), a dish as simple as it is thought provoking. Long, thin, extra-hot green chillies are given a thick coating of gram-flour batter and then deep fried until crisp. These are served with coconut chutney that has a few more chopped chillies sprinkled through it. Eating this actually hurts. Console yourself by remembering that, however bad, chilli burn lasts only ten minutes.

Covent Garden & Holborn

The Ivy

The Ivy is a beautiful, Regency-style restaurant, built in 1928 by Mario Gallati, who later founded Le Caprice. It has been a theatreland and society favourite ever since and never more so than today. The staff, it is said, notice recessions only because they have to turn fewer people away. And that's no joke: The Ivy is booked solid for lunch and dinner right through the week. It behaves like a club even if it is not one, and to get a booking it helps to proffer a name of at least B-list celebrity. That said, if your heart is set on a visit try booking at off-peak times a couple of months ahead, or at very short notice, or ask for a table in the bar area. It's also less busy for the weekend lunch – three courses for a bargain £17.50 plus £1.50 service charge, with valet parking thrown in.

Cost	£25–60

Address 1 West St, WC2
℡ 020 7836 4751
Station Leicester Square
Open Daily noon–3pm (Sun 3.30pm) & 5.30pm–midnight
Accepts All major credit cards
ⓦ www.caprice-holdings.co.uk

And once you're in? Well, first off, whether you're famous or not, the staff are charming and unhurrying. Second, the food is pretty good. The menu is essentially a brasserie list of comfort food – nice dishes that combine simplicity with familiarity and which are invariably well cooked. You could spend a lot here without restraint; surprisingly little if you limit yourself to a single course and pudding. You might start with split pea and ham soup (£5.50), or the risotto with wild mushrooms (£9.75/14.75), or the eggs Benedict (£5.75/10.75). Then there's deep-fried haddock (£14.75), corned beef hash with double fried egg (£9.50), and well-made versions of classic staples such as the Ivy hamburger with dill pickle (£9), shepherd's pie (£11.25) and salmon fishcakes (£11.75). Even the vegetable section is enlivened with homely delights like bubble and squeak (£2.75). For dessert you might turn to chocolate pudding soufflé (£6.50), Eton mess (£9.50), or perhaps finish with a savoury such as smoked anchovies on toast (£3.25).

The Ivy's present incarnation is the result of a 1990 makeover that meticulously restored the wood paneling and leaded stained glass. It also involved a roll call of British artists. Look around and you may notice works by, among others, Howard Hodgkin, Peter Blake, Tom Phillips and Patrick Caulfield.

J. Sheekey

Sheekey's is one of a handful of restaurants which had shambled along since the war – the First World War. Then, in the late 1990s, it was taken over by the team behind The Ivy and Le Caprice (see p.38 and p.96). After a good deal of redesign and refurbishment, it emerged from the builders' clutches as J. Sheekey, with much the same attitudes and style as its senior siblings, but still focused on fish. The restaurant may look new, but it certainly seems old, and its series of interconnecting dining rooms gives it an intimate feel. The cooking is accomplished, the service is first-rate, and the fish is fresh – a good combination!

Cost £18–70

Address 28–32 St Martin's Court, WC2
℡ 020 7240 2565
Station Leicester Square
Open Mon–Sat noon–3pm & 5.30pm–midnight, Sun noon–3.30pm & 5.30pm–midnight
Accepts All major credit cards
ⓦ www.caprice-holdings.co.uk

The long menu presents a seductive blend of plain, old-fashioned, classic fish cuisine, such as lemon sole belle meunière (£17.50), with more modernist dishes like yellow-fin tuna with peperonata and rocket (£16.50). There are always hand-written dishes on the menu, "specials" which change on a weekly basis. To start with, there are oysters, crabs and shellfish, plus everything from jellied eels (£4.75) and potted shrimps (£9.75) to seared rare tuna (£9.50) and char-grilled squid with chorizo and broad beans (£9.50). Main courses, like pan-fried wing of skate with capers and brown butter (£14.25), or Cornish fish stew with celery heart and garlic mayonnaise (£19.50), are backed up by classics such as roast cod (£14.75) and Sheekey's fish pie (£9.75). Puddings go from spotted dick with butter and golden syrup (£5.25) to raspberry trifle (£5.75) and orange Muscat jelly with Jersey cream (£8.50).

The set menus are good value. At the weekend, lunch costs just £13.75 for two courses, or £17.50 for three (plus a £1.50 cover charge in the main dining room). You could tuck into Italian black figs with Parma ham; then escalope of salmon with mixed courgettes and tomato vinaigrette; and finish with chocolate and Grand Marnier tart. In a further bid to make life at the weekend hassle-free, the restaurant operates a valet parking system on Sunday.

NORTH AMERICAN

Joe Allen

By some inexplicable alchemy, Joe Allen continues to be the Covent Garden eatery of choice for a wide swath of the acting profession. It is a dark, resolutely untrendy place that dishes up American comfort food. So saying, you can never have anything better than exactly what you want and, if your heart is set on a Caesar salad, chilli con carne or eggs Benedict, this is a great place to come. Joe Allen also has a splendid attitude to mealtimes: the à la carte runs all

Cost	£16–35

Address 13 Exeter St, WC2
℡ 020 7836 0651
Station Covent Garden
Open Mon–Fri
noon–12.45am, Sat
11.30am–12.45am, Sun
11.30am–11.30pm
Accepts All major credit cards
except Diners
ⓦ www.joeallen.co.uk

day, so you can have lunch when you will. There's a special menu offering two courses for £13 and three for £14 (noon–4pm), plus a pre-theatre menu (Mon–Sat 5–6.45pm) which delivers two courses for £14 and three for £16.

The food is the kind of stuff that we are all comfortable with. Starters include smoked salmon with scallion and herb fritters and crème fraîche (£7), chopped chicken liver (£5), and black bean soup (£4.50). They are followed on the menu by a section described as "salads/eggs/sandwiches" in which you'll find some of Joe Allen's strengths: Caesar salad (£5/7); roast chicken salad with Chinese leaf, carrots, onion, red apple and a peanut dressing (£8); and eggs Joe Allen (£8.50), a satisfying combination of poached eggs, potato skins, Hollandaise sauce and spinach. Main courses range from grilled swordfish with pak choi and black bean dressing (£13.50), through barbecue spare ribs with rice, wilted spinach, black-eyed peas and corn muffin (£11), to pan-fried calves' liver with mashed potatoes, grilled bacon and red wine gravy (£12.50). The side orders, including mashed potatoes with gravy (£2.50) and green beans with toasted almonds (£2.50), are most attractive. And the desserts are serious – go for the brownie (£4.50), with hot fudge sauce as an extra (£1.50).

Joe Allen is also home to its very own urban legend. The hamburger is very highly rated by aficionados everywhere, but you have to be in the know to order one, as it has never been listed on the menu.

Mela

(🍴) In the colourful brochure, Mela is described as "Indian cuisine – Country style". What they really mean is "Indian cuisine – Indian style". This is one of the new breed of Indian restaurants that doesn't follow the time-honoured tradition of Bangladeshi restaurants, with their familiar dishes carefully developed solely for the Brits. At Mela the attitude is more "If it's good enough for Delhi..." The

Cost	£5–40

Address 152–156
Shaftesbury Ave, WC2
℡ 020 7836 8635
Station Covent Garden
Open Mon–Sat noon–11.30pm,
Sun noon–10.30pm
Accepts All major credit cards
🖳 www.melarestaurant.co.uk

result is a restaurant serving very attractive and remarkably good-value Indian food. Mela may even have cracked the great lunch conundrum – Indian restaurateurs find it very difficult to persuade Londoners to eat curry for lunch. There's a "Paratha Pavilion" at lunchtime, which may sound a bit kitsch but lists a variety of delicious set lunches, from the insubstantial at £1.95, to the jolly good at £4.95. Stellar value in WC2.

At lunch the set meals revolve around bread – parathas to be precise – much as in Delhi's famous Parathey Wali Gali, which is a street of snackers' heaven. Choose bread made from maize, sorghum, millet, whole-wheat flour, or chilli- and coriander-flavoured chickpea flour. The latter is particularly good. They come with dal or curry of the day for £1.95! Or with a savoury stuffing at £2.95. There are other breads, too, such as roomalis (large and thin, wholemeal handkerchief bread), puris (fried chapatis), uttapams (rice flour pancakes) and naans. Dosas come in at £3.95. At these prices you can experiment. The main menu, which is available at lunch but comes into its own in the evening, is full of good things. Calamari paktooni (£4.50) is fiery chilli squid. Tandoor dishes like chukandar kalam ke kebab (£9.25) – a boned chicken leg marinated in beetroot and chillies – are very tasty indeed. There is also a good Allepey prawn curry (£10.95), and an exemplary rara gosht rogan josh (£8.95).

The decor here is on the bright side, but this is a large and modern restaurant that disowns the flock wallpaper tradition and bustles along, happily dishing out good, fresh food to happy customers. It is also located in the West End, and open throughout the afternoon, which is something of a boon. Service is slick and friendly.

INDIAN

Punjab

In 1951, Gurbachan Singh Maan moved his fledgling Indian restaurant from the City to new premises in Neal Street in Covent Garden, his plan being to take advantage of the trade from the nearby Indian High Commission. It was a strategy that has worked handsomely. Today, his grandson Sital Singh Maan runs what is one of London's oldest curry houses, though one which has always been at the forefront of new developments – in 1962 the Maan family brought over one of the first tandoor ovens to be seen in Britain, and in 2002 they celebrated forty years in the business with a new extension and a lick of paint. Despite these forays into fashion, the cuisine at the Punjab has always been firmly rooted where it belongs – in the Punjab.

Cost	£15–35

Address 80–82 Neal St, WC2
☎ 020 7836 9787
Station Covent Garden
Open Mon–Sat noon–3pm &
6–11.30pm, Sun noon–3pm &
6–10.30pm
Accepts All major credit cards
🌐 www.punjab.co.uk

Punjabi cuisine offers some interesting, non-standard Indian dishes, so start by ordering from among the less familiar items on the menu. Kadu and puri (£2.10), for instance, a sweet and sharp mash of curried pumpkin served on a puri; or aloo tikka (£2.10), which are described as potato cutlets but arrive as small deep-fried moons on a sea of tangy sauce; or chicken chat (£2.60), which is diced chicken in rich sauce. To follow, try the acharri gosht (£7.50), or the acharri murgha (£7.80). The first is made with lamb, and the second with chicken, and the Maan family are very proud of the acharri; the meat is "pickled" in traditional Punjabi spices and, as a result, both meat and sauce have an agreeable edge of sharpness. Chicken karahi (£7.10) is good, too – rich and thick. The anari gosht (£7.50) combines lamb with pomegranate, while from the vegetable dishes, channa aloo (£4) offsets the nutty crunch of chickpeas with the solace of potatoes. For refreshment, turn to a satisfyingly large bottle of Cobra lager (£3.60), which originated in Bangalore but is now, rather more prosaically, "brewed in Bedford".

On the menu you'll also find benaam macchi tarkari (£7.50), a "nameless fish curry, speciality of chef". This curry may be nameless but it is certainly not flavourless, with solid lumps of boneless white fish in rich and tasty gravy.

Rules

Rules would be a living cliché but for one essential saving grace – all the fixtures, fittings and studied eccentricities which look as if they have been custom-made in some modern factory are real. Rules is the genuine article, a very English restaurant that has been taking its toll of tourists for two hundred years. Dickens, Betjeman, H.G. Wells, Thackeray, Graham Greene and King Edward VII are just a few of the celebs who have revelled in Rules. In 1984 the restaurant passed into the hands of John Mayhew, and in 1997, he brought in David Chambers as head chef. Rules' proud boast is, "We specialize in classic game cookery". Indeed they do, and the restaurant has become more of a bustling brasserie than the mausoleum it once was, despite instituting a resolute non-smoking policy which has upset as many people as it has pleased.

Cost	£25–65

Address 35 Maiden Lane, WC2
℡ 020 7836 5314
Station Covent Garden
Open Daily noon–midnight
Accepts All major credit cards
🖳 www.rules.co.uk

BRITISH

First of all you should note that Rules is open from noon till late, which is very handy when circumstances dictate a four o'clock lunch. There is also a competitive pre-theatre offer – £19.95 for two courses. Start with Cornish crab with coriander, avocado, tomato and fennel dressing (£9.50), a Stilton and celeriac soup (£5.95), or an outstanding parfait of chicken liver and foie gras (£8.95). Go on to game in season; whatever the time of year, you'll find something good here. The menu changes with the seasons but the steak and kidney pudding with mash (£16.95) is a banker. As is the grilled Dover sole for two (£37.90) and the roast rib of beef for two (£39.90). Also noteworthy is the poached Finnan haddock in a mussel and saffron sauce (£17.95). Puddings, such as treacle sponge or sticky toffee (both £6.50), are merciless. Why not go for the traditional blue Stilton cheese with celery and a glass of port (£9.95)?

And all this in a beautiful Victorian setting. Should you face entertaining out-of-town relations, or foreign visitors in search of something old and English, Rules is a good place to indulge your nostalgia to the full.

Euston & King's Cross

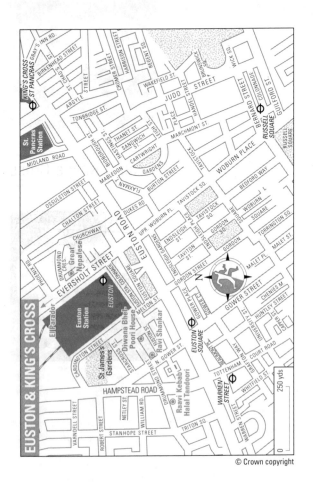

© Crown copyright

Diwana Bhel-Poori House

All varnished pine and shag-pile carpets, the Diwana Bhel-Poori House puts you in mind of a late-1970s Wimpy bar. Only the Indian woodcarvings dotted around the walls give the game away – that and the heady scent of freshly blended spices. It's a busy place, with tables filling up and emptying at a fair crack, though the atmosphere is con-

Cost	£5–18

Address 121 Drummond St, NW1
☏ 020 7387 5556
Station Euston
Open Daily noon–11.30pm
Accepts All major credit cards
ⓦ www.diwanarestaurant.com

vivial and casual rather than rushed. There's no licence, so you can bring your own beer or wine (corkage is free) and a full water jug is supplied on each table. This, the low prices (the costliest dish will set you back just £6.20), a chatty menu listing "tasty snacks", and fast, friendly service combine to create a deceptively simple stage for some fine Indian vege-tarian cooking. There's even a set lunch buffet at £5.45.

Starters are copious, ladled out in no-nonsense stainless steel bowls. The dahi bhalle chat (£2.30) is a cool, yoghurty blend of chickpeas, crushed pooris and bulghur wheat, sprinkled with "very special spices". The dahi poori (£2.30) is a fragrant concoction of pooris, potatoes, onions, sweet and sour sauces and chilli chutney, again smothered in yoghurt and laced with spices. Stars of the main menu are the dosas, par-ticularly the flamboyant deluxe dosa (£4.60), a giant fan of a pancake with coconut chutney, potatoes and dhal nestling beneath its folds. Also superb is the house speciality, thali annapurna (£6), a feast of dhal, rice, vegetables, pickles, side dishes, mini bhajees and your choice of pooris or chapatis – divine but unfinishable, especially if you make the mistake of ordering some monstrously proportioned side dishes as well.

Whatever feast you put together, do leave room for dessert, as there's a heavenly kulfi malai (£1.70) to dig into – a creamy pyramid of frozen milk flavoured with kevda, nuts and herbs. Alternatively, try the Kash-miri falooda (£2.20) – cold milk with china grass and rose syrup topped with ice cream and nuts. Though strictly speaking a drink, this is surely pudding enough for anyone.

Great Nepalese

This bit of London behind Euston station is distinctly seedy, and the shops that are neighbours to the Great Nepalese offer strange products for probably quite strange people. After completing the new shopfront, the decorators have now strayed as far as the dining room, which in 2001 was painted an orangey colour. The giant wall photo showing the Queen and Prince Philip standing with five Gurkha holders of the Victoria Cross has survived the refurb. This place combines friendly and homely service with authentic Nepalese food and, should your nerve falter, the menu also has a buffer zone littered with standard curry house favourites – lamb rogan josh is helpfully subtitled "a very popular lamb curry".

Cost	£8–22

Address 48 Eversholt St, NW1
℡ 020 7388 6737
Station Euston/Euston Square
Open Mon–Sat noon–2.45pm
& 6–11.30pm, Sun
noon–2.30pm & 6–11.15pm
Accepts All major credit cards

But don't order the lamb curry unless feeling profoundly unadventurous. It may be a very nice, popular lamb curry but the authentic Great Nepalese dishes are nicer still. Start with masco bhara, a large frisbee-shaped doughnut. It is made from black lentils, but without their black skins, so the result is a nutty-tasting, fluffy white mass with a crisp outside. It comes with a bowl of curry gravy for dipping (£3.50 plain, £3.85 with a hidden core of shredded lamb). Or try haku choyala (£3.75), diced mutton with garlic, lemon juice and ginger. It's spicy and agreeably sharp. For mains, the staff direct you to the dumba curry (£4.95), a traditional Nepalese-style curry, reliant on the same rich gravy as the masco bhara, or the chicken ra piaj (£5.25), with onions and spices. Both are highly recommended. Another very typical Nepalese dish is the butuwa chicken (£5.25). It combines ginger and spices with garlic and green herbs and is delicious. And if you like dhal, you shouldn't miss the kalo dal (£2.95), nutty and dark with black lentils.

A single note of caution. Beware the Coronation rum from Kathmandu. This firewater was first distilled in 1975 for the coronation of his majesty, the late King Birendra Bir Bikram Shah Dev, and it comes in a bottle shaped like a glass kukri. You probably have to be a Gurkha to appreciate its finer points.

El Parador

El Parador is a small, no-frills Spanish restaurant and tapas bar, slightly stranded in the quiet little enclave around Mornington Crescent, between King's Cross and Camden. It serves very tasty tapas at very reasonable prices and has a friendly, laid-back atmosphere, even on busy Friday and Saturday nights. It's a good place to spend a summer evening, with a lovely garden out the

Cost	£9–22

Address 245 Eversholt St, NW1
☎ 020 7387 2789
Station Mornington Crescent
Open Mon–Thurs noon–3pm & 6–11pm, Fri noon–3pm & 6–11.30pm, Sat 6–11.30pm, Sun 7–10.30pm
Accepts All major credit cards

back, though this is no secret and the sought-after tables here should be booked in advance.

As ever with tapas, the fun part of eating here is choosing several dishes from the wide selection on offer, and then sharing and swapping with your companions. The plates are small, so allow yourself at least two or three tapas a head – more for a really filling meal – and go for at least one of the fish or seafood dishes, which are treats. Highlights include chipirones salteados (£4) – baby squid pan fried with sea salt and olive oil; gambas al pil-pil (£4.90) – nice fat tiger prawns pan fried with parsley, paprika and chilli; and salteado de pez espada (£5) – fresh swordfish sautéed with garlic and coriander. Carnivores shouldn't miss out on the jamón serrano (£4.80) – delicious Spanish cured ham; or the morcilla de Burgos (£4.20) – sausages that are a cousin of black pudding. Also good is the potaje de cordero con lentejas (£4) – a classy lamb stew with lentils. The numerous vegetarian tapas include judias salteadas (£4) – green beans sautéed with braised leeks, red peppers and wine; paella del Parador (£4) – a vegetable paella with peas, corn and green beans; and buñuelos de patatas (£4) – mashed potato cooked with sun-dried tomatoes, cumin and Manchego cheese. Desserts keep up the pace: marquesa de chocolate (£3.30) is a luscious, creamy, home-made chocolate mousse; flan de naranja (£3) is a really good orange crème caramel.

Try a glass of the dry Manzanilla (£2.90) to start or accompany your meal. It's a perfect foil for tapas. Or delve into El Parador's strong selection of Spanish wines. Enjoyable choices include Muga Crianza '99 (£16.50), a smooth white Rioja, and the Guelbenzu Crianza '99 (£16), a rich and fruity red.

Raavi Kebab Halal Tandoori

This small restaurant has been a fixture for more than 25 years, during which time Drummond Street has become one of the main curry centres of London. Competition here is more than just fierce, it is ludicrous, as well-established vegetarian restaurants compete to offer the cheapest "eat-as-much-as-you-can" lunch buffet. It is lucky that vegetables are so cheap. But the Raavi is not just about bargain prices – or vegetables, come to that. It is an unpretentious Pakistani grill house that specializes in halal meat dishes, and on the menu shyly offers "probably the best grilled and cooked items in London". And indeed, when you fancy tucking into an item, this is a great place to come.

Cost	£6–15

Address 125 Drummond St, NW1
℗ 020 7388 1780
Station Euston/Euston Square
Open Daily 12.30–10.30pm
Accepts All major credit cards

The grills here are good but hot – hot enough for the wildest chilli-head. Seekh kebab (£2.50) – juicy and well-flavoured, straight from the charcoal grill in the doorway – is hot. Chicken tikka (£2.50) is hot. Mutton tikka (£2.50) is hot. And with the kebabs comes a khaki-coloured dipping sauce that is sharp with lemon juice, strongly flavoured with fresh coriander and, as you'd expect, hot with fresh chillies. Lamb quorma (£4.75) is not so fierce; its rich sauce with fresh ginger and garlic is topped with a sprinkle of shaved almonds. Chicken daal (£3.95) brings chunks of chicken on the bone, bobbing on a sea of savoury yellow split-pea dhal, and is thoroughly delicious. Nan breads (90p) are light and crispy. Nihari (£4.95), the traditional Muslim breakfast dish of slow-cooked curried mutton vies with haleem for the title of bestseller here. Haleem (£4.95) is a dish whose origins are shrouded in mystery. Some say that it was invented in the Middle East, which is certainly where it is most popular today; other devotees track it back to Moghul kitchens. The recipe is arduous. Take some meat and cook it, add four kinds of dhal, a good deal of cracked wheat, and two kinds of rice, plus spices. Cook for up to seven hours, then add some garam masala. The result is a gluey slick of smooth and spicy glop from which any traces of the meat have all but disappeared.

And how does it taste? You'd be hard pushed to be more enthusiastic than "not bad".

Ravi Shankar

🍴 As a hotbed of Indian dining, Drummond Street is still a magnet for curryholics and anyone else seeking a good, cheap meal. The Ravi Shankar opened in the 1980s, and its decor is still firmly wedged in an era when plain enough was good enough. The Ravi Shankar may look ordinary, and the seating may not be ultra-comfortable, but the vegetarian food is very honest and very cheap – something that weighs heavily with the loyal clientele.

Cost	£4–15

Address 133 Drummond St, NW1
℡ 020 7388 6458
Station Euston
Open Daily noon–10.45pm
Accepts Major credit cards except AmEx and Diners

On a Monday, the daily special consists of cashew nut pillau rice and cauliflower curry, served with salad and mint yogurt chutney for the princely sum of £3.95. There are not many sub-£4 meals left anywhere in London, let alone a meal at such a price that is well cooked and satisfying. The cashew nut pillau is rich and nutty, and the cauliflower curry has been made substantial by the addition of chunks of potato. On Tuesday, there's vegetable biryani with curry (£4.25), Wednesday brings aloo palak with chapati (£3.95), and the specials wind onwards to the extravagance of chana batura (£4.50) on Saturday – a delicious fried bread with a chick pea curry. The main menu starters fall into two categories. There are hot snacks from Western India, including samosas (three for £2.30), bhajia (£2.30) and potato bonda (£2.50) – a solid, tasty, deep-fried sphere made from potato and lentils. Then there are cold "snacks and chat", billed as coming from Bombay's famed snack city, Chowpatty beach. At Ravi Shankar there are bhel puri, pani puri and potato puri (all £2.30). Try the pani puri – a plate of tiny spherical shells arrives with a bowl of cooked chickpeas in tamarind and date sauce. You punch a hole in the top of the puri then add a spoonful of chickpeas. Good fun. Breads are good – treat yourself to an ace stuffed paratha (£1.95).

Or try a thali – these complete meals come on stainless steel trays, and range from rice and dal (£3.95) to the Shankar thali (£6.95), which comes with dhal soup, four different curries with rice, raita, a pappadom and puris or chapatis, plus a dessert.

Kensington

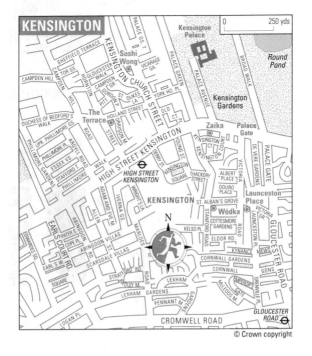
© Crown copyright

Launceston Place

Launceston Place is one of those small, chic streets where you cannot help feeling a pang of envy for anyone rich enough to live in the slick little houses. As the road curves you'll find a sprinkling of high-ticket shops on one side and the Launceston Place restaurant on the other. The restaurant sprawls its way through a nest of rooms and is pleasantly formal. Or perhaps that should be formal and pleasant. Service is efficient but not in your face and there is a traditional feel to everything. This is a neighbourhood restaurant, but one that is the product of a very swish neighbourhood, which makes some sense of the fact that a couple of years after opening here the team went on to create Kensington Place (see p.453) – another establishment very much in tune with its surroundings.

Cost	£18–65

Address 1a Launceston Place, W8
℗ 020 7937 6912
Station High Street Kensington
Open Mon–Fri 12.30–2.30pm & 7–11.30pm, Sat 7–11.30pm, Sun 12.30–2.30pm
Accepts All major credit cards

The menu changes every six weeks or so and dishes match traditional combinations with fashionable ingredients in an unstuffy way. Starters range from a classic dish such as baked oysters Florentine (£9), to quail's eggs and broccoli salad with crispy pancetta and Parmesan (£6), or clam and sweetcorn chowder (£6). Mains range from plain dishes such as grilled monkfish brochette with gremolata (£17), to pan-fried sea bass with Jerusalem artichoke, truffle ravioli and watercress sauce (£18), and on to meatier offerings like oxtail stew with baby onions, bacon and button mushrooms (£16), or possibly sirloin steak with ceps, garlic and parsley butter (£17.50). The dessert menu ticks all the appropriate boxes: there's blueberry cheesecake (£6.50) and a Mississippi mud pie with crème fraîche (£6.50). The wine list is strong in traditional areas, so think French.

The set lunch is much beloved by local ladies-who-lunch and is priced reasonably at £15.50 for two courses and £18.50 for three. Caesar salad, seared salmon with dill and cucumber dressing, chocolate mousse cake, coffee, a tsunami of chilled white wine and gossip – just about perfect.

Sushi Wong

(icon) Sushi Wong is the kind of name you either love or hate but, whichever side you take, it is certainly slick – just like this deceptively sized restaurant. On the ground floor there's a modernist Japanese restaurant-cum-sushi-bar seating about 25 people. Downstairs there's a teppan-yaki table and room for a further sixty diners. Looking in from the street it's hard not to admire the stark blue and bright-yellow colour scheme, and the tables, each topped with ground glass backed by a blue neon tube. In the face of all this brightness and modernity, the service is so low-key that it almost seems timid, but Sushi Wong is a confident and efficient place for all that.

Cost	£15–40

Address 38c–d Kensington Church St, W8
⊕ 020 7937 5007
Station High Street Kensington
Open Mon–Sat noon–2.30pm & 6–10.30pm, Sun 6–9.30pm
Accepts All major credit cards

Sushi is delicious here. Ordering the sushi matsu set (£19) brings a round lacquer tray with six pieces of salmon or tuna roll flanked by ten pieces of various sushi – the chef's selection. The fish is fresh, the wasabi strong, the gari delicious and the sushi well prepared. A good array at a fair price. The menu emphasizes hosomaki (roll sushi), ranging from edo (£4.20) – crab meat, salmon and cucumber – to "Kensington roll" (£3.80), which is a crispy salmon and asparagus concoction "specially made for Kensington dwellers!" There is also a wide range of à la carte selections: starters like agedofu dengkaku (£3.90), which are thick-sliced tofu grilled on skewers; deep-fried soft-shell crab (£6.20); yakitori (£4.90); and age-gyoza (£4), which are deep-fried dumplings. Mains include stir-fried lobster tail (£10.80); chicken teriyaki (£8.80); pork tonkatsu (£8.80); and the Sushi Wong tempura selection (£12.80), which includes king prawns, fish and vegetables. Among the noodle dishes you'll find nabeyaki udon (£7.50) and Sushi Wong ramen (£6.50) – egg noodles with chicken, prawns, egg and vegetables in miso broth.

The set menus make life simpler. The Sakura (£26) gets you sashimi, tempura, salmon steak or beef teriyaki, rice and miso soup, plus dessert. There's also a seven-course Sushi Wong Dinner (£36). Or book one of the hibashi tables for a teppan-yaki dinner cooked in front of you – five courses for £33.

The Terrace

The Terrace is a small, modern restaurant hidden among the residential streets north of Kensington High Street. Its dining room is small but, as the name proclaims, there is a terrace fronting onto the street, where a handful of tables await any diners who have the nerve to brave the British weather. The food is simple, seasonal and modern.

Cost	£18–30
Address	33c Holland St, W8
☎	020 7937 3224
Station	High Street Kensington
Open	Mon–Sat noon–2.30pm & 7–10.30pm, Sun 12.30–3pm
Accepts	All major credit cards

Presentation is unfussy and the standard of cooking is generally high. Elsewhere you would probably expect the prices to be a tad lower, but here in Kensington, on the way to Holland Park, they represent quite decent value.

The menu changes regularly. Starters like a quiche Lorraine with a lamb's lettuce salad (£7.50) are well executed, while there might be a terrine of confit quail, foie gras and salsify (£11.50). Or there's an open ravioli of seared scallop (£8.50) which is served with a crab bisque and baby spinach. The Terrace salad (£6.50) could be anything from a competently made Caesar to a combination of grilled spiced aubergines, plum tomatoes and goat's cheese. Soups veer towards the exotic, such as cream of butternut squash with sage and Parmesan croutons (£5.50). At first glance the main courses look like standard fare – steak, pork, monkfish, lamb – but they're all made from fresh ingredients which deliver good, strong flavours. Slow roast loin of pork comes with Japanese fried rice, shitake mushroom and braised aubergine (£17.50), and is particularly good. Char-grilled grass-fed rib-eye steak with duck-fat roast potatoes, parsley butter and red wine sauce (£19.50) is a rich and straightforward combination. A bourride of monkfish and clams (£18.50) comes with new potatoes and leeks. The dessert section ranges from chocolate mousse with vanilla cream (£5.50), via gooseberry fool (£5.50), to raspberry crème brûlée (£5.50).

Regulars are easily spotted: they're the ones tucking into the excellent-value (and constantly changing) set lunches – £14.50 for two courses, £17.50 for three.

Wódka

Wódka is a restaurant that lies in wait for you. It's calm and bare, and the food is better than you might expect – well cooked, and thoughtfully seasoned. The daily lunch menu represents extremely good value at £10.90 for two courses and £13.50 for three, a large proportion of the dishes being refugees from the evening à la carte. Where, you wonder, is the streak of madness that helped the Polish cavalry take on German tank regiments with sabres drawn? On the shelves behind the bar, that's where, in the extensive collection of moody and esoteric vodkas, which are for sale both by the shot and by the carafe.

Cost	£14–42

Address 12 St Albans Grove, W8
ⓣ 020 7937 6513
Station High Street Kensington
Open Mon–Fri 12.30–2.30pm & 7–11.15pm, Sat & Sun 7–11.15pm
Accepts All major credit cards
ⓦ www.wodka.co.uk

The soup makes a good starter: Ukrainian barszcz (£4.50) is a rich, beetrooty affair. Blinis are also the business: they come with smoked salmon (£6.90/8.90), aubergine mousse (£5.50/6.90) or 40g of Oscietra caviar (£23.50). A lunchtime selection will get you all except the caviar. Also good is the kaszanka (£5.90) – grilled black pudding with pickled red cabbage and pear puree. For a main course, the fish cakes (£10.90) with leeks and a dill sauce are firm favourites with the regulars. In line with the Polish love of wild game, when partridge is available it is roasted and served with a splendid mash of root vegetables – the mashed potato is also worthy of special praise. Or there may be haunch of venison with sour cherries and honey-roasted pears (£13.90). Puddings tend to be of the oversweet, under-imaginative gateaux variety, but the vodka will ensure that you won't be worrying about that.

Consider the list of vodkas with due attention – there is a host of them: Zubrówka (made with bison grass); Okhotnichya (for hunters); Jarzebiak (that's rowan berries); Cytrynówka (lemon); Sliwowica (plum); Sliwówka (plum, but hot and sweet); Czarna Porezecka (blackcurrant); Ananas (pineapple); Krupnik (honey, and served hot); Roza (rose petals); Goldwasser (made with flakes of gold and aniseed); Soplica (which is a mystery). They cost from £2.25 to £2.75 a shot, and from £33.90 to £39.90 per 50cl carafe. Remember this simple test: pick any three of the above names and say them quickly. If anyone shows signs of understanding, you need another shot.

Zaika

(icon) Zaika is an upmarket Indian restaurant that gives the lie to any snobs who still maintain that Indian food can never amount to anything. Not content with netting one of the first Michelin stars to be given to an Indian restaurant, this establishment upped sticks and moved across London from the Fulham Road to its current home. The head chef is Vineet Bhatia and he is an accomplished cook. The spicing is well balanced, the presentation above average and though your bill will not be a small one it will not be a West End wallet-breaker either. There are novel dishes to be sampled but they sit alongside classics – you can still enjoy an impeccable rogan josh served on the bone.

Cost   £12–60

Address 1 Kensington High
St, W8
℗ 020 7795 6533
Station High Street Kensington
Open Mon–Fri noon–2.45pm
& 6.30–10.45pm, Sat 6.30–
10.45pm, Sun noon–2.45pm
& 6.30–10pm
Accepts All major credit cards
except Diners
⊛ www.zaika_restaurant.co.uk

Start with the dhungar machli tikka (£6.95) – it is hard to praise this dish highly enough. A well-marinated chunk of salmon is cooked in the tandoor and served when just right. Wonder of wonders, not over-done! Or there is the murghabi seekhe (£6.50), which is a dish of minced duck rolls. A good deal of thought goes into the main courses. This is not a seasonal menu in the strictest sense of the term, but in season the grey mullet will switch with sea bass or the cauliflower may be changed for broccoli. The nariyal jhinga (£12.95), made from prawns cooked in a coconut masala tempered with lime leaves, stands out. Or there's lal mirch murg (£9.95), a spicy chicken dish made with fennel and coriander seeds. The koh-e-rogan josh (£12.95) is very good. Samundri khazana (£21.50) is most interesting – this is a crispy, Hawaiian, soft-shell crab with spiced scallops and an Indian risotto. Inspirational stuff. The simpler dishes are also good – try the dubkiwale aloo (£4.95), a straightforward dish of potatoes with cumin. And the breads are splendid. Try the malai nan (£2.95) with your starters – it's cheesy, sticky, self-indulgent. On the dessert menu you may find the chocomosa – crisp samosas containing an admirably bitter melted chocolate.

As well as elaborate multi-course set dinners at £45 per person Zaika offers an express lunch for £7.95. Is this the cheapest way to eat Michelin-starred food in London?

Knightsbridge & Belgravia

© Crown copyright

The Capital

(❗) The Capital Hotel has quietly gone about its business since 1971. The cooking has always been top flight, but it took the arrival of a voluble and passionate French chef called Eric Crouillère-Chavot to lift things to the current exalted level. In January 2001 Mr Michelin gave the Capital two stars, putting it firmly in the top half-dozen restaurants in London, and for once he was right. The dining

Cost	£35–150

Address 22–24 Basil St, SW1
(☎) 020 7589 5171
Station Knightsbridge
Open Mon–Sat noon–2.15pm
& 7–11pm, Sun noon–2.15pm
& 7–10.15pm
Accepts All major credit cards
(🌐) www.capitalhotel.co.uk

room looks a tad old fashioned, but pilgrims come for the food not the decor. This is not a cheap restaurant. In the evening all starters cost £18, mains £25, and puds £10. The five-course dégustation menu costs £65. All of which makes the £27.50 three-course lunch a bargain!

Chavot's menu is an exciting one. Dishes are full flavoured and elegantly plated. Sometimes presentation strays into the fussy zone beloved of the Michelin inspectors, but expect classically rich and satisfying flavours. Starters may include a truffle and pecorino risotto; scrambled eggs with potato and Parmesan beignet. The risotto is a masterpiece, with buckets of flavour and a slight crunch to the rice. The scramble is served in a brown eggshell, and is very, very good. A fricassée of Jersey Royals and green asparagus with pea jus is simple but richly flavoured, and truly delicious. Main courses range from Dover sole fillets served on top of broad beans that have been cooked with bacon – a grand combination; to roast veal cutlet with truffle cheese, glazed carrots, girolles and salsify; or corn-fed chicken leg stuffed with mushrooms and served with tagliolini; or roast brill with tapenade, courgettes and aubergine and deep fried mozzarella. Puds are elaborate, sculptural and satisfying – Chavot's interpretation of bread and butter pudding is small, rectangular, fussy and tastes of essence of bread and butter pudding.

The terminal cup of dodgy coffee has ruined many a good meal, but not at The Capital. Choose to have your personal cafetière loaded with Colombian Medellin Excelsor, Mount Kenya AA, Ethiopian Mocha Djimmah, or Prime Honduras.

La Tante Claire

At the end of 1998, Pierre Koffman gathered up his kitchen brigade and moved to the Berkeley Hotel in Knightsbridge. After a lengthy bedding-in period, things have settled down, Tante Claire has regained form and is as sublime as ever. Perhaps it is his Gascon heritage, but Koffman's food pulls off an amazing treble whammy: it is sophisticated but earthy and rich in flavour; dishes are both elegant and satisfying; things look good but they taste better. There is only one way to find out how he does it, and that is to go and eat. Every chef with aspirations should try the set lunch here – £29 for three courses, with coffee and petits fours.

Cost	£35–150
Address	Wilton Place, SW1
☎	020 7823 2003
Station	Hyde Park Corner
Open	Mon–Fri noon–2pm & 7–11pm, Sat 7–11pm
Accepts	All major credit cards

What an amazing deal! There are two choices for both starter and main, so you might find yourself agonizing between a salade Niçoise – a large bowlful with small potatoes, runny egg and marinated tuna – and chicken liver parfait with Sauternes jelly. Choosing the main is no easier – herb-crusted cod versus perfect double lamb chop. If these dishes sound simple, that is because they are. They are also perfectly judged, strongly flavoured, well balanced and well presented. Come back at dinner and prices move briskly upwards. There are usually six starters, five fish and six meats on offer. Starters like tranche de foie gras poêlée, enrobée de cacao, sauce cappuccino (£24); and coquilles St Jacques grillés, sauce à l'encre de seiche (£25) pave the way for filet d'àgneau cuit au four, oignon confit au citron, amandes et pruneaux brochette d'abats (£29); and canard de Challans (£29) – roast duck with a Banyuls and foie gras sauce. Or perhaps you should try Koffman's signature dish, the pied de cochon farci aux morilles (£28), and see the fabled dish from which so many chefs have drawn inspiration for so long.

The service here is slick and unobtrusive, the petits fours are good and the puddings are amazing. There's also a minimum charge of £50 a head in the evening, plus a 12.5% service charge and a wine list that starts sensibly and ends up stratospheric. All in all this is the real thing. So start saving now and treat yourself.

Zuma

Zuma was launched in the summer of 2002 with the unstated but obvious aim of out Nobu-ing Nobu (see p.83). A stylish triumvirate of investors enlisted the Japanese uber-design team Super Potato to create this huge restaurant. This firm may sound more like an ingredient than a group of designers, but

Cost	£25–120

Address 5 Raphael St, SW7
℡ 020 7584 1010
Station Knightsbridge
Open Mon–Sat noon–3pm &
6–11pm, Sun noon–4pm
Accepts All major credit cards

they have made a decent job of the place and now the premises that once used to be home to the Chicago Rib Shack are all stone, rough-hewn granite and unfinished wood. This is a seriously trendy place, and the bar buzzes with the glad cries of both the A list and their wannabe disciples. The approach to eating is modernist – with Japanese dishes, macrobiotic options and pick-and-mix nibbles portions.

The menu is a long one, and complicated to boot. Start by nibbling some edamame Zuma style (£3.50). These are soya beans which have been boiled in the pod – you strip the beans out with your teeth and leave the pods. Or there is tosa dofu (£4.50), which is deep-fried tofu with daikon and bonito flakes. Shake no zukeyaki (£9.50) is a most accessible dish of sesame-coated seared salmon. The skewers from the robata grill are fresh and appealing. Try asparagus and cured pork (£4), or ginko nuts with sea salt (£4.80). Then there are seafood dishes, meat dishes, sashimi, sushi, tempura … every dish is presented stylishly, and while prices are high the ingredients are commendably fresh. Nobu fans will be interested to compare and contrast the respective black cod (£18.50) dishes; the Zuma version is marinated and then cooked wrapped in a hoba leaf. One outstanding dish is the very tender rib-eye no daikon ponzu fuumi (£9.80), which really does melt in the mouth.

This is a restaurant with a complicated sake list of 22 varieties – it even has a sake sommelier. Ozeki (£2 per 50ml) is your starting point, and the only one to be served hot, but experts will prefer the Zuma Daiginjo (£5 per 50ml), which is made from rice that has been finely milled. It has been described as having a flowery and even peachy taste.

Marylebone

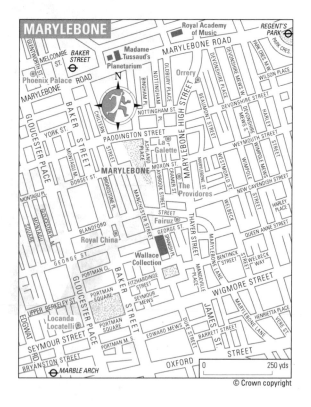

Fairuz

🍴 Squeezed in between two self-consciously hip and groovy Blandford Street eateries, Fairuz happily carries on doing its own thing, which is Lebanese cooking. As you open the front door, jolly souk music, the smell of Eastern spices and the light of the warm, mud-coloured room assault and beguile the senses.

Cost	£15–35

Address 3 Blandford St, W1;
with branches
☎ 020 7486 8182
Station Bond Street
Open Daily noon–11pm
Accepts All major credit cards

This is one of London's more accessible Middle Eastern restaurants.

The menu is set out in traditional style. There's an epic list of mezze, both hot and cold, to start, followed by a selection of charcoal grills and a couple of oven-baked dishes. You can leave the selection up to the restaurant and order a set mezza (minimum two people, £16.95 per head), or a set menu (minimum two people, £24.95 per head) which combines a mezza with a mixed grill – plus a glass of fiery arak thrown in. The set mezza delivers eight or ten little dishes, plenty for lunch or a light supper. But if you prefer to make your own selection, the menu lists 39 different mezze to choose from: cold dishes all cost £3.95; hot dishes £4.95. Particularly recommended are the wonderfully fresh and herby tabbouleh; the warak inab – stuffed vine leaves; the hummous Beiruty; and makanek – spicy lamb sausages. Even that most dangerously indigestible of delicacies, the felafel, is fine here. Main course grills are generous and well prepared. Kafta khashkhash (£10.95) – lamb minced with parsley and grilled on skewers – is unexpectedly delicate and fragrant, but stands up well against its accompanying chilli sauce, while the shish taouk (£10.95) – chicken marinated in garlic and lemon – really is finger-licking good. Round off your meal with excellent pastries (£4.25), and real Lebanese coffee (£2).

Fairuz is a comfortable place, full of sleek and contented Marylebonians. It's not the most authentic, the cheapest or the best Lebanese food that you'll eat in town (best head to the nearby Edgware Road for that). But the ambience at Fairuz is better suited to novice Westerners – staff are friendly and helpful, and the wine list, though short, is offered willingly. If you can, get there early to secure one of the nook and crannyish, tent-like tables.

La Galette

The proprietors of La Galette have obviously given some thought to the potential of pancakes. La Galette opened at the end of June 2001, and it's a bright, modern place with a paint scheme that starts light and gets dark as you travel towards the bare brick wall and the open kitchen at the rear. There's an appealing breakfast served between 10am and 4pm, and then there's the main menu, which plunges into the galettes with little more ado.

Cost	£7–22
Address	56 Paddington St, W1
☎	020 7935 1554
Station	Baker Street
Open	Daily 10am–11pm
Accepts	All major credit cards except Diners
⊛	www.lagalette.com

The hors d'oeuvres are delightful – very simple, and very French. The charcuterie plate (£6) teams some saucisson sec with Bayonne, Jésus and garlic sausage; the hors d'oeuvres plate (£6) majors in those delightful shredded raw vegetable salads – finely grated celeriac with a good mayonnaise, carrot with a light dressing, pickled beetroot and hard-boiled eggs; and there's a good feisty tapenade (£2.50). Or there's soupe du jour (£3.50). The bread is a good chewy-crusted sourdough. When you feel you cannot put off that pancake moment any more launch into a galette. These large buckwheat pancakes come with a dozen different fillings, and in this instance the use of the word filling is not an exaggeration. The "complet" (£6.50), with ham, cheese and a fried egg winking from the centre, is simple and satisfying. Or there's a galette with smoked salmon and crème fraîche (£8). Or naked except for rather good Normandy butter (£2.75). Or with Toulouse sausage, caramelized onions and roast tomatoes (£8.50). You can even opt for a galette with scallops, leek and mushrooms (£8.60). This is not fancy cooking but the portions are generous and the quality of the ingredients seems agreeably high, while the large pancakes are as crisp as you could wish for. However appealing the galettes, there are still puddies who will proceed directly to the crêpes – "Normandy" comes with caramelized apple and crème (£4.50).

There's a Francophile wine list, but much more appealing is the range of Breton ciders served in *pichets* – small jugs – and which must be drunk out of traditional *bollées* – think of a thick, earthenware breakfast cup with the handle knocked off.

ITALIAN

Locanda Locatelli

Giorgio Locatelli is the chap who won a Michelin star at Zafferano, so it comes as no surprise that the opening of his new restaurant in a corner of the Churchill Hotel kicked off a feeding frenzy among the critics. It opened on Valentine's day 2002 and by the end of the first week everybody from the Prime Minister to Madonna had been in to sample the startlingly good and surprisingly cheap North Italian food. The room is elegant, the cooking terrific, the prices modest. No wonder it is booked up way ahead.

Cost	£25–60

Address 8 Seymour Street, W1
☏ 020 7935 0672
Station Marble Arch
Open Mon–Sat noon–3pm & 7–11pm
Accepts All major credit cards except Diners

There is a large turnover of dishes on the menu but the cooking is always spurred on by the seasons. There may be starters like the ox tongue with green sauce (£5) – tender and delicate meat with a light, fresh, green dressing. Mackerel fillets crop up rolled in pork belly (£5.50), and there may be a salad of swordfish with leeks (£6.50). Pasta dishes delight: tiny fluffy potato gnocchi (£8) come with artichokes; home-made ravioli (£8) are filled with lemon cream and pork ragu. Chickpea soup (£8) is rich and wholesome, and comes with ravioli stuffed with bottarga. Every dish looks elegant on the plate, and combines tastes and textures to their best effect. Main courses may include a dish of pike fillets (£15.50), marinated and then cooked and served with the mildly pickled veg from the marinade. And there's pork fillet (£13.50), with a crust made from preserved mustard fruits. The service is slick, and the restaurant has an established and comfortable air, which belies its status as the new kid on the block. The see-and-be-seen crowd discovered this place on day one, yet for such a talked-about restaurant, everything is still astonishingly good value – wine starts at £3 a glass.

Revel in the basket of breads. This is a co-production, the honours being shared by Giorgio Locatelli and master baker Dan Leppard of Baker & Spice. Seven or eight different breads, all fresh, all majestic, plus metre-long, home-made, cheese-dusted grissini. With a start like this, any meal has a lot to live up to. Locatelli's meets the challenge.

Orrery

There is no doubt that Sir Terence Conran has gone to great lengths to ensure that the public don't see a "formula" in his restaurants. There are large ones, small ones, short ones, tall ones; Italian, French, British; loud music, no music. Even so, Orrery stands out. This is a very good restaurant indeed, driven by a passion for food, and the mainspring is the head chef, Chris Galvin. It may be part of a large group, but they still change the menu daily if need be. Orrery cherishes its own network of small suppliers, going for large, line-caught, sea bass above their smaller, farmed cousins, and selecting the best Bresse pigeon and Scottish beef. The service is slick and friendly, the dining room is beautiful, the cheeseboard has won prizes and the wine list is exhaustive. And the cooking is very good indeed. All of the above is reflected in the bill. For once, you do get what you pay for.

Cost	£29–90

Address 55 Marylebone High St, W1
℡ 020 7616 8000
Station Baker Street/ Regent's Park
Open Mon–Sat noon–3pm & 7–11pm, Sun noon–2.30pm & 7–10.30pm
Accepts All major credit cards
🌐 www.orrery.co.uk

What a pleasure to see such a short menu, with simple starters like velouté of Jerusalem artichoke, cèpes Bordelaise (£9.50); or a first-rate terrine of foie gras served with Sauternes jelly and toasted sourdough (£16.50); or seared scallops teamed with pork belly and cauliflower (£16.50). Mains feature well-judged combinations of flavours: saddle of venison, black pudding, pumpkin fondant and sauce amère (£22.50); Barbary duck with pain d'épice, red onion and foie gras Tatin, Banyuls jus (£22); supreme of halibut, braised lettuce, Puy lentils and pancetta (£24.50). Presentation is ultra-chic, flavours are intense – this is serious stuff. Puddings span the range from classics such as baked chocolate fondant (£8) to the nouvelle délice of liquorice and pear (£9).

One way to eat well here is to rely heavily on the set menus: the three-course menu du jour is £23.50; while Sunday dinner, also three courses and including a glass of champagne, costs £28.50. The Menu Gourmand (which must be ordered by the entire table) brings six courses, coffee and petits fours for £45, rising to £75 when you opt for the specially matched glasses of wine. A stress-free bargain.

Phoenix Palace

To find a large, bright, busy Chinese restaurant just to the north of the Marylebone Road is very unusual. This site was formerly an Indian eatery called the Viceroy of India and, in the transition, the rather smart Indian carvings have been left behind. The result is a large room with some tables on a raised dais running around the room, the obligatory feng shui fish tank, and the little wooden idols looking down. This is a very North London sort of place; it may be only just over the river of traffic that flows past Madame Tussaud's, but it has North London attitudes and North London punters.

Cost	£12–45

Address 3–5 Glentworth St, NW1
℡ 020 7486 3515
Station Baker Street/ Marylebone
Open Mon–Sat noon–11.30pm, Sun 11am–10.30pm
Accepts All major credit cards except Diners

The menu is a huge one, and stretches off into the farthest corners of Chinese chefly imagination. The food is well presented and portions are large – something for which we must thank those North London attitudes? Starters include all the old favourites, but steamed fresh scallops at £3 each are no bargain. Stick to chicken wrapped in lettuce leaf (£5.50), which is well flavoured, if a little short on lettuce leaves. Or order a main-course portion of the deep-fried squid in light batter (£8), which makes a fine opening move. The menu chunters on for over two hundred dishes and is worth a careful read, as there are some interesting discoveries to be made. Salt-baked chicken (£10/20) is a wonderful, savoury roast chicken with juicy meat and crisp skin. The fried minced pork cakes with salted fish (£6.50) are very classy, the salt-fish seasoning the pork mix successfully. The dual seasonal greens with curry (£5.50) is a novelty item – baby sweetcorn and broccoli lurk in a yellow and pretty fierce curry sauce. Very inscrutable. The stewed beef flank (£5.50) is that old favourite, braised brisket – very dark and very rich. The range of noodle dishes is extensive.

The standard of cooking here is good and would not be out of place in the better Chinatown eateries, even if the decor might raise an eyebrow. The Phoenix Palace makes a brave attempt to cheer up a whole tranche of North London.

The Providores

There's only one chef working in London who has a 24-carat, bankable reputation for fusion food and that is Peter Gordon, the amiable New Zealander. Together with a consortium of friends, Gordon opened the Providores and the Tapa Room in mid-August 2001. Downstairs, all is informal – you can even have breakfast in the bar before the menu segues gracefully into a host of small dishes for the rest of the day. The resto part occupies a plain and elegant room on the first floor. Chairs are modern but comfortable, tablecloths are white and simplicity rules – which is just as well, as the dishes are amongst the most complicated in town. But what may look like an untidy and arbitrary assemblage on paper becomes wholly satisfying the moment you pop a forkful into your mouth. These dishes all taste fresh, every flavour is distinct, and each combination is cunningly balanced.

Cost	£7–22

Address 109 Marylebone High St, W1
☏ 020 7935 6175
Station Baker Street/Bond Street
Open Mon–Fri noon–3pm & 6–11pm, Sat & Sun brunch noon–3pm & dinner 6–11pm
Accepts All major credit cards except Diners
🌐 www.theprovidores.co.uk

The menu descriptions read more like lists: spicy coconut laksa with green tea noodles grilled tiger prawn, deep-fried quail egg and crispy shallot (£7.50). Puzzled? The rich, creamy, sweet coconut broth is covered with a scattering of crisp bits of shallot and laced with the contrasting textures of ribbon noodles, tiger prawns and the egg. Or how about a plate of Teruel jamon with Arbequina olives and a glass of Manzanilla (£8.20)? Mains may include pan-fried swordfish on wokked sugar snaps, back beans, Piquillo peppers and coriander with tomato chilli jam (£14.60), or roast New Zealand venison on spicy cabbage, potato and chorizo stew (£15.70). Or, for a dish to ponder over, roast Trelough duck breast crusted with bee pollen, with honey glazed plums and roast celeriac (£16.10). Desserts are more accessible: hokey pokey ice cream with a ginger snap (£6.20)!

This is a place where they understand the majesty of ingredients and give each and every flavour and texture full scope. The Providores will doubtless have its detractors, but this is outstandingly good and original food – something so rare in London that you shouldn't be surprised if it is not recognised for what it is.

Royal China

Like its more famous sibling, on Queensway, this Royal China is a black-and-gold palace. The effect is a kind of cigarette-packet chic and smacks of the 1970s. But don't let that put you off. The food is not as expensive as the decor would have you believe, the service is efficient and brisk (rather than that special kind of rude and brisk you may encounter in Chinatown) and the food is really good. One knowledgeable chef-critic describes the Royal China's sticky rice wrapped in a lotus leaf as the "best ever".

Cost	£14–27

Address 40 Baker St, W1; with branches
℡ 020 7487 4688
Station Baker Street/Bond Street
Open Mon–Thurs noon–11pm, Fri & Sat noon–11.30pm, Sun 1–10pm
Accepts All major credit cards except Diners

You could eat well from the full menu, which, like everything else in the Royal China, is bound in gold. It goes from "Today's Chef Special" through dim sum to lunchtime noodle and rice dishes, but it is the dim sum (served daily until 5pm) that is most enticing here. The roast pork puff (£1.90) is famous, and unusual in that it is made from puff pastry; it is very light and has a sweetish char sui filling. From the "specials", try the lobster dumpling (£3.90) and Thai-style fish cake (£2.50), both of which are tasty. Also worth noting are the prawn and chive dumpling (£2.30), pork and radish dumpling (£1.90), and seafood dumpling (£2.30) – or a selection of three. Also the turnip paste with dried meat (£1.90), and the sesame paper prawn roll (£2.30). The glutinous rice in lotus leaves (£2.80) really is the best ever – it's rich and not too gamey, and two parcels come in each steamer. The Royal China cheung fun (£2.70) is another sampler providing one of each filling – prawn, pork and beef. They take their cheung fun seriously here, with a total of seven variants including mushrooms and dry shrimp (£2.30). The fried rice dishes and the noodles are well priced (£4.50–7.50).

This may well be the place finally to take the plunge and try chicken's feet. Spicy chicken feet (£1.90) come thickly coated in a rich, spicy goo and, to be frank, this sauce is so strong that – were it not for the obvious claw shapes – you could be eating almost anything.

Mayfair & Bond Street

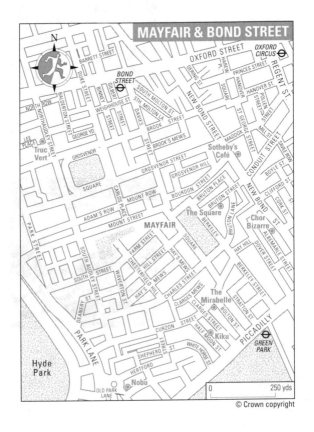

MAYFAIR & BOND STREET

© Crown copyright

Chor Bizarre

Chor Bizarre is something of a novelty in London as one of a handful of Indian restaurants that has a "head office" in India. Indeed the London Chor Bizarre is a straight copy of the one in the Broadway Hotel in Delhi. Its name is an elaborate pun (Chor Bazaar translates as "thieves' market") and, like the Delhi branch, the London restaurant is furnished with an amazing clutter of Indian antiques and bric-a-brac. Every table, and each set of chairs, is different, and you may find yourself dining within the frame of an antique four-poster bed. The food is very well prepared and encouragingly authentic. Care is taken over the detail, and wine expert Charles Metcalfe has devised a striking wine list. Chor Bizarre does, however, carry the kind of price tag you'd expect of Mayfair.

Cost	£24–45

Address 16 Albemarle St, W1
℡ 020 7629 9802 or 8542
Station Green Park
Open Mon–Sat noon–3pm & 6–11.30pm, Sun 6–10.30pm
Accepts All major credit cards
ⓦ www.chorbizarre.net

Start with simple things such as pakoras (£5), which are tasty vegetable fritters, or Punjabi samosas (£5.50), which are fresh, full of potato and peas, and served with fine accompanying chutneys. Kebabs are taken seriously here, too: try gilouti kebab (£6) – lamb with saffron and served with a white radish salad. Or gazab ka tikka (£11), a best-seller in Delhi, which is a kind of chicken tikka deluxe. Then, for your main course, choose dishes like baghare baingan (£8), a Hyderabadi dish combining aubergine, peanuts and tamarind. Or bater ka achaar (£14.50), a dish made with pickled quail; or goshtaba (£15), the famous Kashmiri lamb curry – very velvety. Breads are also impressive, including an excellent naan (£2.50); pudina paratha (£2.75) – a mint paratha; and stuffed kulcha (£2.75) – choose from cheese, potato or mince.

The many imposing set menus are a good way to tour the menu without watching your wallet implode. South Indian Tiffin (£24) features chicken Chettinad, Kerala prawn, poriyal and sambal, served with rice and Malabari parathas on a banana leaf. Kashmiri tarami (£24) is a copper platter with goshtaba, mirchi korma, rajmah, al yakhni, tamatar chaaman and nadru haaq on rice. Or there is the Maharaja Thali (£24, or £22 vegetarian) – a meal on a tray! TV dinners will never be the same again.

Gordon Ramsay at Claridges

FRENCH

The entrance of abrasive foot-baller-chef Gordon Ramsay to Claridges in 2001 would have made a great Bateman cartoon. But the transition from faded and gentile dining to mega-busy gastro temple seems to have slipped through on the nod. The dining room is still large, the service is still slick, but the food is much better than it used to be and, it could be argued, better

Cost	£30–120

Address Brook St, W1
℡ 020 7499 0099
Station Green Park
Open Mon–Fri noon–3pm & 5.45–11pm, Sat & Sun noon–3.30pm & 5.45–11pm
Accepts All major credit cards
⊕ www.gordonramsay.com

value too. The £25 set lunch here is an even better bargain than the £35 set lunch at Ramsay's Chelsea flagship (see p.412). Unfortunately, like its sibling, Claridges is booked up far in advance. The à la carte offers three courses for £50 and there is a "prestige menu" option that takes you through six courses for £60.

While Gordon Ramsay has his name over the door, the head chef here is Mark Sargeant, who won his spurs in the hothouse of Mr Ramsay's three-star establishment. Starters range from smoked haddock Vichyssoise with confit new potatoes and poached quail's eggs; to fricassée of calves' sweetbreads with wilted rocket, Jerusalem artichokes and truffle cream – a grand combination of tastes and textures. Presentation on the plate is elegant and seasoning spot on. Main courses include civet of brill poached in red wine with creamed potatoes, glazed salsify, baby spinach and roasted shallots – a good combo; or pigeon from Bresse, poached and grilled, and served with caramelized parsnips, Vichy carrots and port wine sauce enriched with puréed dates – the texture of the meat is a revelation, like soft red velvet. The desserts are equally considered: caramelized pineapple with its own granite; or a stunning hazelnut and Marsala parfait with white chocolate ice cream. This is classy cooking in a classy restaurant in a classy location, but at agreeably accessible prices.

If you thought it was hard to get a booking in the restaurant, don't even consider the chef's table. This seats six comfortably in an air-conditioned alcove overlooking the kitchen. You get to watch the blood, sweat and tears from a safe distance while toying with a special multi-course menu.

Kiku

There's no doubt it sounds like a bit of a porky. Kiku is a Japanese restaurant (translates as pricey), deep in the heart of Mayfair (translates as very pricey) and one that serves top class sushi with a classical ambience – without charging the earth. Your bill will prove it. In helpful, Oriental fashion it lists the huge number of sushi portions you are alleged to have consumed and then the average price. For one memorable meal this figure was an awesomely low £2.93 per dish. What's even more appealing is that Kiku is laid out around a traditional sushi bar where you can sit and wonder at the dexterity of the knife man, who effortlessly keeps pace with the appetites in his section. Go along smack on opening time, snatch a seat at the counter and go for it.

Cost	£16–55

Address 17 Half Moon St, W1
☎ 020 7499 4208
Station Green Park
Open Mon–Sat noon–2.30pm
& 6.30–10.15pm, Sun
5.30pm–9.45pm
Accepts All major credit cards

Knowledgeable Japanese folk always start a meal of sushi with tamago (£1.50) – the sweetish, omelettey one which allows the diner to properly assess the quality of the rice before getting serious with the fishy bits. Who knows? The toro (£5), or tuna belly, is good; the suzuki (£2.70), or sea bass, is good; the amaebi (£2.30), or sweet shrimp, is ... sweet. Hiramei (£2.70), or turbot, is very delicate. You must have the hotate (£2.70) – slices of raw scallop, translucent and subtle, very good indeed. From the rolled sushi section, pick the umeshiso maki (£3.20), made from rice perked up by pickled plums and fresh green shiso leaves. There are so many good things here that you might feel emboldened to try some of the more challenging sushi, like akagai (£3), or ark shell; or uni, which is sea urchin roe (£4.50). Verging on the "experts" category is tobiko (£2.70), which is flying fish roe and really rather good. A successful strategy might be to try a few sushi and then turn to the main menu: perhaps tempura moriawase (£9.50), which is mixed tempura; or sake teriyaki (£6.80), which is grilled teriyaki salmon. Drink the very refreshing Asahi beer and only venture into the realms of sake if you understand it.

If you feel your nerve breaking, there is a grand assortment of sushi combinations such as tokujyo nigiri (£27) or jyongiri (£20). You can share these to minimize the risk.

The Mirabelle

Anyone hoping to open their own restaurant should have lunch at The Mirabelle. It's not just the touch of Marco Pierre White, London's own culinary Rasputin, the whole operation is superlative. Forgive them the mind-numbingly arrogant and extensive wine list – surprisingly no-one has yet ordered the 1847 vintage Chateau d'Yquem at £30,000 – and concentrate on the food, which is quite reasonably priced for this kind of cooking. The ingredients are carefully chosen. The presentation on the plate is stunning. The surroundings are elegant, and the service attentive. There's a very elegant bar, too, which really does invite a pause for a drink before and maybe after a meal. Go on, splash out.

Cost	£25–110

Address 56 Curzon St, W1
℡ 020 7499 4636
Station Green Park
Open Mon-Fri noon–2.30pm
& 6–11.30pm, Sat noon–3pm
& 6–11.30pm, Sun noon–3pm
& 6–10.30pm
Accepts All major credit cards
ⓦ www.whitestarline.org.uk

Start with a classic: omelette "Arnold Bennett" (£9.50). It's no wonder that Arnold liked these so much – they're rich, buttery and light, made with smoked haddock. Or there's ballotine of salmon with herbs (£8.95). Or fresh asparagus with sauce mousseline (£10.50). Step up a level for some triumphant foie gras "en terrine" dishes: with green peppercorns, gelée de Sauternes and toasted brioche (£16.95); or "parfait en gelée" (£9.95). Believe it or not, these two are actually bargains. For a fishy main course, how about fillet of red mullet Niçoise jus ossobuco (£16.95)? Or the classical grilled lemon sole served on the bone with sauce tartare and creamed potatoes (£18.95)? In the meat section, choose from roast venison au poivre, sauce grand veneur (£16.50); or grilled calves' liver raisin sec, Madeira roasting juices (£15.95); or grilled cutlet of veal à la forestière (£18.50). Puddings (all at £7.95) are deftly handled. The star is tart sablée of bitter chocolate.

Choose the set lunch, don't let the wine list sneak up on you (there's a decent enough Montes Sauvignon Blanc for £15.50) and you could be enjoying a fine meal of ceviche of mackerel with tomato in vinaigrette, followed by confit leg of duck with beetroot salad, and finally Bakewell tart with vanilla ice cream. Monday to Saturday, two lunchtime courses go for £16.50, and three for £19.95; at Sunday lunch three courses cost £19.50.

CENTRAL

FRENCH

Nobu

It's hard to know just what to make of Nobu. On the face of it, a restaurant owned by Robert de Niro, Drew Nieporent and Matsuhisa Nobuyuki sounds like the invention of a deranged Hollywood producer. And then there is the cocoon of hype: the restaurant is amazingly expensive, it has a broom cupboard Boris Becker qualified for his paternity suit and it's within the mega-cool Metropolitan hotel. As is often the case with hype, some of the above is gossip and some is gospel, but which is which? Don't worry, the food is innovative and superb. Ingredients are fresh, flavour combinations are novel and inspired, and presentation is elegant and stylish. See for yourself – the lunchtime bento box, which includes sashimi salad, rock shrimp tempura, black cod and all the trimmings costs just £25.

Cost	£30–100

Address 19 Old Park Lane, W1
Ⓣ 020 7447 4747
Station Hyde Park Corner
Open Mon–Thurs
noon–2.15pm & 6–10.30pm,
Fri & Sat noon–2.15pm &
6–11pm, Sun 6–9.30pm
Accepts All major credit cards

Chef Matsuhisa worked in Peru, and South American flavours and techniques segue into classical Japanese dishes – some of the dishes here defy classification. There are lists of Nobu "special appetisers" and "special dishes"; the problem is where to begin. Tiradito Nobu style (£10.50) is a plate of wafer-thin scallop slices, each topped with a dab of chilli, half a coriander leaf and a citrus dressing – delicate and utterly delicious. The sashimi is terrific: salmon (£10) is sliced and just warmed through to "set" it, before being served with sesame seeds – the minimal cooking makes for a superb texture. The black cod with miso (£24) is a grandstand dish – a piece of perfectly cooked, well-marinated fish with an elaborate banana-leaf canopy. Other inspired dishes are the rock shrimp tempura (£8.75), and, for dessert, the chocolate and almond parfait with red berry compote (£7.95).

Nobu is probably the only place in London where none of the customers fully understands the menu. No one on a first visit could hope to make sense of it. For once it is no cop-out to opt for the omakase (chef's choice) menu, which costs £70 in the evenings and £50 at lunch. Don't be intimidated: book your table well in advance and settle back for a stunning gastronomic experience.

Sotheby's Café

🍴 If you like the idea of eating in an
art collection attached to a famous
auction house, and rubbing shoulders
with international art dealers and collec-
tors, you will enjoy Sotheby's Café.
Quintessentially English, it manages to
retain an air of peace despite being sited
on one side of the main hall of Sotheby's.
For once, mumblings about an oasis of

Cost	£12–35
Address	34–35 New Bond St, W1
☎	020 7293 5077
Station	Bond Street
Open	Mon–Fri 9.30–11.30am, noon–3pm & 3–4.45pm (tea)
Accepts	All major credit cards

calm are entirely appropriate. The Café is also that rarity among London
restaurants nowadays – a place where you can get a fine English afternoon tea.

The lunch menu is short, and changes daily with seasonal variations.
Ricotta and spinach crêpe (£6.25) comes with a tomato and basil coulis
and rocket; or there may be carrot, coriander and poppy seed soup (£5).
There are also trad items with a bit of twist, such as bubble and squeak
with a soft poached egg and Mesclun salad (£11). The fabled lobster
club sandwich (£14.50) has been ever present since the restaurant
opened, and makes for an ideal light lunch. The large chunks of fresh
lobster are served in a club sandwich with fresh mayonnaise, and it is so
popular that it's worth ordering it in advance. Puddings include brûléed
lemon tart (£4.75), and a delightfully fresh-tasting pear and almond
crumble with crème fraîche (£4.75). There is also a large range of teas,
herbal teas and other infusions. Wines are chosen by Serena Sutcliffe, the
Master of Wine who also runs Sotheby's wine auction department, and
are well suited to the dishes that they accompany. For afternoon tea you
can choose delicacies like Welsh rarebit (£6.25) or Dumfries smoked
salmon with brown bread (£7.95). There is also Sotheby's Small Tea at
£5.25, which includes toasted tea loaf and clotted cream. Breakfast
extends to scrambled eggs with toast (£4.95), and smoked salmon with
scrambled eggs and toast (£8.95), but sadly no bacon and eggs.

Whatever time of day, visitors who come just for the food are made
very welcome – there's no pressure to feel that you need to go home
with an old master. However, in keeping with the reverential atmosphere, a notice whispers "please, no smoking or mobile phones".

The Square

The Square is very French: food is terribly important here. And in the gastro first division – an arena where almost every commentator bows to the supremacy of French chefs and French cuisine – you cannot help a slight smirk that head chef Philip Howard, an Englishman, has got it all so very, very right. At the Square, the finest ingredients are sought out, and then what is largely a classical technique ensures that each retains its essential character and flavour. Eating here is a palate-expanding experience.

Cost	£25–110

Address 6–10 Bruton St, W1
☎ 020 7495 7100
Station Green Park
Open Mon–Fri noon–3pm & 6.30–10.45pm, Sat 6.30–10.45pm, Sun 6.30–9.30pm
Accepts All major credit cards

This is a very gracious restaurant. Service is suave, silent and effortless. Seasoning is on the button. Presentation is elegant. The wine list seems boundless in scope and soars to the very topmost heights (where mortals dare not even ask the price). Go for lunch and experience real excellence. For £20 you might have an assiette of duck and foie gras, or a risotto of pea and morels with scallops; followed by either roast salmon with a ragout of Jersey Royals, mussels, saffron and leeks, or navarin of lamb with creamed potato and spring vegetables. Add the extra fiver and go on to chocolate fondant with malted milk ice cream. In the evening three courses cost £55 (plus a few supplements for the wildest extravagances). The menu changes on a broadly seasonal basis but you will choose from eight starters – dishes like sauté of scallops and langoustines with sauce Nero; or a game consommé with tarragon dumplings and a bacon cream; or millefeuille of red mullet and aubergines with a vinaigrette of sardines and wild rocket. Then nine mains, which may include fillet of turbot with a risotto of cured salmon, cucumber and dill and a caviar beurre blanc; or roast pigeon from Bresse with a stuffed Savoy cabbage leaf and Madeira. Puddings – such as a fondant and croustillant of chocolate with orange – are classics. Howard is an able man and Michelin's two-star measure of his worth is an underestimate.

There's also a six-course "taster" menu for £75 plus service (for the entire table only). Book now. This is one treat you will never regret.

Truc Vert

Truc Vert is one of those hybrid restaurants. You want it to be a deli, with fine cheeses, artisan chocolate and obscure wild boar salami? Then it's a deli. You want it to be a restaurant, with proper starters, mains and puds? Then it's a restaurant. The Truc is open all day during the week, and it makes a very decent fist of being all things to all customers. The quality, provenance and freshness of all the ingredients gets top priority, and the menu changes daily. It comes in two halves: "From the shop" means quiche, salads, chicken from the rôtisserie, patés, cakes, pastries and cookies. There is also a novel approach to the magnificent cheese counter: you nominate a few different cheeses, they make up an elegant plateful and then weigh it, and you are charged by weight. The same deal works for charcuterie. With all these instant goodies you would expect the "From the kitchen" section to be a poor relation, but the cooking seems adept and the seasoning spot on.

Cost	£12–40

Address 42 North Audley St, W1
① 020 7491 9988
Station Bond Street
Open Mon–Fri 7.30am–9pm, Sat noon–4pm, Sun 1–3pm
Accepts All major credit cards except Diners

The menu is re-written daily, but by way of starter you could be offered a Jerusalem artichoke soup (£4.25); warm smoked kippers with new potato, roast broccoli and poached egg salad (£7.25); and asparagus and wild mushroom frittata with red chard salad (£7.25). Mains run the gamut from grilled tuna loin steak with braised chicory and pesto dressing (£12.95); to penne pasta with marinated prawn, mussels and semi-dried tomatoes (£10.50); and char-grilled lamb steak with roast beetroot, shallots, mushrooms and balsamic (£12.95). Puds are accomplished – try warm fig and plum tart (£4.25), or poached pears and plums with coffee ice cream (£4.50) – but they pale beside the prospect of the epic array of fine cheeses.

Wines also get a very sympathetic treatment here. You pay the shop price and they add on £4.50 corkage, so a 1996 Vosne Romanée tips the scales at around £40 – a bit young, maybe, but at a fair price.

Paddington & Edgware Road

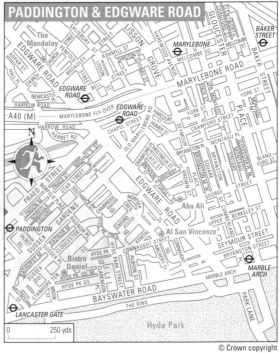

PADDINGTON & EDGWARE ROAD

The Mandalay

Edgware Road

Marylebone

Marylebone Road

Baker Street

Abu Ali

Al San Vincenzo

Paddington

Bistro Daniel

Bayswater Road

The Ring

Lancaster Gate

0   250 yds

Hyde Park

© Crown copyright

Abu Ali

You can only suppose that, in the Lebanon, going out to eat is man's work. That certainly seems to be the case around the Oxford Street end of the Edgware Road, where you'll find Abu Ali's bustling café. This is an authentic place, the Lebanese equivalent of a northern working man's club, and men gather to smoke at the pavement tables. Despite a recent refurb, it's still a bit spartan in appearance, but the food is honest and terrific value. Although you are unlikely to find many Lebanese women here, female diners get a dignified welcome. There's nothing intimidating about the place or its clientele.

Cost	£7–25

Address 136–138 George St, W1
☎ 020 7724 6338
Station Marble Arch
Open Daily 9.30am–11pm
Accepts Cheque or cash only

You will want a selection of starters. Tabouleh (£2.50) is bright green with lots of fresh parsley, lemon juice, oil and only a little cracked wheat – it even tastes healthy. Hommos (£2.50) is rich and spicy, garnished with a few whole chickpeas and Cayenne pepper. Warak inab (£3) are thin and pleasantly sour stuffed vine leaves, served hot or cold. Kabis is a plate of tangy salt and sour pickles – cucumber, chillies and red cabbage – that comes free with every order. For main dishes there's kafta billaban (£5.50) – minced lamb kebabs served hot under a layer of sharp yoghurt and with a sprinkling of pine kernels. Or there's kibbeh bissiniyeh (£5), which is a strange dish: a ball of mince and pine kernels coated with a layer of mince and cracked wheat, then baked until crispy in the oven. The plain grilled meats are also good: try the boned-out poussin – farrouge moussahab (£7). To drink, there is mint tea (£2) – a Lipton's teabag and a bunch of fresh mint in every pot – or soft drinks.

At Abu Ali's, bubble pipes cost £5 a go, and you can choose apple or strawberry. The long strands of black tobacco are mixed into a squelchy mess with chopped fruit and then covered with a piece of foil, on top of which is placed a chunk of blazing charcoal – you are on your way to clouds of sweet-smelling smoke. Some of the cognoscenti take this procedure a step further and replace the water through which the smoke bubbles with ice and Appletise. It certainly makes for a perfumed environment from which to watch the world go by.

Bistro Daniel

Bistro Daniel is the baby brother of Daniel Gobet's smarter restaurant, Amandier. The bistro occupies the basement while the restaurant is on the ground floor. Both are dedicated to French gastronomy with a Provençal bias and they share the same kitchen. Daniel served in the kitchens of Mon Plaisir before opening his own place, La Ciboulette, in Chelsea, which gained an enviable reputation in a very short space of time. Both establishments were resolutely French; Bistro Daniel, while still offering accomplished cooking, introduces some less traditional touches. It is an informal restaurant and the cool basement makes for an intimate atmosphere.

Cost	£13–50

Address 26 Sussex Place, W2
℡ 020 7723 8395
Station Paddington/Lancaster Gate
Open Mon–Fri 12.30–2.30pm & 7–10.30pm, Sat 7–10.30pm
Accepts All major credit cards

Starters might include home-made country-style terrine and gherkins (£4.50); half a dozen snails in their shells with garlic parsley butter (£4.95); a pukka French onion soup with croutons and cheese (£3.50); and a tartare of avocado and Atlantic prawns (£4.95). Main courses may include braised knuckle of lamb, carrots and thyme jus (£10.95); fricassée of Scottish scallops and chicory with a herb butter sauce (£13.50); and Barbary duck breast with soft polenta and a black olive sauce (£8.95). There's also croustillant of cod fillet with sweet red pepper sauce (£8.50); pan-fried Scottish sirloin steak with a peppercorn sauce (£12.50); and, on a lighter, vegetarian note, fricassee of fine tagliatelle with chanterelle mushrooms (£7.50). Side dishes of gratin Dauphinoise, pommes frites and carrots with cumin seeds (all £1.95) are generous and tasty. Puddings (all £3.95) include pear and ginger bread-and-butter pudding; profiteroles and vanilla ice cream; and chocolate cake with pistachio ice cream. Trifling with the selection of French cheeses will set you back £5. There's a daily set lunch at £9.95 for two courses and £12.95 for three.

Bistro Daniel shares a wine list with the Amandier restaurant upstairs. So you can venture all the way from sensible to serious. Listed here are wines as grand as Bâtard Montrachet Grand Cru (£110) or even a Château Latour (£350), if the fancy takes you and your wallet concurs.

The Mandalay

In the Edgware Road desert – north of the Harrow Road but south of anything else – Gary and Dwight Ally, Scandinavian-educated Burmese brothers, have set up shop in what must be an ex-greasy spoon. The resulting restaurant is rather bizarre, with just 28 seats, the old sandwich counter filled with strange and exotic ingredients, and greetings and decoration in both Burmese and Norwegian. Gary is in the kitchen and smiley, talkative Dwight is front of house.

Cost	£6–16

Address 444 Edgware Rd, W2
℡ 020 7258 3696
Station Edgware Road
Open Mon–Sat noon–2.30pm & 6–10.30pm; closed Sun & bank holidays
Accepts All major credit cards
⊛ www.bcity.com/mandalay

BURMESE

The Ally brothers have perhaps correctly concluded that their native language is unmasterable by the English, so the menu is written in English with a Burmese translation – an enormous help when ordering. But the food itself is pure unexpurgated Burmese, and all freshly cooked. The local cuisine is a melange of different local influences, with a little bit of Thai and Malaysian, and a lot of Indian, and a few things that are distinctly their own. To start there are popadoms (two for £1.20) or a great bowlful of prawn crackers (£1.90), which arrive freshly fried and sizzling hot (and served on domestic kitchen paper to soak up the oil). First courses range from spring rolls (from £1.90 for two) and samosas (£1.90 for four), to salads like raw papaya and cucumber (£3.90) or chicken and cabbage (£3.90). There are soups, noodle soups and all manner of fritters as well. Main courses are mainly curries, or rice and noodle dishes, spiced with plenty of ginger, garlic, coriander and coconut, and using fish, chicken and vegetables as the main ingredients. The cooking is good, flavours hit the mark, portions are huge, and only a handful of dishes costs over £6.50. Vegetable dishes are somewhat more successful than the prawn ones, but at this price it's only to be expected.

Even with its eccentric setting, tiny room and rigorous no-smoking policy, The Mandalay has built up a loyal following over the years. The tables are minuscule and the acoustics are good, so be careful what you talk about and keep your ears open – you are just as likely to sit next to a dustman as an ex-pat Burmese diamond dealer.

Al San Vincenzo

Al San Vincenzo is not a cheap restaurant. But then you'll find it smack bang in the middle of a patch of serious affluence near the bottom end of the Edgware Road, so the local clientele are not over bothered. This is a very passionate place with a small dining room and a single-minded chef in the kitchen, which perhaps accounts for the mercifully simple dishes and good seasonal food. The front-of-house attitudes are more relaxed, but if there were a motto over the door it would probably read "No compromise". The pricing is straightforward: two courses may be had for £27.50 and three courses cost £33.50; supplements are rare but some of the more expensive ingredients, like fresh fish, can bump the price up a bit.

Cost	£35–65
Address	30 Connaught St, W2
☎	020 7262 9623
Station	Marble Arch
Open	Mon–Fri 12.15–3pm & 7–11pm, Sat 7–11pm
Accepts	Major credit cards except AmEx and Diners

The menu changes to reflect the seasons, but there are usually six or seven starters to choose from. Dishes range from the plain but satisfying, such as potato and lentil soup, to interesting and unusual combinations like slivers of breast of goose with a pomegranate sauce and rocket salad. Flavours are intense and presentation gloriously unfussy. The perfect example is fresh eels pan-fried with chilli, onions and lemon – the richness of the boneless eel fillets is cut by the lemony tang and a belt of chilli. This tastes as good as it sounds. Main courses are in similar vein: fillet of brill with mussels, saffron and potato puree; rack of venison with red cabbage and green beans; or risotto of cannellini beans, celery and Parmesan cheese. Vegetarians are well-served here, and the lasagne starter of porcini mushrooms, buffalo Mozzarella and pumpkin is particularly fine. The dessert menu ranges from the expected – vin santo with biscotti – to more surprising puds such as fresh dates stuffed with marzipan, rolled in pistachio and served with a bitter chocolate sauce and vanilla ice cream.

The wine list covers the mid-ground well, with a well-chosen series of Italian wines priced at between £15 and £35. Look out for the light and bright Vernaccia, which is a good option at lunch. Beer-lovers will be intrigued by the full-flavoured Ichinusa beer from Sardinia – this is a real treat.

Piccadilly & St James's

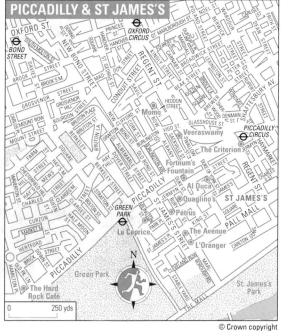

© Crown copyright

The Avenue

The Avenue was one of the first banker-led restaurants in London – a bunch of City chums set up the kind of restaurant where they would choose to eat. Now it's part of a sprawling empire, including Kensington Place (see p.453) and Circus (see p.123), to name just two. This is a stark yet stylish barn of a place, with white walls and pale cherry-wood chairs, and an enormous video wall of moving images around the bar seating area. Entrance is through a glass door, part of a great glass plate fronting the restaurant, and greeting is by designer-clad hosts. Inside it's very noisy, with an upbeat atmosphere. There is not much subtlety about this place – wear your choicest clobber to feel most at home and do not be afraid to gawp.

Cost	£25–50

Address 7–9 St James's St, SW1
℗ 020 7321 2111
Station Green Park
Open Mon–Thurs noon–3pm & 5.45pm–midnight, Fri & Sat noon–3pm & 5.45pm–12.30am, Sun noon–3.30pm & 5.45–10pm
Accepts All major credit cards
⊛ www.theavenue.co.uk

MODERN BRITISH

Cooking is well executed and the menu is a fashionable mix of English and Italian. First courses are generally salads and pastas: buffalo mozzarella and roast tomato salad (£6); warm salad of wild mushrooms with Brie and truffles (£5.95/10.95); or tagliatelle with roast red peppers (£6/11). They are offered in two sizes to give more choice to vegetarians, who otherwise may feel the choice here is a little cramped. Main courses are generally more substantial, and lean towards nursery food: fish fingers (£12); salmon fishcakes with buttered vegetables (£14.50); or calves' liver with champ and bacon (£14.25). Anyone watching their weight might like to try the seared tuna with rocket salsa (£15). And for those with a hearty bent, there's roast rump of lamb with fondant potato and onion marmalade (£16.25). Puddings (all £5.75) range from fruit Pavlova to pecan tart, and black cherry and chocolate mousse cake. They are generally unchallenging, and will appeal to those with a seriously sweet tooth.

The Avenue is huge, so even if you haven't booked it's likely you'll get a table for dinner. Call to check if there have been any cancellations. At lunch there's a good set menu at £17.50 for two courses, and £19.50 for three. Pre- or post-theatre (5.45–7.30pm and 10.15pm–midnight), you can choose from three starters and three mains, at £14.50 for two courses and £16.50 for three.

Le Caprice

Every London socialite worth their salt is a regular at this deeply chic little restaurant, and everyone from royalty downwards uses it for the occasional quiet lunch or dinner. That's not because they'll be hounded by well-wishers or because photographers will be waiting outside. They won't. This restaurant is discreet enough to make an oyster seem a blabbermouth. It's not even particularly plush or comfortable, with a black-and-white tiled floor, a big black bar and cane seats. What keeps Le Caprice full day in, day out is its personal service, properly prepared food and a bill that holds no surprises.

Cost	£25–55

Address Arlington House, Arlington St, SW1
℡ 020 7629 2239
Station Green Park
Open Mon–Sat noon–3pm & 5.30pm–midnight, Sun noon–4pm & 5.30pm–midnight
Accepts All major credit cards
ⓦ www.caprice-holdings.co.uk

The much-copied menu is enticing from the first moment. Plum tomato and basil galette (£6.75) is simplicity itself, but with decent ingredients that taste of what they should. Crispy duck comes with watercress salad (£8.75), while dressed Cornish crab with celeriac remoulade (£13.75) is so fresh and clean it makes you wonder why other restaurants can't manage this. In season, there's usually game, such as a grouse salad with elderberries (£14.50) – perfectly hung breast of grouse with tender salad leaves. Or perhaps char-grilled squid with Italian bacon (£13.75) tempts, or braised knuckle of lamb (£9.75), or deep-fried haddock with minted pea puree, chips and tartare sauce (£14.75). If you are still up for pudding, try the sherry trifle with summer fruits (£5.75) or the blackberry summer pudding (£6.50) to see just what classic English puds are about. In the winter there is an array of more solid rib-stickers.

Expense aside, the only trouble with Le Caprice is the struggle to get a table. It is so permanently booked up that they only really accept reservations from people they know, or people who book well in advance. If you are able to plan far enough ahead, you should go just for the experience, otherwise you'll have to befriend a regular. But this has its advantages, too. It's too chic and grown up to attract the fly-by-night fashion people, and you won't find wall-to-wall hip designer-wear. All you need to look the part is a Continental tan, a little jewellery, Italian clothes and a few old-fashioned laughter lines.

The Criterion Brasserie

The Criterion is one of London's most beautiful restaurants. Covered up and used as a shop for decades (it was a 24-hour Boots branch for years), in its latest incarnation it has been restored to its full-on belle-époque glory. Dining areas are divided by classical arches, and the impossibly high ceiling is decorated with gold mosaics and flower-like lamps. And a trip to the loo is de rigueur, simply to be able to walk the whole length of the room viewing the romantic paintings on the walls. Tables are laid with linen and silver in a modern version of traditional perfection, and are set far apart from each other. Diners are a mix of young romantic couples, middle-aged gourmets and a few business people clearly plotting. All of them hope that while Marco Pierre White doesn't cook here personally, he's keeping an eye on the food.

Cost	£28–55
Address	224 Piccadilly, W1
T 020 7930 0488	
Station	Piccadilly Circus
Open	Mon–Sat noon–2.30pm & 5.30–11pm, Sun 6–10.30pm
Accepts	All major credit cards except Diners

Start with the warm salad of smoked eel, bacon and pommes sautées with creamed horseradish (£9.50), or the risotto of Cornish crab with chives (£9.95), and you will see how a reputation is earned. Main courses are created from simple combinations of good ingredients – ingredients that have been combined so that each enhances the other. Try the fillet of red mullet à la Marocaine, salad vert, sauce cumin (£14.95); braised pork cheeks in ginger and spice (£13.75); smoked haddock, Colcannon beurre Nantaise (£13.95); or grilled calves' liver with bacon pommes purées sauce Lyonnaise (£13.95). Puddings (all £7.50) include sticky toffee pudding with vanilla ice cream; tarte Tatin au pommes (for two); and strawberry sorbet shortcake. You'll find that over-indulgence seems strictly necessary.

The Criterion doesn't come cheap. With wines up to £225 on the ordinary list (there is a fine wine list at much higher prices) you could blow your monthly salary here, but there are some bargains too. The daily set lunch at £14.95 for two courses, and £17.95 for three is good value, considering the quality and venue. Booking for dinner is essential.

Al Duca

This restaurant hit the West End scene, to warm applause, in 2000. High quality, sophisticated food, agreeable setting, slick service, and all at prices that represent real value – what you get here seems to be far more than you pay for. It's unlikely, however, that Al Duca makes a loss, being part of talented restaurateur Claudio Pulze's mini-group. What seems more likely is that prices elsewhere may be a tad higher than they should be. The formula here is a simple one: at lunch, two courses cost £16.50, three cost £19.50, and four £22.50. In the evening the prices go up to £19, £23 and £27. A four-course dinner for £27 within stumbling distance of Piccadilly? More like this please!

Cost	£20–40

Address 4–5 Duke of York St, SW1
℡ 020 7839 3090
Station Piccadilly Circus
Open Mon–Fri noon–2.30pm & 6–11pm, Sat 12.30–3pm & 6–11pm, Sun 6.20–10pm
Accepts All major credit cards except Diners
ⓦ www.alduca-restaurant.co.uk

Anyone who eats out regularly in London might feel cynical about such an offer, doubtful that the cooking and portion sizes could remain uncompromised by the low prices. But do not think London, think Italy. Such regularly changing menus are commonplace there. There are usually six starters at Al Duca: dishes like poached egg with organic polenta and Taleggio cheese; or salad of French beans, marinated tomatoes and warm goat's cheese. Then there are six dishes under the heading pasta: boccoli all'ortolane (garden vegetables); linguine with clams; or reginette with peas and bacon. Followed by six main courses: pan-fried salmon with green beans and aged balsamic; sea bass; chicken; roast leg of rabbit. Finally, six desserts, ranging from an indulgent tiramisù to a classic, simple plate of fresh pear and pecorino cheese. The standard of cooking is high, with dishes bringing off that difficult trick of being both deceptively simple and satisfyingly rich. The home-made pasta and polenta are fresh and good. The fish is perfectly cooked. Overall there is much to praise here, and the slick service and stylish ambience live up to the efforts in the kitchen.

As seems to be the case with every "all-in" menu, the dreaded supplements do put in an appearance, but they are on the small side and seem fair – £2 extra for the rabbit or for a starter made with truffles.

Fortnum's Fountain

The main entrance to Fortnum's Fountain Restaurant is at the back of the store, on the corner of Jermyn Street. This makes it a draw for those working and shopping in the surrounding area, though the core clientele of this rather traditional English restaurant are well-to-do retired folk who use Fortnum & Mason to shop. The Fountain reflects their taste and is utterly dependable, delivering just what you expect – well-prepared, very English breakfasts, lunches, teas and early dinners. The ingredients, as you'd expect of London's smartest and most old-fashioned food shop, are top-class. And the Fountain itself is a very pretty room, with classical murals all around.

Cost	£15–30

Address 181 Piccadilly, W1
T 020 7973 4140
Station Piccadilly Circus/
Green Park
Open Mon–Sat: breakfast
8.30–11.30am, lunch
11.30am–3pm, tea 3–5.30pm,
dinner 5.30–8pm
Accepts All major credit cards
® www.fortnumandmason
.co.uk

The Fountain is deservedly famous for its selection of Fortnum's teas and coffees accompanied by cream teas and ice cream sundaes, and on any given afternoon you will see small children being treated to their idea of heaven by elderly relatives. And beware, the splendid Knickerbocker glory (£4.75) has a terrifying ability to turn even grumpy middle-aged men into small children. But the restaurant also serves a very decent breakfast. The full English, called Fortnum's Farmhouse Breakfast (£11.95), is rather better than that found in many hotels, and the grilled kipper with brown toast (£7.95) will gladden the dourest heart. The dishes on the Fountain Menu (which serves for both lunch and dinner) reflect the ingredient-buying power of the food department and, sensibly enough, tend to the straightforward. The excellent London smoked salmon with soda bread (£13.25) is a real treat, as is Fortnum's Welsh rarebit on Cheddar bread with grilled tomato, back bacon or poached egg (£8.75). There are also simple classics such as grilled Dover sole with side salad and new potatoes (£19.50); grilled sirloin steak with peppercorn sauce and chips (£14.75); and Highland scramble (£10.25), which teams scrambled eggs with smoked salmon.

The restaurant is always busy and, though they turn tables, you will not be hurried. The downside is that there is no booking. That's great for shoppers, but anyone on a schedule should avoid the lunchtime peak. Give breakfast serious consideration.

The Hard Rock Café

The Hard Rock Café is a genuine celebration of rock 'n' roll, which makes its location, in Hyde Park's trad hotel strip, all the more strange. Perhaps it was chance, or clever marketing, as the bulk of the café's customers are tourists. Whatever the reason, this is the original Hard Rock Café, here since the 1970s, and it's the original theme restaurant. As such, it's a hard act to follow. The queue to get in is legendary. There is no booking and you will find a queue almost all day long, every day of the year – and it kind of adds to the occasion. Once in, there is a great atmosphere, created by full-on rock music, dim lighting and walls dripping with rock memorabilia. The Hard Rock food is not bad, either, predominantly Tex-Mex and burgers.

Cost	£8–35

Address 150 Old Park Lane, W1
℡ 020 7629 0382
Station Hyde Park Corner
Open Mon–Thurs & Sun 11.30am–midnight, Fri & Sat 11.30am–1am
Accepts All major credit cards
🌐 www.hardrock.com

Scanning the menu is a serious business here, dishes get short but complex essays attached to them, so boneless bodacious tenders (£5.75) are explained as "boneless chicken tenders, lightly breaded and coated in our Classic Rock (medium), Heavy Metal (hot) sauce or tangy Bar-B-Que sauce. Served with celery and Bleu cheese dressing" – the job of copywriter is an important one here. The burgers knock spots off those at the high-street chains and cover the spectrum from natural veggie burger (£7.25) to HRC burger (£7.75) and hickory Bar-B-Que burger (£9.25). There are also Tex-Mex specials like the grilled fajitas (£11.95), which are a pretty good example of the genre (they are billed as HRC's famous grilled etc – everything is famous here). Further along, among the Smokehouse Specialities, there's the Tennessee pulled pork sandwich (£9.25) and Braco's famous Bar-B-Que ribs (£10.95). Puddings are self-indulgent, and the hot fudge brownie (£4.25) elevates goo to an art form.

Elderly Lords and Ladies who used to totter up Piccadilly in search of the branch of Coutt's bank that stood on the opposite corner will be deeply puzzled to find that it is now the Hard Rock's memorabilia shop. Perhaps they could try for a T-shirt and cashback?

Momo

Momo is an attractive and very trendy Moroccan restaurant tucked away in a backwater off Regent Street. For dinner, you usually have to book at least a week in advance and to opt for an early or late sitting. If you apply for the late shift, be prepared for a noisy, night-club ambience, especially on Fridays and Saturdays. The design of the place is clever, with bold, geometric, kasbah-style architecture, decked out with plush cushions and lots of candles. Downstairs there's an even more splendid-looking Moorish bar, annoyingly reserved for members only – a shame, as Momo is the kind of place where you could happily carry on the evening, especially if you're booked in for the earlier (7–9pm) of its two dining slots.

Cost	£30–50
Address 25 Heddon St, W1
ⓣ 020 7434 4040
Station Piccadilly Circus/ Oxford Circus
Open Mon–Fri noon–2.15pm & 7–10.30pm, Sat 7–10.30pm, Sun 6.30–9.45pm
Accepts All major credit cards

Whenever you arrive, get into the mood with a Momo special (£6), a blend of vodka, lemon juice and sparkling water, topped with a pile of chopped mint. While you're downing that, you can check out the starters. Briouat aux trois fromages, coulis de poivron (£7.50) are mouth-watering little parcels of paper-thin pastry filled with cheese and served with a pepper sauce, while Méchouia (£6.50) is made with grilled peppers, tomatoes, cumin and coriander. Or you might go for chiprons farcis à la mode Algeroise (£10.50) – stuffed baby squids in a spicy tomato sauce. For main course, choose from four tagines, which are North African-style stews served in a large clay pot. Try the tagine of chicken with preserved lemons (£14.50) or the tagine of lamb with dried figs and walnuts (£15). Alternatively, opt for couscous: brochette de poulet (£14.50) combines the staple with marinated spicy chicken and a pot of vegetables; couscous Méchoui (£32 for two) is based around roasted spiced lamb. Or treat yourself to the Fès speciality of pastilla (£10), the super-sweet pigeon pie in millefeuille pastry – a main course that has been relegated to the starters list. Desserts (all around £5.50) include pastries, deep-fried filo parcels of fruit, pancakes and meringues.

Finally, even if you don't make it into the seclusion of the member's bar, don't miss a trip to the toilets downstairs – the men's urinal is an installation of some beauty.

L'Oranger

From the outside, L'Oranger looks like a very expensive French restaurant dedicated to expense-account diners. While it's not cheap, the inclusive menus do bring serious cooking within reach. At lunch you pay £20 for two courses or £24.50 for three, and dinner is set at £39.50 for three courses. For your

Cost	£28–70
Address	5 St James's St, SW1
T	020 7839 3774
Station	Green Park
Open	Mon–Fri noon–2.30pm & 6–11pm, Sat 6–11pm
Accepts	All major credit cards

money you can expect modern Provençal cooking of a high standard. The saucing leans towards light olive-oil bases rather than the traditional "loadsa-cream" approach and, for cooking of this quality, it is most competitively priced.

Starters may include split pea soup and smoked bacon; open ravioli of wild mushrooms, asparagus and bacon; endive salad with lemon and olive oil; ballotine of salmon and soft cheese cream; and sautéed scallops with lettuce velouté and Iberico ham. In the main, these are well-judged combinations of flavours. For main courses, try roasted duck magret with fondant potato and foie gras sauce – delicious, and not as rich as you might imagine. There's also roasted filet of John Dory with crushed coco beans, jus de ceps; rump of lamb with braised potatoes, artichoke and confit of tomato; whole sea bass baked "en croute de sel" with oysters tartare; and roasted fillet of venison. Puddings include lemon and thyme crème caramel; warm Caraibe chocolate fondant; and tartlette de "poires aux vins". It's one of those menus where you want everything, even though some of the more elaborate dishes carry a small supplement. Side dishes of seasonal vegetables are also served. At lunch the menu is shorter, with slightly simpler dishes. The wine list is encyclopaedic, starting at £16 for a Chardonnay and going up to £450 for a bottle of La Tâche de la Romanée-Conti. But there's plenty of good choice at the lower prices.

L'Oranger is refined and elegant with attentive service but a relaxed and unstuffy atmosphere. There's also a secret outside courtyard, which is open at dinner only, and a private function room for twenty. The set prices policy turns what would be an expensive treat menu into accessible dining. More restaurants copy please.

Pétrus

St James's once used to bristle with stuffy clubs for English gentlemen, but has achieved a new role as something of a restaurant centre. As the older restaurants – some of which, like Prunier's and Overton's, had been around since the war – upped sticks, so modern establishments arrived. And now, despite the terrible shortage of parking, there's a small coterie of restaurants offering fine dining. This site's transformation has not been simple: the first restaurant here, 33, opened to fanfares in 1996, but never quite made it, and at the beginning of 1999, after a serious refurb, it reopened with new owners as Pétrus. It has bedded in well – well enough to attract a star from the tyre people.

Cost £30–100

Address 33 St James's St, SW1
☎ 020 7930 4272
Station Green Park
Open Mon–Fri noon–2.45pm & 6.45–10.45pm, Sat 6.45–10.45pm
Accepts All major credit cards

FRENCH

This is a restaurant that gives the impression of being old-established, and it has a loyal and suitably St James-ish following. Head chef Marcus Wareing is a skilled cook. Dishes have a grand intensity of flavour, presentation is targeted at two stars, and each dish is a well-balanced affair – both in terms of taste and texture. Even more miraculous, dishes here have a quirk of originality about them. Pricing is simple: three courses for £50. Starters are often elaborate and "haute cuisine", such as fricassée of frogs' legs, cèpes, baby spinach and pan-fried foie gras served with a velouté of Jerusalem artichokes; or white crabmeat ravioli with a fennel and cucumber salsa, ginger cream velouté. Main courses may include a roasted fillet of turbot with brandade of salt cod, braised fennel and red wine sauce; roast breast of Anjou pigeon on a parsnip galette, with caramelized red onion, game tourte, garlic, rosemary and a truffle game jus; or braised pork belly with pan-fried foie gras, spinach, shallots and baby leeks, with truffle pomme mousseline and braising jus. The puddings and pastrywork are accomplished.

There's a terrific set lunch – how about velouté of Jerusalem artichoke and foie gras served with tortellini of sweetbread and mushrooms; followed by roast pavé of salmon on baby gems, with braised root vegetables and lobster bisque; and millefeuille of macerated figs with vanilla ice cream? And for £26? Outstanding.

Piccadilly & St James's

Quaglino's

In 1929 Giovanni Quaglino opened a restaurant in Bury Street which became an instant success. He was a daring innovator and is reputed to have been the first person to serve hot dishes as hors d'oeuvres. The thing his new restaurant had, above all else, was glamour. When Sir Terence Conran redesigned and reopened Quaglino's, more than sixty years later, his vision was essentially the same. Love it or loathe it, Quaglino's is glamorous, and when it first opened it attracted a sophisticated crowd. Inevitably, with such a huge restaurant, that early exclusivity is no more. And although the food no longer tops the first division, the ambience is still at the top of the Premiership – the elegant reception, the sweeping staircase into the bar that overlooks the main restaurant, and the second stairway down to restaurant level. If this kind of thing rings your bell you will be happy here.

Cost	£16–70

Address 16 Bury St, SW1
℡ 020 7930 6767
Station Green Park
Open Mon–Thurs noon–3pm & 5.30pm–11.30pm, Fri & Sat noon–3pm & 5.30pm–1am, Sun noon–3pm & 5.30pm–11pm
Accepts All major credit cards
🌐 www.conran.com

The menu is simple, classy and brasserie-style, with very little to scare off the less experienced diner. Given the size of the restaurant, it is best to go for the simpler dishes that need less finishing and exactitude – with this number of people to feed, the head chef is not going to have a chance to get to every plate. The plateau de fruits de mer (£30 per person, minimum two people) is as good as you would hope, as is the whole lobster mayonnaise (£29). Fish and chips (£13.50) is served with home-made chips and tartare sauce, and is excellent, while a 10oz rib-eye steak with Béarnaise sauce (£17.50) is a treat when served, as it is here, properly cooked. Puddings are straightforward and agreeably predictable – hazelnut tart with red wine plums (£6); double chocolate pudding (£6.50).

Quaglino's staff can be brusque, but then marshalling large numbers of glamour-seekers is a testing enough job which would make anyone a little tetchy. You can avoid this altogether by staying in the bar, which offers highlights from the menu – including all the seafood. Furthermore, Quaglino's is open late, which makes it perfect for a genuine after-theatre dinner. There's a prix-fixe menu at lunch and pre- or post-theatre: two courses for £13, three for £15.50.

Veeraswamy

Veeraswamy is Britain's oldest-surviving Indian restaurant, founded in 1927 by Edward Palmer following a successful catering operation at the British Empire Exhibition. Its next owner was Sir William Steward, who pulled in the rich and famous throughout the postwar boom – their numbers included the King of Denmark, whose penchant for a glass of Carlsberg with his curry is said to have first established the link between Indian food and beer. The latest owner is Namita Panjabi, who also owns Chutney Mary (see p.409) and Masala Zone (see p.126). She has swept Veeraswamy into the modern era: the old and faded colonial decor has gone, along with the old and faded dishes. In their place there's an elegant, fashionable restaurant painted in the vibrant colours of today's India, and an all-new menu of bold, modern, authentically Indian dishes of all kinds.

Cost	£20–50

Address Victory House, 101 Regent St, W1
☏ 020 7734 1401
Station Piccadilly Circus
Open Mon–Fri noon–2.30pm & 5.30–11.30pm, Sat 12.30–3pm & 5.30–11.30pm, Sun 5.30–10.30pm
Accepts All major credit cards
🌐 www.realindianfood.com

You'll need to adjust your pattern of ordering. Main dishes come as a plate with rice, and sometimes vegetables too. They're not designed for sharing, and you will definitely need one each. Street food makes great starters: pani puri (£5.25), rich with tamarind; or ragda pattice (£5.25) – spiced potato cakes with chickpea curry. Or there's machli ki tikki (£6) – fish cakes; and fresh oysters (£7.75), exquisitely stir-fried with Keralan spices. The main-dish curries are well spiced and have a good depth of flavour. Apple dopiaza (£13.50) is lamb curry with chillies, caramelized onions and apples. You could also try the Malabari lobster curry (£17), with fresh turmeric and raw mango; or chicken salaan (£13.50), a Keralan dish that's hot with black pepper. The biryanis are a revelation, too, and particularly good is the moghlai masala biryani (£13.50), a dish of lamb and rice cooked slowly in a sealed pot with lots of green herbs and nuts. Vegetarian dishes are also grandstand affairs and include tarkari Hyderabadi biryani (£11) – vegetables and mushrooms slow-cooked with rice.

Like its sister restaurant, Chutney Mary, Veeraswamy does an excellent Sunday lunch, and there is also a "tasting menu" at £30 per person.

Queensway & Westbourne Grove

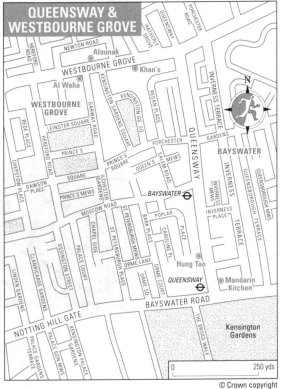

QUEENSWAY & WESTBOURNE GROVE

PORCHESTER ROAD

QUEENSWAY

HATHERLY GROVE

HEREFORD ROAD

NEWTON ROAD

Alounak

WESTBOURNE GROVE

Khan's

Al Waha

WESTBOURNE GROVE

KENSINGTON GARDENS SQUARE

KENSINGTON GS SQ

REDAN PLACE

INVERNESS TERRACE

GARWAY ROAD

LEINSTER SQUARE

REDE PLACE

HEREFORD ROAD

PRINCE'S

PORCHESTER

GARDENS

BAYSWATER

PRINCE'S SQUARE

SQUARE

QUEEN'S MEWS

SALEM ROAD

QUEENSWAY

INVERNESS

INVERNESS MEWS

QUEENSBOROUGH MWS

QUEENSBOROUGH TERRACE

CHEPSTOW PLACE

DAWSON PLACE

PRINCE'S MEWS

ILCHESTER GARDENS

BAYSWATER ⊖

INVERNESS PLACE

INVERNESS TERRACE

MOSCOW ROAD

ST PETERSBURGH MEWS

BARK PLACE

POPLAR PLACE

CLANRICARDE GARDENS

OSSINGTON STREET

PALACE COURT

CHAPEL SIDE

ST PETERSBURGH PLACE

ORME LANE

CAROLINE PL.

Hung Tao

QUEENSWAY ⊖

Mandarin Kitchen

LINDEN GARDENS

ORME COURT

ORME SQ

NOTTING HILL GATE

PALACE GARDENS TERRACE

PALACE GDN MWS

KENSINGTON PALACE GARDENS

BAYSWATER ROAD

THE BROAD WALK

Kensington Gardens

0   250 yds

© Crown copyright

Al Waha

Anissa Helou, who has written the definitive book on Lebanese cuisine, nominates Al Waha as London's best Lebanese restaurant. And after cantering through a few courses here you will probably agree with her. Lebanese restaurants are all meze-obsessed, and Al Waha is no exception. What is different, however, is the way in which the chef at Al Waha is obsessive about the main course dishes as well!

Cost	£12–35

Address 75 Westbourne Grove, W2
℡ 020 7229 0806
Station Bayswater/ Queensway
Open Daily noon–midnight
Accepts All major credit cards

When you sit down, a dish of fresh, crisp crudités will be brought to the table. It includes everything from some quartered Cos lettuce through to a whole green pepper. Get the healthy eating part over early. As always with Middle Eastern food, choosing is the problem – there are 22 cold starters and 24 hot ones. Go for a balance and always include one that you have never had before. Hummus (£3) is good here; tabouleh (£4) is heavy on the parsley; the kabees (£3) are moreish if you like the Lebanese style of heavily salted pickles; and the foul moukala (£4) is good, despite its name – it's a dish of broad beans with garlic, coriander and olive oil. From the hot section, try manakeish bizaatar (£3.75), which is a freshly baked mini-bread topped with thyme, like a deluxe pizza, or maybe haliwat (£4.50), a dish of grilled sweetbreads with lemon juice and herbs. Or there's batata harra (£3.75), which combines potatoes with garlic and peppers. The makanek ghanam (£4.50) are tiny Lebanese lamb sausages, like a very refined cocktail sausage. For main courses, grills predominate, and they are all spanking fresh and accurately cooked. Tasty choices include shish taouk (£8.75), made with chicken, and samakeh harrah (£18), with sea bass. Star turn is kafta khashkhash (£8.75), a superb cylinder of minced lamb with parsley, garlic and tomato. Drink the good Lebanese beer or the very good Lebanese wines.

Al Waha's greatest strength is in its superb home-style dishes of the day. Monday means dajaj mahshi – stuffed chicken with rice and pine nuts. Tuesday gets you a good artichoki mozat, which is lamb stewed with artichoke bottoms. Friday is fish – sayadieh is a fillet of fish cooked with herbs and rice. They are all priced at £9.

Alounak

Westbourne Grove has always had
a raffish cosmopolitan air to it,
which makes it the perfect home for this,
the second branch of Alounak (actually
the third, if you count its early years in a
Portakabin opposite Olympia station).
Don't be put off by the dated sign outside
– this place turns out really good, really
cheap Iranian food. The welcoming smell

Cost	£8–20
Address	44 Westbourne Grove, W2; with branches
☎	020 7229 0416
Station	Bayswater/ Queensway
Open	Daily noon–midnight
Accepts	All major credit cards

of clay-oven-baked flat bread hits you the moment you walk through the
front door, creating a sense of the Middle East that's enhanced further by
the gentle gurgling of a fountain, and the strains of Arabic music.

The sizeable contingent of Middle Eastern locals dining here testifies
to the authenticity of the food on offer. As an opening move, you can do
no better than order the mixed starter (£8.40), a fine sampler of all the
usual dips and hors d'oeuvres, served with splendid, freshly baked flat
bread. And then follow the regulars with some grilled meat, which is
expertly cooked. Joojeh kebab (£6.90) is melt-in-the-mouth baby
chicken, packed with flavour. The kebab koobideh morgh (£6.90) is a
tasty kebab made from minced chicken "reassembled" into long cylin-
ders. As you would expect from a Middle Eastern restaurant, lamb dishes
feature heavily, and they are simply grilled without fuss or frills. A good
way to try two in one is to order the chelo kebab koobideh (£11.10),
marinated lamb fillet coupled with minced lamb kebab, which is deliciously rich and oniony. For those with an inquisitive bent there is the
innocuous-sounding "mixed grill" (£30 for two), which brings a vast
platter best summed up as grilled everything. It's worth looking out for
the daily specials, too – especially good on a Tuesday, when they offer
zereshk polo (£6.20), a stunning chicken dish served on saffron-steamed
rice mixed with sweet-and-sour forest berries.

Round things off with a pot of Iranian black tea (£3), sufficient for
six and served in ornate glass beakers. Infused with refreshing spices, it
does a great job of cleaning the palate, leaving you set for a finale of
select Persian sweets. Beware, however, of musty-tasting yoghurt drinks
with unpronounceable names.

Hung Tao

It is easy to find the Hung Tao: just look out for the much larger New Kam Tong restaurant, and two doors away you'll see this small and spartan establishment. They're actually part of the same group, as is another restaurant over the road (which is where all those singularly appetizing ducks hanging up in the windows of the three establishments are roasted). The reason to choose the Hung Tao above its neighbours is if you fancy a one-plate (or one-bowl) meal. Despite a long and traditional menu, featuring mainly Cantonese and Szechuan dishes, its strengths lie in barbecued meat with rice, noodle dishes and noodle soups. All attract the hungry and are keenly priced.

Cost	£4–20

Address 51 Queensway, W2
☏ 020 7727 5753
Station Bayswater/ Queensway
Open Daily 11am–11pm
Accepts Cash and cheques only

The very first thing on the menu is delicious – hot and sour soup (£1.90). Uncannily enough, this is both hot, with fresh red chillies in profusion, and sour. There are also a dozen different noodle soups, priced between £4.20 and £5. Then there are twenty dishes that go from duck rice (£4.20) to shrimps and egg with rice (£5.25). Plus about thirty noodle, fried noodle, and ho fun dishes, priced from £3 to £6. The fried ho fun with beef (£4.50) is a superb rich dish – well-flavoured brisket cooked until melting, on top of a mountain of ho fun. And the barbecued meats displayed in the window are very tasty, too: rich, red-painted char sui; soya duckling; and crispy pork or duck.

Towards the front of the menu, and hailing from Canton, you'll find a succession of congee dishes. Congee is one of those foods people label "interesting" without meaning it. It is a thick, whitish, runny porridge made with rice, stunningly bland and under-seasoned, but tasting faintly of ginger. Plunge in at the deep end, and try thousand-year egg with sliced pork congee (£4.50). As well as containing pork, there's the "thousand year" egg itself, the white of which is a translucent chestnut brown and the yolk a fetching green. Inscrutably, it tastes rather like an ordinary hard-boiled egg. Pundits will tell you that far from being a thousand or even a hundred years old, these eggs acquire their bizarre, slightly cheesy taste after being buried for just one hundred days.

Khan's

If you're after a solid, inexpensive and familiar Indian meal, Khan's is the business. This restaurant, in busy Westbourne Grove, is a long-standing favourite with students and budget-wary locals who know that the curries here may be the staples of a thousand menus across Britain, but they're fresh, well cooked and generously portioned. Just don't turn up for a quiet evening out. Tables turn over in the blink of an eye,

Cost	£6–20

Address 13–15 Westbourne Grove, W2
℗ 020 7727 5420
Station Bayswater
Open Mon–Thurs noon–3pm & 6–11.45pm, Fri–Sun noon–midnight
Accepts All major credit cards
⊛ www.khansrestaurant.com

service is perfunctory (this isn't a place to dally over the menu), and it's really noisy. Try to get a seat in the vast, echoey ground floor, where blue murals stretch up to the high ceilings – it feels a bit like dining in an enormous swimming pool; the basement is stuffier and less atmospheric. Wherever you sit, be prepared to be fed briskly and hurried on your way.

There are some tasty breads on offer. Try the nan-e-mughziat (£1.60), a coconut-flavoured affair with nuts and sultanas, or the paneer kulcha (£1.45), bulging with cottage cheese and mashed potatoes. You might also kick off with half a tandoori chicken (£2.75), which is moist and well cooked, or a creditable chicken tikka (£3.80). For main dishes, all those curry house favourites are listed here – meat madras or vindalu (£3.20), prawn biryani (£5.25), chicken chilli masala (£3.20), king prawn curry (£6.20) – and they all taste unusually fresh. Especially good is the butter chicken (£4.70), while for lovers of tikka masala dishes, the murgh tikka masala (£3.70) will appeal. There's a typical array of vegetable dishes too: bhindi (£2.70), sag aloo (£2.60) and vegetable curry (£2.60). Desserts include kulfi (£2.15), chocolate bombe (£1.60) and various ice creams – or you could try the lemon or orange delight (£1.70). A pint of lager will set you back £1.90, and there's a small selection of wines: a bottle of Chardonnay costs £8.50, or you can get a glass of house white or red for £1.60.

Cast your eye around the tall, tiled ground floor and front windows and you'll find enough architectural clues to confirm that this was once a Kardomah coffee bar. On a more enterprising note, this is one of very few curry houses that has a special children's menu. Excellent, start them young.

Mandarin Kitchen

London has its fair share of French fish restaurants, and there are famous English fish restaurants, so why does it seem odd to come across a Chinese fish restaurant? Part of the mystique of the Mandarin Kitchen, which you'll find at the Kensington Gardens end of Queensway, is the persistent rumour that they sell more lobsters than any other restaurant in Britain. (When questioned about this myth, the management will confirm that they regularly have 100-lobster days!) This is a large restaurant, busy with waiters deftly wheeling four-foot-diameter table tops around like giant hoops as they set up communal tables for large parties of Chinese who all seem to be eating ... lobster. What's more, as the menu observes, "we only serve the finest Scottish wild lobsters, simply because they are probably the best in the world".

Cost	£15–35
Address	14–16 Queensway, W2
☎	020 7727 9012
Station	Queensway
Open	Daily noon–11.30pm
Accepts	All major credit cards

Whatever you fancy for the main course, start with as many of the steamed scallops on the shell with garlic soya sauce (£1.80 each) as you can afford. They're magnificent. Then decide between lobster, crab or fish. If you go for the lobster, try ordering it baked with green pepper and onion in black bean sauce (it is priced at about £15 per pound depending on the season), and be sure that you order the optional extra soft noodle (£1.20) to make a meal of it. The crab is tempting, too. Live crabs are shipped up here from the south coast, and a handsome portion of shells, lots of legs and four claws baked with ginger and spring onion is a pretty reasonable £14. Fish dishes require more thought – and an eye to the per-pound prices, which do reflect the gluts and shortages of the fish market. The menu lists "the fish we normally serve" as sea bass, Dover sole, live eels, live carp, monkfish, Chinese pomfret and yellow croaker. Sea bass comes steamed whole at £17–19 per pound, depending on season. The steamed eel with black bean sauce (£10.90) is notably rich. The monkfish (£10.90) is meaty and delicious.

After seafood, the never-ending menu wanders off down a road of old favourites, and even features a number of veal dishes such as roasted veal chop with Mandarin sauce (£8.90) – so a seafood allergy is no reason for you to miss out.

Soho

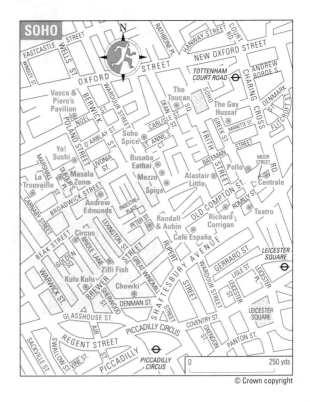

SOHO

N

EASTCASTLE STREET
WELLS ST.
OXFORD STREET
RATHBONE PL.
HANWAY STREET
COURT RD.
NEW OXFORD STREET
ANDREW BORDE S.

WINSLEY ST.
WARDOUR STREET
BERWICK
TOTTENHAM
COURT ROAD
CHARING CROSS

Vasco &
Piero's
Pavilion
NOEL
DEAN ST.
SOHO
SQ.
The Toucan
The Gay
Hussar
DENMARK
FLITCROFT

POLAND STREET
D'ARBLAY ST.
CARLISLE ST.
ST. ANNE'S CT.
FRITH STREET
GREEK ST.
MANETTE ST.
STREET

Yo!
Sushi
Soho
Spice
Busaba
Eathai
BATEMAN
Pollo
MOOR
ST. RD.

La
Trouvaille
MARSHALL
DUFOUR'S PL.
LIVONIA ST.
Masala
Zone
Mezzo
Spiga
Alastair
Little
ROMILLY ST.
Centrale

BROADWICK STREET
Andrew
Edmunds
INGESTRE PLACE
OLD COMPTON ST.
Teatro

CARNABY STREET
BEAK STREET
PETER ST.
Randall
& Aubin
Café España
Richard
Corrigan

Circus
GOLDEN SQ.
LEXINGTON ST.
GREAT WINDMILL STREET
RUPERT ST.
SHAFTESBURY AVENUE
GERRARD ST.
WARDOUR STREET
LISLE ST.
LEICESTER PL.
LEICESTER ST.
LEICESTER SQUARE

WARWICK ST.
BRIDLE LANE
Zilli Fish
Kulu Kulu
BREWER
SHERWOOD
Chowki
DENMAN ST.
STREET
COVENTRY ST.
OXENDON ST.
LEICESTER SQUARE
PANTON ST.

GLASSHOUSE ST.
AIR ST.
PICCADILLY CIRCUS

SACKVILLE ST.
SWALLOW ST.
VINE ST.
REGENT STREET
PICCADILLY
PICCADILLY CIRCUS

0   250 yds

© Crown copyright

Alastair Little

ITALIAN

(icon) This restaurant was Alastair Little's first, opened back in those days when the London eating public was moving hesitantly out of a world where visiting an Italian restaurant meant gasping at the size of the peppermills and the clever way that the straw-wrapped Chianti flasks had been

Cost	£30–65

Address 49 Frith St, W1
℡ 020 7734 5183
Station Leicester Square
Open Mon–Fri noon–3pm &
6–11pm, Sat 6–11pm
Accepts All major credit cards

transformed into lamps. The sparse decor and unfussy, modern lines of Little's Frith Street joint seemed little short of revolutionary at the time. Today, the place looks much the same as every other trendy eatery. Most importantly, Alastair Little was the man who showed us a new style of Mediterranean food: simple, strong flavours; fresh produce; joyful meals. And today his two restaurants continue to fly the flag for these admirable values (you'll find the other one reviewed on p.445).

Unlike the decor, the menu changes twice a day. Not radically, although there may be one extra starter or main course to choose from at dinner. Pricing is simple: at lunch £27 buys you three courses; at dinner £35 gets you three courses. The wine list is a largely sub-£30-a-bottle affair, with a sprinkling of more ambitiously priced famous names. The menu runs the gamut – the charcuterie may come from Spain, and there will be French classics mixed in with resolutely Italian dishes – but everything is seasonal. So starters may include celeriac and celery soup with crème fraîche; salad of Jerusalem artichokes, bacon and a soft boiled egg; and, at something of a tangent, "sashimi" of tuna with "oshitashi" vegetables and wasabi. Or how about breast of pigeon, rosemary and apple pancake? The main courses are in a similar vein, and may feature dishes like red-wine-glazed, slow-roast belly of pork with cavolo nero; or calves' liver with bacon, button mushrooms and onions. Fish dishes, such as baked brill with buttered leeks and grain mustard sauce, are well handled. And there is always an appealing vegetarian option – perhaps leek and potato ravioli with porcini sauce.

To end your meal there are splendid puds, like a blood orange tart or the truly wonderful affogato al caffe – and the satisfying alternative of a plate of British cheeses with oatcakes.

Andrew Edmunds

Andrew Edmunds' wine bar, as it is called by Soho locals, has been an institution in the area for some fifteen years – a long time when you consider how speedily so many restaurants come and go. It all started when the lease on the wine bar next door to his print gallery became vacant and he decided that as he wanted to go on eating there himself, he should take it on. The restaurant now has a loyal band of regulars who like the imaginative bistro-style dishes. It's cosy, dark and very crowded, a place where people wave to friends across the room.

Cost	£20–35

Address 46 Lexington St, W1
℡ 020 7437 5708
Station Oxford Circus
Open Mon–Fri 12.30–3pm &
6–10.45pm, Sat 1–3pm &
6–10.45pm, Sun 1–3pm &
6–10.30pm
Accepts All major credit cards
except Diners

The menu changes weekly and combines solid favourites with bright new ideas, so that regular diners can either comfort themselves with the familiar or head off into the unknown. Start with sweet potato, coconut and chilli soup (£2.95); or spiced mackerel fillet with couscous and coriander yoghurt (£4.25); or a pigeon breast salad with roast pinenuts and caramelized apples (£4.75). Main courses may include stalwart and straightforward dishes such as roast pork chop with gratin Dauphinoise (£9.50); or an impressively strongly flavoured vegetarian option like penne with leeks, broccoli, spring onion, dolcelatte, garlic and chilli oil (£7.95); as well as lighter combinations like a whole Dover sole with roast new potatoes, green beans and lemon butter (£13.50). This is very like stumbling on a neighbourhood restaurant in an affluent suburb, only in the very heart of Soho. Puddings include chocolate mousse cake (£3.50), the ubiquitous tiramisù (£3.50), and plum and almond tart (£4).

Wines are a passion with Andrew Edmunds. The constantly changing, broker-bought list is long and special and, because of his low mark-up policy, there are some genuine bargains. There is an additional list of halves of sweet wines and daily special wine offers are chalked on a blackboard. Expect to pay a bit more and get much more in return. Booking, especially for the tiny upstairs dining room, is essential.

Busaba Eathai

Busaba occupies a West End site that was once a bank – you remember the days when banks were conveniently positioned all over the place? Former customers stumbling into 106 Wardour St would be more than a little surprised by the dark, designery and implacably trendy Thai eatery that is now bedded in. One of the gents behind this new establishment is the brains behind the original Wagamama (see p.18), and regulars there will find all sorts of echoes and resonance at Busaba Eathai. There's the same share-a-table and no bookings policy, and there's the same half-cod philosophy: "sanuk is busaba's living ethos. Based upon traditional Bhuddist values..." You need read no further. The place is saved by serving pretty decent Thai food at low prices, and with consummate lack of pretension. For all the fake Zen, this is a jolly and energetic restaurant and you will probably have a very good time.

Cost	£8–22

Address 106–110 Wardour St, W1
☎ 020 7255 8686
Station Piccadilly Circus
Open Mon–Thurs noon–11pm, Fri & Sat noon–11.30pm, Sun noon–10pm
Accepts All major credit cards except Diners
ⓦ www.busaba.com

Food, grouped into categories, veers towards one-pot dishes, and vegetarians are particularly well served. If you want starters you need to peruse the side dishes. Choose from such things as a good green papaya salad (£5.60); or po-pea jay (£2.90), which are vegetable spring rolls; or fish cakes (£4.20); or Thai calamari (£4.20), which are not unlike everyone else's calamari. There are curries: crab claw and baby cuttlefish (£8.80); green chicken (£6.90); green vegetable (£6.50); and red lamb (£7.90). You'll find genuine Thai veg, such as pea aubergines, sweet basil and lime leaves, although dishes do tend to be on the sweet side. Or there's phad Thai (£5.90), and thom yam chicken (£6.50). Stir-fries range from char-grilled duck in tamarind sauce with Chinese broccoli (£7.60); ginger beef (£6.60); and deep-fried cod with chilli and basil sauce (£7.80).

The power juice phenomenon has reached Busaba. Nam polamai (£2.70) is organic, and combines carrot, apple and celery with dandelion and nettle extract. Or there's Thai San Sam whiskey with ice (£3.50).

Café España

🍴 Situated as it is, at the heart of Soho's pink strip at the Wardour Street end of Old Compton Street, and nestled among the hard-core shops and video stores, Café España is a remarkably balanced restaurant. From the outside it looks rather small and shabby – not very prepossessing at all, in fact, and much like the more tourist-focused trattorias. But once through the door, tripping over the dessert trolley, you can sense you're in for something good. You'll be greeted by a friendly maître d' and led up the stairs to join a hubbub of hungry Soho folk with a nose for a bargain.

Cost	£10–20
Address	63 Old Compton St, W1
☎	020 7494 1271
Station	Piccadilly Circus/ Tottenham Court Road
Open	Mon–Sat noon–midnight, Sun noon–11pm
Accepts	MasterCard, Visa

The menu does give a nod to the trattoria, with a short list of pastas, but it is Spanish, not Italian cooking that you should be going for here – and if you are anything less than seriously hungry, it's best to stick with the tapas. Mejillones a la marinera (£4.50) delivers enough mussels for a small main course; a portion of tortilla (£4) is the size of a saucer and is likely to be cooked especially for you; ordering the jamón serrano (£6.25) brings a decent portion at a price you'd be hard to match wholesale. For something more substantial, there's plenty of choice, mostly in the form of simple grills. Try chuletas de cordero a la brasa (£9.95) – lamb chops; higado de ternera (£8.95) – calves' liver and bacon; or rodaballo a la plancha (£12.95) – grilled turbot. Or there are the traditional Valenciana and marinera paellas (£22, to feed two), though these are slightly less exciting. Service is swift, if a little harassed. Keeping food prices this low means a rapid turn-around of custom, but the waiters are nonetheless friendly and polite. And given the number of people in the place, you can be sure that whatever you are eating is freshly prepared – the volume of ingredients they get through must be huge.

To enjoy Café España to the maximum, go mob-handed and allow yourself the luxury of running amok with the tapas selections before pouncing on the paella. But be warned: it is very unwise to try and re-create the glorious abandon of your last Iberian holiday here – the sangria is a dark and dangerous West End concoction that is really quite horrid.

Centrale

(🍴) In a grid of streets full of bottom-dollar belly-fillers, Centrale stands out. It has an idiosyncratic charm beloved by its regulars. But don't be misled by its down-at-heel exterior – there's something special about sweeping through the plain glass door and sliding into one of its cracked vinyl banquettes, forced into cosy, chatty

Cost	£5–15

Address 16 Moor St, W1
ⓣ 020 7437 5513
Station Leicester Square/
Tottenham Court Road
Open Mon–Sat noon–9.30pm
Accepts Cash and cheques
only

proximity with strangers across a narrow red Formica table. A lick of paint at Christmas 2001 doesn't seem to have made any difference. Maybe it's the small size of the place, maybe it's the crush of students, maybe it's just the cappuccino in smoked-glass cups, but Centrale is not only effortlessly friendly but also strangely glamorous. Odd, really, when this is basically a place to line your stomach with cheap pasta before going on to a pub or club.

Centrale's menu is artless – orange juice (£1) appears as a starter – and the portions are substantial. Appetisers include home-made minestrone (£2.25), salami (£3.75) and pastina in brodo (£2.25) – short pasta snippets in a clear, slightly oily soup. There's a fair spread of diner staples to follow, including pork chop (£4.75) and fried scampi (£4.75), each partnered by an inevitable sprinkling of chips, but the main event here is the pasta. The Bolognese dishes – spaghetti, tagliatelle, rigatoni and ravioli (all £3.75) – are equally dependable, adequately spicy and chewily meaty, as is the lasagne al forno (£4.25). The "specials" include spaghetti vongole (£4.50), and rigatoni Alfredo (£4.25) – a pungent swirl of cream, mushrooms, cheese, tomato and lots and lots of garlic. Rather than a small salad (£1.75), a side order of spinach (£2.25) adds something green to the solid bulk of the pasta.

The menu gives up the ghost a bit when it comes to dessert, sticking to just three old favourites: banana split (£1.75), apple pie (£1.75) and ice cream (£1.50), the last being a tripartite scoop of chocolate, strawberry and vanilla. Still, you're not here for puds. You're here for a fix of cheap food – and cheap wine. There's no licence, so you can bring your own bottle for 50p corkage (£1 for a big bottle), from the off-licences just around the corner in Old Compton Street.

Chowki

Chowki is chef Kuldeep Singh's first venture after the runaway success of Mela (see p.41), and it opened in July 2002 to immediate acclaim. This is a large, cheap restaurant serving authentic homestyle food in stylish surroundings. The menu changes every month in order to feature three different regions of India.

Cost	£6–15
Address	2–3 Denman Street, W1
☎	020 7439 1330
Station	Piccadilly
Open	Daily noon–midnight
Accepts	All major credit cards

Thus the first month featured Kashmir, Chettinad and Lucknow, then it was all change to the Punjab, Goa and Hyderabad for the second. During a whole year Chowki will showcase 36 different regional styles of food! All the dishes come with accompaniments, they are all authentic, and they are stunning value. Chowki has 120 seats spread across three dining areas, but you'll still probably have to wait for a table at peak times. Cheer up – like Mela, this place is astonishingly good value.

There are three or four starters and three or four mains from each region. When the menu showcased the cuisine of Kashmir, Chettinad and Lucknow, starters included a pair of epic kabarga lamb chops from Kashmir (£3.50); a dish of spicy mussels from Chettinad (£2.95); and a chicken tikka malai from Lucknow (£2.95). This would be a very good standard of cooking at three times the price. Mains follow the lead and come with an appropriate vegetable and the correct rice or bread. From Kashmir comes a vegetable dish made with a kind of yam called colocassia (£4.95). From Chettinad is chicken in cream and poppy seeds (£5.95). From Lucknow there is a rich curry of lamb on the bone (£6.95). All the dishes have the unmistakable stamp of homely cooking – rich, simple, appetizing flavours. Service is friendly, and this is a comfortable, modern place. Finding anywhere this good – and this cheap – within earshot of Piccadilly Circus is little short of miraculous.

Go for the "regional feast": £9.95 buys you a complete meal, which turns out to be all three main courses plus the side dishes from a particular region. So if you and two companions each ordered a different "feast" your table would get to try the entire menu!

Circus

When it opened towards the end of the 1990s, Circus was everything a fashionable fin-de-siècle restaurant should be. The decor was cool shades of black and white, there was a de rigueur members' bar downstairs, open till the wee hours, and there were spiky "statement" flower arrangements. The service was efficient and good looking, and the food was competent, clean and very much of the moment. It took little time for Circus to become a destination restaurant for media and design professionals. A few years and several trends later, Circus has proved that it can stand the test of time. It still has the attributes with which it started, it's still pulling the punters in, and it maintains a gloss of confidence that rubs off on its customers.

Cost	£16–60

Address 1 Upper James St, W1
℡ 020 7534 4000
Station Oxford Circus
Open Mon–Fri noon–3pm & 5.45pm–midnight, Sat 5.45pm–midnight
Accepts All major credit cards
🌐 www.circusbar.co.uk

The menu works hard to offer something for everyone. Tucked in alongside the pan-fried risotto with smoked haddock and soft poached egg (£6), and the aged Feta, aubergine and pepper terrine (£5.80), you'll find starters as diverse as pea and ham soup (£5) – for those spies coming in from the cold – or 30g of Iranian caviar with trimmings (£50). Main courses offer the traditional – roast rump of lamb (£15.50), rib-eye steak with mash and chasseur sauce (£16.50) – as well as more modern dishes such as fried squid with bok choy, chilli and tamarind (£13.80). Everything about this place suggests that whatever you choose will be well executed and pleasing to the eye. The kitchen is obviously at ease, cooking good quality ingredients properly and with predictable results. This being an expense-account eatery ideal for business lunches and dinners, desserts are often skipped. Which is a shame, as the pastry chefs obviously delight in flights of fancy.

Be aware that the sometimes ambitiously priced wine list can further inflate an already not inexpensive dinner bill, but a meal at Circus needn't always be a costly affair. There's a competitively priced set lunch (£17.50 for two courses, £19.50 for three) available throughout the week, and an early dinner or lunchtime bar menu which at £10.50 (or £12.50 for late dinner) is a positive steal.

The Gay Hussar

As you walk in off the street, the ground floor dining room of the Gay Hussar stretches before you: there are banquettes, there are waiters in dinner jackets, there is panelling and the walls are covered with political caricatures. "Aha!" the knowledgeable restaurant-goer murmurs, "How very retro – some fashionable designer has replicated an entire 1950s restaurant dining room." Not so. Granted, it has been spruced up, and the room is clean, neat and comfortable, but The Gay Hussar is the real thing, right down to the faded photo of a naked Christine Keeler.

Cost	£18–40

Address 2 Greek St, W1
☏ 020 7437 0973
Station Tottenham Court Road
Open Mon–Sat 12.30–2.30pm & 5.30–10.45pm
Accepts All major credit cards
ⓦ www.gayhussar.co.uk

Perhaps the politicos like the food, which is solid, dependable, comfortable and tasty. It's also good value: at lunch there is a prix fixe of two courses for £15.50, and three for £18.50. In the evening, dishes get a trifle more complicated. Starters include a well-made disnó sajt (£3.90) – pressed boar's head; and hási pástétom (£3.90) – a fine goose and pork pâté; but the most famous (a house speciality that has featured in various novels) is the chilled wild cherry soup (£3.80), which is like a thin, bitterish, sourish yoghurt and is rather good. Main courses are blockbusters. Try the hortobagyi palacsinta (£13.50), a pancake filled with a finely chopped veal goulash and then sealed, deep-fried and served with creamed spinach. Very tasty. Or there are fish dumplings (£11.50), which are served with rice and a creamy dill sauce. Or there's cigány gyors tal (£13.75), billed as a gypsy fry-up of pork and peppers. The food here is tasty and filling, and best eaten in the chill of winter. Puds are also fierce – poppy-seed strudel comes with vanilla ice cream (£4.50). The home-made liptoi (£3.50), a savoury amalgam of cream cheese, herbs, paprika and a whiff of onion, is very good. The wine list is gently priced. Try the good, dry Hungarian whites like the Castle Island Furmint (£14.50).

Sometimes, there are questions that just have to be asked. Does the Transylvanian mixed grill (erdély fatányéros, £35 for two people) include a stake?

Kulu Kulu

Kulu Kulu is a conveyor-belt sushi restaurant that pulls off the unlikely trick of serving good sushi without being impersonal or intimidating. It is light and airy and there are enough coat hooks for a small army of diners. The only thing you might quibble over is the rather low stools, which are so heavy they feel fixed to the floor – anyone over six feet tall will find themselves dining in the tuck position favoured by divers and trampolinists. The atmosphere is Japanese utilitarian. In front of you is a plastic tub of gari (the rather delicious pickled ginger), a bottle of soy and a small box containing disposable wooden chopsticks. After that, as they say at Bingo, it's eyes down, look in, and on with the game.

Cost	£10–30
Address	76 Brewer St, W1
☎	020 7734 7316
Station	Piccadilly Circus
Open	Mon–Fri noon–2.30pm & 5–10pm, Sat noon–3.45pm & 5–10pm
Accepts	MasterCard, Switch, Visa

The plates come round on the kaiten, or conveyor, and are coded by design rather than colour, which could prove deceptive: A plates cost £1.20, B plates are £1.80, C plates are £2.40, and D plates £3. All the usual sushi favourites are here, and the fish is particularly fresh and well presented. Maguri, or tuna, is a B; Amaebi, or sweet shrimp, is a C; Hotategai, or scallops, is a C, and very sweet indeed. Futomaki, a California, cone-shaped roll with tuna, is a B. The Ds tend to be ritzier fishes such as belly tuna. The eye-watering wasabi factor, however, is a bit hit or miss. Just as you're wishing for a bit more wasabi, you bite into something that makes you long for a bit less. As well as the sushi, the conveyor parades some little bowls of hot dishes. One worth looking out for combines strips of fried fish skin with a savoury vegetable puree. It counts as an A, as does the bowl of miso soup. To drink there is everything from Oolong tea (£1.50) to Kirin beer (£2.60).

Kulu Kulu also offers a range of set options, which represent excellent value and take the strain off keeping your eye fixed on the conveyor belt. They include mixed sashimi (£10) and mixed tempura (£8.60). Look behind the bar and you may see a stack of cardboard cases containing sake supplies. It is strange but true that one of the premium sakes is made in the Rocky Mountains!

Masala Zone

Masala Zone is impossible to pigeonhole. The food is Indian, but modern Indian, with a commendable emphasis on healthy eating – as would be the norm in India, there's a long list of attractive vegetarian options. The dining room is smart and large, but the prices are low. There are fast-food dishes on the menu, but they tend to be the roadside snacks of Bombay. The playlist was put together by one of India's top club DJs. In all, this is an informal, stylish and friendly place, serving food that is simple and delicious.

Cost	£5–18
Address	9 Marshall St, W1
☎	020 7287 9966
Station	Oxford Circus/ Piccadilly Circus
Open	Daily noon–2.30pm & 5.30–11.30pm
Accepts	MasterCard, Visa

The gentle informality extends to the menu, which begins with small plates of street food (all around £2.50). There are sev puris, dahi puris, samosas, a particularly fine aloo tikki chaat, and tokir chaat – an amazing potato basket filled with veg, salad and fruit. Pick several dishes and graze your way along – at these prices it doesn't matter if there's the occasional miss amongst the hits. At lunch there are some splendid Indian sandwiches, including a giant masala chicken burger (£4.50) and a superb Bombay layered-vegetable grilled sandwich (£3.25). There are also half a dozen curries that are well balanced and richly flavoured – served simply, with rice, they cost between £4.75 and £6.50. But you should move straight on to the thalis, which are the authentic option. At Masala Zone these are steel trays with seven or eight little bowls containing a vegetarian snack (to whet the appetite), a curry, lentils, a root vegetable, a green vegetable, yoghurt, bread, rice and pickles. You just choose the base curry and a complete, balanced meal arrives at table. Choose from chicken thali (£8.50), lamb thali (£9), prawn thali (£8.50), or vegetarian thali (£7.50).

The wall decorations are striking. After the surface had been rendered with a close approximation to mud, two tribal artists were flown in to do the painting. The mural depicts their people's history from hunters, to gatherers, to farmers selling to the cities. The artists have also featured their trip to London – look out for the stretch limo, which impressed them quite as much as Buckingham Palace.

Pollo

You won't find haute cuisine at Pollo, but you do get great value for money. As at its neighbouring rival, Centrale (see p.121), this is comfort food, Latin-style – long on carbohydrate and short on frills. Sophistication is in short supply, too – the interior design begins and ends with the lino floors and tatty pictures. But no matter, devotees return time and again for the cheap platefuls of food and the friendly, prompt service. Diners are shoehorned into booths presided over by a formidable Italian mama who tips you the wink as to what you should order. Downstairs there's more space, but you still might end up sharing a table.

Cost	£5–16

Address 20 Old Compton St, W1
Ⓣ 020 7734 5917
Station Leicester Square
Open Daily noon–midnight
Accepts Cash or cheque only

The spotlight at Pollo's lengthy menu falls on cheap, filling pasta in all its permutations. Tagliatelle, rigatoni, ravioli, papardelle, tortelloni and fusilli are all available. Your choice is basically down to the pasta type, as most of them are offered with the same selection of sauces. The tortelloni salvia (£3.80), which comes with a wonderfully sagey butter sauce, is very good, as is the tagliatelle melanzana (£3.60), whose rich tomato sauce is boosted by melt-in-the-mouth aubergine. Meat courses are less successful: anchovies, for instance, are few and far between in the bistecca alla pizzaiola (£6) – steak in capers and anchovy sauce. But vegetarians are very well catered for here. Meat-free highlights include spaghetti aglio, olio e peperoncino (£3.50), a hot mix of garlic, olive oil and chilli. Meanwhile, a hearty plateful of gnocchi (£3.80) would curb even the most flamboyant appetite. Then there are pizzas – perhaps not the elegant, wood-fired-oven type that are all the rage, but solid and substantial nonetheless, like the Regina (£4.10), which is a hammy, cheesy, mushroomy kind of experience. There is even a selection of risotti (all £3.70) to choose from. A bottle of house wine is a bargain at £7.45; and so are the puddings, at £1.60. After a substantial hit of pasta, the imposing portion of tiramisù is a challenge for even the greediest diner.

As if Pollo wasn't cheap enough as it is, it offers the same menu as takeaway, on which all the pasta dishes cost just £3.

Randall & Aubin

Formerly a butcher's, Randall & Aubin was recast as a sharp restaurant – as its seafood counter and champagne buckets groaning with flowers suggest – but it's also a rotisserie, sandwich shop and charcuterie to boot. It's the oysters that draw you in, along with the 1900s shop decor. The original white tiles have been cleverly

Cost	£12–40

Address 16 Brewer St, W1 ;
with branches
℡ 020 7287 4447
Station Piccadilly Circus
Open Mon–Sat noon–11pm,
Sun 4–10.30pm
Accepts All major credit cards

adapted with touches of the French and American diner, such as the cool marble table tops, and the high stools that look characterful, though they don't exactly lend themselves to relaxed dining. But that's part of the plan – Randall's serves good food speedily to folk without a lot of time. In summer, the huge sash windows are opened up, making this a wonderfully airy place to eat, especially if you grab a seat by the window.

There's an extensive menu. An eclectic choice of starters roams the globe, with soupe de poisson (£3.90), Japanese fish cakes (£5.95), and salt and pepper squid with fresh coriander and teriyaki dressing (£7.85). Main courses range from "original" Caesar salad (£6.85), spit-roast herb chicken (£10.50), and sausage with butter bean mash and onion gravy (£10.50), to organic sirloin steak with pommes frites (£12.50) – sauce Béarnaise £1 extra. There are also some interesting accompaniments, such as pommes Dauphinoise (£2.85), or zucchini frites with basil mayonnaise (£3.95). If you don't mind crowds, drop in at lunchtime for a hot filled baguette (£6.70–7.85). How about a lamb souvlaki, tzatsiki and salad baguette (£7.85)? Also available in the evening, the baguettes provide an inexpensive yet satisfying meal. The list of fruits de mer offers well-priced seafood, ranging from a whole dressed crab (£11.50), through grilled lobster, garlic butter and pommes frites (half £12.50, whole £20) to "the works" (£26 per head, minimum two people). Puddings all cost £3.95 and range from tarts and brûlées to the more adventurous pear and caramel galette, or chocolate truffle cake. Many of these dishes are also on the inexpensive takeaway menu, which makes for exciting picnicking.

Hard-core traditionalists with a penchant for chewing gobbets of resilient rubber which taste remarkably like the aroma of pumped-out bilge water will relish the fresh whelks with lemon and vinegar (£8.50).

Richard Corrigan at The Lindsay House

Even among chefs – not usually held to be overly calm and level-headed people – Richard Corrigan is regarded as something of a wild man. He arrived at this deservedly Michelin-starred restaurant in Soho via a spell bringing haute cuisine to a dog track in the East End, but at The Lindsay House

Cost	£30–110

Address 21 Romilly St, W1
℡ 020 7439 0450
Station Leicester Square
Open Mon–Fri noon–2.30pm
& 6–11pm, Sat 6–11pm
Accepts All major credit cards

he seems to have found his niche. The restaurant is split into a series of small rooms, the service is attentive, and the food is very good indeed. The menus are uncomplicated and change regularly to keep in step with what is available at the market. Dinner means a choice of seven starters, six main courses and six puddings, and costs £44, while at lunch the line-up is smaller, as is the price – a real bargain at £23 for three courses. There is also an epic eight-course tasting menu for £65.

Only a fool would try to predict what dishes Richard Corrigan will have on his menu tomorrow, but you can be sure that they will combine unusual flavours with verve and style. Starters surprise – ravioli of hen's egg, braised celery and truffle froth – or are lusciously opulent – sweet sherry-marinated foie gras with fig compote. Or there are combinations that seem familiar but come with a twist, like sautéed veal kidney, couscous and harissa spice. Main courses follow the same ground rules (or lack of them!), so you might be offered ballotine of sea bass, cabbage and oyster cream; or red mullet, fennel purée and crème fraîche. Or, on a more classical note, roast haunch of venison, creamed sprouts and celeriac fondant. The puddings soar towards dessert lover's heaven with the enigmatic "banana and bananas", warm steamed apple pudding with vanilla cream, or poached pear with Sauternes jelly and blue cheese bavarois. The wine list is extensive and expensive.

If there is one thing that marks out the cuisine at the Lindsay House, it is Corrigan's love affair with offal. Sweetbreads, kidneys and tongue all find their way onto the menu, in dishes that perfectly illustrate his deft touch with hearty flavours.

Soho Spice

Soho Spice is the new face of Indian restaurants. It's large – seating one hundred in the restaurant and forty in the bar – and takes bookings only for parties of six or more. It's busy, with loud music and late opening at the weekends, the decor is based around a riot of colour, and it is very, very successful – which must be mainly down to food that is a large step away from curry house staples. The main menu features contemporary Indian cuisine, while a regularly changing special menu showcases dishes from particular regions. What's more, when you order a main course it comes on a thali – with pulao rice, naan, dhal and vegetables of the day – which makes ordering simple and paying less painful.

Cost	£10–28

Address 124–126 Wardour St, W1
℡ 020 7434 0808
Station Leicester Square/ Piccadilly Circus
Open Mon–Thurs 11.30am– midnight, Fri & Sat 11.30am– 3am, Sun 12.30–10.30pm
Accepts All major credit cards

On the main menu, starters include Bhopali seekh kebab (£3.50), murg malai tikka (£3.50), and mahi lasooni tikka (£5.25), which is salmon cooked in the tandoor. Commendably enough, prices here have actually fallen a little since our last edition. Main courses represent good value, given their accompaniments. Good choices are the tandoori champ (£12.50) – spicy lamb chops; and daba murgh (£9.95) – chicken in turmeric gravy. Or how about the sarson machali (£12.50) – salmon cooked with tomatoes and onions and given bite by mustard seeds? Gentler palates will enjoy the gosht pasanda (£11.95), rich with yoghurt and almonds. Desserts offer mango or pistachio kulfis (£2.95) – Indian ice creams made with boiled milk – and that sweetest of comfort foods, gulab jamun (£2.95), which is a dumpling soaked in rose syrup.

The special regional menu, called "Seasonal Colour", offers three courses plus tea or coffee for £14.95 and changes every month – so it may be recipes from Rajasthan or dishes from Bengal. For example, when the chosen region was the North West Frontier there were starters like gilafi kebab – lamb dumplings with pearl onions and button mushrooms. Mains included the celebrated murg malai Peshwari – a kebab of chicken breast and cheese; and Kandhari pasanda – lamb with onions, tomatoes, almonds and saffron.

Spiga

Spiga has an impeccable pedigree. It comes from the same stable as Aubergine, L'Oranger and Zafferano, and has that piece of kit that long identified any Italian restaurant as serious – a wood-fired oven. But despite its credentials you don't need to pay a king's ransom to eat here, nor do you have to dress up. This is a pleasantly casual affair. The atmosphere is lively – sometimes the music is too lively – and the look is cool. Spiga may have cut the prices but they haven't cut corners – the tableware is the latest in Italian chic.

Cost £14–30

Address 84–86 Wardour St, W1
℡ 020 7734 3444
Station Leicester Square
Open Sun–Tues noon–3pm & 6–11pm, Wed–Sat noon–3pm & 6pm–midnight
Accepts All major credit cards

ITALIAN

Menus change monthly, with occasional daily specials, but there's a definite pattern. Starters will get you in the mood. The buffalo mozzarella (£6/9) is served with thyme, perfumed zucchini and sun-dried tomatoes. Or try something like the speck d'anatra con carciofi e casarau (£7/9.50), which is duck ham, or the legumi griglia (£6/9). But the home-made pasta course is where it's really at. What's good is that, like the starters, most pasta dishes come in large or small portions. Think Italian and enjoy an extra course, such as gnocchi di spinaci e patate al taleggio (£7/9), or ravioli di faraona (£7.50/9.50), which are pasta parcels of guinea fowl in a Castelmagno cheese sauce. Then consider a pizza – thin crust, crispy and the size of a dustbin lid. Pizza buffala (£9.60) is rich with genuine mozzarella; pizza Gorgonzola e speck (£8.50) is topped with Gorgonzola cheese and cured ham; pizza porchetta (£9.50) comes with smoked cheeses and suckling pig. Alternatively, main courses offer up char-grilled and pan-fried dishes: filetto d'orata con funghi (£13.50) teams pan-fried sea bream with mushrooms; while palliard di pollo con patate e spinaci (£12.50) is a simple but good char-grilled chicken breast. If you aren't already full, the pudding section is well worth a look, too. Highlights include a wickedly indulgent lemon and mascarpone tart (£5.50) and an excellent tiramisù (£6.50).

Full marks to the person who can identify the weird loofah-like objects hanging on the walls.

Soho

Teatro

This restaurant has both celebrity owners (Lee Chapman and Leslie Ash) and celebrity customers. The latter may be spotted not only hiding in the members' bar, but also plying the knife and fork in the main arena. Given such potential distractions, the food is remarkably good and not too extravagantly priced. 2002 saw the end of the set lunch menu – indeed all lunches are now served in the less formal "Glenfiddich" area.

Cost	£30–70

Address 93–107 Shaftesbury Ave, W1
☏ 020 7494 3040
Station Leicester Square
Open Mon–Fri noon–3pm & 6–11.45pm, Sat 6–11.45pm
Accepts All major credit cards
🌐 www.teatrosoho.co.uk

On the main menu, starters can be substantial, with favourites like salmon and sorrel fishcakes with a horseradish cream dressing (£7.50). Or if you're a foie gras fan, try it pan fried with spiced quince (£13.50). For lovers of the simple, there's a leek and potato soup with chive crème fraîche (£5.50). Other dishes have some good combinations of flavour, such as flaked mackerel with beetroot, Asian pear and balsamic dressing (£6.95). Main courses take the favourites theme further, with whole roast loin of suckling pig with creamed potatoes and mustard sauce (£16.35), and pan-fried skate wing with capers, crab, beurre noisette and new potatoes (£15.75). Or perhaps roast breast of poulet noir with fettuccine of wild mushrooms (£15.50) appeals? Puddings (all £6) veer towards the rich and comforting: baked English apple comes with short-bread and rum raisin ice cream, and there's banana toffee cheesecake. The wine list, which starts at £14 for a house bottle and climbs doggedly to £250 for a Chateau Margaux 1989, is well chosen, with some bargains in the £20 to £40 region. There are twenty wines by the glass (£3.50–9.50) and fourteen cigars.

Like many smart restaurants, Teatro now has a bargain corner. Until 7.30pm there's a special pre-theatre menu at £11.50 for two courses and £14 for three. You might be presented with grilled Manouri cheese, rocket and pesto; then smoked haddock fillet with a Welsh rarebit crust; then iced lemon and Amaretto parfait. For cooking of this standard, this is very good value.

The Toucan

(🍴) When they opened The Toucan the proprietors' first priority was to approach Guinness and ask if they could retail the black stuff. They explained that they wanted to open a small bar aimed single-mindedly at the drinking public, just like the ones they had enjoyed so much in Dublin. Guinness replied that, providing they could shift two barrels a

Cost	£7–14

Address 19 Carlisle St, W1
ⓣ 020 7437 4123
Station Leicester Square/
Tottenham Court Road
Open Mon–Sat 11am–11pm
Accepts MasterCard, Visa
ⓦ www.thetoucan.co.uk

week, they'd be happy to put them on the list. Neither party imagined that the regular order would end up at more like thirty barrels a week! It's an impressive intake, but then The Toucan is an impressive place, serving home-made, very cheap, very wholesome and very filling food, along with all that Guinness. Its success has meant expansion from the original hot, dark, cellar premises to include the ground floor.

Start with six Rossmore Irish oysters (£5), or the vegetable soup with bread (£2). Go on to a large bowl of Irish stew with bread (£5), or Guinness pie and champ (£6) – champ is a kind of supercharged Irish mashed potato with best butter playing a leading role alongside the spring onions. It features in a couple of novelty items – you can have chilli and champ (£5), or garlic mushrooms and champ (£3). And just when you think you have the measure of the place, there's Thai chicken curry and rice (£5.50). The JPs (jacket potatoes, from £3.50) come with various fillings, and there's an array of sandwiches. There's also a great-value smoked salmon salad plate (£6.50). One thing to bear in mind if you've come here hungry is that there are times when The Toucan becomes so packed with people that you can scarcely lift a pint. At those times, all attempts at serving food are abandoned.

Of course, if things have got out of hand, you could spend a happy evening at The Toucan without actually eating. As some Irish sage once remarked, "There's eating and drinking in a pint of Guinness". And if it's a chaser you're after, then be aware that The Toucan also makes a feature of Irish whiskeys, including some exotic and stratospherically expensive Tullamore Dews – 38, 41 and 42 year-olds. If you have to ask how much it costs, you cannot afford it.

La Trouvaille

Think back to those stalwart English archers who won the famous victories at Agincourt and Crècy. Unfortunately, those away wins were forgotten within a couple of hundred years, and ever since the French have got their own back and given England a bit of a culinary drubbing. Food-wise, French haute cuisine has topped the European Champions League for about a century, and

Cost	£20–50

Address 12a Newburgh St, W1
☎ 020 7287 8488
Station Oxford Circus
Open Mon–Sat noon–3pm & 6–10.30pm, Sat 6–10.30pm
Accepts All major credit cards except Diners

although the English may resent such total dominance, there is a particular kind of French eatery they still adore. At La Trouvaille the proprietors understand the English need for really French Frenchness, they even know that they should provide one or two dishes that are a step *too* authentic for most Brits. They know that waiters who would be considered too over the top for "Allo, Allo" are admired here. They know that their clientele want good food at a price that doesn't break the bank.

The set lunch is £16.75 for two courses and £19.50 for three courses – very good value for this quality of cooking. Starters may include a cardoon and potato soup, or artichoke vinaigrette, which comes with an improbably large artichoke that is all the better for simple presentation. Grilled salsify comes with a herb aioli – very delicious. If you hanker after a "dangerously French" dish, try the presse de tripailloux; this is a terrine made with tripe and is absolutely authentic – cold, with a chewy-gluey texture and an unsettling absence of real flavour. Main courses stay in character: boudin blanc with Périgueux sauce; roast pigeon with figs. Someone in the kitchen has a truly French respect for the integrity of ingredients, and suppliers are listed at the foot of the menu. So pick onglet à l'échalotte and then revel in excellent Aberdeen Angus beef.

When considering the puds – choccy mousse, crème brûlée, roast pears – divert to the weekly cheese plate, which is outstandingly good. Three cheeses – perhaps a chunk of melting Livarot, a wedge of waxy Brebis, and a richly blued Fourme d'Ambert – plus a little pot of truffled honey. Anyone who hasn't tried that last speciality should do so immediately, it is stunning – a wipe-your-finger-round-the-bowl-unashamedly experience.

Vasco and Piero's Pavilion

Very much a family-run restaurant, the Pavilion has been a Soho fixture for the past twenty years. But there's nothing old or institutional about the cooking or decor. Vasco himself cooks for his regulars, and the establishment has long been a favourite with diners who appreciate his food, which is fairly simple but made with top-class ingredients.

Cost   £15–30

Address 15 Poland St, W1
☎ 020 7437 8774
Station Oxford Circus
Open Mon–Fri noon–3pm &
6–11pm, Sat 7–11pm
Accepts All major credit cards
🌐 www.vascosfood.com

Dishes are biased towards Umbrian cuisine. Customers include the great and the good, and the Pavilion's modern yet comfortable atmosphere guarantees them anonymity.

There's only an à la carte menu at lunch (plus a two course "light menu" which doubles as pre-theatre and costs £12.50), but in the evening the basic deal is that you choose either two courses for £18.50 or three for £22.50. Given the quality, freshness of ingredients and attention to detail, this proves exceptional value. A starter of carpaccio of tuna with avocado and ginger dressing is a moreish and clever variation on traditional carpaccio. Or there may be a simple bruschetta with garlic, tomato and basil. Duck salad, mixed leaves and mostarda di Cremona is plate-wipingly good, with the duck shreds crispy yet moist. Pastas, all home-made, are excellent, too, particularly the tagliolini with king prawns and zucchini – perfectly cooked and with a sauce that is prepared from fresh ingredients and tastes like it. Or perhaps tagliatelle with mixed mushrooms and cream? Simple is good. For carnivores, however, there is nothing to beat the calves' liver with fresh sage – paper-thin liver that literally melts in the mouth. Piscivores should turn to the scallopine of swordfish with garlic, parsley and cannellini beans; or sautéed monkfish with saffron and lentils.

Puddings continue the theme – they are simple and top quality. A panna cotta is gelatinously creamy, a praline semi-freddo is rich and soft as well as being crunchy, and a torta della nonna reveals buttery sponge pastry and custard, flavours that remind you of bread and butter pudding and ambrosia. There is a good selection of the less usual Italian wines, as well as some good Italian pudding wines.

Yo!Sushi

When Yo!Sushi burst upon the scene it was to fanfares and a tidal wave of publicity. This was an event beyond just another kaiten (conveyor-belt) sushi bar. Robotic sushi-makers, robotic drinks trolleys, video screens – and not many restaurants credit "sponsors" like ANA, Sony and Honda. In among all this there is even some food and, while purists may shudder, it's more consistent than the hype would have you suspect.

Cost	£8–25

Address 52 Poland St, W1;
with branches
℡ 020 7287 0443
Station Oxford Circus/
Piccadilly Circus
Open Daily noon–midnight
Accepts All major credit cards
🖥 www.yosushi.co.uk

Plates are marked in lime (£1.50), blue (£2), purple (£2.50), orange (£3) and pink (£3.50). When satiated you call for a plate count, and your bill is prepared. You sit at the counter with a little waiters' station in front of you – there's gari (pickled ginger), soy and wasabi, plus some little dishes and a forest of wooden chopsticks. Kirin beer costs £3, a small warm sake £3, and unlimited Japanese tea is £1. You're ready to begin. Yo!Sushi claim to serve more than one hundred sushi, so be leisurely and watch the belt – and, if in doubt, ask. The nigiri sushi range from fruit and crabstick (both £1.50); through salmon, French bean and mackerel (£2); and tuna, prawn and squid (£3); and so on up to yellow-tail and fatty tuna – which carry the warning that they are "as available" and a pink price tag of £3.50. There are about twenty different maki rolls (with vegetarians well catered for), at all prices. The ten different sashimi and five different gunkan all command the higher orange and pink prices. As do the isorolls – which are bound with nori and can provide some pretty advanced combinations such as teriyaki chicken and enoki mushroom. It's always worth asking the server what hot dishes are available as they vary from day to day. Dining at Yo!Sushi does call for some restraint and deft mental arithmetic, as the tower of brightly badged empty plates building up in front of you can end up costing more than you expected.

Yo!Sushi is at the forefront of restaurant merchandising and no age group is safe. There are Yo!Sushi T-shirts, books, and even baby-gros. Even a badged mouse mat has been sighted.

Zilli Fish

Bright, brittle and brash, Zilli Fish is a part of Aldo Zilli's growing Empire. You can see into the surprisingly calm kitchen through a large window as you walk along Brewer Street. Inside, in a hectic atmosphere, the restaurant serves a modern Italianate fish menu to London's media workers and the rest of the young Soho crowd. Tables are close and everything is conducted at a racy pace. Not ideal for a secret conversation or for plighting your troth, unless you want the whole place to cheer you on.

Cost	£25–60
Address	36–40 Brewer St, W1
☏	020 7734 8649
Station	Piccadilly Circus
Open	Mon–Sat
	noon–11.30pm
Accepts	All major credit cards
⊛	www.zillialdo.com

The menu features a modestly entitled section, "what we are famous for". These are dishes like seared tuna Niçoise (£22); traditional deep fried cod, chips and tartare sauce (£15.90); spaghettini with fresh lobster (£22); and wild salmon stuffed with crab and spinach, and steamed in ginger and soya (£18.50). Or baked sea bass fillet (£19), wrapped in banana leaf and cooked with cherry tomatoes, ginger, garlic, basil, olive oil and lemon dressing. From the side orders, mixed salad (£3.25) is simple but well made. While the list is dominated by fishy favourites, in keeping with the name, there are some modern Italian vegetarian and meat options as well, including risotto with wild and field mushrooms and white truffle oil (£12.90), and chicken breast stuffed with Taleggio (£15). Puddings (all £6.50) include a ricotta and amarena cherry tart with cherry coulis; a home-made tiramisù with Pavesini; and, rather incongruously, a fried banana spring roll with white chocolate ice cream.

Aldo Zilli has built up a reputation in Soho that guarantees that his bar and restaurants are almost always packed. Zilli Fish offers good food, but also good fun. In keeping with so many restaurants nowadays, Signor Zilli is quite happy to give away his secrets, so signed copies of his latest book are always available in the restaurant. Gastronauts will probably wish to visit Zilli Fish on a Sunday, when the suckling pig comes into its own and there's a set lunch at £20 for three courses.

South Kensington

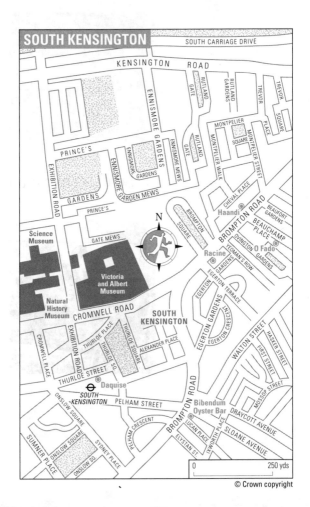

Bibendum Oyster Bar

Bibendum Oyster Bar is one of the nicest places to eat shellfish in London. The 1911 building, a glorious tiled affair that was a former garage for the French tyre people, is Conranized throughout, but the oyster bar is housed in what looks like the old workshop on the ground floor, and they've done precious little to it. On the old forecourt stand two camionettes: one is used as a

Cost	£12–30

Address Michelin House, 81 Fulham Rd, SW3
℡ 020 7589 1480
Station South Kensington
Open Mon–Sat noon–10.30pm, Sun noon–10pm
Accepts All major credit cards
Ⓦ www.bibendum.co.uk

SEAFOOD

shellfish stall, selling lobsters, oysters and crabs to the good people of Chelsea; the other is a flower stall, with lilies, ginger flowers and roses rather than carnations. It all looks rather quaint, but it's very attractive, and it gives a much-needed initial splash of colour which stays with you in the plain oyster bar, with its cream walls, marble tables and stone floor.

The menu is a shellfish lover's heaven. Here you'll find three different types of rock oyster (£7.50–8 per half-dozen) – you can choose your favourite or order a selection to find out the difference. The crab mayonnaise (£9) comes in the shell, giving you the enormous fun of pulling it apart and digging through the claws. Or you can have it done for you in a crab salad (£9.50) – probably just as good, but not nearly so satisfying. If you're really hungry, there's a particularly fine plateau de fruits de mer (£28.50 per head, minimum two people), which has everything: crab, clams, langoustines, oysters, prawns and shrimps, as well as winkles and whelks. There is plenty of choice for those allergic to claw crushers, though surprisingly there is practically nothing that uses crustacea in hot dishes. Instead there are simple combinations such as lemon chicken with chickpeas (£12.80), and devilled mackerel with spiced cucumber salad (£10). The daily-changing set menu follows suit – smoked haddock and leek tart with green salad (£10); rump of lamb with vegetable chutney and herb oil (£12.50). Desserts are simple and seasonal – raspberries and Jersey cream (£5.50); cheese (£5.50); and the inevitable crème brûlée (£5.50).

Given the nature of the place, there's a sensible wine list, mostly given over to white wine and champagne, with a decent smattering of half-bottles and wines by the glass.

POLISH

Daquise

(❯❮) Daquise is more old-fashioned than you could possibly imagine. High ceilings, murky lighting, oilcloth table covers, charming service, elderly customers – the full Monty. During the day it serves coffee, tea and rather good cakes to all comers, breaking off at lunchtime and in the evening to dispense

Cost	£8–25
Address 20 Thurloe St, SW7	
☎ 020 7589 6117	
Station South Kensington	
Open Daily 11.30am–11pm	
Accepts MasterCard, Visa	

Polish home cooking, Tatra Zwiecka beer, and shot glasses of various vodkas. Several novels have been completed here by penniless writers seeking somewhere warm to scribble – buying a cup of coffee gets you a full ration of patience from the management, all you need supply is a little inspiration. The food is genuine here, and does evolve, albeit at a glacial pace. Regulars were shocked when the magnificent "herrings with potato" became the almost as good "herrings with bread". Portions are serious here, but prices are very reasonable, even if you don't take advantage of Daquise's hospitality to while away the day.

Start with Ukrainian barszcz (£2.50), rich and red, or the new starter, herrings with bread (£3.50) – the herring fillets are amazingly good here. Thick cut, pleasantly salty and with a luxurious smooth texture. Go on to the kasanka (£6), a large buckwheat sausage, cousin to black pudding, made using natural skins. Or, for the fearless, there is giant golonka (£8.80), a marinated pork knuckle which is boiled and served with horseradish sauce. Also welcome back an old friend, Vienna schnitzel (£9.50), with a fried egg on top. And it is hard not to be tempted into ordering an extra dish of potato pancakes (£5.50), which are large, flat and crispy, and come with sour cream or apple sauce. The other side-dish options are an odd kind of sauerkraut (£1.50), served cold and very mild; cucumbers in brine (£1); and kasza (£1.60), the omnipresent buckwheat.

Since the first edition of this guide we have reported on the planning wrangles which crop up every now and then when a speculator proposes to redevelop this entire chunk of Thurloe Street. On such occasions the locals and regulars band together to defend the Daquise. Thankfully, to date they have always been successful.

Haandi

East African Punjabi restaurants are famous for simple dishes, rich, intense sauces and a welcome belt of chilli heat – the kind of food that hitherto has meant a trek to Southall or Tooting. This is a brave initiative. The management decided to expand an empire based on successful establishments in Nairobi and Kampala by adding the long and narrow space which, in a bygone age, was a Sloaney haven known as the

Cost	£17–40

Address 136 Brompton Road, SW3
℡ 020 7823 7373
Station Knightsbridge
Open Mon–Fri 6–11pm, Sat & Sun noon–3pm & 6–11.30pm
Accepts All major credit cards accepted
🌐 www.haandi-restaurants.com

Loose Box. The decor is curry-house smart, the room is as light and bright as a nearly-basement can be, and you can see into the kitchen through a curved glass wall. The menu and chefs have been flown in from East Africa. The curries are incredibly rich, and got that way by being reduced gradually rather than being thickened with powdered nuts.

Start with some kebabs. Machli mahasagar (£8.50) is a dual-purpose dish – it makes a grand, if pricey, starter or a sensible main course; it is a fish kebab, with large chunks of white fish that are marinated and then cooked in the tandoor. The tandoor man knows his job, and every mouthful has a light overshirt of spices and is still moist in the middle. The murg malai tikka (£8.80) is also very good. Another star turn from the tandoor is the Kashmiri kabarga (£8.80), which are implausibly tender lamb chops, richly spiced, with good crispy bits to gnaw. The curries are also very satisfying. Try the lasoni prawns masala (£12.80) – good-sized prawns, which are cooked firm and retain some bite, inhabit a very rich, very strongly flavoured, almost dry masala. Or how about the gosht-ki-haandi (£8.10)? This is a trad lamb curry, chilli hot. The vegetable dishes are equally good. Dum aloo Kandahari (£6.20) is made with potatoes that have been stuffed with dried fruit before being curried in a rich tomatoey sauce containing apricots – implausible but delicious. The breads are excellent.

Service is smiley. Haandi may be a much more expensive proposition than almost all of London's other East African/Asian restaurants, but such price tags seem less rapacious so close to Harrods, and at Haandi the food is very good.

O Fado

O Fado seems somewhat out of place in the chic environs of Beauchamp Place. In a street lined with some very pretentious establishments, this Portuguese restaurant flies the flag for simpler things. O Fado is owned, staffed and largely frequented by Portuguese, though the waiters also need to speak Japanese, or at least refer to the food glossary on the wall when taking orders from the regulars, who come here for the seafood. Pretty in pink, and bedecked with hand-painted azulejos, it is quite a romantic restaurant, seductively lit with a few nooks and crannies that are bagged quickly – so book.

Cost	£25–45

Address 45–50 Beauchamp Place, SW3
⊤ 020 7589 3002
Station Knightsbridge
Open Daily noon–3pm & 6.30pm–1am
Accepts All credit cards except Diners

Both the menu and wine list are exhaustive. Favourite dishes among Japanese diners include octopus salad (£7.50) and arroz de marisco (£28 for two) – the Portuguese take on paella. But those wanting to get in the mood for their summer holiday should try the crisp and salty grilled sardines (£4.85), or caldo verde soup (£4.50), followed by a spicy piri piri chicken and fries (£9.90), and finish off with the comfortingly named pudin flan (£4) – crème caramel Portuguese-style. Less holiday-inspired options are the shellfish crêpe with brandy sauce (£5.60) and the mussels (£6.90) with a twist – served in olive oil and coriander together with the usual wine and garlic. The range of salt cod specialities is popular with Portuguese families for Saturday lunch: bacalhau a cataplana (£13.95) is a dish of salt cod and clams, pressure-cooked in a rich tomato sauce, and it's surprisingly delicious. Among the meat specials, look out for the strange dish that teams fillet steak and prawns in a cream and brandy sauce (£13.95). If you still have room after the sumo-wrestler portions, try the arroz doce (£4), a wonderful rice pudding. The tarta da laranja (£4), a moist, eggy orange cake, and Molotof (£4.80) – not a bomb but an egg-white soufflé – are both good as well.

This place is called O Fado for a reason: mid-evening the house singer begins the haunting, lyrical strains of fado ballads, with guitar accompaniment, and diners listen appreciatively if they know what's good for them. It's all a lot quieter at lunchtime.

Racine

Racine opened with suitable fanfares in June 2002, as it brought together what was something of a foodie "dream team." The chef half of the partnership is Henry Harris (previously at Hush and the 5th Floor at Harvey Nicols), and the front of house is run by Eric Garnier (of Bank and more recently Fish!). The food is French. Not just any old French, but familiar, delicious, nostalgic dishes from the glory days of French cooking. The dining room at Racine is dark brown and comfortable. The service is friendly and Gallic. The prices are reasonable. It was no surprise that by the end of the first fortnight this place was busy enough to make booking imperative.

Cost	£17–50

Address 239 Brompton Rd, SW3
℡ 020 7584 4477
Station Knightsbridge/South Kensington
Open Mon–Sat noon–3pm & 6–10.30pm, Sun noon–3.30pm & 6–10pm
Accepts All major credit cards

Henry Harris is a very good cook and his menus are invariably skilfully written. Everything tempts, everything is priced reasonably, and he takes a great deal of trouble to source and buy top quality seasonal ingredients. To start with, expect simple but glorious combinations such as jambon de Bayonne with celeriac remoulade (£6); salade Lyonnaise (£5); a stunning chilled tarragon and lemon soup (£5); and an old-fashioned chicken liver terrine (£5.75). Or a truly wonderful warm garlic and saffron mousse with wild mushrooms (£7) – light and airy, with a triumphant texture and a delicate taste. Mains continue the "classical" theme: a grilled rabbit leg with mustard sauce (£9.50); roast skate with broad beans and capers (£11.50); tete de veau with a well-made sauce ravigote (£9); marmite Dieppoise (£12.50); plus chicken, chops, steak and fish – but all given the kind of treatment you would expect from the kitchen of a respected restaurant in provincial France. The dessert menu deals in classics: petit pot au chocolat (£6); strawberries in Beaujolais (£5); and Mont Blanc (£5), which is a rich chestnut purée with meringue and chocolate sauce. The wine list is Francocentric but merciful – even the smart bottles seem reasonably priced.

There is a good and bourgeois (in the best possible way) set lunch to tempt Knightsbridge ladies away from a salad of mixed leaves – two courses at £12.50; three courses £15.

Victoria & Westminster

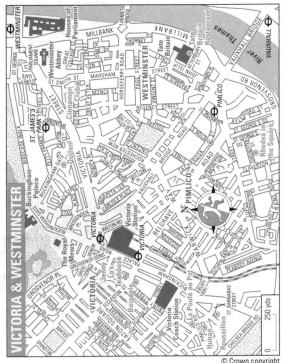

VICTORIA & WESTMINSTER

© Crown copyright

Boisdale

Boisdale is owned by Ranald Mac-donald, who is next in line to be the Chief of Clanranald, and if that information gives you a premonition of what the restaurant is like you are probably thinking along the right lines. This is a very Scottish place, strong on hospitality, and with a befuddlingly large range of rare malt whiskies. Fresh produce – correction, fresh Scottish produce – rules wherever possible, and it is no wonder that the clubby atmosphere and reliable cooking makes this a haven of choice for local businessmen, who are also likely to be found in the ultra-Scottish back bar, home to the formidable malt whisky collection.

Cost	£15–50

Address 15 Eccleston St, SW1
℗ 020 7730 6922
Station Victoria
Open Mon–Fri noon–1am, Sat 7.30pm–1am
Accepts All major credit cards
⊛ www.boisdale.co.uk

There are three Boisdale menus, one of which is the admirably simple "Flying Scotsman" lunch menu – for £14, diners can enjoy leek and potato soup or soused mackerel, followed by crofter's pie, salmon kedgeree or breast of chicken with stoved potatoes, and finally rhubarb crumble. Or there's the "Boisdale" menu – a choice of six starters and seven mains for £17.45 (yes, just like the rebellion!). Starters range from Hebridean lobster bisque and mini roast Macsween haggis to the slightly less Scottish salad of asparagus with new potatoes and green beans. Main courses veer from Aberdeen Angus beef olives to smoked haddock and cod, or from smoked haddock and Scottish salmon fish cakes to – you've guessed it – roast Macsween haggis. The à la carte includes a good many luxury ingredients. As well as Lochcarnan smoked salmon from South Uist (£10.90), and Rannoch Moor smoked venison with black truffle dressing (£9.90), there's spiced potted lobster with rocket and warm toasted brioche (£10.50). Commendably, the mains feature fresh fish of the day, fresh offal of the day, and today's roast game. There are various Aberdeen Angus beef steaks: fillet with Béarnaise sauce and chips (£19.90), or rib-eye with black truffle, pommes Dauphinoise, spinach and wild mushrooms (£20).

Sensibly enough, you can mix and match all of these menus as you work towards an after-dinner malt, or malts. Perhaps in the Macdonald bar and cigar club, next door, which features jazz every evening from Monday to Saturday (cover charge £3.95)?

The Cinnamon Club

It had to happen. Those brave people who set up smart new restaurants were eventually bound to run out of bank premises to convert. It seems we are entering the next phase, as the Cinnamon Club occupies what was formerly Westminster Library. Banks and libraries have a good deal in common – lofty ceilings, large doors, old wood floors, plenty of panelling – just the stuff to make a cracking formal restaurant. The Cinnamon Club is elegant, substantial and very pukka. Service is polished and attentive, the linen is snowy white, the cutlery is heavy, the ashtrays stealably elegant, the toilets opulent, and there are huge flower arrangements. The cooking is accomplished, and each dish offers a finely judged combination of flavours, every one distinct. There's an informed wine list. And yes, unlikely as it may sound, this is an Indian restaurant.

Cost	£25–70

Address Old Westminster Library, Great Smith St, SW1
℡ 020 7222 2555
Station St James's Park/ Westminster
Open Mon–Fri 7.30–10am, noon–3pm & 6–11pm, Sat 6–11pm, Sun noon–3.30pm
Accepts All major credit cards
🖳 www.cinnamonclub.com

From the "Appetisers" section of the menu, Nile perch is spiced with clove, fennel and coriander (£7.50); or there is chicken with sandalwood (£6); or half a lobster, Bengali style (£14). Such dishes and prices set the tone. Mains are also well conceived. Mustard flavoured king prawns are teamed with a saffron flavoured kedgeree (£18.50); or there is pan-seared Gressingham duck breast with a sesame tamarind sauce (£17); or roast scallops with fennel and chilli (£24) – a Keralan curry sauce and not something you'd find on the High Street. There's also a hot, Hyderabadi biryani made with beef (£15). Go for the basket of breads (£3) as a side dish, a selection of unusual parathas, nans and rotis. Desserts are elegant: try the warm apple lassi with champagne granita (£6), or the spiced banana tart Tatin (£6.50), which comes with a deep-purple berry sorbet.

Politicos have already been sighted here prowling amongst the grazing foodies. And to cater for power breakfasters, the Cinnamon Club offers the choice of full English (£16) or Bombay scrambled eggs on layered bread (£11). Perhaps this is a sign that refined and elegant Indian food will soon take its place as the lobbyist's weapon of choice?

Hunan

The Hunan is the domain of Mr Peng. As you venture into his restaurant you put yourself into his hands, to do with you what he will. It is rather like being trapped in a 1930s B-movie. You order the boiled dumplings ... and the griddle-fried lettuce-wrapped dumplings turn up, "because you will like them more". And most likely you will.

Cost	£25–50
Address	51 Pimlico Rd, SW1
☎	020 7730 5712
Station	Sloane Square
Open	Mon–Sat noon–2.30pm & 6–11.30pm
Accepts	All major credit cards except Diners

Probably at least ninety percent of Mr Peng's regular customers have given up the unequal struggle, submitting themselves to the "feast" – a multi-course extravaganza, varied according to the maestro's whims and the vagaries of the market, that might include pigeon soup. Or goose. Or a dish of cold, marinated octopus. This fine food and attentive service is matched by the Hunan's elegant surroundings, but be warned – the prices are Pimlico rather than Chinatown, and they continue to escalate.

If you want to defy Mr Peng and act knowledgeable, you could actually try asking for the griddle-fried lettuce-wrapped dumplings (£6.50), which are exceedingly delicious. Or there are frogs' legs in rich and hot Hunan sauce (£7); or smoked chicken slices (£6.50); or grilled salt and pepper squid (£7). Alternatively, try the camphor-wood-and-tea-smoked duck (£18 for a half, £33 for a whole). Once again, this dish is as interpreted by Mr P, so as well as a southwestern Chinese version of crispy duck (with pancakes etc) there's a sweet and sourish sauce (apparently his regulars felt that it was "too dry" without). Other standouts include hot and spicy beef (£7), and stir-fried squid (£8), which is accurately cooked. Also on offer are sizzling prawns (£8), braised scallops in Hunan sauce (£8) and spicy braised eggplant (£6).

However, for all but the strongest wills, resistance is useless and you'll probably end up with what is described on the menu as "Hunan's special leave-it-to-us-feast – minimum two persons, from £28 a head. We recommend those not familiar with Hunan cuisine and those who are looking for a wide selection of our favourite and unusual dishes to leave it to the chef Mr Peng to prepare for you his special banquet. Many of the dishes are not on the menu." Quite so.

Jenny Lo's Teahouse

Jenny Lo's Teahouse in Victoria is the complete opposite of those typically stuffy, over-designed Chinese restaurants. This place is bright, bare and utilitarian – and stylish and fashionable, too. From the blocks of bright colours and refectory tables to the artifice of framing the emergency exit sign like a picture over the door, this is a somewhat smart, but comfortable, place to eat. And that just about sums up the food too. Service makes you think that you're in the politest cafeteria in the world and the prices don't spoil the illusion. Although portion sizes and seasoning can vary, the food is freshly cooked and generally delicious. All of which meets with unqualified approval from a loyal band of sophisticated regulars.

Cost	£7–22

Address 14 Eccleston St, SW1
☎ 020 7259 0399
Station Victoria
Open Mon–Fri 11.30am–3pm & 6–10pm, Sat noon–3pm & 6–10pm
Accepts Cash or cheque only

The menu is divided into three main sections: soup noodles, wok noodles and rice dishes. Take your pick and then add some side dishes. The chilli beef soup ho fun (£6.95) is a good choice. A large bowl full of delicate, clear, chilli-spiked broth which is then bulked out with yards of slippery ho fun – ribbon noodles like thin tagliatelle – plus slivers of beef and fresh coriander. The black bean seafood noodles (£6.95) are an altogether richer and more solid affair, made from egg noodles with prawn, mussels, squid and peppers. Rice dishes range from long-cooked pork and chestnuts (£6.50), to gong bao chicken with pine nuts (£6.95) and the simpler Szechuan aubergine (£5.75). The side dishes are great fun, with good spare ribs (£3.50) and guo tie (£4.25), which are pan-cooked dumplings filled with either vegetables or pork. Spring onion pancakes (£2) are a Beijing street food made from flat, griddled breads laced with spring onions and served with a dipping sauce.

Try the tea here, too. As well as offering Chinese and herbal teas, Jenny Lo has enlisted the help of herbalist Dr Xu who has blended two special therapeutic teas: long-life tea (£1.85), described as "a warming tonic to boost your energy", and cleansing tea (£1.85), "a light tea for strengthening the liver and kidneys". It tastes refreshing and faintly gingery, and is doubtless cleansing, too.

La Poule au Pot

You are in trouble at the Poule au Pot if you don't understand at least some French. It is unreservedly a bastion of France in England, and has been for more than three decades. What's more, several of the staff have worked here for most of that time, and the restaurant itself has hardly changed at all, with huge dried-flower baskets and a comfortable

Cost	£17–40
Address	231 Ebury St, SW1
T	020 7730 7763
Station	Sloane Square
Open	Mon–Sat 12.30–2.30pm & 7–11.15pm, Sun 12.30–2.30pm & 7–10.30pm
Accepts	All major credit cards

rustic atmosphere. The wide windows make it bright at lunch, but by night, candlelight ensures that La Poule is a favourite for romantic assignations.

A small dish of crudités in herb vinaigrette is set down as a bonne bouche. Different fresh breads come in huge chunks. The menu is deceptive, as there are usually more additional fresh daily specials than are listed. The patient waiters struggle to remember them all and answer your questions about the dishes. As a starter, the escargots (£7.50) deliver classic French authenticity with plenty of garlic and herbs. The soupe de poisson (£8.25) is not the commonly served thick soup, but a refined clear broth with chunks of sole and scallop, plus prawns and mussels. A main course of bifteck frites (£13.75) brings a perfectly cooked, French-cut steak with red-hot chips. The gigot aux flageolets (£13.50) is pink and tender, with beans that are well flavoured and not overcooked. There's calves' liver (£13.25), and carré d'agneau à l'ail (£16) – rack of lamb with garlic. The pudding menu features standards like crème brûlée (£4.50) – huge, served in a rustic dish, and classically good – and banane à sa façon (£4.50), which is lightly cooked with a caramel rum sauce. There is also a selection of good pudding wines: a glass of Monbazillac (£2.95) makes an excellent companion to the richness of the desserts.

If you are a Francophile, you'll find all your favourites, from French onion soup to boeuf Bourguignon, from quiche to cassoulet. And, such is the atmosphere of the place that, for a few hours at least, you forget that you are in England, particularly if you take advantage of the prix-fixe lunch (£14.50 for two courses and £16 for three).

INDIAN

Quilon

Quilon is about as swish as Indian restaurants get – as you'd expect when you learn that it is owned by the Taj Group, which also runs a dozen of India's most upmarket hotels. This elegant, modern 92-seater opened in September 1999, and anyone who still unfairly pigeonholes all Indian restaurants as cheap and cheerful should pop along for

Cost	£20–60

Address 41 Buckingham Gate, SW1
℡ 020 7821 1899
Station St James's Park
Open Mon–Fri noon–2.30pm & 6–11pm, Sat 6–11pm
Accepts All major credit cards

a reality check. Quilon has the appearance of a sophisticated restaurant, you get the service you'd expect in a sophisticated restaurant, and you get the quality of cooking you'd expect from a sophisticated restaurant. And, unsurprisingly, you get the size of bill you'd expect from a sophisticated restaurant. The menu, built around "Coastal Food", showcases the splendid cuisine of Kerala – lots of fish, seafood, fresh peppercorns and coconut. The food is very good indeed.

Start with the Coorg chicken (£5.50) – chunky chicken with rich spicing and a hint of Coorg vinegar. Or pepper shrimps (£6.50) – prawns fried in batter with plenty of chilli and a touch of aniseed. In season there may be partridge masala (£5.50), cooked in really fresh spices. Moving on to the mains, seafood tempters include clam chilli fry (£14.25) and prawns Byadgi (£18.50); the latter are enormous prawns grilled with the specially imported and pleasantly hot Byadgi chillies. Or try Canara lamb curry (£15.95) – very, very rich with a clean and honest heat; or the guinea fowl salan (£13.75), cooked with coconut milk and yoghurt. These are all fairly spicy choices, but there is also gentler fare, with plenty of chicken options and several duck dishes. All the main courses come with a vegetable of the day. Standouts include masala stuffed aubergine (£7.50) – whole baby aubergines stuffed with coconut and poppy seeds; and a spinach poriyal (£7.50), made with freshly grated coconut, mustard leaves and split Bengal gram.

In the middle of the dining room there is an outpost kitchen where a busy chef works at an array of burners making fresh appams (£1.95), feathery rice pancakes which are stunning when hot and so-so when cold. Good value set-lunch menus were introduced in 2002 – £12.95 for two courses and £15.95 for three.

Rhodes in the Square

Get him away from all that television hype, and Gary Rhodes is actually a very good cook. In his restaurants there is a real respect for genuine British ingredients, and the resulting dishes are good to eat. It's hard to understand why restaurant critics tend to rank his food below that of his more French-inspired peers. Rhodes in the Square is the place to make up your mind. It underwent its first refurb (a rite of passage for all restos) in summer 2002, and re-opened suitably slick. This is not a cheap restaurant, though you could maybe console yourself by thinking of all the bond dealers tucking in at Gary's City restaurant – they tend to pay a bit more for this kind of grub. And, as always seems to be the case, this quality of food is most wallet-friendly at lunch: two courses for £17.80 and three courses for £19.80 is not so bad.

Cost	£20–75

Address Dolphin Square, Chichester St, SW1
☎ 020 7798 6767
Station Pimlico
Open Tues–Fri noon–2.30pm & 7–10pm, Sat 7–10pm
Accepts All major credit cards
🌐 www.rhodesrestaurants.com

MODERN BRITISH

In the evenings, dinner costs £36.50 for three courses, with only a couple of supplements. Starters are simple and stunning: warm wild mushroom tartlet on a Jerusalem artichoke and walnut salad; steamed monkfish "scampi" with minestrone sauce; cream of cauliflower soup with pan-fried fillet of red mullet. But the one starter on the dinner menu that every self-respecting hedonist must try is the lobster omelette thermidor (£2.50 supplement). Presented in its own little pan, this is a melting omelette with a rich sauce and chunks of lobster. Main courses are equally rich and reassuring: squab pigeon on a game and foie gras toast; poached loin of lamb on a shallot tarte Tatin with a marjoram cream sauce; tournedos of cod on shrimp spinach with saffron tomato and capers. For pudding, you could pass up the famous Rhodes bread and butter pudding – though it is a signature dish – and try the warm soft chocolate pudding with steeped cherries and an ivory ice cream.

Since the opening in 1998, the menu here has become somewhat simpler and, if anything, prices have not increased as rapidly as they have elsewhere. Anything that makes this kind of honest cooking more accessible is to be applauded.

FRENCH

Roussillon

Roussillon is a restaurant that got off to a slow start but has quietly gone on to earn a growing reputation and a cupboard full of awards. The mainspring is a young French chef called Alexis Gauthier who is obsessed with the quality and freshness of his ingredients. His dishes invariably combine strong flavours, and make good use of fine English foods. To see the advantages of being season- and market-driven, try the terrific-value set lunch at Roussillon, at £15 for two courses and £18 for three. The main menu runs in at two courses for £29, three for £35, and four for £42. At which point you will probably feel the urge to splash out on one or other of the seven-course showing-off menus – the vegetarian "Garden Menu" (£45) and the "Seasonal Menu" (£60).

Cost	£20–90

Address 16 St Barnabas St, SW1
℡ 020 7730 5550
Station Sloane Square/ Victoria
Open Mon–Fri noon–2.30pm & 6.30–10.45pm, Sat 6.30–10.45pm
Accepts All major credit cards except Diners
® www.roussillon.co.uk

The menu has five sections to it: the classics, the seeds, the garden, the sea and the land – and changes with the seasons. Overlook the rather coy names and listen to your taste buds. Open with a terrine of duck foie gras with conference pear. Into "the garden": ceps and bone marrow ravioli with grated cheese and beef jus; or autumn vegetables and fruits cooked together in a pot with aged balsamic. Fish dishes may include roast monkfish, with larded salsify, crisp onion rings and chicken jus; or grilled John Dory, with bitter green and white dandelion, chervil root and crustacean sauce. "The land" brings beef that is organically raised Aberdeen Angus from Donald Russell, served with larded vegetables and thick French fries; and pan-fried fillet of Highland venison with caramelized pumpkin, and truffle and celeriac purée. This is gastronomic stuff. Onwards to cheese, fruit and chocolate.

You have to warm to anyone that puts a separate section of chocolate dishes on the menu. There's chocolate fondant, chocolate praline finger and chocolate soufflé. It is only eclipsed by the Parthian shot – spicy soufflé of organic duck egg with gingerbread fingers and maple infusion.

Tate Britain Restaurant

In these days of a "sandwich at the desk" office culture, you have to think very long and hard before recommending a restaurant that is only open for lunch, especially when it has the potential to be a pretty wallet-challenging affair. For the foodie, the Tate Britain Restaurant is worth a visit; for the winey it is an essential pilgrimage. This restaurant's love affair with wine began in the 1970s, when the food was dodgy and it seemed as if the only customers were wine merchants marveling at the impossibly low prices. Today there are fewer florid gents enjoying a three-bottle lunch, but the atmosphere is soothing and the wine list is not only fascinating – but offers outstanding value as well.

Cost	£25–100

Address **Tate Britain, Millbank, SW1**
℡ **020 7887 8877**
Station **Pimlico**
Open **Mon–Sat noon–3pm, Sun noon–4pm**
Accepts **All major credit cards except Diners**
ⓦ **www.tate.org.uk**

The menu changes on a regular basis and offers admirably seasonal dishes. There's also a set lunch, with two courses at £16.75 and three at £19.50. Although there is no indication on the menu, there are dishes to suit the oenophiles, and dishes for civilian diners. Thus wine folk might choose simple starters like organic smoked salmon with wholemeal bread (£9), or sauté of wild mushrooms (£7.95), while the others can opt for pan-fried foie gras with caramelized orange and brioche (£10.50). Mains touch most of the bases and dishes are straightforward: roast cod fillet with herb crust and boulangère potatoes (£14.50); pan-fried duck breast with Swiss chard and thyme-roasted carrots (£13.50); or linguine with spring greens vegetables and pesto (£11.50). The cooking is good. The food is fresh and unpretentious. There are enough tempting puddings to team with dessert wines although the caramelized lime and clove tart sets up a wine-matching conundrum.

The wine list is wonderful, and constantly changing as bins run out. It takes the form of a vast book, but do not be intimidated and take your time. The wine waiters are both knowledgeable and helpful. Bottles are served at the right temperature and decanted without fuss when necessary. As a strategy, how about picking a few good half-bottles? For example, a Côte de Nuits-Villages Blanc 1997 from Louis Jadot (£15.50), and Chorey-les-Beaune Château de Chorey 1998 Domaine Germain (£14).

Waterloo & The South Bank

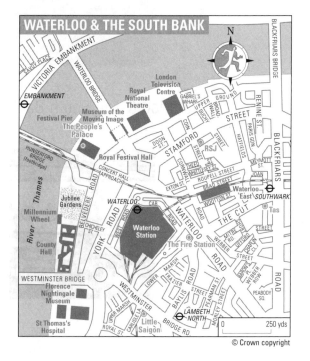

WATERLOO & THE SOUTH BANK

N

BLACKFRIARS BRIDGE

SAVOY PLACE

VICTORIA EMBANKMENT

WATERLOO BRIDGE

EMBANKMENT

London Television Centre

Royal National Theatre

GABRIEL'S WHARF

RENNIE ST

PARIS GDN

Festival Pier

Museum of the Moving Image

The People's Palace

UPPER GROUND

STAMFORD STREET

HATFIELDS

BLACKFRIARS

HUNGERFORD BRIDGE (footbridge)

DOON ST

CORNWALL

RSJ

THEED

WHITTLESEY ST

MEYMOTT ST

Royal Festival Hall

CONCERT HALL APPROACH

EXTON ST

ROUPELL STREET

BRAD STREET

JOAN

Thames

Jubilee Gardens

BELVEDERE ROAD

WATERLOO

CAB

WOOTTON ST

Waterloo East

SOUTHWARK

Millennium Wheel

YORK ROAD

WEST ROAD

CHICHELEY ST

Waterloo Station

THE CUT

Tas

River

County Hall

The Fire Station

WATERLOO ROAD

MITRE RD

OXFORD

STREET

GREY COAT CL

OXFORD ROAD

WESTMINSTER BRIDGE

LOWER MARSH

Florence Nightingale Museum

WESTMINSTER

BAYLIS

FRAZIER ROAD

STREET

PEARMAN ST

MORLEY STREET

WEBBER ROW

PEABODY SQ.

St Thomas's Hospital

UPPER MARSH

CARLISLE LA

ROYAL ST

Little Saigon

LAMBETH NORTH

BRIDGE RD

0   250 yds

© Crown copyright

The Fire Station

MODERN BRITISH

When you arrive at The Fire Station it's hard to imagine that the food will be of much distinction. This is a big barn of a place with pumping music, and to get to the restaurant at the back you have to fight your way through noisy waves of colourful-drink-swillers. Decoration is scant, consisting mostly of red and cream paint, and blackboards painted with popping champagne corks. At first glance, it looks exactly like a theme hamburger bar. But if you look a little closer you'll see an open-plan kitchen preparing good-looking food, and a lot of happy diners. It's worth persevering.

Cost	£18–35

Address 150 Waterloo Rd, SE1
T 020 7620 2226
Station Waterloo
Open Mon–Fri noon–2.45pm & 5.30–11pm, Sat noon–10.45pm, Sun noon–9.30pm
Accepts All major credit cards

The menu changes daily but there are some simple things that often feature, including starters such as carrot, orange and coriander soup with croutons (£4.25); Cajun King prawns with mixed leaves and mustard citrus dressing (£6.50); smooth liver terrine (£5.75); and dressed crab on a bed of mixed leaves with lemon dressing (£6.50). Equally appealing are mains such as roast spiced pork belly with sticky rice, pak choi and soy sauce (£10.95); pan-fried salmon fillet with crushed new potatoes and lemon butter sauce (£11.95); and tandoori-seared yellow-fin tuna loin (£12.50). Or how about parsley-crusted calves' liver (£12.50)? Or the Fire Station bouillabaisse (£15.50), a large casserole containing a rather unauthentic mix of prawns, calamari, crab, mussels and salmon? The cooking is sound enough, and the service is friendly. The only problems stem from a tendency towards "sorlin" cooking (it's-all-in) and, though it seems churlish to comment on over-generosity, the seriously large portions. Thankfully, puddings are simple, but there are four huge scoops for one helping of caramel ice cream with butter-scotch sauce (£3.95). To wash it all down, there's a decent wine list with five reds and whites by the glass, as well as a 50cl carafe (£7.95 for the house white, £9.80 for Rioja).

There's a set menu (available up to 7pm) of two courses for £10.95 and three for £13.50, which makes The Fire Station a sensible place to visit on the way to the Old Vic or the National Theatre. It's a little less frenetic then, as well.

Little Saigon

After ten years running a restaurant in Frith Street, the Long family had had enough. Soho rents were hitting the stratosphere and the lease was up for renewal. So Mr Long and his wife opened Little Saigon, just behind Waterloo Station, a homely restaurant serving good Vietnamese food from a comprehensive menu. Stick to the indigenous dishes, and take the opportunity to get to grips with Vietnamese spring rolls – both the crispy deep-fried kind and the "crystal" variety. The latter are round discs of rice pastry like giant, translucent communion wafers, which you soak in a bowl of hot water until pliable and then roll around a filling made up of fresh salady things, interesting sauces, and slivers of meat grilled on a portable barbecue.

Cost	£15–35

Address 139 Westminster Bridge Rd, SE1
℡ 020 7207 9747
Station Waterloo/Lambeth North
Open Mon–Fri noon–3pm & 5.30–11.30pm, Sat & Sun 5.30–11.30pm
Accepts All major credit cards

Run amok with the starters. Sugar-cane prawns (two for £3.20) are large prawn "fish cakes" impaled on a strip of sugar cane and grilled. Vietnamese imperial spring rolls (£2.60) are of the crispy fried variety, but they are served cut into chunks and with lettuce leaves to roll them up in. Also good is the strangely resilient Vietnamese grilled squid cake (£3.50). Topping the bill are special spring rolls (four for £2.60) – delicate pancakes, thin enough to read through, filled with prawns and fresh herbs – which in this case have been "pre-rolled" and are quite delicious. It's as if each of the starters comes with its own special dipping sauce, and the table is soon littered with an array of little saucers – look out for the extra-sweet white plum sauce and the extra-hot brown chilli oil. For mains, ha noi grilled chicken with honey (£5.30), special Saigon prawn curry (£6.40), and the house special, fried crispy noodles (£4.80), can all be recommended.

Do try and master the "specialities". Make an intermediate course of the crystal pancakes and use them to wrap the crunchy salads and the meats barbecued at the table. You have to soak your own pancakes and it is trickier than it looks. Soak them too long and they stick to the plate; not long enough, and they won't wrap. Grilled slices of barbecued beef (£12) and grilled slices of pork in garlic sauce (£12) both make splendid fillings.

The People's Palace

When this restaurant first opened, there were tales of diners who had finished their dinner late being locked into the Festival Hall and of others wandering for ages between levels. It is still not the most straightforward venue to find, but it has its own entrance now, opposite Hungerford Bridge. And it's worth seeking out. It's a very large place, run with the high standards you would hope for – considering that it is within the South Bank Centre and many diners are either pre- or post-concert, which makes timing crucial. The food is well presented and accurately cooked. There are occasional flashes of innovation but the menu is mainly composed of well-balanced, satisfying dishes at reasonable prices. Add the fabulous view overlooking the Thames, the sound service, a child-friendly policy (they're nice to kids, and provide highchairs and children's menus), and it all adds up to an attractive package.

Cost	£16–45

Address Level Three, Royal Festival Hall, South Bank, SE1
☎ 020 7928 9999
Station Waterloo
Open Daily noon–3pm & 5.30–11pm
Accepts All major credit cards
🌐 www.peoplespalace.co.uk

The bargains at The People's Palace are its fixed-price menus. Lunch menus are available daily at £12.50 for two courses, while the pre-theatre menu is £17 for two courses, and the all-day Sunday menu is £16.50 for two courses. For this, you choose from a good spread of daily selections. On the à la carte you'll find starters like warm Stilton and red onion tart with pear and watercress salad (£6.50); seared tuna with Asian vegetables, coriander and soy (£8.75); and smoked duck with mozzarella and quince salad (£8.50). Mains may include a cassoulet of fish and shellfish with Manzanilla (£15.50); roast venison loin with peppered pear, chicken mousse and fig wine jus (£17.50), or a pot au feu made with topside of beef, poussin and bacon (£14.75). Puddings (£5) ring the sweet tooth bell: fig and ginger pudding with cinnamon custard; or banana and pecan pudding with clotted cream and toffee sauce.

It's worth figuring the Festival Hall's concert programme into your plans. On a popular night, you'll need to book for pre- or post-concert sittings. When you call to make a reservation, ask the receptionist, who will know just what's on and when it finishes.

RSJ

Rolled Steel Joist may seem a curious name for a restaurant, but it is appropriate – they can point out the RSJ holding up the first floor if you wish! What's more interesting about RSJ is that it's owned by a man with a passion for the wines of the Loire. Nigel Wilkinson has compiled his list mainly from wines produced in this region, and it features dozens of lesser-known Loire reds and whites – wines which clearly deserve a wider following. Notes about recent vintages both interest and educate, and each wine is well described.

Cost	£19–55

Address 13a Coin St, SE1
℗ 020 7928 4554
Station Waterloo
Open Mon–Fri noon–2.30pm & 5.30–11pm, Sat 5.30–11pm
Accepts All major credit cards
⊛ www.rsj.uk.com

The menu is based on classical dishes, but with a light touch and some innovative combinations as well. The starters might include tagliatelle of buttered Savoy cabbage, cep mushrooms and oregano (£5.95); boiled bacon and winter vegetable soup (£5); or guineafowl terrine with shallots, mushrooms, bacon and home-made piccalilli (£5.25). Moving on to the main courses, typical choices might include roast cod fillet with a casserole of butter beans, and fennel flavoured with rosemary (£12.95); roast rump of lamb with Savoy cabbage, and celeriac, carrot and garlic mash (£14.95); and rib-eye of beef with marinated red onion and Stilton cheese salad, plus pommes frites (£14.95). The menu also features an above-average number of vegetarian options, some of which are carefully thought out, like a broccoli and blue cheese tart with a spicy tomato and mint salsa, parsnip potato cakes and Savoy cabbage (£10.95). The puddings can be the kind of serious stuff that you really should save room for, such as white chocolate tart with raspberry coulis (£5.75); or sticky toffee pudding with toffee sauce (£5.25).

Like The Peoples' Palace (see p.163), RSJ is situated close to the South Bank Centre's cinema, concert halls and theatres, and is clearly enjoyed by patrons. It appears to cater for both the hastier pre-theatre crowd and a late crowd who are not rushed in any way – always a good sign. The set meals at £15.95 for two courses and £16.95 for three represent jolly good value. Use the Web site to check out the RSJ Wine Company, whose list is a joy to anyone devoted to the fine wines of the Loire.

Tas

Tas is a bright and bustling Turkish restaurant where eating is cheap, the menu and the set menus have proliferated until there is an almost baffling choice, and there is often live music. All of which explains why the place is heaving with office parties, birthday bashes and hen nights every night of the week. The management is obviously alert to the possibilities of a modern restaurant serving Turkish dishes – the feel of this place is closer to a busy West End brasserie than to your standard street-corner Turkish grills. Expect colourful crockery and an overdose of noise. If lively is what you like then Tas will do just fine.

Cost   £8–35

Address 33 The Cut, SE1; with branches
℡ 020 7928 1444
Station Southwark
Open Mon–Sat noon–11.30pm, Sun noon–10.30pm
Accepts All major credit cards except Diners
🌐 www.tasrestaurant.com

TURKISH

The menu is a monster. Four soups, followed by twelve cold starters, twelve hot starters, ten salads, eight rice dishes, four side orders, six pasta dishes, ten vegetarian dishes, fourteen grills, ten casseroles (including moussaka, which is stretching things a bit), fourteen fish and shellfish dishes, and nine desserts. Overwhelmed? Everyone else is. Which is probably why Tas also offers four set menus starting at three courses for £6.95 and peaking at a combo of six mezze, a grill, dessert and a coffee at £18.50 (for a minimum of two people). Now you can see why the parties flock here. The first thing to say about the food is that it is well presented and tastes wonderfully fresh. From the cold starters, favour the zeytin yagli bakla (£3.25), which is a fine dish of broad beans with yoghurt; or the cacik (£2.95), a simple cucumber and yoghurt dip. The bread is very good. Stars of the hot starter menu are the borek (£3.25), which is filo pastry filled with cheese and deep fried; and the sucuk izgara (£3.25), a Turkish garlicky sausage. Unless you have particular likes or prejudices to pander to, go on to the good, sound grills: bobrek izgara (£6.25) are lambs' kidneys; and tavuk shish (£7.25) is a chicken kebab. The fish dishes are accurately cooked and come in large portions: grilled halibut (£8.95) comes with tomato sauce; while the kalamari (£7.25) brings squid with a walnut sauce.

The menu announces, "Tas is our traditional Anatolian cooking pot, used to prepare casseroles". So try one.

City & East

Brick Lane & Spitalfields

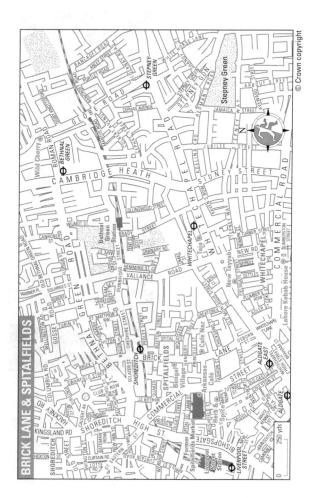

BRICK LANE & SPITALFIELDS

© Crown copyright

Arkansas Café

🍴 As you approach the Arkansas Café the glow from its steel-pit barbecue invites you in. Bubba Helberg and his wife Sarah claim that they serve the best barbecue this side of the pond, and they may just be right, for they are regularly in demand as the US Embassy's barbecue experts (they will also open here for evening parties of twelve or more). Their

Cost	£10–20

Address Unit 12, Old Spitalfields Market, E1
☏ 020 7377 6999
Station Liverpool Street
Open Mon–Fri noon–2.30pm, Sun noon–4pm
Accepts MasterCard, Visa

food is fresh and simple, and Bubba only uses the highest–quality ingredients, choosing his own steaks individually from Smithfield market to make sure that the meat is marbled enough for tenderness. The provenance of his lamb and sausages is listed for all to see. He marinates and smokes his own beef brisket and ribs, and his recipe for the latter won him a soul food award back home. His secret home-made barbecue sauce is on every table, but he won't sell the recipe to anyone.

Decor is spartan – clean-scrubbed tables, canvas chairs and paper plates – but this does not intrude on the quality of the food. There are no starters, so you just get stuck in. Any of the steaks – Irish steak platter (£9.50), USA steak platter (£13.50) – are good bets, char-grilled with Bubba's special sauce and served with potato salad and a vegetable salad. Note that the price is genuinely market sensitive and can rise and fall. Corn-fed French chicken (£7) is tender and full of flavour, and a side order of chilli (50p) provides a spicy sauce-like accompaniment. Most of the other dishes on the menu are platters or sandwiches, the latter including choices like char-grilled Barbary duck breast sandwich (£6); free-range pork sandwich (£5); beef brisket Texas-style sandwich (£7), which comes meltingly tender and smoky; and, of course, hot dog (£4). Puddings (all £2.50) include New York-style lemon cheesecake and New Orleans pecan pie. They are as sweet and as solid as they should be. The wine list is short and to the point, but the beer list is long, with a large selection of serious brews including Budvar and Budweiser (both £3.25), and the American Anchor Steam (£2.50).

Diners at Arkansas usually include expat Americans homesick for authentic barbecue, which has to be a good sign. Eat in and take an extra order home.

Bengal Village

Cost	£8–18
Address	75 Brick Lane, E1
ⓣ	020 7366 4868
Station	Aldgate East/ Liverpool Street
Open	Daily noon–midnight
Accepts	All major credit cards
ⓦ	www.bengalvillage.com

No doubt about it, Brick Lane is becoming more sophisticated. Where once all was BYOB restaurants serving rough-and-ready curries at bargain-basement prices to impoverished punters seeking chilli and all things familiar, you will now find a crop of slick new establishments serving authentic Bangladeshi cooking. The Bengal Village is one such place. There's a blonde wood floor and modernist chairs, but it's about more than just design. The menu touches all the bases: trad curryholics can still plough their way through more than a hundred old-style curries – korma, Madras, vindaloo – but now they can also try some more interesting Bangladeshi dishes, too.

Bucking what seems to be becoming the trend, starters are not the best dishes at the Bengal Village. The onion bhajis (£1.95) are, well, onion bhajis, and the chicken tikka (£2.10) is no more than sound. Move straight along to the Bangla specialities. Bowal mas biran (£5.80) is boal fish that has been deep fried with a rich sauce. There are four shatkora curries – the shatkora being a small green fruit that has a delightful bitter citrus tang and goes very well with rich meats – lamb shatkora (£4.85), for example. Then there are ureebisi dishes, traditionally made with the seeds of a large runner-bean-like plant – in the UK butter beans are often substituted and nobody seems to mind. Try chicken ureebisi (£4.85). There are also some rather splendid vegetarian options: chalkumra (£3.95) – subtitled "ash-ground", and supposed to be made with a pumpkin-like gourd – in practice turns out to be slices of marrow in a korma-ish sauce. The marrow kofta is a curry with large and satisfactorily dense vegetable dumplings floating, or rather sinking, in it. There are two thalis available, offering a complete meal (either vegetarian or non-vegetarian) for £6.75 or £9.70.

The wine list comes on a small card which makes splendid reading. "Bolinger Champaign – £39.95"; "Moet and Chandan – £40.95"; "Jacobs Greek (Red Wine) – £8.75". Go for a large Cobra beer (£2.95) or follow the great Brick Lane tradition and take your own refreshment with you in a carrier bag.

Café Naz

Café Naz dominates Brick Lane with its elegant facade complete with an all-glass staircase and spacious upstairs dining room. "Contemporary Bangladeshi Cuisine" is what it says on the menu, and generally speaking that is what you get, though you will find some of the Indian restaurant standards – a list

Cost	£9–22

Address 46–48 Brick Lane, E1
℡ 020 7247 0234
Station Aldgate East
Open Daily noon–midnight
Accepts All major credit cards
🖰 www.cafenaz.com

of baltis and, of course, chicken tikka masala. The decor is certainly contemporary: bright colours, modern furniture and a gleaming open kitchen where you can watch the chefs at work. Prices are low – thirty curry restaurants within a stone's throw makes for serious competition – and service is attentive.

Start with the boti kebab (£2.95), either lamb or chicken, cooked in the tandoor and served with a plateful of fresh salad. Or there's adrok chop (£3.95), small pieces of lamb chop which have been marinated in ginger and garlic before getting the treatment in the clay oven. Fish cutlet (£2.95) brings pieces of a Bangladeshi fish called the ayre, deep fried and served with fried onions. These could be called goujons if they weren't so big and didn't contain a good many large bones. For main courses, the dhansak (£4.50) comes as either mutton or chicken and is very tasty – it's cooked with lentils and turns out at once hot, sweet and sour. Or how about palak gosht (£4.95), a simple dish of lamb and spinach? Then there's gosht kata masala (£5.95), a splendidly rich lamb curry; or chicken sour masala (£5.95), which is chicken in a very tomatoey tomato sauce sharpened with a little vinegar. Naan bread (£1.35) is freshly cooked and wiped with butter – delicious. And there are a range of vegetable dishes (all £2.75) – niramish, mutter aloo, bindi, sag aloo, brinjal. Very sound and very good value.

Weekdays, the lunch is a buffet – your chance to go through the card for £7.95, sampling curries, tandoori chicken, rice dishes and a constant flow of hot naans. If you want to do this justice, pick a day when all is serene – a nap after such a lunch is obligatory.

Herb & Spice

Do not let the tiny, rather gloomy dining room and huge swags of plastic flowers put you off this treasure of a curry house on Whites Row, a small road just off Commercial Street and tucked in behind Spitalfields. A loyal clientele from the City means that to secure one of the 22 seats you'll probably have to book! The menu here

Cost	£7–15
Address	11a Whites Row, E1
☎	020 7247 4050
Station	Aldgate East/ Liverpool Street
Open	Mon–Fri 11.30am– 2.30pm & 5.30–11.30pm
Accepts	All major credit cards

includes all the curry classics, plus one or two dishes you may not have spotted before, but what sets Herb & Spice apart from the pack is that the dishes are freshly cooked and well prepared and yet the prices are still reasonable. When the food arrives it will surprise you: it's on the hot side, with plenty of chilli and bold, fresh flavours.

It's not often that the popadoms (55p) grab your attention. They do here. Fresh, light and crisp, they are accompanied by equally good home-made chutneys – perky chopped cucumber with coriander leaf, and a hot, yellowy-orange, tamarind-soured yoghurt. The kebabs make excellent starters: murgi tikka (£2.75) – chicken, very well cooked; shami kebab (£2.75) – minced meat with fresh herbs; gosht tikka (£2.55) – tender lamb cubes. For a main course you might try the unusual murgi akhani (£6.95), a dish of chicken cooked with saffron rice and served with a good, if rather hot, vegetable curry. Or there's bhuna gosht (£4.95), a model of its type – a rich, well-seasoned lamb curry with whole black peppercorns and shards of cassia bark. Murgi rezalla (£5.95) is chicken tikka in sauce; it's much hotter and comes with more vegetables than its cousin, the chicken tikka masala. The breads are good, too: from the decent naan (£1.65) to the shabzi paratha (£1.95), a thin, crisp wholemeal paratha stuffed with vegetables.

For a real tongue-trampler, try the dall shamber (£2.75), a dish of lentils and mixed vegetables which is often overlooked in favour of that popular garlicky favourite, tarka dhal. Traditionally served hot, sweet and sour, at Herb & Spice dall shamber comes up very hot, with an almost chemical bite from the large amounts of chilli, and very, very sweet indeed. Not for the faint-hearted.

Lahore Kebab House

(Y) For years, the Lahore has been a cherished secret among curry-lovers, a nondescript, indeed downbeat-looking, kebab house serving excellent and very cheap fare. Recent years, however, have seen a few changes. Thankfully, the food is still good and spicy, the prices are still low, and the service brusque enough to disabuse you

Cost	£4–15

Address 2 Umberstone St, E1
℡ 020 7481 9737
Station Whitechapel/Aldgate East
Open Daily noon–midnight
Accepts Cash or cheque only
Ⓦ www.lakoe.com

of any thoughts that the new round marquetry tables, posh shop front, and even the threat of further expansion in the summer of 2002 will take the Lahore upmarket. What they do here, they do very well indeed. And if you need any further proof, look at all the other similarly named places which have sprung up all over town.

Rotis (50p) tend to arrive unordered – the waiter watches how you eat and brings fresh bread as and when he sees fit. For starters, the kebabs are standouts. Seekhe kebab (50p), mutton tikka (£2.50) and chicken tikka (£2.50) are all very fresh, very hot and very good, and served with a yoghurt and mint dipping sauce. The meat or chicken biryanis (£6) are also splendid, well spiced and with the rice taking on all the rich flavours. The karahi gosht and karahi chicken (£5.50 for a regular portion or £11 for a huge one) are uncomplicated dishes of tender meat in a rich gravy. The dal tarka (£3.50) is made from whole yellow split peas, while sag aloo (£3.50) brings potatoes in a rich and oily spinach puree. A sad loss from the menu is paya (an awesome dish of long-stewed sheeps' feet, thought by some to be the hallmark of any genuine Pakistani restaurant) – apparently it's impossible to get top-quality sheeps' feet nowadays. Much more palatable, if you want a very Lahore kind of delicacy, is the home-made kheer (£2), which is a special kind of rice pudding with cardamom.

This Lahore is unlicensed, but happy for customers to bring their own beer or wine – and there's a nearby off-licence ready to oblige. You will certainly need some complement to the generally hot food, though note that alcohol isn't the best cooling agent. For that, order a lassi.

New Tayyab

(🍽) The Tayyab Empire has come a
long way since those first days in
1974. After the initial café came the
sweet shop, and then the New Tayyab
took over what was once the corner pub.
In 2001, number 83 was transformed
from a scruffy converted pub crammed
with too many tables and uncomfortable

Cost	£4–15

Address 83 Fieldgate St, E1
Ⓣ 020 7247 9543
Station Whitechapel/Aldgate
East
Open Daily 5pm–midnight
Accepts Cash or cheque only
Ⓦ www.tayyabs.co.uk

chairs into a smart new designer restaurant. Now there's art on the walls, smart lighting and the chairs are
leather and chrome. Miraculously the food remains straightforward Pakistani fare: good, freshly cooked and served without pretension. And
more miraculous still, the prices have stayed lower than you would
believe possible. Booking is essential and service is speedy and slick.
This is not a place to umm and er over the menu.

The simpler dishes are terrific, particularly the five pieces of chicken
tikka (£2.40), served on an iron sizzle dish alongside a small plate of
salady things and a medium-fierce, sharp, chilli dipping sauce. They do
the same thing with mutton (£2.40), or there's a plate of four splendid
and large lamb chops (£3.80). Sheekh kebabs (70p) and shami kebabs
(60p) are bought by the skewer. There are round fluffy naan breads
(60p), but try the wholemeal roti (40p), which is deliciously nutty and
crisp. The karahi dishes are simple and tasty: karahi chicken (£4 normal
portion, £7.80 large) is chicken in a rich sauce; karahi batera (£4/8) are
quails; and karahi aloo gosht (£4) is lamb with potatoes in another rich
sauce, heavily flavoured with bay leaves. Or there's karahi mixed vegetables (£3). A list of interesting daily specials includes dishes such as the
splendidly named meat pillo (£4), which is served every Wednesday, and
features chunks of mutton slow-cooked in rice; it's rich, satisfying and
seeded with whole peppercorns for bite. Or, for genuine specialists,
there's paya (£3.80) – slow-cooked sheep's feet, available on Mondays.

The Tayyab is strictly BYOB if you want alcohol. But whether you're
going for beer or Coke, make sure you try the Tayyab lassi anyway. A
yoghurt drink served in a pint glass, it comes sweet or salted (£1.50),
and with mango or banana (£2).

Taja

Taja's exterior of black and white vertical stripes certainly jolts the eye. Venture in and you find a dining area accommodating sixty covers across two floors. The counter is ultra-modern in stainless steel and the seating has recently been upgraded from stools to comfy chairs. On the ground floor, large windows look out onto the hurly-burly of passing traffic just inches away. The food tastes very fresh, and is markedly cheap.

Cost	£5–12
Address	199a Whitechapel Rd, E1
℡	020 7247 3866
Station	Whitechapel
Open	Mon–Wed & Sun 11am–midnight, Thurs–Sat 11am–12.30am
Accepts	All major credit cards
∰	www.taja.net

So far so good. By now, those in the know will have recognized that the restaurant in question is a converted toilet in the Whitechapel Road. And, as if that is not novelty enough, Taja is a genuine rarity – a thoroughly modern Bangladeshi restaurant. The menu is both enlightened and lightened, with a host of vegetarian dishes balancing the traditional favourites.

Start with that great test of a tandoor chef, chicken tikka (£1.95). At Taja you get half a dozen sizeable chunks of chicken, cooked perfectly – not a hint of dryness – with the obligatory salad garnish (a waste of time) and a yellowish "mint sauce". Or try chotpoti (£1.95), described on the menu as "green peas and potatoes with spices, served with a tamarind chutney – high in protein". Move on to a biryani of mixed vegetables, lamb, chicken or prawn (all £4.95); a good-sized portion comes with a dish of really splendid vegetable curry by way of added lubrication. There are also a host of curry-house favourites. Chicken bhuna (£4.29) is an outstanding choice, with a really fresh sauce, hot but not too hot, and with lots of fresh herbs. The naan breads – plain, peshwari or keema (£1.50) – are large, thick-rimmed and very fresh, as a naan should be. The Taja got its licence in 1999 but you can still bring your own for a small corkage. Healthier types will enjoy the fresh juices – orange and carrot (£1.95) is especially good.

Taja offers all sorts of set meals and deals. The "fast set snack – ready in five to ten minutes" weighs in at £5.50 for veggies, £6.50 for omnivores. Or you can organize a takeaway or delivery by mouse – the website offers a bewildering array of options.

Wild Cherry

Wild Cherry is a vegetarian restaurant that, as the mission statement by the door proclaims, "exists firstly to provide fresh home-cooked vegetarian meals for the local community". It's part of the London Buddhist Centre around the corner and was once a soup kitchen for workers and devotees.

Cost	£5–20
Address **241 Globe Rd, E2**
⊤ 020 8980 6678
Station **Bethnal Green**
Open **Mon 11am–3pm,**
Tues–Fri 11am–7pm
Accepts **All major credit cards**
except Diners

It's a bright, clean, self-service venue with modern wooden tables and Arne Jacobsen chairs. A blackboard lists the daily menu and you choose from selections like cauliflower and almond cheese pie with one salad (£4.50); spaghetti with creamy pea, mushroom and fresh mint sauce (£4.25); hot quiche of the day with two salads (£4.25); and polenta pie with roasted vegetables and one salad (£4.50). There's a choice of three different salads every day, and there's always a soup and a quiche and two hot dishes. Baked potatoes include a choice of comforting fillings like humous (£2.40), grated cheddar (£2.80) and tzatsiki (£2.80). Salads (large mixed £3.50, regular mixed £2.40, single scoop £1.20) include choices like arame rice; ruby chard, cherry tomato and fresh chive; mixed leaf; Moroccan chickpea with rocket; and coleslaw with vegan mayonnaise. Puddings include chocolate and beetroot cake (£1.40); prune and honey cake (£1.25); and banoffee pie (£2.25). There's no liquor licence, but you can bring your own for £1 corkage. There are, however, fourteen different teas (80p or 90p), ten of them herbal, plus Free Trade coffee (£1.10 per mug, £1.80 per cafetiere), and a choice of soya or cow's milk. Daily choices often include wheat-free and sugar-free dishes and some are vegan. The portions are huge, it all tastes wholesome and it's amazing value. The resto is relaxed and you can have anything from a full meal to a refreshing cup of camomile tea.

Reading the full mission statement is a must. You learn that "We promote vegetarianism by making it both available and, hopefully, irresistible". You read on and discover that Wild Cherry is run by seven Buddhist women whose "working practices are based on the Buddhist principles of non-violence, honesty and generosity". Surely worthwhile aims in any restaurant kitchen?

City

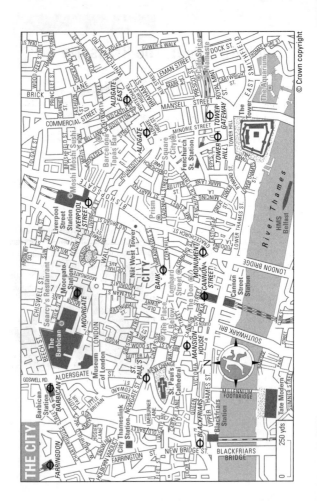

© Crown copyright

1 Lombard Street, The Brasserie

The Brasserie at 1 Lombard Street was formerly a banking hall and the circular bar sits under a suitably imposing glass dome. This is a brasserie in the City, of the City, by the City and for the City. It is connected to Bloomberg – a sort of elitist Ceefax-cum-email system which keeps City traders in touch with each other, rather like passing notes at school – and messages flash in and out. The brasserie menu is a model of its kind, long but straightforward with a spread of dishes that is up to any meal occasion – starters and salads, soups, egg and pasta, caviar, fish, crustacea, meat, puddings. It delivers on pretty much every front, serving satisfying dishes made with good fresh ingredients, and surprisingly it manages to be both stylish and unfussy at the same time. The bar, meanwhile, is like any chic City watering hole – loud, brisk and crowded, with simultaneous conversations in every European language.

Cost	£25–65

Address 1 Lombard St, EC3
℡ 020 7929 6611
Station Bank
Open Mon–Fri 11.30am–3pm & 6–10pm
Accepts All major credit cards
🖳 www.1lombardstreet.com

The brasserie menu changes every couple of months to satisfy the band of regulars, and there are daily specials in addition. The starters can be ambitious, like pig's trotter galette with seared foie gras (£9.95), or simple, like yellow pea soup with ham knuckle (£6.50), while further down the menu there will be some even more comfortable options like a soft-boiled free-range egg (£8.25 or £12.95 main course) served with baked potato, smoked haddock, and English mustard sauce. There's enough listed under shellfish and crustacea to fuel even the wildest celebrations, including sautéed scallops with fennel and Pernod (£22.50), and casserole of mussels and clams (£7.95/£14.50). Then the meat section features a very well-made coq au vin à la Bourguignon (£14.95) plus steaks, sausages, liver and chops. During the season you may also find fricassée of pheasant in puff pastry (£18.95).

There is a smaller, forty-seater room at the back of the bar set aside for fine dining at fancy prices. It's interesting to note, however, that caviar is a brasserie dish – 50g of beluga served with blinis, steamed potatoes and sour cream will set you back £120.

The Aquarium

St Katharine's Dock is a strange place, part tourist trap and part haven for millionaire yachties, so the medieval banquet (complete with fighting knights and wenches) rubs shoulders with big boats. The Aquarium is run by Christian and Kerstin Sandefeldt, a Swedish husband and wife team, and at the beginning of 2002 they refurbished the dining room. This is a fish restaurant and a rather good one. The underlying premise of the place is that the quality of ingredients is of paramount importance so you may see langoustines from the Outer Hebrides, and sea bass from Devon jostling for star billing with Swedish perch and Arctic char. The restaurant is pretty but plain, and has pleasant views across the water. Dishes are well conceived if elaborately presented.

Cost	£18–60

Address **Ivory House, St Katherine's Dock E1W**
℡ **020 7480 6116**
Station **Tower Hill/Tower Gateway**
Open **Mon noon–3pm, Tues–Fri noon–3pm & 6.30–11pm, Sat brunch noon–4pm, dinner 6.30–11pm**
Accepts **All major credit cards**
🌐 **www.theaquarium.co.uk**

There is a very sound lunch menu: two courses for £14.50 and three courses for £17.50. On the à la carte, the starters include Thai crab salad with toasted almond and sautéed veal sweetbreads (£7.75) – this dish sounds a mess and tastes terrific, the sharpness of the salad complements the sweet crabmeat, and the sweetbread offers a crisp counterpoint to both. Gravad lax (£7.50) is good here, or you could try the seared scallops with caviar and horseradish velouté (£9.75). Main courses are presented in fanciful fashion. Steamed Arctic char with seafood risotto cake and citrus and truffle salad (£13) is a grand dish of precisely cooked fish atop a rich rice pediment. Pot-roast monkfish with palourde clams, dill and butter beans (£13) comes to table in a casserole and is then transferred to a soup bowl. It is jolly good – and you'll need a spoon. Or perhaps grilled tuna with crispy shitake roll (£12.50) appeals? There's a tempting array of desserts, including one dish disarmingly called "lots of chocolate" (£7.50) – the line up is a choccy crème brûleé, a choccy fondant bun, a choccy milkshake, a choccy orange sorbet, and a three-choccy terrine.

If ever a competition were held to determine the world's silliest restaurant plate, the Sandefeldts would probably win. Picture a punt – those old, smelly, rectangular wooden boats. Then think smaller, about 600mm long, and imagine it was made of white china.

Barcelona Tapas Bar

At the start of the East End, not a hundred yards from the towering buildings of the City, you find yourself among the market stalls of Petticoat Lane and Middlesex Street. On one of the less salubrious corners you'll see a banner bearing the legend "tapas". Note that the arrow points down. As you descend the stairs into a cramped base-

Cost	£12–30

Address 1a Bell Lane, E1;
with branches
℡ 020 7247 7014
Station Aldgate
Open Mon–Fri 11am–11pm
Accepts All major credit cards
ⓦ www.barcelona/tapas.com

ment, which seats about twenty, try to still the thought that this is an inauspicious start to your lunch or evening. Barcelona is, in fact, one of London's best tapas bars. The range of snacks wouldn't be sniffed at in Barcelona or Madrid, and includes a fair few Catalan specialities – including the classic tomato- and garlic-rubbed bread, a good accompaniment to any tapas session.

You'll find a number of tapas lined up in typical Spanish style along the back half of the bar – these are just a few of the selection on offer. The Barcelona has a vast (in more ways than one) menu, written in Spanish and Catalan with English translations. Many are simple, like Serrano ham (£8.50), or queso Manchego (£4.95), or aceitunas (£1.75–2.95) – olives – and rely on the excellent quality of the raw ingredients. Then there are peasant dishes like fabada Asturiana (£3.50), a stew of white beans with chorizo. More skill is involved in creating the paellas; the paella Valenciana (£11.95 per person) is particularly good. And there is also a chicken brochette (£6.95). Be warned, the Spanish seem blithely unaware of the havoc they wreak with the social lives of unsuspecting diners, and here, as well as being delicious, the gambas al ajillo (£6.95) are pungent enough to give you heartburn and the kind of breath that gets you elbow room in a thronged rush-hour tube.

Unusually for such a small place with such a huge choice, there's no need to worry about freshness. There is a bigger, smarter, newer and less charming Barcelona nearby, and the apparent lull between ordering and receiving your dish may be because the girl is running around the corner to the other kitchen to fetch a portion.

Café Spice Namaste

During the week this restaurant is packed with movers and shakers, all busily moving and shaking. They come in for lunch at 11.59am and they go out again at 12.59pm. Lunchtimes and even weekday evenings the pace is fast and furious, but come Saturday nights you can settle back and really enjoy Cyrus Todiwala's exceptional cooking. What's more, with the City "closed for the weekend", parking is no problem. It is well worth turning out, for

Cost	£20–50

Address 16 Prescot St, E11; with branches
℡ 020 7488 9242
Station Aldgate East/Tower Hill
Open Mon–Fri noon–3pm & 6.15–10.30pm, Sat 6.15–10.30pm
Accepts All major credit cards
ⓦ www.cafespice.org

this is not your average curry house. The menu, which changes throughout the year, sees Parsee delicacies rubbing shoulders with dishes from Goa, North India, Hyderabad and Kashmir, all of them precisely spiced and well presented. The tandoori specialties, in particular, are awesome, fully flavoured by the cunning marinades but in no way dried out by the heat of the oven.

Start with a voyage around the tandoor. The murg kay tikkay (£4.75/9.95) tastes as every chicken tikka should, with yoghurt, ginger, cumin and chillies all playing their part. Or there's venison tikka aflatoon (£6.50/12.50), which originates in Gwalior and is flavoured with star anise and cinnamon. Also notable is the papeta na pattice (£3.95), a potato cake perked up with coconut, green peas and Parsee-style hot tomato gravy. For a main course, fish-lovers should consider the tareli machchi nay leeli curry (£12.75) – tilapia fillets marinated and then grilled, and served with a coconut curry. Choose meat and you should try the dhansak (£11.75). This is an authentic version of the much-misrepresented Parsee speciality of lamb curried with lentils; it is served with a small kebab and brown onion-rice. Breads are also excellent, and some of the accompaniments and vegetable dishes belie their lowly status at the back of the book-sized menu. Try baingan bharta (£4.50/7.25), an aubergine classic.

It's a good idea at Café Spice Namaste to do as the in-the-know diners do, and choose from the speciality menu that changes every week. Also make a note to try the pickles – they are very good indeed.

The Don

George Sandeman first took over the cellars at 20 St Swithin's Lane in 1798. And very fine cellars they are too, complete with an ornate, black, iron "Capital Patent Crane" for lowering barrels into the depths. The latest incumbent to occupy the site is The Don restaurant and bistro, which takes its name from the trademark portrait of Sandeman port's "Don" which has been re-hung, with due ceremony, at the gateway to this hidden courtyard. The vaulted brick cellars make a grand backdrop for the bistro, while the lofty room on the ground floor makes a striking restaurant. The restaurant floor is real wood – so real that it squeaks underfoot – and the walls are hung with suitably enigmatic modern art. The whole place reeks of aspiration.

Cost	£25–65
Address	20 St Swithin's Lane, EC4
☎	020 7626 2606
Station	Bank
Open	Mon–Fri noon–3pm & 6–10pm
Accepts	All major credit cards

The food in the upstairs restaurant is good – it is setting its cap at great things by aiming directly for the fine dining market. This is a strategy that may well work in the long term, as the food is accomplished and you couldn't ask for a better-heeled catchment area. Starters range from a terrine of foie gras with Sauternes jelly and toasted brioche (£9.95), and a mosaic of peat-smoked Scottish salmon with grilled artichokes and confit shallots (£6.75) – both of which show skill in the charcuterie department – to a salade paysanne of boudin noir with Cox's apples and Calvados dressing (£6.25). Mains may include roast cod Lyonnaise on a potato galette with rosemary jus (£14.50); loin of young New Zealand venison with roast fig and fondant potato "Oporto" (£16.95); and a well-judged dish of calves' liver with braised chicory and champ potatoes (£15.75). The cooking is good but the presentation is ambitious and tends towards old-fashioned "tall food". Puds are comforting: dark chocolate tart with eau de vie Mandarine sorbet (£5.75); hazelnut pistachio parfait (£5.50). And there are savouries, including a delicious French rarebit (£7.75) of grilled Reblochon on toast.

The bistro downstairs offers simpler, cheaper food, and there is a grand private room in the next-door cellar.

Moshi Moshi Sushi

Moshi Moshi Sushi serves healthy fast food, Japanese style – its dishes circulate on a kaiten or conveyor belt. There are a dozen or so such places in London these days, but this one claims to have been the first. Its location, inside Liverpool Street railway station, meshes perfectly with the concept. With its glass walls and ceiling, and no-smoking policy, it is a great place to eat before setting off on a train journey. It is, however, much more than a refuelling stop for commuters and, reassuringly, you'll find both local office workers and Japanese diners enjoying leisurely meals. Either sit at the bar and watch your dinner circulate, or opt for table service, with some nice views of the old station arches. Set menus range from £6.80 to £11.50.

Cost	£10–25

Address Unit 24, Liverpool Street Station, EC2 1; with branches
☎ 020 7247 3227
Station Liverpool Street
Open Mon–Fri 11.30am–9.30pm
Accepts MasterCard, Visa
🖥 www.moshimoshi.co.uk

If you opt for a bar seat, the ordering system is child's play – just pluck your chosen dishes from the conveyer belt as they trundle past. You'll be charged according to the pattern on each individual plate you end up with. All the sushi is good and fresh, and there's a decent range of authentic dishes, from the somewhat acquired taste, or texture, of uni (£2.50) – sea urchin – through to flying fish roe (£2.50). There are some delicious California hybrids too, such as avocado and crabstick (£2), which is combined with sweet, sticky sushi rice and rolled with sesame seeds. Regular sushi choices – such as negitoro temaki (£2.90), which is a seaweed-wrapped roll of tuna and spring onion, or shakemaki (£2), which is salmon roll – are done well, too, as is the Nigiri sushi (£1.20–2.50). Of the puddings (all £2.50), the custard pancake, or dorayaki, is good, as are the various ice creams. Unless you're a fan, avoid adzuki dishes, no matter how dark, sticky and mysterious they look; they consist of over-sweetened red-bean paste – definitely an acquired taste.

Look out for the cartoons on the laminated cards, which give handy tips spelling out which sushi are best for beginners and which are "challenging". There are also helpful hints on just how to treat the fiery, ground wasabi that will clear your sinuses faster than anything else on the planet.

The Place Below

Bill Sewell started the Place Below in 1989, and yes, it is a vegetarian restaurant, and yes it is in the crypt of the St Mary-le-Bow church. But persevere, it has a splendidly low worthiness rating. If and when you find the restaurant – wander into the wonderfully elegant Wren church and look for the staircase down to the crypt – you'll see that it is split into two halves. The first has an open kitchen at one end and acts as coffee shop and servery. Good pastries and breakfast buns. The restaurant proper is open at lunch (with prices a pound or two cheaper between 11.30 and noon). Choose from the daily changing menu, push a tray along the canteen-style rails, and the chefs will fill a plate for you.

Cost	£6–15
Address	St Mary-le-Bow Church, Cheapside EC2
☎	020 7329 0789
Station	Bank/St Paul's
Open	Mon–Fri 7.30am–10.30am & 11.30am–2.30pm
Accepts	All major credit cards except Diners

The menu is reassuringly short – if everything is freshly cooked, if the menu is seasonal, and if prices are to be kept low, then a short menu is your guarantee. The dining room is lofty, with the large, central communal dining table being the only one with a tablecloth. The menu changes daily. There are a couple of soups, a hot dish, a quichey option, a salad of the day, good trad puds and that's about it. A soup such as carrot and saffron (£2.90) is rich and has a good texture, and you get a big bowlful. Splash out on bread (60p), which is very good indeed – nutty with a good crust. The salad of the day (£7.50) can be triumphant: crisp green beans, a rich savoury dollop of wild rice, shredded carrot with sesame seeds, and plenty of fresh leaves. Or how about a hot dish like the chilli bean casserole (£7)? It's rich and light, with a good spike of chilli, topped with a blob of very decent guacamole and served with Bulghur wheat. The field mushroom, fennel and Gruyère quiche (£6.50) is also well made. At the Place Below the cooking is of a high standard, and prices are commendably low.

No alcohol here, so make a bee-line for the home-made lemonade (£1.50), which is very good indeed.

Prism

The question we should ask our-selves is: where have all the banks gone to? And the answer is probably that they have vanished into cyberspace behind hole-in-the-wall machines, leaving free all these tantalizing banking halls with the kind of lofty ceilings and grandiose pillars that make restaurant designers drool. Prism, part of the Harvey Nichols plan for world domination, is an expensive City restaurant. Whether you find it a soul-satisfying experi-ence is probably something that can only be settled by a long interrogation of your wallet (or more probably your expense account). If you work in the City it is undeniably handy. Eating here is rather like being inside a towering, white-painted cube; it's very slick, and very much an old banking hall. The food is a well-judged blend of English favourites and modernist influences. There is the obligatory long bar and the obligatory suave service. As a restaurant it has no pronounced character but rather leaves an impression of modernity – no bad thing considering where it is.

Cost	£35–110
Address	147 Leadenhall St, EC3
ⓣ	020 7256 3888
Station	Bank
Open	Mon–Fri 11.30am–3.30pm & 6–10pm
Accepts	All major credit cards
ⓦ	www.harveynichols.com

Starters are well executed. White bean and Parmesan rind soup (£7.50) – they must be leftovers. Belgian endive salad with crisp pancetta and Asian pear (£10). Perigord truffle risotto (£13). Tempura of Whitby cod with pea puree (£10). When it comes to main courses, the menu splits half fish and half meat. On the fish side are dishes like roast salmon with salt cod cakes, shrimps and herb beurre blanc (£18.50), as well as more adventurous offerings such as monkfish wrapped in Carpegna ham with minestrone of vegetables (£22). The meat side offers roast veal chop with Roquefort butter (£22), rib-eye steak with onion rings and horseradish ketchup (£21.50), and honey-roast duck breast with Dauphinoise potatoes and sherry jus (£21.50). Puddings (all £7) include carmelized pineapple, crème brûlée, and chocolate mousse served with orange jelly and cocoa and orange sor-bets.

Like the pricing, the wine list is for bankers. There are a few bottles to be had for sensible prices but the main thrust is towards whatever the traffic will bear.

Searcy's Restaurant

Over Easter 2002, Searcy's tweaked the layout of this restaurant, adding a new, re-designed bar area to the new dining room and new-style cuisine that were brought into play the year before. This restaurant, hidden deep within the bowels of the Barbican Centre, has improved out of all recognition in the last couple of years. It may seem contradictory, but the food has sped upmarket while the service and ambience have become less formal. These were both welcome changes. As far as the service goes, Searcy's is now an agreeable place to eat, full of cheery gourmets rather than hushed aesthetes. And the kitchen is really going for it. The dishes are ambitious and well cooked, carefully plated but with none of that "tall food", over-fussy nonsense.

Cost	£25–80
Address	Level 2, The Barbican Centre, Silk St, EC2; with branches
	020 7588 3008
Station	Barbican
Open	Mon–Fri noon–2.30pm & 5.30–10.30pm, Sat 5–10.30pm
Accepts	All major credit cards

The chef manages to combine classic principles with some iconoclastic touches. Everything is well seasoned and technically very good; reductions are rich but not over-gluey. Starters include roast foie gras with cep tart and anise jus (£8.95), and ravioli of scallops with truffle and pea emulsion (£13.50). Or how about warm salad of skate with brandade (£8)? Or Tatin of roast beetroot with pigeon (£6.50)? Mains are also accomplished. There's a braised pig's trotter with caramelized sweetbreads and pommes purées (£17) – good trotter, good gravy, good mash. Or casserole of roasted lobster with baby vegetables (£24.50). Or roast sea bass with salsify and parsley cream (£21.95). Or loin of veal with truffle faggot (£19.95). These are very good combinations. Desserts (all £6.50) are very elegant: passion fruit parfait with pistachio mousse; roast fig Tatin with tea-soaked prunes; thin apple tart with Calvados bavarois. Add smiling service, the smart new bar and a long wine list and you have a very good restaurant.

There is a bargain table d'hôte menu and, for once, the restricted choice is more than compensated for by the quality of the grub; two courses at £19.50 and three at £22.50.

Thai Square City

When this restaurant opened in 2001, PR fanfares proclaimed that it was Europe's largest Thai restaurant, and it is plausible enough. In a vast room decorated with temple bells, Buddhas, pots, carved panels, teak, wooden flowers and gold-mosaic rooftop dragons, friendly staff greet customers with a genuine smile. Downstairs there's a 100-seater cocktail bar with a 4–7pm happy hour and a massive bar stocked with brightly coloured drinks. On Thursday and Friday, downstairs at Thai Square turns into a club with a 2am drink and dancing licence.

Cost	£12–45

Address 136–138 The Minories, EC3
℡ 020 7680 1111
Station Aldgate/Tower Hill
Open Mon–Thurs noon–10pm, Fri noon–11.30pm
Accepts All major credit cards

The eighty-dish menu lists both familiar favourites and more novel ideas. Toong thong (£4.00) is a dish of minced prawn and chicken in purse-like little sacks, and very moreish. Tod man poo (£5.00), or Thai crab cakes, will satisfy connoisseurs seeking this favourite, and tom yam kung (£4.50) will delight lovers of the classic lemon grass soup. Moo ping (£5.00), or barbecued pork served with a sweet and incredibly hot sauce, is tender and good. The menu suggests that it's especially good with sticky rice (£1.75), and it is. Five Thai curries (all £6.25) offer a choice of red or green and different main ingredients, which boosts the number of menu choices significantly. Other treats include Chu-chee lobster (£16.00), which is deep-fried lobster with special curry paste, coconut milk and lime leaves; frogs legs with garlic (£12.00), which is served with Thai salad; and roasted duck curry (£6.25), a clay pot of duck with spiced coconut milk, lychee and pineapple. There's a 20-dish vegetarian menu and a wine list that starts at £9.95, threads its way through some decent choices at around the £15–20 mark and rockets to cosset city boys with Krug Grand Cuvée champagne (£140), and a Chateau Cheval Blanc St Emilion (£245). Puddings include banana with coconut syrup and sesame seeds (£3.50), Thai egg custard (£3.00), and ice creams and sorbets (£3.00).

There's a bargain "Lunch Express" midday menu (noon–4pm), too, which brings you a meal for £6.50.

Clerkenwell

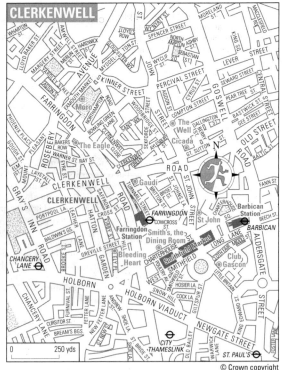
© Crown copyright

Bleeding Heart

Just a glance around the deeply traditional basement rooms at Bleeding Heart Yard will tell you instantly what kind of a place this is. The clientele is from the City, the wine list is for the City, and the menu is written for, and priced for, the City. And that's not the mufti-wearing, dressing-down, informal sort of City but the pukka, suit-wearing, claret-loving kind. Even during a glorious summer these paneled dining rooms will still be packed, and should the forecast veer towards the windy and rainswept this place makes a very agreeable refuge indeed.

Cost	£28–80

Address Bleeding Heart Yard, off Greville St, EC1
℗ 020 7242 2056
Station Farringdon/Chancery Lane
Open Mon–Fri noon–2.30pm & 6–10.30pm
Accepts All major credit cards

The menu changes seasonally and is written in resto-French with Brit subtitles, which may be old-fashioned but obviously suits the customers. Starters may include a little soufflé made with suckling pig, pancetta and a coddled egg (£6.50); home-smoked salmon with a quail egg and Caesar salad (£7.95); and a terrine of foie gras with a spiced brioche and a roast fig vinaigrette (£9.50). The mains range from a pot au feu of poulet noir (£15.45); or rack of lamb on crisp potato cake with roast tomato and field mushrooms (£15.45); to tournedos of salmon, basil pomme purée and tapenade (£12.95). The Bleeding Heart empire – restaurant, bistro, tavern, crypt, plus the Don restaurant (see p.185) – also extends to a vineyard in New Zealand, so it's no surprise to see "filet de chevreuil de Nouvelle Zealand avec charlotte de pommes de terre au Reblochon" (£16.75). There's a good, if Franco-centric, cheese trolley, and sound trad puds (all £5.75). The chef's cooking is precise and unfussy, quality ingredients are left to speak for themselves, and thankfully they speak out loudly. The wine list is an epic tome.

Like every one else, Bleeding Heart is proud to quote the press, and two hyperbolic comments particularly appeal. According to the Wine Spectator, this place has "one of the most outstanding restaurant wine lists in the world", and according to the New Yorker, Bleeding Heart Yard is "bleeding hard to find". For once these quotes may even be true.

Cicada

Once Clerkenwell was where you went for printing and watch repairs, but it's fast becoming London's coolest City-fringe dormitory – a fact that is reflected in its growing choice of restaurants and bars. Cicada was one of the first establishments to cater to the growing local population. Part bar, part restaurant, it offers an unusual menu loosely based in Southeast Asia that changes three or four times a year and allows you to mix and match from small, large and side dishes. This suits a lot of modern tastes, as everyone can share dishes and different flavours.

Cost	£17–40

Address 132 St John St, EC1
℡ 020 7608 1550
Station Farringdon
Open Mon–Fri noon–11pm,
Sat 6–11pm
Accepts All major credit cards
⊛ www.cicada.nu

In its mission to be all things to all customers, soups lead on to dim sum, and then on to small dishes, salads, large dishes and side dishes before topping out at desserts. The dim sum are served all day: try the prawn and chive open-topped dumplings (£6), or crispy seaweed (£4). Small dishes are more eclectic – Thai betel leaves with pomegranate (£5) or chicken (£5.50). Chilli-salt squid comes with adjud sauce (£6), and crispy fried fish with chilli and lime leaf (£5.50). Moving on to the large dishes, how about a big bowl of phad Thai – vegetable (£7.50) or prawn (£8.50)? Or whole wok-fried crab with Shaoxing wine, chilli and coriander (£11)? Other good choices might be the sweet ginger noodles (£2.50), a tasty bowlful; the monkfish jungle curry (£11); or tempura cod with ponzu soy (£10)? Puddings include tempting offerings like white chocolate and forest fruit dumplings (£5), and steeped fruit plate with coconut sherbet (£4.50). There is a good selection of mid-priced wines and beers, including Tiger beer (£2.50), if you want to go Oriental.

Cicada has a friendly, bar-like atmosphere, and staff members are young and easy-going. If the weather is good it's a great place to sit outside – it's set back from the main part of the street so the pavement tables give a degree of privacy. All in all, it makes a good bridge between going to a bar for a drink and going to a restaurant for a meal, and a sound precursor to the night ahead.

Club Gascon

(🍴) It's hard to believe it, but Club Gascon opened as long ago as 1998. This place still seems new and still seems fresh, although a vast scrapbook of glowing reviews and a cabinet full of awards testifies to how amazingly successful it has become. If you want a booking, they advise calling two or three weeks ahead, though you may strike

Cost	£35–75

Address 57 West Smithfield, EC1
℗ 020 7796 0600
Station Farringdon
Open Mon–Fri noon–2pm & 7–10pm, Sat 7–10.30pm
Accepts MasterCard, Visa

lucky with a cancellation. Pascal Aussignac is the chef here, and his cooking is that of the southwest of France, tidied up a little but generally authentic. The menu is set out as six sections and the portions are larger than some starters but smaller than most mains, the idea being that you indulge in your very own dégustation, trying several dishes – which isn't the cheapest way of eating.

The sections are "La route du sel" – cured meats and charcuterie; "Le potager" – vegetables and cheese; "Les foies gras"; "L'océan" – fish and shellfish; "Les pâturages" – mainly duck and cassoulet; "Le marché" – game and offal. There are forty different dishes. It's important to spread your ordering. Here are some promising combinations: farmhouse jambon du Bearn (£8); grilled foie gras of duck with grapes (£10.50); three oysters with grilled chipolata (£5.50); beef fillet a la plancha, Madeira sauce and stuffed pimento (£8.50); roast confit of duck, crème forte (£7). Or maybe marinated fresh salmon, dill and pastis des landes (£6); or home-made French fries with fleur de sel (£3.80) appeal? The problem with eating like this is that you can hit on a dish that is amazing and therefore too small. You must have the confidence to order a second or even third serving.

If you feel daunted, try the tasting menu, which changes monthly: five courses for £30 (but everyone at the table must order it). One such menu might lead you from a foie gras dish to grilled oysters, a crisp risotto of Aquitaine smoked eel and a casserole of guinea fowl, culminating in black cherry shortbread and smooth cheese. A pretty good way to shed £30. Dig deep and up the ante to £50 and you can have specially selected wines as well.

Clerkenwell

The Eagle

The Eagle was for years a run-down pub in an unpromising part of London. Then in 1991 it was taken over by food-minded entrepreneurs who transformed it into a restaurant-pub turning out top-quality dishes. They were pioneers: there should be a blue plaque over the door marking the site as the starting place of the great gastro-pub revolution. In a decade or so of existence, the Eagle has remained a crowded, rather shabby sort of place, and the staff still display a refreshing full-on attitude. The kitchen is truly open: the chefs work behind the bar, and the menu is chalked up over their heads. It changes daily, or even hourly, as things run out or deliveries come in. The food is broadly Mediterranean in outlook with a Portuguese bias, and you still have to fight your way to the bar to order and pay.

Cost	£8–20
Address	159 Farringdon Rd, EC1
☏	020 7837 1353
Station	Farringdon
Open	Meals served Mon–Fri 12.30–2.30pm & 6.30–10.30pm, Sat 12.30–3.30pm & 6.30–10.30pm, Sun 12.30–3.30pm
Accepts	No credit cards

This is a pub with a signature dish. Bife Ana (£8.50) has been on the menu here since the place opened and they have sold tens of thousands of portions. It is a kind of steak sandwich whose marinade has roots in the spicy food of Portugal and Mozambique, and it is delicious. The rest of the menu changes like quicksilver but you may find the likes of the famous caldo verde (£4.50) – the Portuguese chorizo and potato soup which takes its name from the addition of spring greens. There may be a grilled plaice with roast vegetables, and shallots with honey and balsamico (£9.50); or a delicious and simple dish like roast spring chicken with celeriac, celery, cream and bay "al forno" (£9.50); or a shoulder of lamb "en sofrito" with chilli and caraway seeds, and couscous with dried fruit and nuts (£10). To finish, choose between a fine cheese – perhaps a Sardinian pecorino served with flatbread and marmalade (£6.50), or the siren charms of those splendid, small, Portuguese, cinnamony custard tarts – pasteis de nata – at £1 a piece.

Even with pavement seating providing extra capacity in decent weather, the Eagle is never less than crowded. The music is always loud and the staff are busy and brusque. A great place nonetheless.

Moro

This modern, rather stark restaurant has slipped effortlessly from being new and iconoclastic to occupying a place on the list of London's "must visit" eateries. In feel it's not so very far away from the better pub-restaurants, although the proprietors have given themselves the luxury of a slightly larger kitchen. This has also become a place of pilgrimage for disciples of the wood-fired oven, and as the food here hails mainly from Spain, Portugal and North Africa, it is both Moorish and moreish. There is also a grand list of moody sherries. The only problem lies in Moro's popularity. It's consistently booked up, which places a bit of a strain on both kitchen and waiting staff. A relatively new development is the tapas menu, which is available all day and offers a good range of small dishes priced between £2.50 and £4 – a good way to test things out.

Cost	£18–48
Address	34–36 Exmouth Market, EC1
☏	020 7833 8336
Station	Farringdon/Angel
Open	Mon–Fri 12.30–2.30pm & 7–10.30pm, Sat 7–10.30pm
Accepts	All major credit cards

Soups are among Moro's best starters. How about caldo Gallego (£4.50), a ham-bone broth with turnip tops, white beans and potatoes? The menu changes fortnightly and you may be offered starters such as charcoal-grilled sardines with Tahini sauce and sumac (£6); warm leeks and broad beans with goat's curd and mint (£5.50); or huevos revueltos (£6) – a grown-up scrambled egg with prawns and parsley. Main courses are simple and often traditional combinations of taste and textures. As with the starters, it's the accompaniments that tend to change rather than the core ingredients. Look out for pollo al ajillo (£14.50) – chicken braised with garlic, Fino sherry and potatoes; or wood-roasted loin of pork with black beans and pimientos de Padrón (£14.50); or perhaps charcoal-grilled sea bass with roast beetroot, spinach and almond and sherry vinegar sauce (£15.50). There are usually some other fishy options too, along the lines of wood-roasted whole sea bream with pine-nut and raisin pilaf and yoghurt and dill sauce (£14).

Do not miss the splendid Spanish cheeses (£5) served with membrillo – traditional quince paste. And there's no excuse to avoid the Malaga raisin ice cream (£4), or the serious chocolate tart (£4).

Clerkenwell

St John

One of the most frequent requests, especially from foreign visitors, is "Where can we get some really English cooking?" Little wonder that the promise of "olde English fare" is the bait in so many London tourist traps. The cooking at St John, however, is genuine. It is sometimes old-fashioned and makes inspired use of all those strange and unfashionable cuts of meat which were once commonplace in rural Britain. Technically the cooking is of a very high standard, while the restaurant itself is completely without frills or design pretensions. You'll either love it or hate it. But be forewarned, this is an uncompromising and opinionated kitchen, and no place to take a hard-core vegetarian.

Cost	£25–60

Address 26 St John St, EC1
℡ 020 7251 0848
Station Farringdon
Open Mon–Fri noon–3pm &
6–11pm, Sat 6–11pm
Accepts All major credit cards
🖥 www.stjohnrestaurant.co.uk

The menu changes every session but the tone does not, and there's always a dish or two to support the slogan "nose to tail eating". Charcuterie, as you'd imagine, is good: a simple terrine (£6) will be dense but not dry – well judged. Or, for the committed, what about a starter of roast bone marrow and parsley salad (£6.20)? Antony Bourdain claimed this as his "Desert Island Dish". Or salted venison liver, radishes and boiled egg (£6.40)? Or lamb, fennel and butterbean broth (£5.80)? Be generous to yourself with the bread, which is outstanding (the bakery is in the bar, and you can purchase a loaf to take home). Main courses may include a pigeon pie (for two, £27.80), or smoked eel, bacon and mash (£14.80). Maybe there will be rabbit saddle with carrots and aioli (£14.60), or a dish of butterbeans and courgettes (£10.80); perversely, in this den of offal, the veg dishes are a delight. Puddings are traditional and well executed: rice pudding with plums (£5.40), or a slice of strong Lancashire cheese with an Eccles cake (£5.50). Joy of joys, sometimes there is even a seriously good Welsh rarebit (£5).

St John has won shedloads of awards, and booking is a must. How encouraging to see a party of Japanese businessmen forsaking tourist pap for roast sirloin, dripping toast and horseradish (£16)! Whatever your feelings about meat and offal cookery, be assured that St John serves food at its most genuine.

Smiths, the Dining Room

Calling Smiths of Smithfield an ambitious project is like saying that pyramid building calls for a large workforce. First take a Grade II listed warehouse overlooking Smithfield Market, then gut it. Rebuild the inside in ultra-modern meets Bladerunner style and – hey presto – you have two restaurants, two bars, private rooms, kitchens and whatever, spread over four floors. On the ground floor there's a bar and café serving drink and good, sensible food from breakfast to bedtime. At the top is the "rooftop restaurant", a 70-seater which pays particular attention to quality meat with good provenance. On the second floor is the 130-seater "Dining Room". The culinary mainspring is John Torode, who should be congratulated on his enlightened buying policy – quality, quality, quality.

Cost £18–50

Address 67–77 Charterhouse St, EC1
☎ 020 7236 6666
Station Farringdon
Open Café Mon–Fri 7am–11pm, Sat & Sun 10.30am–5pm; restaurants Mon–Fri 11am–3pm & 6–11pm, Sat 6–11pm
Accepts All major credit cards
🌐 www.smithsofsmithfield.co.uk

MODERN BRITISH

The Dining Room is a large space around a central hole which looks down onto the smart bar area. Eating here is rather like sitting at the centre of a deactivated factory – a tangle of exposed pipes and girders. The menu is divided into Larder (which means starters), Soups, Mains, Grills, Daily Market Specials, Sides, and Sweet Tooth. The way the prices are expressed, however, is coy and irritating – Larder "all at 4 3/4 Pounds"; "Sides 2 1/2 Pounds". Bah humbug. But the starters are simple and good: cured Cumbrian ham, pears and watercress (£4.75); spaghetti with clams, garlic, lemon and parsley (£4.75); spiced duck and green papaya salad with Thai herbs and chilli dressing (£4.75). Main courses show off the careful buying policy: crisp belly of pork with mashed potato and green sauce (£10.50); Smiths 10oz beef burger with cheese and Old Spot bacon (£11.50); roast cod with green pea puree and garlic mayonnaise (£10.50). The lunch specials are from the comfort-eating school, and feature such delights as shepherds' pie (£10.50). Puds are good. Try hot waffles, bananas, toffee and double cream (£4).

There's a decent breakfast on offer downstairs, with porridge (£2) or bacon, egg, beans, sausage, mushrooms, black pudding, tomatoes, bubble and toast (£6.50). And it is available all day, so Dr Johnson would have been happy.

The Well

Taking its name from the well that served the clerken hereabouts and so inspired the name of the area, The Well is a buzzy bar-cum-gastropub where the diners, staff and owner Tom Martin all appear to be friends having a good time. Scrubbed tables and old church chairs give a fresh, accessible feel to this corner venue which is open as a bar throughout

Cost	£30–70

Address 180 St John St, EC1
☎ 020 7251 9363
Station Angel/Farringdon
Open Mon–Fri noon–3pm & 6–10.30pm, Sat noon–10.30pm, Sun noon–10pm
Accepts All major credit cards

the day and as a restaurant during kitchen hours. A couple of daily specials on a blackboard complement the modern mixed menu, which appears to be geared to everyone's favourite dishes rather than any particular cuisine. The wine list runs from a respectable Italian house red or white at £10.95 to Dom Perignon 1993 champagne at £85, for the Clerkenwell heeled.

The menu changes regularly, but starters may include broccoli and ginger soup with roasted almond cream (£4.50); "pint o' prawns" with mayonnaise (£5.50); confit of tomatoes with avocado puree and deep-fried won tons (£6.25); and Vietnamese shredded chicken with crispy vermicelli (£6.50). Main courses are equally considered. Sausages come with creamed mash and onion gravy (£9.95), but these are Merguez sausages; or there may be braised lamb shank with potato gnocchi, pancetta, olives and tomatoes (£12.95); or smoked duck breast (£12.95), which comes with prosciutto and roasted fig salad. Fish dishes get good representation: roast turbot with creamed salsify, clams, shrimps and spinach (£10.50); or creamed spaghetti with saffron, rocket, roasted peppers and mixed seafood (£10.50). The desserts (all £3.95) range from the classic – chocolate brownies with vanilla cream, or whisky bread-and-butter pudding with custard – to the more adventurous – like cranberry and cinnamon crème brûlée. Cheeses (£5.50) are from the admirable Neal's Yard Dairy.

The Well attracts an unusually varied crowd from the surrounding dotcom millionaire loft roosts and council estates, but they all seem to enjoy its lively atmosphere and good value.

Docklands

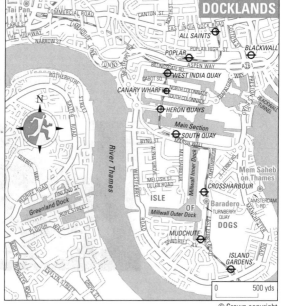

Baradero

Baradero is modern, light, tiled and airy. And, as far as the view of Mill-wall dock and proximity to the London Arena will permit, you could almost think yourself in Spain. Essentially a tapas bar, it offers main courses too, and both are of restaurant quality. Take a seat at the bar or at one of the well-spaced tables, order yourself a bottle of Estrella beer or

Cost	£15–30
Address	Turberry Quay, off Pepper St, E14
☎	020 7537 1666
Station	DLR Crossharbour
Open	Mon–Fri noon–11pm, Sat 6–10.45pm
Accepts	All major credit cards

a glass of Fino sherry, and set about the tapas. There is even a floor show of sorts in the form of the balletic automatic orange juicer, called a Zumm, which seems to wave the whole oranges about for inspection before squashing them for juice.

Start with an order of pan con aioli (95p) – good bread with a pot of fearsome but seductive garlic mayonnaise. Or pan con tomate (£1.45) – Catalan-style toast drizzled with olive oil and rubbed with garlic and tomato. Add some boquerones (£3.50) – classic white anchovies, sharp with vinegar and garnished with raw garlic slices; and jamón Serrano (£5.50) – a large portion of dark, richly flavoured, dry-cured ham. Then follow up with hot tapas such as croquetas de pollo (£4.25). Whoever would have thought that croquettes could taste so good? Or pulpo a la Gallega (£5.25) – octopus boiled and seasoned in Galician style. Or the particularly delicious fabada Asturiana (£4.95), an Asturian bean stew loaded with chunks of sausage, black pudding and ham hock. Also lurking on the tapas menu is paella Valenciana (£17.50). This is the real thing, with chicken and shellfish, and it feeds two. If you can restrain your ordering and don't end up crammed full of tapas, move on to the list of main courses, which changes weekly. Try patita de cordero al horno (£16.50), which is a whole roast leg of baby lamb. Or maybe salmon a la parrilla (£11.50) – grilled salmon with fresh vegetables. There is also a convenient special offer of prix-fixe hot and cold tapas (from £19.50 per person), which runs all day.

As well as adding new tapas and main courses each week, to keep regulars from getting bored, there is dancing to live music on Friday and Saturday nights.

Mem Saheb on Thames

Mem Saheb on Thames has certainly got an evocative address. "Amsterdam Road" conjures up pictures of old-fashioned docks and wharves, rolling fog banks and cheery East-enders. In practice, this bit of Docklands is a lot like Milton Keynes: Amsterdam Road (along with nearby Rotterdam Drive and Rembrandt Court) are all part of the new Docklands. Not truly "new" any longer,

Cost	£15–30

Address 65–67 Amsterdam Rd, E14
℡ 020 7538 3008
Station DLR Crossharbour
Open Mon–Fri noon–2.30pm & 6–11.30pm, Sat & Sun 6–11.30pm
Accepts All major credit cards

but new enough for you to notice that some of the paintwork is starting to get chipped. The redeeming factor is the river. As the Thames sweeps round in a majestic arc, the restaurant has a superb view across the water to the Millennium Dome. Mem Saheb is certainly "on-Thames". As a result there's a good deal of squabbling for the middle table in the non-smoking section (pole position as far as the view is concerned). Ultimately, however, the lucky winner must balance the grandstand view of the Millennium folly with the piped-music speaker that hovers directly above the table.

Start by sharing a tandoori khazana (£8.95), which is a platter of mixed kebabs from the tandoor, including good chicken tikka. Or perhaps some salmon samosas (£2.50)? Also tasty is the kabuli salad (£2.95), a winning combination of chickpeas and hard-boiled egg in a sharp tamarind dressing. Of the main courses, boal dopiaza (£6.95) teams meaty steaks of boal fish from Bangladesh with an onion-based sauce. Chicken bemisal (£6.95) is sweet and sour, with a welcome belt of green chilli. Prawn and pumpkin (£6.95) balances hot and sweet, although it is rather let down by the small and undistinguished prawns. The breads and vegetable dishes are good, particularly the aloo chana (£4.50) – a simple dish of potatoes and chickpeas. The chef is to be commended for avoiding artificial additives and colourings.

The spicy dhal (£2.50/4.50) is made with yellow split peas and small, red dried chillies. The chilli flavour infuses the dhal and this is a very successful dish... until the moment when the unwary diner bites into one of these little red booby traps. The ensuing pain is enough to banish any calm induced by the restful river view.

Tai Pan

As anyone who has followed the adventures of Sherlock Holmes will know, Limehouse was London's first Chinatown, complete with murky opium dens. So, despite the well-intentioned efforts of the Docklands Development Board to promote the area, today's Limehouse seems pretty tame in comparison. It can, however, boast about the Tai Pan. This restaurant is very much a family affair – the ebullient Winnie Wan is front of house, running the light, bright dining room, while Mr Tsen commands the kitchen. He organizes a constant stream of well-cooked, mainly Cantonese dishes, and slaves over the intricately carved vegetables, which lift their presentation. He's a good cook, and the menu hides one or two surprises as well as all the old favourites.

Cost	£15–30
Address	665 Commercial Rd, E14
☎	020 7791 0118 or 0119
Station	DLR Limehouse
Open	Mon–Thurs & Sun noon–11.15pm, Fri noon–11.45pm, Sat 6–11.45pm
Accepts	All major credit cards

After the complimentary prawn cracker and seriously delicious hot-pickled shredded cabbage, start with deep-fried crispy squid with Szechuan peppercorn salt (£6.90), or fried Peking dumplings with a vinegar dipping sauce (£4.30) – both are delicious. Or try one of the spare-rib dishes (£5.40), or the soft-shell crabs (£4.80 each), or the nicely done, crispy, fragrant aromatic duck with pancakes and the accoutrements (£15.50 for a half). Otherwise, relax and order the Imperial mixed hors d'oeuvres (£8.80 per person, for a minimum of two), which offers a sampler of ribs, spring rolls, seaweed, and prawn and sesame toast, with a carrot sculpture as centrepiece. When ordering main dishes, old favourites like deep-fried shredded beef with chilli (£5.80), and fried chicken in lemon sauce (£5.30) are just as you'd expect. Fried seasonal greens in oyster sauce (£4.30) is made with choi sum, and delicious, while the fried vermicelli Singapore-style (£5.10) will suit anyone who prefers their Singapore noodle pepped up with curry powder rather than fresh chillies.

Sometimes there are "specials" which don't feature on the main menu. They're generally worth trying. There are also some bargains to be had among the special lunch deals. Asking Winnie to recommend something is always a good idea. Sinking your teeth into the carved vegetables is not.

Hackney & Dalston

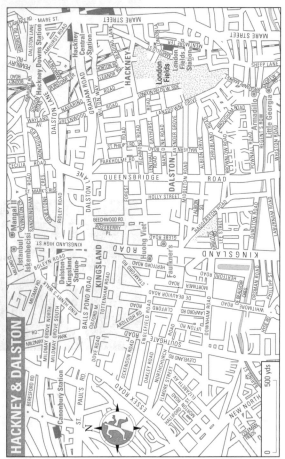

HACKNEY & DALSTON

© Crown copyright

Armadillo

Armadillo is that rare thing – a small neighbourhood restaurant with an unusual menu and staff who care. Chef-owner Rogerio David, from Brazil, has based his dishes on South American home cooking with influences from Spain, North Africa and even Asia. This means adventurous cooking with a modern twist, and if you're looking for unusual combinations of ingredients cooked with a spicy background then Armadillo is an agreeable addition to your list. The dining room is bright, colourful and filled with a lively Broadway Market clientele. The menu uses some unfamiliar South American terms, but after a couple of Armadillo's excellent Caipirinhas (made with a fierce white spirit called Cachaçà, with sugar, crushed limes and ice) the friendly explanations from the staff seem to make sense.

Cost	£18–50

Address 41 Broadway Market, E8
℡ 020 7249 3633
Station Bethnal Green
Open Tues–Sat 6.30–10.30pm; brunch Fri–Sun noon–3pm
Accepts All major credit cards
✉ www.armadillorestaurant.co.uk

Coconut sancocho with a peanut and coriander aji sauce (£4) is a rich chunky vegetable soup-stew with a dollop of tasty green chilli and coriander sauce in the middle. Roast artichoke, red onion, new season garlic and red peppers en escabeche with goat's cheese (£4.70) is a clever way to boost the blandness of an artichoke. Seafood menestron with beans, sugar snaps and noodles (£12.50) is a clean-tasting broth made with fresh fish in season, and has a tangy but sweet bite. Roast belly of pork al achiote, with black beans, boniato potatoes and mojo (£12.50) is slow-roasted to melting point with annato spice and South American sweet potatoes. Mojo is the sauce that lubricates – so now you know. Puddings continue in the same vein. Spicy chocolate ice cream and amaretti (£3.90) is home-made and delivers what it promises; squash picarones in a chilli syrup with pomegranate (£3.90) brings little deep-fried squash dumplings with a chilli-hot sweet syrup and fresh pomegranate seeds. Wines are mainly from South America and Spain and are very reasonably priced, from £10.50 to a maximum of £29 for Heidsieck Dry Monopole champagne.

Weather permitting, there's courtyard dining for ten and a balcony with a table for two. Armadillo is deservedly popular on long summer evenings and booking is essential.

Faulkner's

🍴 Faulkner's is a clear highlight among the kebab shops and chippies that line the rather scruffy Kingsland Road – it's a spotless fish-and-chip restaurant, with a takeaway section next door. It is reassuringly old-fashioned with its lace curtains, fish tank, uniformed waitresses and cool yellow walls lined with sepia-tinted piscine scenes, and it holds few surprises – which is probably what makes it such a hit. Usually Faulkner's is full of local families and large parties, all ploughing through colossal fish dinners while chatting across tables. It also goes out of its way to be child-friendly, with highchairs leaned against the wall, and a children's menu priced at £3.95.

Cost	£6–20

Address 424 Kingsland Rd, E8
℡ 020 7254 6152
Station Liverpool Street
Open Mon–Thurs noon–2pm & 5–10pm, Fri noon–2pm & 4.30–10pm, Sat 11.30am–10pm, Sun noon–9pm
Accepts Visa

House speciality among the starters is the fish cake (£1.50), a plump ball made with fluffy, herby potato. Or there's smoked salmon (£3.75), which comes in two satisfying wads, or prawn cocktail (£3.50). If you fancy soup, you've got soup of the day (80p) or a more exotic French fish variety (£1.90), which is peppery and dark and comes from Perard in Le Touquet. For main courses, the regular menu features all the British fish favourites, served fried or poached and with chips, while daily specials are chalked up on the blackboard. Cod (from £7.50) and haddock (from £8.75) retain their fresh, firm flesh beneath the dark, crunchy batter, while the subtler, classier Dover sole (from £12.50) is best served delicately poached. The mushy peas (90p) are just right – lurid and lumpy like God intended – but the test of any good chippy is always its chips, and here they are humdingers, fat, firm and golden, with a wicked layer of crispy little salty bits at the bottom. Stuffed in a soft doughy roll they make the perfect chip butty. Most people wet their whistles with a mug of strong tea (55p), but there are a few bottles of wine on offer, including a Beaujolais Villages (£9.90) and a Chablis (£17.25).

Though always lively, Faulkner's is particularly fun at Saturday lunchtime, when traders and shoppers take time out from the local market to catch up, gossip, and joke with the waitresses.

Huong Viet

(icon) Huong Viet is the canteen of the Vietnamese Cultural Centre, which occupies a rather four-square and solid-looking building that was once one of Hackney's numerous public bathhouses. It has long had a reputation for really good, really cheap food, and the regulars have stuck with it through a couple of general refurbishments, which have threatened to take the place upmarket.

Cost £7–25

Address An Viet House,
12–14 Englefield Rd, N1
(T) 020 7249 0877
Station BR Dalston Kingsland
Open Mon–Fri noon–3.30pm
& 5.30–11pm, Sat noon–4pm
& 5.30–11pm
Accepts MasterCard, Visa

VIETNAMESE

But this place is never going to be Dalston's answer to Mezzo, it is too firmly rooted in Vietnamese culture and too much a focus for the Vietnamese community, so everyone can breathe a sigh of relief. The food has stayed fresh, unpretentious, delicious and cheap, although prices are creeping upwards. The service is still friendly and informal. And the building still looks a lot like an ex-council bathhouse.

Start with the spring rolls (£3.90) – small, crisp and delicious. Or the fresh rolls (£3.50), which resemble small, carefully rolled-up table napkins. The outside is soft, white and delicate-tasting, while the inside teams cooked vermicelli with prawns and fresh herbs – a great combination of textures. Ordering the prawn and green leaf soup (£3.50/5) brings a bowl of delicate broth with greens and shards of tofu. Pho is perhaps the most famous Vietnamese "soup" dish, but it is really a meal in a bowl. The pho here is formidable, especially the Hanoi noodle soup, filled with beef, chicken or tofu (£3.90/5.50). Hot, rich and full of bits and pieces, it comes with a plate of herbs, crispy beansprouts and aromatics that you must add yourself at the last moment so none of the aroma is lost. The other dishes are excellent too. Look out for mixed seafood with pickled veg and dill (£6.50), which works exceptionally well. You should also run amok with the noodle dishes – choose from the wok-fried rice noodle dishes, or the crispy-fried egg noodles (£4.90 –5.70).

All the food tastes fresh – it has obviously been freshly cooked and the chef has used spankingly fresh ingredients. There is a set lunch (£6) which comprises a starter and a main course accompanied by jasmine tea, mineral water or sweet home-made lemonade.

Istanbul Iskembecisi

The Istanbul Iskembecisi is just across the road from Mangal II (see p.214), and at heart they are singing off the same sheet. Despite being named after its signature dish – iskembe is a limpid tripe soup – the Istanbul is a grill house. Admittedly it is a grill house with chandeliers, smart tables and upscale service, but it is still a grill house. And because it stays open until late in the morning it is much beloved by clubbers

Cost	£8–25

Address 9 Stoke Newington Rd, N16
⊕ 020 7254 7291
Station BR Dalston Kingsland
Open Daily noon–5am
Accepts Cash and cheques only
⊛ www.londraturk.com/istanbuliskembecisi

and chefs – they are just about ready to go out and eat when everyone else has had enough and set off home. The grilled meat may be better over at Mangal II, but the atmosphere of raffish elegance at the Istanbul has real charm.

The iskembe (£2.50), or tripe soup, has its following. Large parties of Turks from the snooker hall just behind the restaurant insist on it, and you'll see the odd regular downing two bowlfuls of the stuff. For most people, however, it's bland at best, and even the large array of additives (salt, pepper, chilli – this is a dish that you must season to your personal taste at the table) cannot make it palatable. A much better bet is to start with the mixed meze (£4.50), which brings a good hummus and tarama, a superb dolma, and the rest drawn from the usual suspects. Then on to the grills, which are presented with more panache than usual. Pirzola (£6.50) brings three lamb chops; sis kebab (£5.75) is good and fresh; karisik agara (£8.50) is a mixed grill by any other name. For the brave there's a whole section of offal dishes, among them kokorec (£5), which is lamb's intestines, and arvnavaut cigeri-sicak (£4.50) – liver Albanian style. Doubtless somebody somewhere is mourning two casualties of what will probably be seen as the "food scares era" – there is no more kelle sogus (roasted head of lamb) or beyin salata (boiled brain with salad).

Just when you think you're on safe ground with the desserts, the menu is still able to spring one last surprise – kazandibi (£2.50) which is a "Turkish type crème caramel, milk based sweet with finely dashed chicken breast". When compared with a chicken pudding served as dessert, boiled brain has much to commend it.

Little Georgia

You could be forgiven for thinking that the Little Georgia was just another pub which had been converted into a trendy restaurant. It is certainly bare. The tables and chairs are certainly resolutely ordinary. But then you clock the blackboards with their unpronounceable specials, and the greeting of the somewhat harassed maître d' who approaches with a beaming smile. Even if you are not intimately familiar with Georgian and Russian food, spotting a genuine welcome is easy enough, and you'll find one here. You'll also find an interesting list of essentially peasant dishes. From the menu it would seem that Georgians live on walnuts, pomegranate and beetroot, and that in order to make something of such basics they are not averse to adding the occasional handful of spice.

Cost	£15–35
Address	2 Broadway Market, E8
☎	020 7249 9070
Station	Bethnal Green
Open	Tues–Sat 6.30pm–midnight, Sun 1–4pm
Accepts	All major credit cards

GEORGIAN

The starters fall into two categories: cold (mainly £4) and hot (up to £4.50). Among the colds there are some exciting dips, or phkalis, which are a kind of pounded mixture – choose beetroot and walnuts, or the one made from spinach and walnuts. They are good, with strong flavours and interesting textures. Then there is the Russian salad. Even if youthful encounters with the tinned, mass-produced variety have left you scarred for life, do try this, as it is terrific. The soups here are also very fine: a couple of varieties of borscht (£4/4.50) and sometimes a soup of the day. Main courses range from chakapuli (£12), which is lamb with coriander, tarragon and white wine, to pheasant kishmish (£12.50) – roast marinated pheasant with a garlic and lemon sauce, and a belt of chilli. Gupta (£9) are described as "Georgian meatballs of pork and beef in a mildly spicy roast red pepper and tomato sauce". Prices have got a little higher and the dishes a little less obscure since this place opened – that's what happens when a place gets busier. There is plenty of choice for vegetarians, and the puddings do not disappoint.

Finally, you should make a point of trying the Georgian red wines: unsubtle, tannic, rich, fruity, almost musty – and cheap!

Mangal II

The first thing to hit you at Mangal II is the smell. The fragrance of spicy, sizzling char-grilled meat is unmistakably, authentically Turkish. This, combined with the relaxing pastel decor, puts you in holiday mood before you've even sat down. The ambience is laid-back, too. At slack moments, the staff shoot the breeze around the ocakbasi, and service comes with an ear-to-ear grin. All you have to do is sit back, sink an Efes Pilsener (£2.50) and peruse the encyclopaedic menu.

Cost	£6–25

Address 4 Stoke Newington Rd, N16
☏ 020 7254 7888
Station BR Dalston Kingsland
Open Daily noon–1am
Accepts MasterCard, Visa

Prices are low and portions enormous. Baskets of fresh bread are endlessly replenished, so it's just as well to go easy on the appetizers. With a vast range of tempting mezeler (starters), however, resistance is well nigh impossible. The 25 options include simple hummus (£2.50) and dolma (£2.50); imam bayildi (£3) – aubergines stuffed with onion, tomato and green pepper; thin lahmacun (£1.75) – meaty Turkish pizza; and karisik meze (£4) – a large plate of mixed dishes that's rather heavy on the yoghurt. There's a fair spread of salads (£2.50–3) as well, though you get so much greenery with the main dishes that it's a wasted choice here. The main dishes (kebablar) themselves are sumptuous, big on lamb and chicken, but with limited fish and vegetarian alternatives. The patlican kebab (£8) is outstanding – melt-in-the-mouth grilled minced lamb with sliced aubergines, served with a green salad of which the star turn is an olive-stuffed tomato shaped like a basket. The kebabs are also superb, particularly the house special, ezmeli kebab (£7.50), which comes doused in Mangal's special sauce. Or if you don't fancy a grill, there's also a choice of three freshly made and hearty "daily stews" (£3.50–5).

After swallowing that lot, dessert might not be feasible, but after a long break – there's no pressure to vacate your table – you might just be tempted by a slab of tooth-achingly sweet baclava (£2). Alternatively, round off the evening with a punch-packing raki (£3). And, for a final blast of Ottoman atmosphere, pay a visit to the bathroom – the no-frills facilities are a real taste of old Istanbul.

Hoxton & Shoreditch

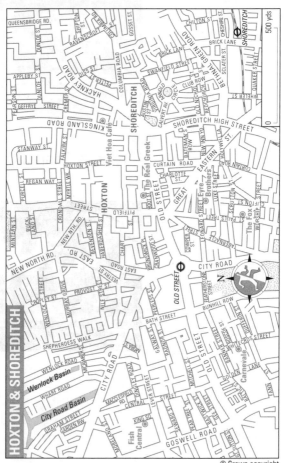

HOXTON & SHOREDITCH

© Crown copyright

Carnevale

🍴 This rather strange little restaurant is tucked into an ordinary shop-like space halfway along a scruffy street which is all street market by day and dingy grubbiness by night. Inside is a clean, light but cramped space, full of blond wood tables and chairs, with carefully selected (if not particularly original) prints on the walls and a faux garden to the rear. The interior has not so much been designed to the hilt, as is the current fashion, but rather put together in workable form to meet the needs of the customers. Mercifully, the enduring tendency of vegetarian restaurants to litter the premises with hippie references has been brought under control.

Cost	£12–22

Address 135 Whitecross St, EC1
☎ 020 7250 3452
Station Old Street
Open Mon–Fri noon–3pm & 5.30–10.30pm,
Sat 5.30–10.30pm
Accepts All major credit cards
🌐 www.carnevalerestaurant .co.uk

Instead, close attention seems to have been paid to the food, which is cooked with care. Take your time over some very good marinated Greek olives (£2) and bread dipped in nutty olive oil while you decide what you'll eat. The menu, which changes every couple of months, is not over-long – ten dishes in all – but is as varied as you could wish for. Starters range from oyster mushroom Niçoise (£5.25); through home-made caramelized pear tortelli with Gorgonzola sauce (£6/9.50); to a celeriac and horseradish spring roll with pickled ginger and black bean dressing (£4.50/7.75). They are good enough to be served in many grander establishments. Main courses are equally eclectic: preserved lemon and goat's cheese tart with baby aubergines tossed in harissa (£9.75); or perhaps okra and red pepper casserole with falafel and lemon Tahini sauce (£9.50). There is a plentiful list of side orders, though given the size of the portions it is unlikely that you'll need any. If your stamina is up to them, puddings (£4.50) are good too: try the dairy-free crème caramel with pineapple and blood oranges, or Pavlova with chocolate mousse, pistachio praline and caramelized banana.

Service is relaxed, coffee is good and there are a number of alternative drinks on offer. But if you are a wine drinker, take care with the short list and aim above the house selection (£9.95), which is unforgiving.

Eyre Brothers

David Eyre will forever be pigeon-holed as one of the creators of the Eagle (see p.196) and, as such, a founding father of the gastro-pub revolution. Which makes it all the more surprising that in August 2001 Eyre and his brother opened a new, very large, very swish, very elegant eighty-seat restaurant. Eyre Brothers is on Leonard Street, deep in the trendy part of EC2. There is a long bar with comfortable seats and a sensible footrail so that eating at the bar is a pleasure rather than a contortion. There is a good deal of dark wood and leather and the overall feel is one of comfortable clubbiness. The food is ballsy, with upfront flavours and textures, and scarcely a day goes by without some dishes falling off the menu and being replaced by new ones.

Cost	£25–70
Address	70 Leonard St, EC2
☎	020 7613 5346
Station	Old Street/Liverpool Street
Open	Mon–Fri noon–3pm & 6.30–11pm, Sat 6.30–11pm
Accepts	All major credit cards

David's cuisine is hard to categorize – there are a few Spanish and Italian dishes, a lot of Portuguese specialities and some favourites from Mozambique. Starters range widely, from marinated salt cod with chickpeas, potato salad, pimentos de piquillo, parsley, olives and a boiled egg (£8), to scrambled eggs and Portuguese blood sausage on toast with mint (£7.50)! Or penne with ricotta, Parmesan and purple sprouting broccoli (£7.50). You will also be offered jamón Iberico "Joselito" gran reserva (£14) – quality is the watchword here. Main courses lead off with grille Mozambique prawns piri-piri (£23) – these are monsters from the deep waters of the Mozambique channel, scarily large and meaty with a belt of heat from the Portuguese chilli. Or there may be grilled best-end new season's lamb chops (£17), served with aubergine salad with mint and couscous. Or cozido (£13), the famous Portuguese stew made with white beans, cabbage and belly pork, and bulked up with ham, sausage, chorizo and blood sausage; it's delicious, and not for wimps. Puds are classics with a twist, such as lemon and ricotta rice pudding with poached apricots (£4.50), or espresso and cardamom crème brûlée (£4.50).

This is one place where you can indulge in really good sherry. A rare Manzanilla Passada, a Palo Cortada or an old Oloroso all cost £4 a glass, or £18 for a half bottle.

Fish Central

(icon) The Barbican may appear to be the back of beyond – a black hole in the heart of the City – but perfectly ordinary people do live and work around here. Apart from the theatres and concert hall and the proximity to the financial district, one of the main attractions of the place is Fish Central, which holds its own

Cost	£8–20

Address 151 King's Square, Central St, EC1
☎ 020 7253 4970
Station Barbican
Open Mon–Sat 11am–2.30pm & 4.45–10.30pm
Accepts All major credit cards

with the finest fish-and-chip shops in town, and indeed a good many snootier restaurants. People tend to be very snobbish about fish and chip shops, but Fish Central is just the place to dispel such delusions.

Though at first sight Fish Central appears just like any other chippy – a takeaway service one side and an eat-in restaurant next door – a glance at its menu lets you know that this is something out of the ordinary. All the finny favourites are here, from cod and haddock to rock salmon and plaice (all £4.95), but there's a wholesome choice of alternatives, including grilled Dover sole (£10.90) and roast cod (£8.25) with rosemary and Mediterranean vegetables. There's no doubt these dishes are cooked to order, as a menu note prepares you for a 25-minute wait, and many of them would not be out of place in much grander establishments. You can eat decently even if you are not in the mood for fish. Try the Cumberland sausages (£4.50), with onions and gravy, or the chicken breast (£5.95). If you think your appetite is up to starters, try the prawn cocktail (£2.95) – the normal naked pink prawns in pink sauce, but genuinely fresh – or grilled sardines with tomato coulis (£3.45), which puts all of those run-of-the-mill Italian restaurants to shame. Chips (£1.45) come as a side order, so those who prefer can order a jacket potato (£1.60) or creamed potatoes (£1.40). Mushy peas (£1.40) are … mushy and Wallies (45p) – pickled gherkins to you – come sliced and prettily served in the shape of a flower.

Fish Central certainly pulls in a crowd of devoted regulars. On any given night, half the customers seem to know each other. Unusually for a chippy, it has an alcohol licence, which means there's a palatable dry house white or even champagne – the perfect partner for mushy peas.

The Fox

(icon) It may raise a few eyebrows amongst biologists, but this fox is the direct descent of an eagle – the Fox is sibling to the original gastro-pub, the Eagle (see p.196). Downstairs it is a grand, pubby sort of pub, with decent real ale and the kind of serious pub food that really appeals. Upstairs is the dining room, which has much in common with

Cost	£15–30

Address 28 Paul St, EC2
℡ 020 7729 5708
Station Old Street
Open Mon–Fri noon–3pm & 6.30–10pm
Accepts All major credit cards except AmEx

the style of the original Eagle: the tables and chairs are an eclectic mix, the cutlery and china are gleefully mismatched, and the whole has a passing resemblance to Steptoe's lair.

The cooking at the Fox is "school of" the Eagle. Dishes are robust, well seasoned, honest and driven by the seasons. The menu changes every day and while there isn't a huge amount of choice there should be something to please everyone. Pricing is straightforward: two courses cost £13.50 and three courses £18. For starters, a typical choice is between a chicken, lemon and dill broth; a dish of courgettes, mint and ricotta; Parma ham served with beetroot; and field mushrooms, wild garlic leaves and a poached egg. Note the homeliness of these dishes, their balance and the use of seasonal elements such as garlic leaves. Main course options include shoulder of lamb with red wine and split peas – an interesting combination of textures; belly pork with a celeriac gratin – the kitchen is good at slow-roasting; baked skate with purple sprouting broccoli; and spring vegetable risotto. There are usually a couple of puds, such as orange and almond cake or hot chocolate pudding, as well as a well-chosen cheese. With food like this, and a sensibly priced wine list, the Fox makes for a pleasant, good-value and unpretentious place to eat.

There is an agreeable little sun-trap terrace, with a few tables for hardened lovers of the al fresco. The view is largely of the surrounding brick walls, but there are tubs with plants and all is suitably casual for a long, lingering lunch.

The Real Greek

(🍴) This particular Real Greek is called Theodore Kyriakou. Traditionally, Greek food has had a pretty rough deal in Britain as most of the restaurants which call themselves "Greek", are usually run by Greek Cypriots with a menu that concentrates on Cypriot food. Thus, for generations of Brits, Greek food has meant greasy, lukewarm moussaka and

Cost	£10–50

Address **15 Hoxton Market, N1**
ⓣ **020 7739 8212**
Station **Old Street/Shoreditch**
Open **Mon–Sat noon–3pm & 5.30–10.30pm**
Accepts **MasterCard, Visa**
🌐 **www.therealgreek.co.uk**

lurid pink cod's roe gloop. Real Greek food is nothing like that, and showing off the authentic dishes of his homeland is the difficult mission Kyriakou has embarked upon. The latter part of 2001 saw The Real Greek spread sideward into what was the old Hoxton Mission Hall. Now the lofty room is a busy *mezedopoliou*, a bar where you can order a few meze (they cost between £2 and £5 a plateful) and try a dozen stunning Greek wines by the glass or *carafaki*. It's a relaxed way to sample some seriously good food.

The restaurant proper goes from strength to strength. The menu changes with the seasons. The first section is "Mezedes" and each platter has three or four components. One such might include duck stuffed with figs and served cold; cured, sliced fillet of beef; a Greco-Jewish cauliflower dish; and tzatziki (£8.45). Or there may be plate with poached monkfish cheek; a Cretan octopus salad; potato and garlic aioli; and beetroots in aged vinegar (£8.20). Or try pork, leek and prune terrine; oven-cooked beans, and pan-fried goat's milk cheese (£7.50). On to "Fagakia": these small dishes could be either starters or sides. Pot-roast crab claws come with an implausibly rich sauce made from ripe tomatoes and Visanto (£8.50). Main courses are a revelation. Slow-cooked calves' liver and sweetbreads are served with oregano potatoes (£16); rabbit hot-pot comes with large dolmades made from cabbage leaves (£16.70); pan-fried fresh fish is served simply, with a warm salad of seasonal leaves, yoghurt and garlic (£17). Then there is a whole range of Greek cheeses and desserts – the figs from Kimi poached in red wine (£5.50) are outstanding.

There is a genuine bargain set lunch and "early doors" dinner (5.30–7pm) which costs just £14.50 for two courses.

Viet Hoa Café

The Viet Hoa dining room is large, clean, light and airy, with an impressive golden parquet floor. The café part of the name is borne out by the bottles of red and brown sauce which take pride of place on each table. The brown goop turns out to be hoisin sauce and the red stuff a simple chilli one, but they have both been put into recycled plastic bottles on which the only recognizable words are "Sriracha extra hot chilli sauce – Flying Goose Brand". Apparently this has made all but the regulars strangely wary of hoisin sauce.

Cost	£8–18

Address 72 Kingsland Rd, E2
☏ 020 7729 8293
Station Old Street
Open Daily noon–4pm &
5.30–11.30pm
Accepts All major credit cards
except AmEx

As befits a café, there are a good many splendid "meals in a bowl" – soups and noodle dishes with everything from spring rolls to tofu. For diners wanting to go as a group and share, an appetizer called salted prawn in garlic dressing (£4.70) is outstanding – large prawns marinated and fried with chilli and garlic. From the list of fifteen soups, pho (£5.50) is compulsory. This dish is a Vietnamese staple eaten at any and every meal, including breakfast. Ribbon noodles and beef, chicken or tofu are added to a delicate broth. It comes with a plate of mint leaves, Thai basil and chillies, your job being to add the fresh aromatics to the hot soup – resulting in astonishingly vivid flavours. Main courses include shaking beef (£6.70) – cubes of beef with a tangy salad; and drunken fish (£6.70) – fish cooked with wine and cloud-ear mushrooms. Both live up to the promise of their exotic names. There are a good many salad and tofu dishes, including tofu with chilli and black bean (£4.95). Bun tom nuong (£5.75) is a splendid one-pot dish of noodles with char-grilled tiger prawns. Also in one-pot-with-vermicelli territory you'll find bun nem nuong (£5), which features grilled minced pork, and that old favourite, Singapore noodles (£4.70).

This is a good restaurant in which to make a first foray into Vietnamese food. It is very much a family-run place, with the grandparents sitting at a table dextrously rolling spring rolls and the younger generations waiting the tables. They're very helpful to novices.

Further East

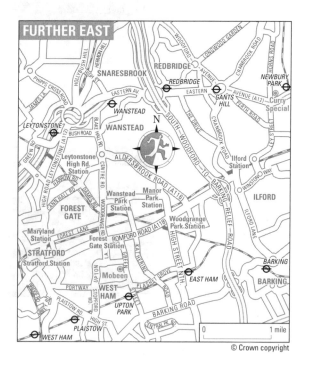

Curry Special

The remote branches of the Anand family (see The Brilliant, p.481) stretch far and wide, and their restaurants all serve a particular kind of Punjabi-meets-Kenyan food. Curry Special is the Eastern outpost in far-off Essex – when interrogated about why they picked Newbury Park when deciding to open a restaurant in 1982, the proprietors talked about "having friends and family in the area". Suffice to say they have had things pretty much to themselves and this restaurant has become a magnet for anyone out east who wants something a bit more interesting than the standard curry-house menu. Rich flavours are achieved by long, slow cooking and carefully chosen spices; there are no instant fixes, no cream, no yoghurt, no handfuls of nuts.

Cost	£10–35
Address	2 Greengate Parade, Horns Rd, Newbury Park, Essex
☏	020 8518 3005
Station	Newbury Park
Open	Tues–Fri 12.30–2pm & 6–11.30pm, Sat & Sun 6–11.30pm
Accepts	All major credit cards

Great pickles. Pause amongst the poppadoms to enjoy the carrot pickle, a genuinely Punjabi-hot super-crunch. Then go on to try the butter chicken (half a chicken £7.50, whole £14), which is suitably, uncannily buttery, and something of a signature dish – as you'd expect, considering the dynastic links with The Brilliant. There's also jeera (cumin) chicken, at the same price, and chilli chicken (half £8, whole £15) – very tasty. Or perhaps one of the less familiar dishes like pili pili bogo (£4.95), which is a dish of mixed vegetable pieces dusted in spiced flour and deep fried. For mains the curries are simple and rich: try methi chicken (for one £6.50, half-chicken £17, whole £34), or the delicious palak lamb (£6.50). From the vegetables section, choose the tinda masala (£4). You will be asked – rather disconcertingly, as how hot is hot? – whether you want your curry mild, medium or hot. Perhaps the spicy Punjabi grub has shocked some previous Essex punters, but whatever the reason, medium here is pretty tame, and you may want to go for hot. Bread-wise, indulge yourself with a hot bhatura (£1.95), which could be subtitled "fried bread meets doughnut".

For all its suburban location opposite B&Q, and its strangely dated name, Curry Special is busy enough to make booking advisable even early in the week. Essex folk seem to know what they like.

Mobeen

If you have never been to West Ham, the whole of Green Street is likely to come as a surprise. It has the feel of Brick Lane and Southall, but everything is much, much cheaper – in the market here you can buy a whole goat for the price of a dozen lamb chops in the West End. Mobeen itself seems to operate at

Cost	£4–16
Address	222–224 Green St, E7
☏	020 8470 2419
Station	Upton Park
Open	Daily 9am–10pm
Accepts	Cash and cheques only

"factory gate" prices, offering a kind of 1950s Asian works canteen ethos – with appropriate decor – and it is a strategy that has been so successful that there is now a chain of these strictly halal Pakistani caffs. As you go in, the kitchen lies behind a glazed wooden partition to your left, while to your right are café tables and chairs. The clientele hits this place like a breaking wave – it can be impressively busy at 11.50am.

The dishes and prices are listed above the servery hatches and the food is displayed below. You go up to the hatch, wait your turn and then order up a trayful, which will be re-animated in the microwave. Then it's off to another hatch for fizzy soft drinks and to yet another port of call to pick up cutlery and glasses. This is workmanlike food in large portions at basic prices, and most things are available in two sizes. Chicken tikka (£2.50/3.40) is red and hot, very hot. Sheekh kebabs (70p) are spicy and piping hot (thanks to the microwave). Meat samosas are just 50p each. Masala fish (£3.30) is rich and good. The biryani (£3/4) is commendably ungreasy and may actually have benefited from being cooked and reheated. There's also spinach and meat curry (£2.70/3.50), a meat curry (£2.70/3.50), and a bhuna meat curry (£2/3). The breads are serviceable, and there is a notable kind of very thick, fried, stuffed paratha (£1), that will tip you over your cholesterol allowance for about a fortnight. This establishment is just up the road from West Ham's home ground. You have to wonder what Alf Garnett would have made of it all.

Mobeen is unlicensed and bringing your own is not allowed, but among the soft drinks and juices are some novelty items: for 50p you can try a fizzy mango juice in a lurid can. Just the thing to tempt a jaded palate.

North

Camden Town & Primrose Hill

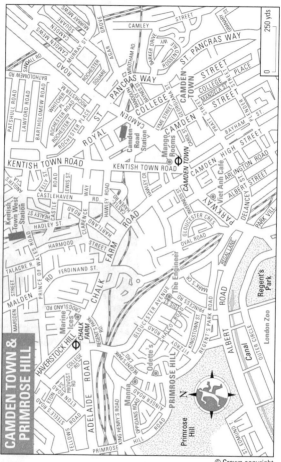

CAMDEN TOWN & PRIMROSE HILL

© Crown copyright

The Engineer

The Engineer is one of that bur-geoning roster of gastro-pubs whose food side has grown and grown – it now has tables in the bar, a more formal restaurant, tables in the garden (for those occasional summer days), and a *salle privée* on the first floor. Wherever you end up sitting, you'll get offered the same menu (which changes every two weeks) and you'll pay the same price. The cooking is accomplished, with good strong combinations of flavours, and a cheerful, iconoclastic approach to what is fundamentally Mediterranean food. The latest development is that they open for breakfast seven days a week. When do they sleep?

Cost	£12–40

Address 65 Gloucester Ave, NW1
☎ 020 7722 0950
Station Chalk Farm
Open Mon–Fri 9–11.30am, noon–3pm & 7–11pm, Sat 9am–noon, 12.30–3.30pm & 7–11pm, Sun 9am–noon, 12.30–3.30pm & 7–10.30pm
Accepts All major credit cards except Diners
🌐 www.the-engineer.com

MEDITERRANEAN/PUB

Your hackles may rise at £2.75 for home-made bread and butter, but the bread is warm from the oven, with a good crust, and the butter is beurre d'Isigny, and, as they refill the basket after you've scoffed the lot, you end up feeling happier about paying. Starters are simple and good. There's soup (£3.75). There may be a summery salad such as Feta cheese, dandelion leaf, watermelon and mint with an orange dressing (£5.95), or char-grilled squid with a ginger and fennel slaw with sweet chilli jam (£6.25). At lunchtime the mains will probably be quite light: eggs Benedict (£9), eggs Florentine (£9), a pan-fried organic beef burger (£10.35). For dinner, expect dishes like char-grilled sea bass fillet with coconut laksa, buckwheat noodles, bok choi and hardboiled egg (£14.50), or free-range baby chicken in jerk sauce, with rice 'n' peas and pineapple salsa (£13.50). There's often a new twist put on familiar ingre-dients, so roast organic lamb chump comes with a herb and spring onion rosti and baba ganoush (£15.50). A side order of baker chips (£2.25) brings thick wedges of baked potato fried until crispy. Thanks to The Engineer's pub status, there is always a decent pint of beer to be had and the coffee is excellent, too. All in all, plenty of reasons why it's so busy, and plenty of reasons why you should book.

At the bottom of the menu it says proudly, "Please note that all our meat is free range and organic". Hurrah! They deserve your support.

Mango Rooms

Mango Rooms is an engaging place, although it does make you wonder why everyone in this part of London is striving so hard to be laid-back. Hereabouts the coolness seems a little forced, and the casualness somehow elaborate. No matter. This restaurant describes itself as offering "traditional and modern Caribbean cuisine". The walls are bright and shabby, the staff gentle and the cooking reliable. If there is a fault to be found, it would be that the spicing and seasoning is somewhat tame, as if the act has been cleaned up a little. Perhaps Camden's restaurateurs simply have an unusually good grasp of what their customers like? Mango Room is certainly very full, and everyone seems to be having a great time, in a laid-back, Camden-cool kind of way.

Cost	£12–38

Address 10 Kentish Town Rd, NW1; with branches
℡ 020 7482 5065
Station Camden Town
Open Tues–Sun noon–3pm & 6pm–midnight, Sun noon–midnight
Accepts MasterCard, Visa

Traditional starters are the most successful, like the salt cod fritters with apple chutney (£4), or crab and potato balls (£4.50) – the exception to the under-spiced rule. Ebony wings, marinated in chilli pepper, garlic and soya with a hot and sweet dipping sauce (£3.80) is a nice dish but not a hot one. For a main course, "Camden's famous curry goat with hot pepper, scallions, garlic, pimento and spices" (£9) is subtitled "A hot, spicy, traditional dish", which it isn't. But it is very tasty: well presented and with plenty of lean meat. For fish eaters there is Creole snapper with mango and green peppercorn sauce (£9.50). The side dishes are excellent – plantain (£2.50), rice and peas (£1.90), white and sweet potato mash (£2.50), and a very good, dry and dusty roti (£2.50). The cooking is consistent and the kitchen makes a real effort with the presentation. If you like your Caribbean food on the sweet side and without the fierce burn of lantern chillies or pepper sauce, you will have a great time here.

Puddings are good – the mango and banana brûlée (£4) sports an exemplary hard top – and the Mango Rooms' special rum punch (£4.50) is sweet enough for most people to class it as a dessert. The bar here is lively and seems to be ever expanding.

Manna

If your new film – the one where a beautiful American business-woman meets a tongue-tied but cute Brit aristo, you know the kind of thing – needed an authentic 1970s veggie restaurant for a crucial hand-holding scene, the decor at Manna would fit the bill perfectly. In this world of chic modern restos and chic modern restaurant designers, it is increasingly hard for anywhere to look old-fashioned and casual without being sneered at. Manna don't care! This stubborn gentle-ness sometimes extends to the service, so don't pitch up here in a hurry, or without a serious appetite – there is no whimsy about the portions here. The cooking is very sound, and if there is such a thing as a pecu-liarly "veggie" charm, this place has it.

Cost	£15–45
Address	4 Erskine Rd, NW1
☏	020 7722 8028
Station	Chalk Farm
Open	Mon–Fri 6.30–11pm, Sat & Sun 12.30–3pm
Accepts	MasterCard, Visa
⊕	www.manna-veg.com

The menu devolves into five sections: starters, salads, mains, sides and desserts. You can also order a selection of any three salads or starters as the "Manna meze" (£13.75). Soup of the day (£3.95) is a sound option, as it comes with the solid but satisfying home-made bread. The menu changes regularly but may include starters like plantain tempura (£5.50) – served with ackee and a coriander and lime salsa. Or how about organic marinated mushroom caviar (£6.75) served on buckwheat blinis? Mains are an eclectic bunch: white bean and chilli tacos (£10.95) come with a wild rice timbale; there's an organic fresh pasta roulade of ricotta, almonds and roast garlic (£11.95) – dishes here do read like recipes; or perhaps oyster mushrooms, tempeh and smoky tofu tom yum (£10.50) appeals? Puds are serious: organic dark chocolate and walnut brownie (£6.25), and lemon and almond drizzle cake (£5.50), are a challenge to all but the stoutest appetites. For the prompt diner there's an early-evening menu that offers two courses for £12.75 and sets out a variety of options drawn from the main menu.

The menu here is decidable: (v) stands for vegan dishes; (vo) means vegan option and adds "please ask"; (org) means an organic dish; and (g) means gluten free. All of which is very helpful. Whether committed veg-etarians or not, we should all take more interest in just what it is that we are eating.

Marine Ices

Marine Ices is a family restaurant from a bygone era. In 1947, Aldo Mansi rebuilt the family shop along nautical lines, kitting it out with wood and portholes (hence the name). In the half-century since, while the family ice cream business has grown and grown, the restaurant and gelateria has just pottered along. All for the good. That means old-fashioned service and home-style, old-fashioned Italian food. It also means that Marine Ices is a great hit with children, for in addition to the good Italian food, there is a marathon list of stunning sundaes, coupes, ice creams and sorbets.

Cost	£8–25

Address 8 Haverstock Hill, NW3
℡ 020 7482 9003
Station Chalk Farm
Open Restaurant Mon–Fri noon–3pm & 6–11pm, Sat noon–11pm, Sun noon–10pm; gelateria Mon–Sat 10.30am–11pm, Sun 11am–10pm
Accepts MasterCard, Switch, Visa

The menu is long: antipasti, salads, pastas and sauces, specialities and pizzas. Of the starters, you could try selezioni di bruschetta (£3.80), which combines one each of three well-made and fresh bruschetta – roast vegetables, sardines and tomatoes. Or go for the chef's salad (£3.95), a rocket salad with pancetta and splendid croutons made from eggy bread. Pasta dishes are home-made: casarecce Aldo (£6.80), from the specials list, has a tasty sauce of spring onions, spinach and ricotta, and it's simple and very good. Main courses range from pollo Valdostana (£7.40) to scaloppa Milanese (£8.60) and fegato alla Veneziana (£8.90). Pizzas are immense, freshly made and very tasty, in whichever of their many guises you choose (£5.20–6.50). And where others may be set on saving Venice, at Marine they support the Roundhouse fund; for every Roundhouse pizza sold – cheese, tomato, ham, mushroom and fresh chilli (all £6.50) – they donate 50p.

When you've had your meal, take a breath and ask for the gelateria menu. There are sundaes from Peach Melba (£2.40) to Knickerbocker Glory (£3.65). There are coppe, including Stefania (£4.40) – one scoop each of chocolate and hazelnut ice cream, covered in nuts and hot fudge sauce. There are bombe, cassate and, best of all, affogati (£4.20) – three scoops of ice cream topped with Marsala or, even nicer, espresso coffee. Or create your own combo from fourteen ice creams and eight sorbets. They're £1.35 a scoop.

Odette's

Odette's is a charming, pictur-esque restaurant, idyllically set in pretty Primrose Hill. The walls are crammed with gilded mirrors and hanging plants, there's a pleasant con-servatory at the back (with a skylight open in warm weather) and candles flicker in the evenings. Add well-judged Modern British food, the odd local celeb, and staff who always try to make you feel

Cost	£20–40
Address	130 Regent's Park Rd, NW1
☎	020 7586 5486
Station	Chalk Farm
Open	Mon–Fri 12.30–2.30pm & 7–11pm, Sat 7–11pm, Sun 12.30–2.45pm
Accepts	All major credit cards

special, and you have all the ingredients for a very successful local restaurant. In summer, try to get one of the tables that spill out onto the villagey street.

The food makes commendable use of seasonal produce, so do not expect to find all the dishes listed every time you visit. However, the olive and walnut bread is a constant – warm and delicious. Starters, if you strike lucky, might include white bean, onion and shallot soup (£4.50), or a risotto of roast pumpkin, ceps and aged balsamic vinegar (£6.50). When in season, six Irish oysters (£8) is a good choice; it arrives well presented, half deep-fried and half "nature", with rice-wine vinegar on the side. Mains generally include at least one choice each of fish, meat, game and chicken. Grilled fillet of halibut comes with but-tered Savoy cabbage (£17.50). Cumin roast neck of new-season lamb, soft polenta and spring greens (£14.50) is another good choice, as is fricassée of rabbit, calves' sweetbreads and smoked bacon (£16), which is served with creamed lettuce and tagliatelle. Monkfish tail is served "au poivre" with creamed potatoes and a brown butter vinaigrette (£16.50), while veggies might go for wild mushrooms and celeriac baked in puff pastry (£10.50). Puddings (all £5) are wonderfully indulgent, and include lemon curd parfait with strawberries, and an outstanding mango and stem ginger sorbet. The set lunch is worth noting: it's available from Monday to Friday and on Sunday, and costs £12.50 for two courses and £15 for three.

Odette's has a very long wine list, with something to suit all tastes and purses. It's also nice to get such a large choice of wines by the glass and half bottle. Try a glass of Argentine Chenin Blanc (£3.40), or a half bottle of Jurancon Sec (£11.25).

VIETNAMESE

Viet-Anh Cafe

Authentic, it says on the card, and authentic it tastes on the plate. Viet-Anh is a bright, cheerful café with oilcloth-covered tables run by a young Vietnamese couple. They cook and give service that's beyond helpful. In complete contrast to the occasionally intimidating feel of some of the more obscure Chinese restaurants, this is a friendly and welcoming place. If there is anything puzzling or unfamiliar they'll tell you what and show you how. It's the sort of place where single diners feel quite at home.

| Cost | £15–40 |

Address 41 Parkway, NW1
℡ 020 7284 4082
Station Camden Town
Open Daily noon–4pm & 5.30–11pm
Accepts MasterCard, Visa

Vietnamese vegetarian spring rolls (£2.95) and Vietnamese meat pancake (£4.95) are classic starters. The former are crisp, well seasoned, and flavoured with fresh coriander; the latter are a delight – two large, paper-thin, eggy pancakes stuffed with vegetables and chicken, and served with large lettuce leaves. You hold these in the palm of your hand and manipulate a slice of the pancake onto the leaf, roll it up together, dip in the pungent lemony sauce and eat. Hot and cold, crisp and soft, savoury and lemony – all in one. Ordering prawn sugar cane stick (£5.50) brings large prawns skewered on a piece of sugar cane. Eat the prawn then chew the cane – it's savoury and sweet in one mouthful. Pho chicken soup, accurately described as the House Special (£4.50), is made with slices of chicken and vegetables plus flat rice stick noodles in broth. Slurp the noodles and lift the bowl to drink the soup. Lemongrass chicken on boiled rice (£4.50) is a more fiery dish – you can have it medium hot or very hot, just ask. There are over a hundred items on the menu, ranging from £1 to £12, and most are complete one-plate meals. Wines come in at around the £15 mark, or there is sake (300ml for £8) as well as various Far East beers. Try the Shui Sen tea (£1.20) – it's more fragrant than jasmine tea, and just as refreshing.

To complete the café feel, huge (1lb 12oz) plastic bottles of sauce with squeezy tops adorn the tables. They are labelled "Sriracha HOT chilli sauce", and the label is as much a warning as an inducement. If you like your food as spicy as the Vietnamese customers do, you're only a squeeze away.

Hampstead and Golders Green

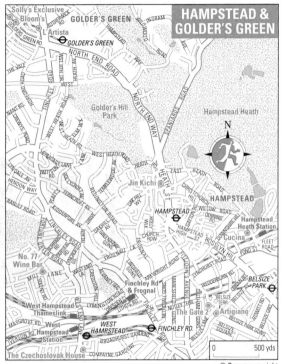

HAMPSTEAD &
GOLDER'S GREEN

Solly's Exclusive
Bloom's
L'Artista
GOLDER'S GREEN
GOLDER'S GREEN
ROTHERWICK RD
INGHAM
GOLDERS GREEN RD
NORTH END ROAD
THE VALE
NORTH END WAY
FINCHLEY RD
WELLGARTH
Golder's Hill
Park
Hampstead Heath
NANT RD
CREWS ROAD
N
HERITAGE LANE
WEST HEATH ROAD
LYNDALE AV
PLATT'S
HEATH DR
EAST HEATH ROAD
HENDON WAY
HAMPSTEAD
FERNCROFT AV
Jin Kichi
HEATH ST
CHRISTCHURCH
RANULF ROAD
REDINGTON ROAD
OAK HILL WY
HAMPSTEAD
WILLOW
DENNING
Hampstead
Heath Station
KIDDERPORE AV
HAMPSTEAD HIGH ST
ROSSLYN HILL
Cucina
FLEET
FERNCROFT AV
FINCHLEY ROAD
HEATH
HENRY RD
DAISY
CHURCH
ROW
FROGNAL
ROAD
No. 77
Wine Bar
FORTUNE GREEN ROAD
WEST END LA
FROGNAL
ARKWRIGHT ROAD
JOHN'S AVENUE
TYNHURST ROAD
BELSIZE
PARK
MILL LANE
CRDIOZ RD
FINCHLEY RD
& Frognal
NETHERHALL GDNS
WEDDERBURN RD
Finchley Rd
& Frognal
MARESFIELD GDNS
BELSIZE
TERR
West Hampstead
Thameslink
LYMINGTON ROAD
NUTLEY TERR
The Gate 2
Artigiano
MAYGROVE RD
West
Hampstead
Station
WEST
HAMPSTEAD
FINCHLEY RD.
BELSIZE SQUARE
BELSIZE PARK GDNS
The Czechoslovak House
BROADHURST GARDENS
COMPAYNE GARDENS

0   500 yds

© Crown copyright

Artigiano

This is one of London's more diffi-cult-to-find restaurants, situated halfway up a dead-end street in the rabbit warren of Belsize Park. Neverthe-less, tracking it down is well worth the effort. When you do find it, you will be confronted with a bright, airy restaurant, glass fronted and with generous sky-lights. There's more chance of seeing a traffic warden than a passing car and the only disturbance from outside is the rustle of leaves. For such an out-of-the-way place the restaurant is surprisingly big, with more than a hundred covers. It's remarkably busy too, full of thirty-something professionals who've sought it out for the same reasons you have – good food and service, convivial atmosphere, and an escape from the rat race.

Cost	£17–28
Address	12 Belsize Terrace, NW3
☏	020 7794 4288
Station	Belsize Park
Open	Mon 6.45–11pm, Tues–Sat noon–3pm & 6.45–11pm, Sun noon–3pm & 6.45–10pm
Accepts	All major credit cards
🌐	www.etruscagroup.com

The menu is longer than you'd expect in such a restaurant, with eight first courses and eight main pastas followed by as many main courses, but it seems that the kitchen can cope. There is an admirable tendency to use spanking fresh ingredients and to let them be themselves. Antipasti might include insalata mista con erbe fresche e vinaigrette all'aceto balsamico (£5.25) – the Italian for mixed leaves! Or prosciutto made from wild boar and served with rocket, orange and walnuts (£8.50), or a good beef carpaccio with a mustardy dressing (£8.50). Pastas are home made and innovative. Casoncelli (£7) are small pasta parcels stuffed with duck and pistachios; stracci di pasta al pesto di carciofi e granchio reale (£8.50) is a mixture of strips of pasta with fresh crab and a basil and artichoke pesto. The "pesce" list also offers a good choice: gilt head bream pan fried with a saffron sauce (£13.50); or seared tuna steak (£14.50). Meat eaters will turn to the ossobuco in gremolata (£13.50), which is served with a timbale of saffron rice; or the grilled wild boar cutlet (£15), which comes with a potato tartlet. The chocolate sorbet (£4) is seductive and the strawberries (£4.50) are marinated in spumante and balsamic vinegar.

Having weathered the first few years, Artigiano looks set fair. If you are able to make it at lunchtime, go for the set menu – £15 for two courses, £18 for three.

L'Artista

Situated opposite the entrance to Golders Green tube, and occupying an arch under the railway lines, L'Artista is hard to miss. With its pavement terrace, abundant greenery and umbrellas, this is a lively, vibrant restaurant and pizzeria that exercises an almost

Cost	£15–24

Address 917 Finchley Rd,
NW11; with branches
☎ 020 8731 7501
Station Golders Green
Open Daily noon–midnight
Accepts MasterCard, Visa

magnetic appeal to the young and not so young of Golders Green. At the weekend it is literally full to bursting and tables spill onto the terrace – a perfect spot to eat alfresco, providing the traffic isn't too heavy on the Finchley Road. Inside, the plain decor is enhanced by celebrity photographs; the waiters are a bit cagey if asked just how many of them have actually eaten here, but the proximity of the tables ensures that you get to rub shoulders with whoever happens to be around you, famous or otherwise.

The menu offers a range of Italian food with a good selection of main courses such as fegato Veneziana (£7.30), a rich dish of calves' liver with onion and white wine. The trota del pescatore (£6.90) is also good, a simple but effective trout with garlic. But L'Artista's pizzas are its forte. They are superb. As well as traditional thin-crust Capricciosa (£5.90) with anchovies, eggs and ham, or Quattro Formaggi (£5.30), there are more unusual varieties such as Mascarpone e rucola (£5.80), a plain pizza topped with mascarpone cheese and heaps of crisp rocket, which is actually very good. The calzone (£5.70) – a cushion-sized rolled pizza stuffed with ham, cheese and sausage and topped with Napoli sauce – is wonderful. Pastas are varied and the penne alla vodka (£5.60), made with vodka, prawns and cream, is well worth a try. For something lighter, try the excellent insalata dell'Artista (£4.90), a generous mix of tuna, olives and fennel, with an order of equally good garlic pizza bread (£2.50).

L'Artista tries hard to bring something of the atmosphere of Naples to Golders Green. By a happy accident this ambience is enhanced by the Vesuvian tremors which occur whenever a Northern-line train rumbles ominously overhead.

Bloom's

Bloom's goes way back to 1920, when Rebecca and Morris Bloom first produced their great discovery – the original veal Vienna. Since then "Bloom's of the East End" has carried the proud tag as "the most famous kosher restaurant in the world". Setting aside the indignant claims of several outraged New York delis for the moment, given its history it's a shame that the East End Bloom's was forced to shut, and that they had to retrench to this, their Golders Green stronghold, in 1965. Nonetheless,

Cost	£12–30

Address 130 Golders Green Rd, NW11
℡ 020 8455 1338
Station Golders Green
Open Mon–Thurs & Sun noon–11pm, Fri 10am–2pm (3pm in summer)
Accepts All major credit cards except Diners
ⓦ www.blooms-restaurant.co.uk

it's a glorious period piece. Rows of sausages hang over the takeaway counter, there are huge mirrors and chrome tables, and you can expect inimitable service from battle-hardened waiters.

So, the waiter looks you in the eye as you ask for a beer. "Heineken schmeineken", he says derisively. At which point you opt for Maccabee, an Israeli beer (£1.90), and regain a little ground. Start with some new green cucumbers (90p) – fresh, crisp, tangy, delicious – and maybe a portion of chopped liver and egg and onions (£4.20), which comes with world-class rye bread. Or go for soup, which comes in bowls so full they slop over the edge: beetroot borscht and potato (£2.90), very sweet and very red; lockshen, the renowned noodle soup (£2.90); or kreplach, full of dumplings (£3.50). Go on to main courses. The salt beef (£13.50) is as good as you might expect, and you can try it in a sandwich on rye bread (£6.90). And there are solid and worthy options like liver and onions (£9.20). Bloom's is now run by Jonathan Tapper, one of the fourth generation of the Bloom family, and despite the occasional refurbishment the inimitable ambience remains intact. You can still order extra side dishes like the dreaded, heart-stopping fried potato latke (£1.90), one of the legendarily substantial dishes that underpins the reputation of Jewish food.

Whatever else you try, don't leave without sampling the tzimmas (£2.20), honeyed carrots so cloyingly sweet that they could claim a spot on the dessert menu. This is filling, wholesome, comforting food. Enjoy!

Cucina

This single-fronted restaurant, next to a bakery near South End Green, looks like the archetypal traiteur, or smart food shop. And that is what it is, at least downstairs, where the Hampstead literati feast upon a range of rather good meals to go. But if you enter and turn right up the stairs you come to a large, brightly painted, wooden-floored, roof-lit dining room. Very modern, very fashionable, very chic. At lunch, all is relatively quiet, and talk at the scattered tables is generally of business. Things hot up in the evening, however, when the à la carte menu takes over. This menu changes every two weeks or so and darts about between cuisines and continents, but wherever you alight you can be sure of well-presented dishes and service that is friendly and efficient.

Cost	£18–40

Address 45a South End Rd, NW3
☎ 020 7435 7814
Station Belsize Park
Open Mon–Thurs noon–2.30pm & 7–10.30pm, Fri & Sat noon–2.30pm & 7–11pm, Sun noon–3pm
Accepts All major credit cards except Diners

Dinner-time starters may include deep-fried quail in a chickpea batter with chermoula and red cabbage (£5.75); roast new potatoes, crispy fried pancetta and Taleggio sauce (£5.75); wok-fried squid with roasted seaweed noodles, chilli and soy (£6.25); or, if that isn't spooky enough for you, Szechuan seared kangaroo shitake, lotus root and mizuna salad with mirin dressing (£6.25). Among the main courses there is always a fish of the day, often something interesting like mahi-mahi. Other fish dishes feature, too, such as char-grilled salmon with fennel, green bean and lemon salad, and artichoke aioli (£12.50). Or how about pan-fried lamb's kidneys, porcini and basil sauce, and truffle-oil mash (£12.75)? Or char-grilled butternut squash and mustard potato curry, with yoghurt and a poppadom (£10.50)? Or confit of duck with sesame-fried courgette noodles, and plum and ginger chutney (£13.50)? For the more traditional diner there is always a very sound char-grilled rib of beef with frites (£26.95 for two).

Puds (all £5) include hot cinnamon doughnuts with apple compote; dried sour cherry, chocolate and hazelnut meringue torte; and treacle tart. Sometimes they have a little note beside them, saying: "Too full! Why not get a pudding to take home?"

The Czechoslovak House

With its low prices and bafflingly retro decor – the kind of ambience where Harry Lime would feel right at home – The Czechoslovak House is always filled with a happy mix of students and locals. It is situated in the old, established Czechoslovak National House (too good an institution to be sundered – or even to adapt its name), and its dining room is a class act. Genuine flock wallpaper gives a unique backdrop for some striking portraits: among them Václav Havel, Winston Churchill and a very young-looking Queen Elizabeth II with her crown and regalia picked out in glitter powder.

Cost	£12–26

Address 74 West End Lane, NW6
℗ 020 7372 5251
Station West Hampstead
Open Tues–Fri 6–10pm, Sat & Sun noon–3pm & 6–10pm
Accepts Cash or cheque only

CZECH/SLOVAK

Menu-writers across London should be forced to study here – it is hard to improve on the concision of "meat soup" (£2.50). Passing that dish by, try starting with tlacenka (£2.50), which is home-made brawn with onions. Or Russian egg (£4) – egg mayonnaise with salad, ham and onions. Or the rather good rollmops (£2.50), again with onions. (You need to like raw onions to do well at the starters.) Main courses deliver serious amounts of home-made, tasty food. Beef goulash (£8.50) is red with sweet paprika, and cooked long and slow until the meat is meltingly tender. Order smoked boiled pork knuckle, (£6.50), and you will be served a vast and tasty ham hock, which comes with a small jug of wildly rich pork gravy to go with your dumplings (£1.50). You can have the dumplings with the roast veal (£6.50) but consider the good fried potatoes (£1.50) or the epic sauerkraut (£2.50). For drink, set your sights on beer: Gambrinus on draught is £2.20 a pint, and there are a number of other bottled Czech beers, including one labelled with a motorcycle and sidecar. There is a story behind this design, which the amiable bartender will explain – not that you will be able to remember the tale after drinking the stuff.

There is one pudding that will have any cholesterol-wary diner clutching at their pacemaker. Apricot dumpling (£3.50) is a cricket-ball-sized lump of dough with an apricot inside. It comes under a coat of sour cream, and sits in a sea of melted butter. It is awesome.

The Gate 2

There are ghetto-like vegetarian restaurants and then there are restaurants in a completely different class that, for one reason or another, happen not to use meat or fish in their cooking. The Gate 2 in Belsize Park, sister to The Gate in Hammersmith (see p.439), is one of the latter, serving excellent and original dishes with intense and satisfying tastes and textures. Even the dedicated carnivore won't miss anything.

Cost	£25–50

Address 72 Belsize Lane NW3
ⓣ 020 7435 7733
Station Belsize Park
Open Mon & Tues 6–11pm,
Wed–Sun noon–3pm &
6–11pm
Accepts All major credit cards
ⓦ www.gateveg.co.uk

Starters may include potato cake filled with spinach and basil pesto (£5.50); tempura (£5.25); or a butternut squash risotto (£5.25/8.50). Or perhaps a three-onion tart (£5.50), which is made with leeks, shallots and roast red onions. Main courses are equally adventurous. A wild mushroom terrine (£10.75) is made from sautéed wild mushrooms, layered on creamed thyme potatoes and enlivened with the crunch of pecan nuts. Or saffron ravioli (£9.50), filled with butternut squash, goat's cheese and spinach before being pan fried in a cream and rocket sauce and served with a dollop of artichoke and hazelnut pesto. An aubergine schnitzel (£10.50) comes layered with smoked mozzarella and is served with pan-fried kale, roast new potatoes and a horseradish cream sauce. There may also be a root vegetable tagine (£9.50) – it is interesting to see veg like celeriac, sweet potato and fennel given the North African treatment. Breads come in five varieties. For pudding, try lemon and fig galette (£5) – a pyramid of caramelized fresh figs, lemon curd and shortbread, the sharpness of the lemon balancing the rich, sweet biscuit and the figs. Otherwise, try the millefeuille (£5.50) – poached apples, dates and roasted pecans on a crisp filo case, with an orange and red-wine syrup. Wines are well priced, with a house wine at £10.50 and a flinty Sauvignon de St Bris 1998 at £14.50.

Decor is modern and minimalist, presentation is decorative but not over fussy and the kitchen downstairs is open to view – always a good sign. If you think vegetarian food is only for the devoted, The Gate 2 might well change your mind.

Jin Kichi

Unlike so many Japanese restaurants, where the atmosphere can range from austere to intimidating, Jin Kichi is a very comfortable place. It's cramped, rather shabby and very busy – tables are booked up (even on the quiet nights of the week) and there is a constant stream of regulars begging for special treatment at the door. It differs

Cost	£12–30

Address 73 Heath St, NW3
℡ 020 7794 6158
Station Hampstead
Open Tues–Fri 6–11pm, Sat 12.30–2pm & 6–11pm, Sun 12.30–2pm & 6–10pm
Accepts All major credit cards

from sushi-led establishments in that the bar dominating the ground floor with the stools in front of it is not home to the sushi master, but rather to a short and fierce charcoal grill and an unhurried chef who uses it to cook short skewers of this and that.

By all means start with sushi. Ordering the nigiri set brings seven pieces of fresh fish for an eminently reasonable £12.70. But then go for the "grilled skewers". Helpfully enough there are two set meals offering various combinations, and each delivers seven skewers (one combo costs £10.80 and the other £8.50). These little, cunningly marinated titbits make for a very splendid kind of eating: each skewer comes hot off the grill; you eat it; it's terrific. Grilled skewer of fresh asparagus (£1.20), and grilled skewer of quail eggs (£1.20) are steady stuff. Be more adventurous – grilled skewer of fresh asparagus and pork rolls with salt (£1.60) is a big seller. Grilled skewer of chicken wings with salt (£1.30) is simple and very good, but grilled skewer of duck with spring onion (£1.80) is even better. Grilled skewer of ox tongue with salt (£1.80) is tender and delicious, while grilled skewer of chicken gizzard with salt (£1.10) is chewy and delicious. The grilled skewer of chicken skin with salt (£1.50) is crisp and very moreish. To drink there is ice-cold draft Kirin beer served in a frosted glass, as well as a range of sake. The remainder of the menu leads off to fried dishes, tempura, different noodle dishes, soups and so forth, but the undoubted star of the show is the little grill.

The art to eating here lies in second-guessing your appetite. Order too little and you face a wait while more food is grilled; order too much and you feel greedy. Go for greedy, it's an inexpensive place.

No.77 Wine Bar

This rowdy and likeable North London wine bar celebrated its twentieth birthday with epic parties in 2002. Looking back over its chequered history, the grub here has gone through various phases, from not-smart to smart and now back to straightforward again. Good news for the locals, the more ambitious stuff has been consigned to the dustbin of gastro-history and the burger formerly known as the "fat bastard" is back. Despite the return to casual dining and a more eclectic, less classical menu, the wine list is long, informed and offers good value.

Cost	£16–38

Address 77 Mill Lane, NW6
℗ 020 7435 7787
Station West Hampstead
Open Mon & Tues noon–11pm,
Wed–Sat noon–midnight, Sun
1–10.30pm
Accepts MasterCard, Visa

Starters range from smoked haddock, pea and saffron risotto cake with tomato confit (£4.55); to hoisin spare ribs with crispy noodles (£4.95); or char-grilled aubergines, goat's cheese and beef tomato with pesto (£4.50). The soupe de jour has come down to earth as "soup of today" (£3.95), while for main course, also in keeping with the old spirit, there is a pasta dish of the day (£7.95). But what about the roasted tandoori salmon with warm vegetable salad, noodles and mango (£9.75)? Or sirloin steak with Portobello mushrooms, baked sweet potatoes and jus (£12.50)? Or confit duck leg with bubble and squeak (£9.65)? Vegetarians might opt for the fresh winter-vegetable stew served with herb and cheese dumplings (£7.95). The new polite name for the Fat Bastard is "No 77 beefburger topped with smoked Cheddar and served with braised capsicum, onions, potato fries and salad" (£8.75). The pud list is littered with familiar faces such as tiramisù with whipped cream (£4.50) and panna cotta with berry compote (£4.50). Lemon brûlée with meringue and berries (£4.50) is a hair's breadth from lemon meringue pie.

Like the menu, the wine list changes as whim and stocks dictate, but look out for delights such as La Grange Neuve de Figeac 1994 (£37.95), or Three Choirs Estate Reserve, lightly oaked, 1997 (£13.95). Anyone visiting Mill Lane for the first time should bear in mind that in this part of North London the busiest night of the week is Thursday, which is when the wine bar will be at its liveliest. They certainly know how to party in these parts.

Solly's Exclusive

What makes Solly's Exclusive so exclusive is that it is upstairs. Downstairs is Solly's Restaurant, a small, packed, noisy place specializing in epic falafel. You'll find Solly's Exclusive by coming out of Solly's Restaurant, turning left, and left again around the side of the building, and then proceeding through an unmarked black door. Upstairs, a huge, bustling dining room accommodates 180 customers, while a back room provides another 100 seats, which lie in wait for functions like bar mitzvahs. The decor is interesting – tented fabric on the ceiling, multi-coloured glass, brass light fittings – while waitresses, all of them with Solly's Exclusive emblazoned across the back of their waistcoats, maintain a brisk approach to the niceties of service.

Cost	£16–35

Address 146–150 Golders Green Rd, NW11
℡ 020 8455 2121
Station Golders Green
Open Mon–Thurs 6.30–10.30pm, Sat (winter only) an hour after sundown–1am, Sun 12.30–10.30pm
Accepts All major credit cards except Diners

The food is tasty and workmanlike. Start with the dish that pays homage to the chickpea – hoummus with falafel (£4.25), which brings three crispy depth charges and some well-made dip. Even the very best falafel in the world cannot overcome the thunderous indigestibility of chickpeas, but as falafel go these are pretty good. Otherwise, you could try Solly's special aubergine dip (£3.25), or the Moroccan cigars (£5), made from minced lamb wrapped in filo pastry and deep fried. Solly's pitta (£1.25) – a fluffy, fourteen-inch disc of freshly baked bread – is closer to a perfect naan than Greek-restaurant bread. Pittas to pine for. For mains, the lamb shawarma (£9.75) is very good, nicely seasoned and spiced, and served with excellent chips and good salad. The barbecue roast chicken (£9.50) comes with the same accompaniments, and is also sound. Steer clear of the Israeli salad (£2.75), however, unless you relish the idea of a large bowl of chopped watery tomatoes and chopped watery cucumber.

Solly's Exclusive is kosher, and under the supervision of the London Beth Din, so naturally its opening days and hours don't follow the same rules as non-Jewish establishments. If you're not fully conversant with the Jewish calendar, check before setting out.

Highgate & Crouch End

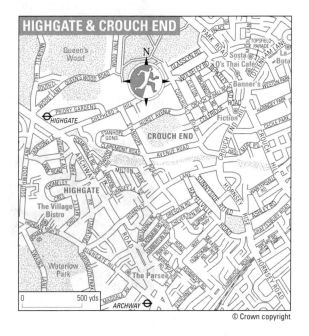

HIGHGATE & CROUCH END

Queen's Wood

Queen's Wood Road

WOOD VALE

SOUTHWOOD LANE

WOOD LANE

PRIORY GARDENS

HIGHGATE

SHEPHERD'S HILL

HURST AVENUE

CROUCH END

STANHOPE GDNS.

CLAREMONT ROAD

AVENUE ROAD

MILTON

JACKSON'S RD

TOWNSEND YD

ARCHWAY RD

HIGHGATE

BROMLEY CRES.

The Village Bistro

HIGHGATE HIGH ST

CHIP

SWAIN'S LANE

HORNSEY LA.

MAKEPEACE AVE

HORNSEY

ROAD

WINCHESTER

HIGHGATE HILL

PROMLEY

Waterlow Park

The Parsee

MAGDALA AV.

ARCHWAY

GLASSLYN RD

WOLSELEY RD

BERKELEY

Sosta

O's Thai Café

CROUCH HALL ROAD

Banner's

WESTON PARK

HARINGEY PARK

COLERIDGE ROAD

Fiction

CECILE PARK

CROUCH END HILL

HASLEMERE RD

CROUCH HILL

LANE

SUNNYSIDE ROAD

HORNSEY RISE

ASHLEY RD

WATERFALL RD

SHAFTESBURY ROAD

HORNSEY ROAD

DRESDEN RD

CRAVEN

LANE

WEALD

PEMBERTON RD

HABBRIDGE

DUNCOMBE RD

ELTHORNE RD

ASHBROOK RD

TOTTENHAM LANE

TOPSFIELD PARADE

La Bota

MIDDLE LANE

0   500 yds

© Crown copyright

Banner's

The 1960s are alive and well at Banner's. This is a characterful restaurant and cocktail bar with a real community feel. Noticeboards proclaim events and accommodation, kids draw using crayons kept in little red wellies, World Music plays ... it's a welcoming kind of place if this slant on life matches velocities with your own.

Cost £10–30

Address 21 Park Rd, N8
☎ 020 8348 2930
Station Highgate
Open Mon–Thurs 9am–11.30pm, Fri 9am–midnight,
Sat 10am–midnight, Sun 10am–11pm
Accepts MasterCard, Visa

With all-day breakfasts, small meals, big meals, kids' meals, sandwiches and no-meat sections, Banner's menu pleases all tastes. Small meals include smoked tuna and coriander fish cake with Thai coconut dip (£4.95); tandoori chicken kebabs with mint raita (£4.25); and Greek salad (£4.75). They're all large enough for a light meal. Bigger meals include rib-eye steak, char grilled with Kentucky black barbecue sauce and peppercorn mash (£10.95); jerk chicken salad with spoon bread and home-made chutney (£9.95); grilled fresh tuna loin with coconut rice and lime butter (£10.65); and Yorkshire sausages and mashed potatoes with cider onion gravy (£8.50) – a generous plateful, tasty and satisfying. Side dishes include cornmeal, sweetcorn and jalapeño spoon bread (£2.75); sweet-potato fries (£2.75); and garlic chips (£2.75) – for the certified lover of the bulb. Desserts include banana cake served warm with ice cream (£4.35); and hot dark-chocolate and walnut brownie with ice cream (£4.75). Ices are from Marine (see p.234). But the all-day-breakfast menu is the star, with choices like two Manx kippers with brown or white toast (£5.25); bubble and squeak with two fried eggs (£4.10); and a proper fry-up with everything, including toast (£6.50).

The "world" feel extends to beers from Lapland and Argentina, exotic cocktails by the glass (£4.95) or jug (£20), cigarettes from the US, and postcards from Crouch End. And, to the relief of other diners, parents are warned, for safety reasons, not to let kids rush around on their own. Easy-going and family-oriented by day, Banner's livens up in the evening to become very busy with a lively, cocktail-drinking crowd; booking is advised.

La Bota

This bustling tapas bar and restaurant enjoys a good evening trade, and with good reason. It's a Galician (northwest Spanish) place, and that's always a good sign, particularly for seafood. The best of its tapas fall into two categories: there are the "raw" ones like Serrano ham, which simply need careful buying and good bread as accompaniment, and there are the stews, which have been made in the morning and reheated as necessary – thankfully, most of the rich, unfussy dishes of Galicia lend themselves well to this treatment. Your first decision is a crucial one: do you go all out for tapas (there are 30 on the menu, plus 17 vegetarian ones, plus another 18 or so daily specials chalked on a blackboard)? Or do you choose one of the main courses – Spanish omelette, paellas, steaks, chicken, fish and so forth? Perhaps the best option is to play to La Bota's strengths and order a few tapas, then a few more, until you have subdued your appetite and there's no longer a decision to make. In the meantime enjoy the air conditioning – and the house wine at a very reasonable £7.60.

Cost	£10–25

Address 31 Broadway Parade, Tottenham Lane, N8
℗ 020 8340 3082
Station Finsbury Park/ Turnpike Lane
Open Mon–Fri noon–2.30pm & 6–11.30pm, Sat noon–3pm & 6–11.30pm, Sun noon–11pm
Accepts All major credit cards except Diners

Start with simple things. Boquerones en vinagre (£3) brings a plate of broad white anchovies with a pleasant vinegar tang. Jamón Serrano (£4.20) is thinly sliced, ruby red and strongly flavoured – perfect with the basket of warm French bread that is on every table. Then move on to hot tapas: mejillones pescador (£3.40) is a good-sized plate of mussels in a tomato and garlic sauce; chistorra a la sidra (£3) is a mild sausage cooked in cider; rinones al Jerez (£3) is a portion of kidneys in a sherry sauce, rich and good. Alas de pollo barbacoa (£3) is an Iberian take on chicken wings. Then there's arroz al campo (£3) – rice cooked with saffron and vegetables; rabbit cazuela (£3.25); chicken Riojana (£3.25); and patatas bravas (£2), the tasty dish of potatoes in a mildly spicy tomato sauce. Just keep them coming…

If you like squid, and don't mind looking at a whole one, opt for chipirones a la plancha (£3.85) – four squidlets grilled to tender perfection.

Fiction

VEGETARIAN

Opposite a hairdresser called Pulp sits the restaurant named Fiction. Fact. But the restaurant was there first, and it was named after the bookshop whose premises it took over – the hairdressers are the film buffs and named their place accordingly. And there's no gore in the tale, as Fiction is strictly vegetarian, although not in the missionary hair shirt and holier-than-thou style. Rather, the idea is to rediscover the use of indigenous herbs, and to cook, with plenty of wine, dishes that were popular in the days when people ate a lot less meat than they do now. All dishes and wines are marked as vegetarian, vegan and organic, where relevant.

Cost	£20–40

Address 60 Crouch End Hill, N8
☎ 020 8340 3403
Station Finsbury Park/ Highgate
Open Wed–Sat 6.30–10.30pm, Sun 12.30–4pm & 6.30–10.30pm
Accepts MasterCard, Visa
⊛ www.fiction-restaurant.co.uk

Fiction's menu changes with the seasons. Starters will include a soup, and often it is an original one, like the Acapulcan three bean, chilli and tomato soup (£4.25). Or try herby onion polenta cake with a cream and sage sauce (£4.95), or chunky cheese, sweetcorn and coriander fritters served with salad garnish and a delicious sweet chilli sauce (£4.45) – a bit like Thai crab cakes without the crab. The signature main courses are wood-roasted butternut squash (£10.95) and "The Good Gamekeeper's Pie" (£10.95). The former is described fulsomely as "a succulent 'steak' of squash filled with lemon-garlic mushrooms", the latter as "chestnuts, wild mushrooms, 'mock duck', leek, carrot and broccoli, prepared in an old English marinade of red wines, and baked in a puff pastry pie". Both are very nicely flavoured. There's also a "Fictional" take on a North African favourite, styled Marrakesh couscous (£9.25) – roast garlic, tomatoes and olives. Side dishes include roast garlic mash with olive oil (£2.70) and the mini power plate (£3.95), a salad of mixed leaves and organic freshly sprouted legumes and alfalfa. The key pudding is triple chocolate terrine with fresh berry coulis (£3.95) – just one taste will tell you why it stays on the menu.

The large outdoor area with its beautifully planted gardens helps make Fiction a summer favourite, but it is essential to book, whatever the season may be.

O's Thai Café

O's Thai Café is young, happy and fresh – just like O himself. With his economics, advertising and fashion-design background, and a staff who seem to be having fun, O brings a youthful zip to Thai cuisine. His café is fast and noisy, and the music is played at high volume. But that's not to say the food is anything less than excellent, and it's very good value too. Order from the comprehensive and well-explained menu or from the blackboard of specials, which runs down an entire wall.

Cost	£10–25

Address 10 Topsfield Parade, N8
☎ 020 8348 6898
Station Finsbury Park
Open Mon 6.30–11pm,
Tues–Sat noon–3pm &
6.30–11pm, Sun noon–3pm &
6.30–10.30pm
Accepts MasterCard, Visa
🌐 www.oscafesandbars.co.uk

Of the many starters you can do no better than order the special (£7.95 for two), which gives you a taster of almost everything. Satay is tasty, prawn toasts and spring rolls are as crisp as they should be, and paper-wrapped thin dumplings really do melt in the mouth. Tom ka chicken soup (£3.75) is hot and sharp, with lime leaf and lemongrass. Main courses include Thai red and green curries – the gaeng kiew, a spicy, soupy green curry of chicken and coconut cream (£5.50), is pungently moreish – as well as an interesting selection of specials such as yamneau, aka weeping tiger (£9.50) – sliced, spiced, grilled steak served on salad with a pungent Thai dressing. If you like noodles, order a pad mee si iew (£5.50), a stir-fry of vermicelli with vegetables, soy sauce, peanuts and the main ingredient of your choice: chicken, beef, pork, king prawn or bean curd. Puddings include khow tom mud – banana with sticky rice wrapped in banana leaf (£1.95), Thai ice cream (£2.50), and fruit fritters served with golden syrup and ice cream (£2.50). There is a wide and varied wine list, with Budweiser, Budvar, Gambrinus and Leffe beers on draught. O's does takeaway too.

If you're new to Thai food, O's is a good place to learn, as the staff are happy to explain how it all works and you can specify how hot you like your food. Most main courses are around £6, which makes for very good value, and all of them are served with a delightfully moulded mountain of rice, which is included in the price. They also offer a discount if you eat early and vacate your table by 8.30pm.

The Parsee

🍴 London has had an acclaimed Parsee chef for some years now. His name is Cyrus Todiwala and his main restaurant is Café Spice Namaste (see p.184). Since 2001, however, London has also had what may be the world's best Parsee restaurant (there have been murmurings about the other one in Bombay). Parsees are Zoroastrians who originally came to India from Persia, and in Indian society they seem to have specialized as surgeons and politicians. They are also renowned for their love of food – and for being the most demanding of customers. They start from the admirable standpoint that nothing beats home cooking and complain vehemently if everything is not exactly to their liking. They will be at home in this part of North London, and happy with Cyrus Todiwala's new restaurant.

Cost	£15–40

Address 34 Highgate Hill, N19
☎ 020 7272 9091
Station Archway
Open Mon–Sat 6–10.45pm
Accepts All major credit cards
🌐 www.theparsee.co.uk

The food here is very good. Honest, strong flavours; rich and satisfying. Start with the admirable home-style akoori on toast (£3.95) – splendid, spiced, scrambled egg; or the tarka na bhajia (£3.95) – light and delicious vegetable fritters; or maybe something from the grill such as marcha nay marina pug (£3.95/8.75) – these are chicken legs that have been marinated with crushed black pepper. Main courses include that most famous of Parsee dishes, the dhansak (£10.95), a rich dish of lamb and lentils served with a pulao flavoured with star anise and little crisp meatballs. Then there's the tareli machchi leel curry nay chawal (£10.50) – tilapia fillets served with a light green curry; or the gos ni curry nay chawal (£10.25), which is a richer-than-rich Parsee lamb curry made with roasted chickpeas, peanuts, cashew nuts and sesame seeds. The breads – rotli (£1.25 for two) – are very good, nutty and moreish. The vegetable dishes are good too: khattu mitthu stew (£3.75/7.25) seems to contain an entire market garden, and is a popular dish at Parsee weddings. Save room for the toffee apricot ice cream (£3.75), rich with concentrated Hunza apricots.

This is a friendly, small, "family" restaurant serving delicious and unfamiliar Indian food. An adventure well worth having.

Sosta

During the 1970s, Silvano Sacchi was at the helm of two of London's more fashionable eateries – the Barracuda (a smart Italian fish restaurant in Baker Street) and San Martino (an Italian tratt in St Martin's Lane). Having sold out to a plc, Sacchi retired to Italy with a bagful of money and happy memories. Just why he would want to return to the maelstrom of the London restaurant scene in the third millennium is a matter for conjecture, but the official party line is that he got bored with doing nothing, and encouraged by his friends' reports of exciting times and record business, decided to return and give it one more go. So he returned in triumph to Crouch End. His restaurant is called Sosta and sticks very firmly to the style that was popular in London during the 1970s – the food comes in large portions and makes no concessions to the modernist school of Italian cooking.

Cost	£12–35

Address 14 Middle Lane, N8
℡ 020 8340 1303
Station Highgate/Finsbury Park
Open Mon–Fri 6.30–10.30pm, Sat noon–3pm & 6.30–10.30pm, Sun noon–10.30pm
Accepts MasterCard, Visa

The antipasti range from insalata tricolore (£4.75) – a mozzarella, avocado and tomato salad; to a monster portion of bresaola (£6.25); or bruschetta (£3.50). Onwards to "primi" where you'll find pasta e fagioli alla Veneta (£3.95), a thick pasta and borlotti bean soup, and pasta dishes such as taglioni con gamberetti (£4.65), gnocchi di patate al dolcelatte (£4.65), and spaghetti rusticana (£4.45). "Secondi" offers five fish and five meat dishes. Orate e cozze in brodetto (£9.95) is sea bream and mussels steamed in a garlic fish broth. Then there's salsiccia al Soave con lenticche e puree di patate (£5.65) – good sausages, good lentils, good mash. Puds are sound: pears poached in Barolo (£2.75); panna cotta (£2.95); and "chef's speciality Tiramisiu" (£2.95). The wine list has some trad Italian bottles that appeal greatly, including a bottle of Masi Campofiorin 1997 (£19.95).

At Sosta the service is slick and the tables are close together. The huge pepper mill of the 1970s may have been replaced by a natty modernist Parmesan grater and the offer of a drizzle of home-made chilli oil from a giant bottle, but everyone is attentive in what now seems like an old fashioned way.

The Village Bistro

Having served French food of varying fashionability for decades, The Village Bistro is something of an institution in Highgate. You can almost forget you're in London here; all is quaint and countrified in this narrow Georgian house approached by a corridor off Highgate's main road. Inside can be a bit of a squeeze, and the decor is all chintzy curtains and crooked paintings, but any sense that you're sitting in an old aunt's living room is swept away by the food, which is Modern French. Presumably this combination of ancient and modern is exactly what hits the spot in Highgate, as this restaurant is, and has been, consistently successful. Downstairs, the windows peek out onto the hilly High Street, while a spindly, winding staircase leads upstairs to the smokers' floor.

Cost	£20–45

Address 38 Highgate High St, N6
☎ 020 8340 5165
Station Highgate/Archway
Open Mon–Sat noon–3pm & 6–11pm
Accepts All major credit cards

Come here hungry: sauces can be rich and dishes very filling. The menu, which changes every few months, includes a range of old stalwarts along with a sprinkling of more contemporary creations. A really tasty starter is deep-fried goat's cheese with dried tomatoes, rocket and green olive dressing (£6.25). Also good is the Parma ham with French beans, pear, soft-boiled egg and walnuts (£6.95). Traditionalists might opt for the fine French onion soup with cheese croutons (£3.95), or, in season, asparagus with Hollandaise sauce (£6.50). There's a good choice of main dishes, and always two specials – dishes like a panaché of seafood with Parmesan, lemon and olive oil (£13.50). For a well-judged mix of flavours and textures, go for the veal fillet with Madeira, wild mushrooms and parsnip purée (£14.50). Or you might try sauté of monkfish and king prawns in garlic butter on a crab and herb tartlette (£15.95), or maybe sirloin steak glazed with Stilton and green peppercorn sauce (£14.95).

Desserts (all £4.50) can be solid and formidable. The white chocolate parfait with dark chocolate truffle is not for anyone wearing tight clothing. The classic crème brûlée, and crêpe filled with vanilla ice cream and hot raspberry sauce, are wiser choices, although still satisfactorily self-indulgent. From Monday to Saturday there is a set lunch at £13.50 for two courses.

Holloway & Highbury

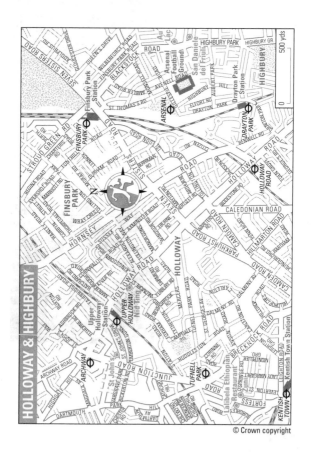

HOLLOWAY & HIGHBURY

© Crown copyright

Au Lac

Vietnamese restaurants in London tend to divide into two camps. On the one hand there is the spartan canteen – no frills, no nonsense and no concessions to non-Vietnamese speakers. And on the other there is a sprinkling of glossy, West End establishments that charge big bucks and would be puzzled if you wanted authenticity. Au Lac doesn't fall into either of these categories. For a start, it is hidden away in Highbury, and what is more, it is a genuinely family-run restaurant – the dining room is comfortable in an informal, shabby sort of way, there are knick-knacks on the walls, and the family cover all the bases from the kitchen to the front of house.

Cost	£8–25
Address	82 Highbury Park, N5
☎	020 7704 9187
Station	Arsenal
Open	Mon–Fri noon–2.30pm & 5.30–11pm, Sat & Sun 5.30–11pm
Accepts	MasterCard, Visa

Start with goi cuon (two for £2.20). These are soft rice-flour pancakes wrapped around crunchy veg and large grilled prawns, and they're fresh and light. Then there's goi tom (£6) – you get large steamed prawns, a small pot of hot and spicy sauce, and several large iceberg lettuce leaves. Take a leaf, add sauce and prawn, wrap, eat, enjoy. The deep-fried monkfish with garlic and chilli (£6) is very good. There are good soups, too. The noodle soups – pho, bun bo and tom hue – come in large portions. They are cheap and tasty, good for eating when alone. For a more sociable, sharing meal, try the chicken with lemongrass and chilli (£5). The noodles are also very good – pho xao do bien (£5.50) is a grand dish of stir-fried rice noodles with fresh herbs and seafood, providing a good combination of flavours and textures. Another very impressive dish is the "minced pork with aubergine in hot pot" (£6.50). Ordering this brings a small casserole whose contents appear almost black. Very dark, very rich, very tasty.

Lurking in the drinks section is "Vietnamese sake". This potion was the one thing from his homeland that the head of the household (now banished to the kitchen) pined for. So the family made it for him. This clear hooch is served warm, and tastes like dry-cleaning fluid. To enjoy it you would have to be very homesick indeed.

Lalibela Ethiopian Restaurant

The real Lalibela is a twelfth-century Ethiopian church carved in the shape of a cross from a huge outcrop of solid rock. Its namesake in Tufnell Park is remarkable for serving uncompromisingly authentic Ethiopian food and for its genuine understanding of hospitality. It has a slightly harassed but still laid-back feel that is a great comfort to the diner. And however ignorant of Ethiopian cuisine and customs you may be, pure ungilded hospitality shines through. The unwary can end up seated on low, carved, wooden seats around traditional low tables (so that you can eat with your hands). If your knee joints won't take that kind of punishment, plead for an ordinary table and resign yourself to dripping sauce down your front.

Cost	£12–34

Address 137 Fortess Rd, NW5
☏ 020 7284 0600
Station Tufnell Park
Open Mon–Sun
6pm–12.30am
Accepts All major credit cards
except Diners

Starters are few, but they banish any inkling you may have about being in an odd kind of curry house. The lamb samosas (£3.75) have very dry, papery pastry and a savoury, spicy filling – delicious. The Lalibela salad (£4) is potatoes and beetroot fried together with a spicy sauce and served hot. Main courses are served traditionally, that is to say as pools of sauce set out on a two-foot-diameter injera bread. Injera is cold, made from fermented sourdough, and thin. You tear off a piece and use it to pick up something tasty. Portions are small, which makes prices seem high. But the flavours are intense. If you prefer, you can have the dishes with rice or mashed potato. What goes on the injera? Wot, that's what. Doro wot (£6.50) is a piece of chicken and a hard-boiled egg in a rich sauce, while begh wot (£6.50) is lamb with a bit more chilli. Lalibela ketfo (£8) is savoury mince with amazing, highly spiced cottage cheese – delicious. King prawn special (£7) is prawns in a tomato, onion and chilli sauce.

Do try the Ethiopian traditional coffee (£5.50), which is not only delicious, but also something of a feast for the eyes. After parading a small wok full of smoking coffee beans through the restaurant, a waiter will bring it to you in a round-bottomed coffeepot on a plaited quoit.

Nid Ting

What are restaurants for? Some pundits would have you believe that restaurants are for posing in, some that their mission is to entertain. Nid Ting is a place that feeds people. Lots of them. And it feeds people well, serving good, unfussy Thai food. The dishes here have not been tamed to suit effete Western palates, and you'll get plenty of chilli heat and pungent fish sauce. You'll also get good value and brisk service – both of which obviously appeal, as the place is usually packed. This is a genuine neighbourhood restaurant at ease with its surroundings.

Cost	£8–20
Address	533 Holloway Rd, N19
⊤	020 7263 0506
Station	Archway
Open	Mon–Sat 6–11.15pm, Sun 6–10.15pm
Accepts	All major credit cards

The starters are neat platefuls of mainly fried food: chicken satay (£3.95) is sound, although the sauce is a bland one; a much better bet is the "pork on toasted" (£3.95) – this is a smear of rich, meaty paste on a disc of fried bread. The prawns tempura (£4.95) are large and crisp, and the peek ka yas sai (£3.95) is very successful – stuffed chicken wings, battered and deep fried. The menu then darts off into numerous sections: there are hot and sour soups, clear soups, salads, curries, stir fries, seafood, rice, noodle dishes and a long, long list of vegetarian dishes – all before you get to the Chef's Specials. From those specials, try the lamb Mussaman curry (£8.75), which is rich and good, made with green chillies and coconut milk. From the noodles, try pad see ew (£5.50), a rich dish made with thick ribbon noodles and your choice of chicken, beef or pork. As a side order, try the som tum (£4.50), which is a pleasingly astringent green papaya salad. Also worth noting is the pla muk kaprow (£6.95), a dish of squid with chilli, garlic and Thai basil; and the koong kra prow (£6.95), which is a dish of prawns that have been given the same treatment.

One of the commonest criticisms of Thai food is that it can be insubstantial, and that dishes can start out looking cheap but end up as pretty bad value when portion size is taken into account. This is not the case at Nid Ting. Here, the cooking is accomplished, and dishes arrive both immaculately presented and in man-sized helpings.

MEDITERRANEAN/PUB

St John's

Archway's unprepossessing Junction Road is an unlikely setting for this fine gastro-pub, where the emphasis is firmly on the gastro rather than on the pub. The food is broadly Mediterranean, with a passion for all things rich, earthy and flavoursome, and there's a real joie de vivre in the combinations of tastes, textures and colours. Not only that, the dining room, which lies beyond the pub itself, looks fabulous – all louche, junk-store glamour with its high, gold-painted ceiling, low chandeliers and plush banquettes. There's an open kitchen at one end of the room, while at the other a giant blackboard displays the long menu. You get lots of food here, so be sure to arrive hungry.

Cost	£12–35
Address	91 Junction Rd, N19
☎	020 7272 1587
Station	Archway
Open	Tues–Fri noon–3.30pm & 6.30–11pm, Sat noon–4pm & 6.30–11pm, Sun noon–4pm & 6.30–10.30pm
Accepts	All major credit cards

As an opening move, the friendly staff bring fresh white bread and bottles of virgin olive oil and balsamic vinegar. The menu changes day by day but you might find starters like smoked halibut with white and green bean and rocket salad, and tarragon dressing (£5.50). The food is robust and piled high on the plate. How about a warm salad of pigeon breast, black pudding, pancetta, quails' eggs and beetroot with mustard dressing (£5.75)? Or, on a simpler note, pea, ham and parsley soup with Parmesan croutons (£4)? Main courses range from the traditional – char-grilled rib-eye steak with roast tomatoes, chips, watercress and green peppercorn sauce (£13.50) – to the adventurous – seared swordfish, chermoula spices, roast red-pepper and herb couscous (£12). The fish is invariably good: perhaps roast dorade, sauté potatoes, spinach, caper, almond and parsley butter (£11). You'll need to take a breather before venturing into pud territory (all £4.25). The rhubarb and raspberry crumble with ginger ice cream is good, but the star turn must be the blissful strawberry and clotted cream fool with shortbread. The intelligent wine list includes a dozen by the glass, with a Cava at £4.

St John's gets more crowded and more convivial as the night goes on, but it is possible to have a dîner à deux; just make sure you're ready to be romantic by 7.30pm, when you've a chance of getting a table. You should book, whatever time you come.

San Daniele del Friuli

Highbury Park is a strange place to find a football club. Lots of grand, renovated houses, wide streets, trees and, just a stroll around the corner, there's the Arsenal. Perhaps that is why they are moving? Until then, don't attempt to go to San Daniele on match days, when it will be packed out with

Cost	£15–40
Address	72 Highbury Park, N5
ⓣ 020 7226 1609	
Station	Arsenal
Open	Mon–Sat noon–2.30pm
	& 6.30–10.45pm
Accepts	MasterCard, Visa

happy, very respectable, middle-class footie fans loading up on Italian grub. San Daniele opened in the summer of 1996, with a chef from Friuli – that bit of Italy in the extreme northeast around Trieste. The dining room is large and airy, and the service is family-restaurant style, both attentive and gracious. The dishes lean that way as well, being substantial and unfussy. The menu is a long one. So unless nostalgia gets the upper hand and you are swept away on a wave of desire for whitebait or insalata tricolore, pay special attention to the "altri Friuliani" (regional delicacies) and to the chef's specials.

The cooking here scales no modern gastronomic heights, and it is not cheap, but portions are large and the hospitality wholehearted. Simple things are well presented, like the vegetali grigliati (£4.50) – grilled vegetables with olive oil; the insalata di mare misto (£6) – a seafood salad; or the excellent prosciutto di San Daniele (£7), served plain or with melon. Or there may be pasticcio alla Friulana (£6.50), a lasagne made with speck and Asagio cheese. There are also risotto and pasta dishes from an imaginative specials board. For a main course you can choose between a dozen different Neapolitan pizzas (£5.50–7), fresh fish dishes and lots of old favourites. A huge portion of calves' liver (£11) comes in a classic butter and sage sauce and is accurately cooked to order. Scallopine di vitello (£8.50) is trad veal escalope and there are several options by way of sauce, including the classic Marsala and black pepper.

For pudding there is an old-fashioned tiramisù (£4), rich with alcohol and mascarpone – delightfully different from the fluffy, faffy fakes that are all the rage in the W-prefixed postcodes.

Zuni

(🍴) On the cover of the book matches, Zuni is described as a "South West" bar and grill. The proprietor is a lady from Los Angeles called Glynis Higgins who says that she was so disappointed in the quality of all things Tex-Mex in London that she determined

Cost	£12–36

Address 134 Fortess Rd, NW5
℗ 020 7428 0803
Station Tuffnell Park
Open Tues–Sun 7–11pm
Accepts MasterCard, Visa

to do better. Zuni is small (under 30 covers), bright and friendly. The walls are covered in a mix of moody sepia photographs of long dead Indian chiefs and bright arty posters of luminaries such as Georgia O'Keefe – this could only be an American restaurant. But whatever its provenance, the locals like it, and they can be seen in some numbers contentedly slurping Margaritas from oversize glasses.

This establishment is pretty much a one-woman band, and as a consequence you are seated, issued with a bowl of nachos plus a bowl of salsa and asked what you are going to drink before you have a chance to think. This strategy makes good sense because single-handed service can get a bit stretched at times. The starters are excellent. There's a decent rough-chopped guacamole (£4.25), and the roast red-pepper hummus (£3.75) is a rich and moreish dip. The duck taco (£5) is a bit of puzzle, and it should probably be called a duck burrito as it is made from a soft, floury tortilla. The cactus quesadillas (£4.50) are dodgy; cactus tastes like overcooked runner beans – certainly not worth air freighting from the desert. Mains include some American-style salads – chicken (£8.75), Caesar (£7.75) – plus burritos (£8.25–9.75), tacos (£8.50–9.50) and enchiladas (£9.25). There are a couple of specials, which can include a splendid traditional Mexican molé (£9.75), made with turkey. This is the famous sauce made with bitter chocolate, and it is very smooth. Puddings include a home-made pumpkin cheesecake (£4) – say no more. Zuni is an easy place to like, and as with most one-man-bands, you have to admire the effort and loving care expended by the proprietor.

You probably need to be American to appreciate the charm of a drink called "Cookies and cream" (£5.25) – Oreo cookies, double crème de cacao and cream, blended with ice.

Islington

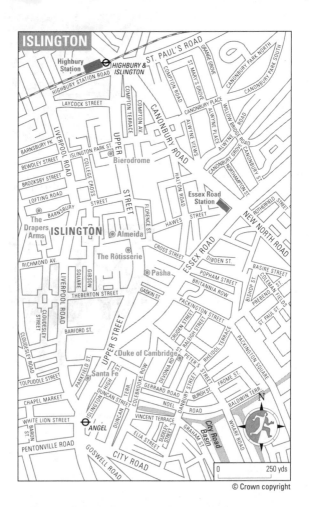

Almeida

It may be located in oh-so-trendy Islington, opposite the home base of the Almeida Theatre, and it may be yet another outpost of Sir Terence Conran's sprawling London empire, but spiritually Almeida is stuck in some faintly remembered rural France. The culinary mainspring behind this restaurant is Chris Galvin of the Orrery (see p.72), and with

Cost	£18–80
Address	30 Almeida St, N1
☎	020 7354 4777
Station	Highbury & Islington
Open	Mon–Sat noon–2.30pm & 6–11pm, Sun noon–3pm & 6–10pm
Accepts	All major credit cards

FRENCH

Almeida's able head chef Ian Wood (also an Orrery man) he has written a menu and opened a restaurant which is a distillation of all that is good about a wonderful, old-fashioned, gently familiar kind of French cooking and eating. On top of which, the large dining room is comfortable and the service is slick without being oppressive. There is a comprehensive wine list, with a good selection available by the glass.

This is a place to overdose on nostalgia. Soupe à l'oignon (£4.50) – the genuine article; six or twelve escargots à la Bourguignonne (£5/9) – garlic heaven; jambon cru, celeriac remoulade (£6); cuisses de grenouilles persillés (£8); oeufs en cocotte Grand'Mère (£4.50); and best of all, the trolley of charcuterie and rillettes (£10.50). This chariot is wheeled round to your table and you can pig out on well-made patés and rillettes to your heart's content. Mains carry the theme forward triumphantly: coq au vin (£14.50); steak au poivre (£19.50); confit de canard, pommes Sardalaises (£11); onglet aux echalottes (£11). Pukka pommes frites (£1.95). For pud there's the tantalizingly named "trolley of tarts" (£5.50), plus marquise au chocolat (£4.50) or fromage blanc à la crème (£4.50). With such a single-minded menu, Almeida could have ended up as something of a French resto theme park, but the kitchen is passionate about the classic dishes, and the mood ends up affectionate rather than reverential. Now wonder it is busy enough to make booking for dinner a prudent idea.

Lunchtime features the twin attractions of a much less crowded restaurant and a grand deal – £17.50 for three courses. There is also a pre-theatre deal: £14.50 for two courses, and £17.50 for three.

Bierodrome

Bierodrome is part of the Belgo empire (see p.32), and shares its emphasis on modernist and iconoclastic architecture. The long, low bar is a temple to beer, and with that beer you can eat if you wish. The menu introduces a change of pace from the other branches – yes, there is life after mussels! Here there are tartines (or smart snacks),

Cost	£7–55

Address 173–174 Upper St, N1; with branches
℡ 020 7226 5835
Station Highbury & Islington
Open Daily noon–midnight
Accepts All major credit cards
🌐 www.belgo.restaurants.co.uk

BELGIAN

along with steaks, lobsters, croquettes and frites. Surprisingly enough, the beeriness runs amok in the dessert section, where, as well as a sorbet made from cherry beer, there is an ice cream made with Leffe blond beer.

It is no surprise that when the Bierodrome first opened they found that the customers were walking off with the beer and wine list. It makes stunning reading, with more than seventy beers to pore over and ultimately pour out. At random, consider: a banana beer – 25cl (£2.55); a very strong beer – Kasteel tripel 11% 35cl (£4.95); and a pretty expensive beer – Gulden Draak 75cl 10.5% (£9.50). As you work your way through your delicious malty glassful, what you will need is some food. Croquettes make good starters: try the Trappist cheese with pic-calilli (£4.50), or the onion tart (£3.95), made with Trappist cheese and Chimay beer, and served on a bed of rocket. Salads are tasty: Liègeoise (£4.95) teams bacon, tomatoes, French beans, onions, boiled egg and new potatoes. Then there are the famous Belgo mussel pots: a kilo pot costs £9.95 and can be had marinière, Provençale, Dijon or even Congo – the latter cooked with creamed coconut and lemongrass. Or there's half a spit-roast chicken with frites (£7.95). Steaks include a 6oz sirloin with frites, salad, tomatoes and garlic butter (£10.95). There are lunch bargains, with a main course for £5, or two courses for £5.95.

The atmosphere in this place is much as you'd expect with such a raft of strong beers on offer. And how about the huge Nebuchadnezzars, which contain fifteen litres of La Veille Bon Secours at a thought-pro-voking £635 a pop? They do not sell those quite so quickly as the others, but you may still need to order ahead!

The Drapers Arms

(🍴) In October 2001, Paul McElhinny and Mark Emberton took over the Drapers Arms in Barnsbury. The Drapers started life as an old-fashioned double-fronted Georgian pub and that is pretty much how it has remained, despite the refurb. There's a bar downstairs and a dining room upstairs, and out the back is a large walled yard which has been paved over and kitted out with tables and chairs, and a pair of huge awnings in case of rain. This "extra dining room" seats another 45 hungry customers, and when the weather is sunny it is a thoroughly charming place. The food at the Drapers is good, much better than standard gastro-pub fare, and that is reflected in the restaurant-ish pricing levels.

Cost	£7–35

Address 44 Barnsbury St, N1
ⓣ 020 7619 0348
Station Highbury & Islington
Open Mon–Fri noon–3pm & 6–10.30pm, Sat noon–4pm & 6–10.30pm, Sun noon–4pm & 6–9pm
Accepts All major credit cards except AmEx

MODERN BRITISH/PUB

The menu changes to reflect seasons and markets, but starters may include a pea, ham and mint soup (£3.80); seared squid, chorizo and artichoke salad (£6); and a chicken liver and foie gras parfait with sourdough and pickles (£5) – this is a skilfully made dish, the parfait light, fluffy and ungreasy. Or how about warm asparagus, smoked eel and lemon butter (£7.50)? The asparagus is cooked perfectly and left with some bite to it, and the eel is a magnificent, well-flavoured, carefully smoked fish. This dish ends up more than the sum of its parts. Mains range from lemon risotto with fennel, soft herbs and crème fraîche (£8.50), and a monster salmon and cod fishcake with spinach and tartare sauce (£9.50), to the laconically named Spring cabbage and bacon (£10.50). This dish could also have been called a smoked pork pot au feu; large chunks of lean smoked bacon are simmered in a pot with fresh herbs, whole shallots, cabbage and carrots. Splendid. Another treat is the roast veal chop with blue cheese gratin, beetroot and baby spinach salad (£14) – a nice firm chop helped out by the tang of cheese. The chips (£2.50) are stellar. Puds are sound, and sensibly the kitchen sticks to favourites.

The sandwiches and bar snacks also punch their weight – grilled steak and Dijon mayonnaise (£6.20); or toasted chicken BLT (£5.50).

Duke of Cambridge

In the canon of organic, things don't get much holier than this, the first gastro-pub to be certified by the Soil Association. Game and fish are either wild or caught from sustainable resources, and the 40-strong wine list is 95 percent organic. As "organic" becomes every supermarket's favourite adjective it is hard to remember that it was tough going in the beginning, and the Duke was there at the start. There's a small, bookable restaurant at the back, but most diners prefer to share the tables in the noisy front bar – the Duke is for the gregarious as well as the organic battalions.

Cost	£15–35

Address 30 St Peter's St, N1
☎ 020 7359 3066
Station Angel
Open Mon–Fri 12.30–3pm & 6.30–10.30pm, Sat 12.30–3.30pm & 6.30–10.30pm, Sun 12.30–3.30pm & 6.30–10pm
Accepts All major credit cards
🖥 www.singhboulton.co.uk

The blackboard menu changes twice daily and is commendably short; you order from the bar. Robust bread with good olive oil and grey sea salt is served while you wait. Starters may include white bean and chilli soup with greens (£4), or chicken liver pâté with pickles, relish and toast (£5). Main courses are an eclectic bunch: a char-grilled whole grey mullet may be partnered with sweetened red cabbage and couscous (£9), while seared scallops come with sautéed potatoes, bacon and spinach (£10.50) – tasty and fulfilling. Roast loin of lamb is stuffed with tapenade and served with pepperonata and polenta chips (£14). Portions are serious, a million miles away from the mean-spirited bar snacks of many old-style pubs. There are vegetarian choices too, such as a potato and mushroom pie with mixed leaves (£7.50). Puddings include plum and apple crumble – with custard, of course (£5), and a chocolate, prune and praline cake with crème fraîche (£5). The wines are well chosen and varied, with a Greek Domaine Spiropoulos Porfyros (£16), and a New Zealand Te Aria Malbec (£21).

There are also many unusual bottled beers and non-alcoholic drinks, all organic. Connoisseurs will seek out the deliciously light and refreshing Eco Warrior ale, or the Freedom Brewery's organic Pilsener. But the zenith of the beer list must be Singhboulton ale. The Pitfield Brewery brews this rich, organic beer exclusively for the Duke of Cambridge, and it is named after the owners, Geetie Singh and Esther Boulton.

Pasha

🍴 If you picture Turkish food as heavy and oil-slicked, think again. Pasha is dedicated to producing fresh, light, authentic Turkish food that's suited to modern tastes. Dishes are made with virgin olive oil, fresh herbs, strained yoghurts and fresh ingredients prepared daily. Pasha doesn't look like a traditional Turkish restaurant either, being open and airy with only the odd brass pot for decoration. The management describes it as "Modern Ottoman". It has clearly adapted well to its Upper Street location – so well, in fact, that the wine list offers a spritzer for £2.95.

Cost £15–30

Address 301 Upper St, N1
☎ 020 7226 1454
Station Angel
Open Mon–Thurs noon–3pm
& 6–11.30pm, Fri & Sat
noon–3pm & 6pm–midnight,
Sun noon–11pm
Accepts All major cards
except Switch

For anyone new to Turkish cooking, the menu is a delight. Dishes are clearly described so that you can try them on a no-risk basis. Staff are helpful and will encourage you to eat in Turkish style with lots of small "meze" dishes. There are set menus (minimum two people) of £10.95 for thirteen meze and £17.95 for a Pasha Feast, which gives diners ten meze plus main courses, dessert and coffee. Meze may include hummus, tarama, cacik, kisir (a splendid bulghur wheat concoction), falafel, courgette fritters, meatballs and a host of others. Other noteworthy starters include Albanian liver (£3.95), which is lamb's liver served with finely chopped onions and sumac. Main courses are more familiar but the choice is better than usual. Try kilic baligi (£10.95) – fillet of swordfish marinated in lime, bay leaf and herbs, and served with rice; Pasha kofte (£7.50) – the standard minced lamb kebab, but well seasoned and well presented; or istim kebab (£8.95) – roasted aubergine filled with cubes of lamb, green peppers and tomatoes with rice; or yogurtlu iskender (£8.45) – a trio of shish, kofte and chicken on pitta bread soaked in fresh tomato sauce with fresh herbs and topped with yoghurt. Though meat undeniably dominates the menu, there are five vegetarian and three fish selections. Puddings include the usual Turkish stickies but once again are light and freshly made.

Wines are priced fairly, and there is Efes beer from Turkey (£2.50), or that powerful spirit raki (£2.95), for a tongue-numbing blast of the real Near East.

The Rôtisserie

The Rôtisserie is buzzing, brightly painted and unpretentious, with a commitment to quality underlying both food and service. Its South African owner makes regular trips to Scotland to lean on the farm gate and make small talk about Aberdeen Angus steers (which, if they did but know it, will soon be visiting his grill), and his menu's claim, "Famous for our steaks", seems well earned. The kitchen also frets about the quality of their chips, which is no bad thing, as the classic combination of a well-grilled steak with decent French fries and Béarnaise sauce is one of life's little luxuries.

Cost	£15–30

Address 134 Upper St, N1; with branches
℡ 020 7226 0122
Station Highbury & Islington/ Angel
Open Mon & Tues 6–11pm, Wed–Fri noon–3pm & 6–11pm, Sat noon–11pm, Sun noon–10pm
Accepts All major credit cards
🖳 www.rotisserie.co.uk

Rôtisserie starters are sensibly simple: a good Caesar salad (£3.95); tiger prawns peri peri (£4.95); grilled mushrooms with garlic and Parmesan (£3.95); char-grilled spare ribs (£4.25). Having brushed aside these preliminaries, on to the steaks, all of which are Scottish Aberdeen Angus: 225g rump (£12.95); 300g sirloin (£14.95); 200g fillet (£14.95); 400g T-bone (£16.95). All are carefully chosen, carefully hung, and carefully cooked. All of them (and all other main courses) come with a good-sized bowl of rather good French fries. If you don't want steak, try one of the other rôtisserie items, such as the French corn-fed chicken leg and thigh (£5.95); or the wonderful spit-roasted Barbary duck (£12.95) – half a duck with fruit chutney. Or perhaps "simply sausages: with creamed mash and onion gravy" (£8.95). The rest of the menu covers the bases for non-meat eaters. There's a grilled fish of the day (£11.95), or grilled Mediterranean vegetable skewers with spiced rice (£8.95). Puddings (all £3.95) are sound, and range from pecan pie to the ubiquitous tiramisù, banoffi pie and home-made ice cream.

The South African influence is a constant lurking presence behind these chunks of grilled meat. Occasional specials feature all manner of exotic meats, and sometimes you can opt for "monkey gland" sauce, which is rich and dark, and made to a secret recipe rumoured to include both Coca-Cola and Mrs Ball's Chutney.

Santa Fe

(logo) Two words are banned at Santa Fe. They are Tex and Mex. The chef (one Rocky Durham – a name which sounds so appropriate that it must be his own) would like the cuisine at Santa Fe to be described as "American Mexican", presumably to distance his creations from the T and M words, and from the strange southwestern dishes that feature on some London menus. The restaurant

Cost	£20–45

Address 75 Upper St, N1
☎ 020 7288 2288
Station Angel
Open Mon–Fri noon–10.30pm, Sat noon–11pm, Sun noon–10pm
Accepts All major credit cards except Diners

is quiet at lunchtimes but gets very busy in the evenings and at weekends. Symbols are used to classify dishes as hot, healthy low fat, and vegetarian.

Lovers of the Margarita (£4.15–20) will be able to indulge, as there are eleven different versions on offer, together with nineteen classic cocktails (£4.15–6.25) and beers like Negra Modelo (£2.95). You are encouraged to plan your meal over drinks and tortilla chips with salsa (£2.95). Start with a flauta – a warm, crisp tortilla – filled with roast chicken, Jack cheese and pico de gallo salsa (£3.95); or shrimp ceviche (£3.95) – tiger prawns marinated in a zesty vegetable relish with lime and chilli. Or try five different starters in a Santa Fe sampler (£9.95). Tastes are fresh and clean, but dishes are hot unless you specify otherwise. For mains, try Santa Fe steak and fries (£12.95), or rack of lamb adovado (£12.95). The steak is spice-rubbed and served with fresh salsa and chilli-dusted chips; the lamb is chilli-marinated, grilled and served with chilli-mashed potatoes and dried fruit chutney. The different chillies bring out the flavours well and make dishes very moreish. It is possible to escape the chilli, but this isn't the place for anyone who likes bland food. There's also a southwest Caesar salad (£4/5.75), served with tortilla chips and, yes you guessed it, a chilli-spiked dressing. Puddings include Santa Fe cheesecake (£3.50), which comes with cinnamon-spiced whipped cream, and a very rich brownie with canela ice cream (£3.65). There are separate lunch and dinner menus, lunch featuring some lighter and more wrap-based dishes.

Santa Fe is a great venue for groups who prefer cocktails and beer to wine, and who like their food chilli-spicy. Quiet and mild it isn't.

Maida Vale & Kilburn

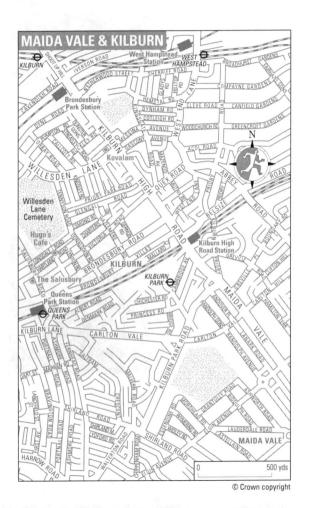

MAIDA VALE & KILBURN

KILBURN

West Hampstead Station

WEST HAMPSTEAD

Brondesbury Park Station

Kovalam

Willesden Lane Cemetery

Hugo's Café

The Salusbury

Queens Park Station

QUEENS PARK

KILBURN

Kilburn High Road Station

KILBURN PARK

MAIDA VALE

0   500 yds

© Crown copyright

Hugo's Café

In 2001 the Organic Café was renamed Hugo's Cafe. But it would take a very perceptive person to pinpoint any differences other than the name. The "mission statement" ticks all the right boxes: organic; seasonal; local produce; non-endangered fish; traditional methods; eco-friendly practices. This place is still a genuine neighbourhood

Cost   £17–35

Address 21–25 Lonsdale Rd, NW6
℡ 020 7372 1232
Station Queens Park
Open Daily 9.30am–11pm
Accepts MasterCard, Visa
🖳 www.organiccafe.co.uk

BRITISH

gem in a quiet, semi-private road. When it is too cold to enjoy one of the pavement tables, enter instead the largish yellow-painted dining room, decorated with twisted fig branches and reclaimed chicken-wire light fittings, and relax.

The menu changes sporadically and is divided traditionally into starters, mains and puds, with the addition of one-course dishes consisting of salads and pastas. But you can mix and match as you wish. Vegetarian choices are exceptionally good, but there is plenty for meat eaters as well. The cooking is reasonably classical and well grounded, with little that is unnecessarily fancy. Expect a couple of soups, pumpkin and coconut (£4.50), perhaps, or an antipasti cold meat platter (£6.50). Or almond pesto galette with citrus confit (£5.50). Thereafter there are three main sections: veggie mains, fish mains and meat mains. Mushroom risotto with rocket and truffle oil (£9.80) vies for attention with pan-fried fillet of bream with ginger and spring onion salsa on green pea mash with purple sprouting broccoli (£13.50). Cumin-spiced rump of lamb with roast vegetables, green beans and cinnamon jus (£13.50) competes with a stunning steak – organic Welsh char-grilled 8oz rib-eye steak, served with potato chips and leaf salad (£14.80). Puddings (£4.80) are on the heavy side: crumble with double cream; sticky toffee pudding; bread-and-butter pudding. The drinks list is short, but there is a range of wines, beers, spirits and juices.

Most of the customers (many of whom are families) are regulars. There is no music to disturb animated conversations (except for occasional jazz nights) and service is informal but efficient. Lunchtime is brunchtime.

Kovalam

In the 1960s and 1970s, Willesden Lane was something of a magnet for curry lovers, as it boasted a couple of London's first authentic South Indian vegetarian establishments. These places shocked diners, who at that time were "curry and chips at closing time" sort of folk, by serving cheap and honest veggie food. Now Willesden Lane is no longer the cutting edge of curry, but that did not dissuade some South Indian entrepreneurs from taking over the curry house at number 12 at the beginning of 2001, and relaunching it as "Kovalam – South Indian cuisine".

Cost	£10–25

Address 12 Willesden Lane, NW6
℡ 020 7625 4761
Station BR West Hampstead/ Brondesbury Park
Open Mon–Thurs & Sun noon–2.30pm & 6–11.15pm, Fri & Sat noon–2.30pm & 6–11.45pm
Accepts MasterCard, Visa

Kovalam is a brightly lit if traditionally decorated restaurant where the best dishes are the specials rather than the curry-house staples that creep onto the list. So think authentic and order accordingly. Start with the ghee-roast masala dosa (£4.95), which is large, crisp and buttery, and has a suitably chilli-hot potato heart. Ordering the cashew nut pakoda (£2.95) brings a good, big helping of the deep-fried nuts. The paripu vada with chutney (£1.90) are very good – crisp lentil cakes with good, coconutty chutney. For your main courses, look closely at the vegetable dishes and the specials: aviyal (£4.25) is creamy with coconut; kaya thoran (£2.50) is green bananas with grated coconut, shallots and mustard. The koonthal masala (£5.25) is a "worth trying" – it's squid in a very rich sauce that has been sharpened with tamarind. Also try the aaterechi fry (£4.95) – dry-fried cubes of lamb with onion, curry leaves and black pepper; it's very tender and very tasty. Or perhaps the kadachachka kootan (£3.90), which is a dish of curried breadfruit, heavy with coconut? The breads are good, as are the scented plain rices – lemon (£1.95) and coconut (£1.95).

Do not be fooled by the terminology of the menu. Aaterechi Madras sounds authentic, but aaterechi is just a South Indian word for lamb, and this is our old friend, meat Madras, in disguise. In fact, the menu includes a good many curry house dishes masquerading under new, "authentic" names.

The Salusbury

On the surface, the Salusbury is a straightforward pub in the middle of a parade of shops. It's fun and friendly, and clearly a home from home for a table-hopping crowd who all seem to know one another. To get to the restaurant, you shoulder your way through the packed bar to find a quieter room filled with the kind of tables your mum had in her living room, stripped and scrubbed, with a display of eclectic art lining the walls.

Cost	£16–35

Address 50–52 Salusbury Rd, NW6
℡ 020 7328 3286
Station Queens Park
Open Mon 7–10.15pm, Tues-Sat 12.30–3.30pm & 7–10.15pm, Sun 12.30–3.30pm & 7–10pm
Accepts MasterCard, Visa

The excellent and varied menu follows a mainly modern Italian theme rather than the more predictable Modern British bias of so many gastro-pubs. Starters (and a wave of dishes that could either be starters or mains) may include sautéed prawns with chilli and garlic (£7/10.50); Tuscan lentil soup (£4); pan-fried asparagus with egg and pangrattato (£7); papardelle with prawns and radicchio (£7.50/9.50); or langoustine risotto (£7/9.50). There's a practical emphasis on pasta and risotto. More mainstream main courses include sea bass cartoccio with spring vegetables (£12.50); cuttlefish nero with saffron mash (£10); roast Pyrenees milk-fed lamb (£15); roast leg of duck with salsa peverada (£10); and rib-eye steak with roast tomatoes, black olives and capers (£10.50). Moving on to pud territory, Amaretto, ricotta and almond pudding (£3.95) vies with sgroppina (£3.95) – a soft lemon sorbet doused in grappa – and pure chocolate tart (£3.95). The wine list is not large, but it is well chosen, and runs from a Chilean merlot (£11.50) to Mersault, Miche Bouzereau 2000 (£38.50). Bread and olive oil are served while you wait, and most of the starters can be had as main courses, though with portions sized the way they are, you would be unlikely to miss the extra.

The Salusbury serves a highly critical crowd with excellent food in stimulating surroundings. If there's one niggle, it's that portion sizes can be daunting. In Yorkshire they call it being "over-faced", but if sound, Italian-accented cooking coupled with excellent value is what rings your bell, you'll like the Salusbury a lot.

St John's Wood & Swiss Cottage

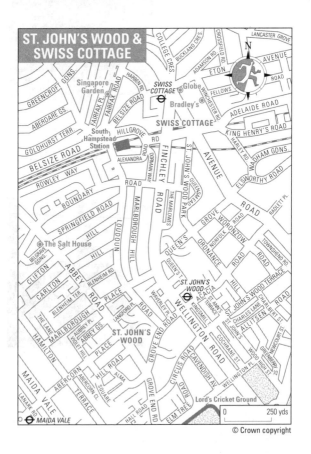

ST. JOHN'S WOOD & SWISS COTTAGE

© Crown copyright

0 — 250 yds

Bradley's

Bradley's, tucked away in a side street behind Swiss Cottage, is hard to find – and you get the impression that the regular clientele would prefer to keep the secret to themselves. The food here is pretty impressive, but that's not all. The atmosphere is warm and inviting, the menu covers and (metal) plates are probably the heaviest in London, and the loos are definitely a must-visit. All of which forms a good backdrop for chef-proprietor Simon Bradley's cooking and presentation. Dishes revolve around a combination of fresh ingredients and are served with a view to making the most of the visual appeal. They can look terrific.

Cost	£15–40

Address 25 Winchester Rd, NW3
℡ 020 7722 3457
Station Swiss Cottage
Open Mon–Fri & Sun noon–3pm & 6–11pm, Sat 6–11pm
Accepts All major credit cards

MODERN BRITISH

The menu works on a prix-fixe basis. Lunch costs £14 for three courses, rising to £18 (or £15 for two courses) on Sunday, when you also get a free aperitif. Dinner costs £22/27, all with mercifully few supplements. Starters range from char-grilled squid with warm potato salad and caper vinaigrette; to pan-fried ox tongue with roasted Jerusalem artichoke and beetroot; or goat's cheese ravioli with oven-dried tomatoes and oyster mushrooms; or a classic Mediterranean fish soup with aioli and croutons. Mains are along straightforward lines: lemon sole fillets with braised leeks, mushroom duxelles and potato gallette; pan-fried scallops with crab risotto; vegetable pot au feu with basil tortellini; venison haunch with braised red cabbage and mustard spätzle; roasted monkfish with braised split yellow peas and crispy pancetta; confit leg and pan-fried loin of rabbit with prunes and potato dumplings. These are enlightened dishes that mix tried and tested combinations of ingredients with flair. Puddings continue the theme: there's a fine apple tart with baked apple ice cream; a blood orange and Campari sorbet with chocolate tuille; and sticky date and ginger pudding with vanilla ice cream.

Bradley's extensive wine list includes some unusual and higher-priced New World wines that can be hard to find. A lively but full-flavoured and biscuity Veuve Delaroy champagne is good value at £29.95, making Bradley's a fine venue for a celebration dinner.

Globe

In 2002 it was out with the bright blue and yellow and in with chocolate and lilac at the Globe, and the private dining room was transformed into a private members' bar, membership of which also gives an edge when it comes to booking tables in the restaurant. This will probably suit the strong local following, as there has always been a clubbish atmosphere at this friendly, buzzy place where the food is based on an accomplished meld of modern and traditional.

Cost	£15–30

Address 100 Avenue Rd, NW3
☎ 020 7722 7200
Station Swiss Cottage
Open Mon & Sat 6–11pm,
Tues–Fri noon–2.30pm &
6–11pm, Sun noon–3pm &
7–10pm
Accepts All major credit cards
except Diners
🌐 www.globerestaurant.co.uk

Among the starters you may find warm duck confit salad with hoisin dressing (£5.50), or tomato, feta and black olive stack with basil oil (£4.50). There may be something simple such as a chicken Caesar salad with crispy bacon, or something colourful like terrine of tuna with sweet, white and purple potatoes, and saffron piccalilli (£4.50). Main courses may include fillet of Scottish beef with Pont Neuf potatoes, pea puree and fried quail's egg (£14.95); pan-fried sea bass with sage tagliatelle and vanilla sauce (£13.95); roast cod on Savoy cabbage with red wine, baby onion and bacon sauce (£12.95); or pan-fried duck breast with Dauphinoise potatoes, thyme jus and crispy leeks (£12.95). Vegetarians are pretty well treated here: perhaps a tomato and mozzarella risotto with green herb pesto and Parmesan wafer (£5.95/11.95), or toasted bruschetta with char-grilled Mediterranean vegetables (£10.95)? Puddings include the ubiquitous crème brûlée, here with chocolate-dipped banana (£4.50), and a mango sorbet with black pepper tuille (£4.50). But the star of the show must be the warm vanilla risotto with sable biscuits and gooseberries (£4.50).

Globe is built like a conservatory, with a glass roof and sliding doors that pull open, and an open-front courtyard for alfresco dining. The lunch menu follows closely on the heels of the dinner menu with many overlapping dishes and a few extra, simpler platefuls. Overall, the lunch menu prices are a pound or so cheaper than the evening prices quoted.

The Salt House

The Salt House combines corner pub, bar, restaurant and flower stall. There is a paved area set back from the road with benches and tables for the few alfresco dining days, the restaurant is reached through a large pub-style bar, and the whole has a relaxed friendliness where women on their own can feel quite at home. The Salt House is part of the Adam Robinson stable of restos (he is proprietor of The Chiswick), and Lee Masters, the chef here, follows the style that has found such favour with Chiswickians. The cuisine is based on what's fresh and in season, prepared simply and with a supporting cast designed to bring out the best in the main players. It is no surprise, therefore, that the menu changes daily according to what is best at the markets.

Cost	£22–50

Address 63 Abbey Rd, NW8
℡ 020 7328 6626
Station St John's Wood
Open Mon–Fri noon–3pm & 6.30–10.30pm, Sat & Sun noon–4pm & 7–10.30pm
Accepts All major credit cards except Diners

BRITISH/PUB

The food is all carefully cooked, well presented and unfussy. Starters may include the simple – French onion soup (£4) – as well as more complex offerings like deep-fried sole with black bean dressing and coriander (£5.50), or a straightforward salad of chicory, walnuts, apple and Cashel blue (£5.50), which contrasts with a technically difficult rabbit and foie gras terrine served with toast and chutney (£6.75). Main courses also appeal: Spanish fish stew comes with saffron potatoes (£10.75); calf's liver comes with semolina gnocchi and sage (£10). Or there may be roast wood pigeon with caramelized baby-onion tart and truffle oil (£10.50). There's also a super trad option for two: rib of beef, chips and field mushrooms (£28) – how very appealing. Puddings include blood-orange jelly with clotted cream (£3.95); rhubarb fool and shortbread (£3.75) – pleasantly tart and creamy at the same time; and, for the unreconstructed sweet tooth, a chocolate and almond torte (£3.95).

The food here is that superb combination of simple and stylish, the service is attentive and friendly, and there's a well-chosen wine list with a welcome absence of extravagant prices. But the real stars at the Salt House are the customers. Everyone seems to be enjoying themselves, and the mood is infectious.

Singapore Garden

🍴 Singapore Garden is a busy restaurant – don't even think of turning up without a reservation – and performs a cunning dual function. Half the cavernous dining room is filled with well-heeled, often elderly family groups from Swiss Cottage and St John's Wood, treating the restaurant as their local Chinese and consuming crispy duck in pancakes, moneybag chicken and but-

Cost	£15–35

Address 83a Fairfax Rd, NW6
℡ 020 7328 5314
Station Swiss
Cottage/Finchley Road
Open Daily noon–2.45pm &
6–10.45pm
Accepts All major credit cards
🌐 www.singaporegarden.com

terfly prawns. The other customers, drawn from London's Singaporean and Malaysian communities, are tucking into the squid blachan and the Teochew braised pig's trotters. So there are cocktails with parasols and there is Tiger beer. But it's always busy, and the food is interesting and good.

Start with a chiew yim soft shell crab (£6.50), which is lightly fried with garlic and chillies rather than annihilated in the deep fryer, like the fresh crab fried in the shell (£15), which does offer exceptional crispy bits. If you're feeling adventurous, follow with a real Singapore special – the Teochew braised pig's trotter (£10), which brings half a pig's worth of trotters slow-cooked in a luxurious, black, heart-stoppingly rich gravy. Or try the claypot prawns and scallops (£12), which delivers good, large, crunchy prawns and a fair portion of scallops, stewed with lemongrass and fresh ginger on glass noodles. Very good indeed. From the Malaysian list you might pick a daging curry (£6.75) – coconutty, rich and not especially hot. You must also try the mee goreng (£5.50), because this is how this noodle dish should be, a meal in itself.

At the bottom of the menu you'll find the "healthy alternative" known as Steamboat (£31.50 per person, for a minimum of two). This is a kind of party game. Eager participants drop tasty pieces of fresh meat and seafood into a cauldron of broth, which bubbles away at the table, then experience agonies of frustration when they find that they haven't the dexterity to fish them out with chopsticks.

Stoke Newington

STOKE NEWINGTON

0   500 yds

Stoke Newington Station

Rasa Travancore

Clissold Park

Rasa

STOKE NEWINGTON CHURCH ST

Anglo Anatolyan

DUMONT RD

N

KYNASTON RD

STOKE NEWINGTON

EVERING ROAD

BARBAULD RD

AMHURST ROAD

BEATTY RD

WALFORD RD

FOWDEN RD

BRIGHTON RD

FARLEIGH ROAD

PALATINE RD

ALLEN ROAD

PRINCE GEORGE RD

BELGRADE RD

HOWARD

PRINCESS MAY R

MATTHIAS ROAD

BARRETT'S GR

ARCOLA ST

POET'S RD

PELLERIN RD

FERNTOWER RD

MILLARD CL

PYRLAND RD

ALVINGTON

BERESFORD RD

MILDMAY ROAD

SANDRINGHAM RD

GROSVENOR AVE

Dalston Kingsland Station

MILDMAY   GROVE NORTH

MILDMAY GROVE SOUTH

RIDLEY ROAD

© Crown copyright

Anglo Anatolyan

The food is sound at the Anglo Anatolyan, the bills are small, and the tables so crowded together that you get to meet all the other diners. But the most intriguing feature of the restaurant is the large and impressive royal crest engraved in the glass of the front door: under it an inscription reads, "By Appointment to Her Majesty Queen Elizabeth II, Motor Car Manufacturers". Why? Do the Windsors slip up to Stoke Newington when they feel a new Daimler coming on? Predictably, asking the waiters for provenance doesn't help much: they look at you seriously and confide that they "got the door secondhand".

Cost	£8–20

Address 123 Stoke Newington
Church St, N16
℡ 020 7923 4349
Station BR Stoke Newington
Open Mon–Fri 5pm–midnight,
Sat & Sun 1pm–midnight
Accepts MasterCard, Visa

Royal warrants aside, the food at the Anglo Anatolyan is usually pretty decent. The bread in particular is amazing: large, round, flat loaves about two inches deep, cut into chunks, soft in the middle and crisp on the outside; it is baked at home by a local Turkish woman and a far cry from the flat, hard, mass-produced pitta pockets of the supermarkets. To accompany it, start with ispanak tarator (£3.15), which is spinach in yoghurt with garlic, and a tremendous, coarse tarama (£2.95). And sigara borek (£3.45) – crisp filo pastry filled with cheese and served hot. And arnavut cigeri (£4.15) – cubes of fried lamb's liver. Dine mob-handed so that you can try more starters. The main courses are more easily summarized: sixteen ways with lamb, one with quails, two with chicken, one with prawn, and two vegetarian dishes. Kaburga tarak (£6.75) is crisp, tasty lamb spare ribs; iskender kebab (£7.75) is fresh doner on a bed of cubed bread, topped with yoghurt and tomato sauce; kasarli beyti (£7.75) is minced lamb made into a patty with cheese and grilled. They are all pretty good.

Like all the Turkish restaurants in this end of town, this is a very laissez-faire kind of place and standards can vary from visit to visit, but when you've eventually had your fill you'll be presented with a handwritten bill, at the bottom of which is printed "Another cheap night out". This, for once, is simply the truth.

Rasa

🍴 Rasa has built up a formidable reputation for outstanding South Indian vegetarian cooking. In fact, when diners stop arguing as to whether Rasa is the best Indian vegetarian restaurant in London, they usually go on to discuss whether it is the best vegetarian restaurant full stop. As well as great food, the staff are friendly and helpful, and the atmosphere is uplifting. Inside, everything is pink (napkins, tablecloths, walls), gold ornaments dangle from the ceiling, and a colourful statue of Krishna playing the flute greets you at the entrance. Rasa's proprietor and the majority of the kitchen staff come from Cochin in South India. As you'd expect, booking is essential.

Cost	£12–30

Address 55 Stoke Newington Church St, N16
☎ 020 7249 0344
Station BR Stoke Newington
Open Mon–Fri 6–11pm, Sat & Sun noon–2.30pm & 6–11pm
Accepts All major credit cards
🌐 www.rasarestaurants.com

This is one occasion when the set meal – or "feast" (£15) – may be the best, as well as the easiest, option. The staff take charge and select what seems like an endless succession of dishes for you. But, however you approach a Rasa meal, everything is a taste sensation. Even the pappadoms are a surprise: try the selection of the crispy things served with six home-made chutneys (£3) – quite simply, a revelation. If you're going your own way, there are lots of starters to choose from. Mysore bonda (£2.50) is delicious, shaped like a meatball but made of potato spiced with ginger, coriander and mustard seeds. Kathrikka (£2.50) is slices of aubergine served with fresh tomato chutney. The main dishes are just as imaginative. Beet cheera pachadi (£3.75) is a colourful beetroot curry, zingy and tasty with yoghurt and coconut; moru kachiathu (£3.85) combines mangoes and green bananas with chilli and ginger. Or go for a dosa – paper-thin crisp pancakes folded in half and packed full with a variety of goodies; masala dosa (£4.75) is filled with potatoes and comes with lentil sauce and coconut chutney. Puddings sound hefty but arrive in mercifully small portions; the payasam (£2.25), a "temple feast", blends dhal with jaggery (raw sugar) and coconut milk. A fine end to a meal.

The word rasa has many meanings in Sanskrit: "flavour", "desire", "beauty", "elegance". It can also mean "affection" – something that the whole of northeast London feels for this wonderful restaurant.

Rasa Travancore

Rasa Travancore is painted glow-in-the-dark Rasa pink, just like the original Rasa which faces it across the roadway. It shows a certain amount of chutzpah on the part of any restaurateur to open a new branch opposite head office, but Das Sreedharan has never been shy. Rasa Travancore moves the spotlight onto a particular facet of Keralan

Cost	£15–35
Address	56 Stoke Newington Church St, N16
☎	020 7249 1340
Station	BR Stoke Newington
Open	Daily 6–11pm
Accepts	All major credit cards
✉	www.rasarestaurants.com

cuisine, Syrian Christian cooking, and a very welcome move it is too. All the South Indian flavour notes are there – coconut, curry leaves, ginger, chillies, mustard seeds, tamarind – but as well as veggie specialities, Syrian Christian dishes feature fish, seafood, mutton, chicken and duck.

The menu is a long one and great pains have been taken to explain every dish, although the language can get a bit flowery. Apparently the king prawns in konjufry (£4.95) have been marinated in "refreshing spices" – whatever. But the prawns are very good – plump and with a rich flavour. Or there's Kerala fish fry (£3.95), a large steak of firm-fleshed kingfish dusted with spice and pan fried. Very delicious. Travancore kozhukkatta (£3.75) is a sort of ninth cousin to those large, doughy Chinese dumplings – steamed rice outside with spiced minced lamb inside. The main course dishes are fascinating and richly flavoured. Kozhy olthu curry (£5.25) – billed as "a famous recipe from Sebastian's mum"! – is a rich, dryish, oniony chicken curry. Lamb stew (£5.95) is a simple and charming lamb curry. Duck fry (£6.95) is dry-fried chunks of duck with curry leaves and onion. Kappayyum meenum vevichathu (£7.95) is a triumph – a soupy fish curry, delicately flavoured and served with floury chunks of boiled tapioca root dusted with coconut. Very moreish. The veg curries are also good: try the Travancore kayi curry (£3.90), "chef Narayanan's signature dish", which is a splendidly richly sauced, coconutty mixed vegetable dish.

Excellent accompaniments are the tamarind rice (£2.50), which has an amazing depth of flavour, and the flaky, buttery Malabar paratha (£2).

Wembley

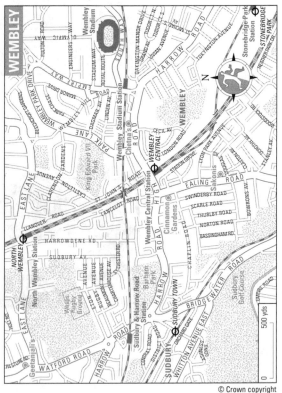

WEMBLEY

© Crown copyright

Chetna's

Chetna's is a remarkable Indian restaurant – busy enough to need a queuing system. You register your interest at the counter and get given a cloakroom ticket, and when your table is ready your number is called. The restaurant has smart wooden tables and chairs, ceiling fans and some seriously ornate brass chandeliers, but despite these trappings it is still awesomely cheap. The food is very good indeed and the menu is a bit of a surprise, opening with a section headed "seaside savouries" – an odd claim in a vegetarian establishment – and moving through to Chetna's Pizza Corner, confirming once again that when Asians go out to dinner they often want a change from the usual fare. The concept of a large "special vegetable hot pizza" (£5.50) cooked by an Indian chef and made with pure vegetarian cheese, onions, and special Chetna sauce – green pepper, corn and hot green chillies – has undeniable charm.

Cost	£4–10

Address 420 High Rd, Wembley
℡ 020 8900 1466
Station Wembley Central
Open Tues–Fri noon–3pm & 6–10.30pm, Sat & Sun 1–10.30pm
Accepts MasterCard, Switch, Visa
🌐 www.chetnassweets.co.uk

INDIAN/VEGETARIAN

Start with a truly amazing mouthful: Chetna's masala golgapa (£2.10). These are small, crisp golgapas filled with potatoes, onions, moong, chana, green chutney and sweet and sour chutney, and topped with sev. You load them into your mouth and, as you chew, different tastes and textures take over. It's an astonishing sensation. Order more portions than you think you'll need. Also try the kachori (£2.10) – a crisp coat encases a well-spiced ball of green peas. Then there are the karela, bhindi and tindora curries (£3). Or there's Chetna's crispy bhajia (£2.90) – slices of potatoes crisp on the outside with a batter containing bits of chilli, and perfectly cooked. The most visually striking dish must be the paper dosa (£3.50), a giant chewy cone of nutty-tasting pancake with a vegetable sambhar and coconut chutney for dipping.

The award for most comprehensive dish must go to the Delhi Darbar thali (£6.50), which is served with one sweet, one farsan, three vegetables, chutney, vegetable biryani, dhal, raita, papadum and paratha. There's a minimum charge of £3.50 per person at Chetna's – presumably to stop a large family sharing one Delhi Darbar thali for dinner.

Cinnamon Gardens

Cinnamon Gardens is a bright and modern restaurant at the Wembley end of Ealing Road. The dining room is all minty green and apricot with a tiled floor and some ostentatiously modern chairs, which thankfully prove comfortable. The walls are also home to a series of murals that seem to be "naive" versions of the classic sun and sand "Muriel" that

Cost	£8–30

Address 42–44 Ealing Road, Wembley

☎ 020 8902 0660

Station Wembley Central

Open Daily noon–midnight

Accepts Cash and cheques only

adorned Vera Duckworth's Coronation Street living room in the 1980s. This is a Sri Lankan restaurant, and things proceed at a Sri Lankan pace. Don't worry, simply relax and assess the relative merits of Lion lager and Lion stout; soon you will be in just the right mood. Teetotallers may want to try the Portello, a lurid purple soft drink with an almost radioactive glow.

Starters include most of the Sri Lankan favourites. There are mutton rolls (two for £1.50), crab claws (£2.75) and the ubiquitous chicken 65 (£4.45), which allegedly must be made with a 65-day-old chicken. There is also a section on the menu devoted to "fried specials", any of which make a great starter when teamed with some bread – try fried mutton (£3.95) or fried squid (£4.40). Another section features devilled dishes, ranging all the way from a devilled potato (£3) to devilled king prawn (£6.25). There is a whole host of hoppers, or rice pancakes, including milk (£2.25 for two), egg (£2.50 for two) and jaggery (£2.50 for two) – the latter rich with unrefined sugar. The Cinnamon special biryani (£5.95) is stunning; dark and richly flavoured, it comes with a bit of everything, including a lamb chop and a hard-boiled egg! From the curries, the chilli chicken (£3.95) is good and hot. Or perhaps crab curry (£4.45), or squid curry (£4.75) appeal? It is also worth noting that the rotis (£1) are very good here, light and flaky, as are the sambols – the seeni sambol (£1.25) is a relatively mild, sweet onion jam, while the katta sambol (£1.75) is an incredibly wild chilli concoction. The service is friendly if a little dozy.

Hidden among the Cinnamon Specials is an intriguing dish, "rubbit curry (when available)". Does Bugs know about this?

Geetanjali's

There are a good many Indian restaurants in Wembley, and it would be easy to write off Geetanjali's as just one more of the same. On the face of it, for sure, the menu is pretty straightforward, with a good many old, tired dishes lined up in their usual serried ranks – chicken tikka masala, rogan josh and so on and so forth. But Geetanjali's has a secret weapon, a dish that brings customers from far and wide. Word on the street is that this place serves the best tandoori lamb chops in North London. And when you've tasted them you'll agree.

Cost £12–26

Address 16 Court Parade, Watford Rd
℡ 020 8904 5353
Station Wembley Central
Open Daily noon–3pm & 6–11.30pm
Accepts All major credit cards
❂ www.geetanjali-restaurant.com

INDIAN

This chop lover's haven has a large, roomy dining room, and the service is attentive, if a little resigned when you pitch up and order a raft of beers and a few portions of chops – or, as the menu would have it, lamb chopp (£4.50). Of course, the chops are good. Very good. Thick-cut, exceedingly tender and very nicely spiced. Accompany them with a luccha paratha (£2.50), warm and flaky and presented in the shape of a flower with a knob of butter melting into its heart. The alternative is the intriguingly named bullet nan (£2.50), which promises to be hot and spicy, and delivers in good measure. You have been warned. Even if you're not a complete chopaholic you can also do well here. Go for starters such as the good chicken tikka haryali (£4.50) – chicken breast marinated in green herbs like coriander and mint before being cooked in the tandoor. Rashmi kebab (£3.90) is also good, made from minced chicken and spices. Main courses include mathi gosht (£6.90), which is lamb with fenugreek, lamb bhuna (£6.50), and lamb badam pasanda (£6.90). And should this emphasis on bread and meat leave you craving some of the green stuff, there's sag aloo (£4.50) or karahi corn masala (£4.50).

This is not the cheapest Indian restaurant in Wembley, but it does have a certain style, even extending to the sophisticated peppermint fondant mints that accompany your bill. And it goes without saying that it's worth travelling for the best tandoori chops in North London.

Sakonis

Sakonis is a top-notch vegetarian food factory. Crowded with Asian families, it is overseen by waiters and staff in baseball caps, and there's even a holding pen where you can check out the latest videos and sounds while waiting your turn. From a decor point of view, the dining area is somewhat clinical: a huge square yardage of white tiling – easy to hose down. Nobody minds – the pre-dominantly Asian clientele is too busy eating. The Indian vegetarian food here is terrific, but it's old hat to many of the Asian customers who dive straight into what is, for them, the most exciting section of the Sakonis menu – the Chinese dishes. These tend to be old favourites like chow mein and chop suey, cooked by Indian chefs and with a distinctly Indian spicing. Unless curiosity overwhelms you, stick to the splendid South Indian dishes.

Cost	£4–10

Address 127–129 Ealing Rd, Alperton; with branches
℡ 020 8903 9601
Station Alperton
Open Mon–Thurs & Sun 11am–11pm, Fri & Sat 11am–midnight
Accepts MasterCard, Switch, Visa

Sakonis is renowned for its dosas. Effectively these are pancakes, so crisp that they are almost chewy, and delightfully nutty. They come with two small bowls of sauce and a filling of rich, fried potato spiced with curry leaves. Choose from plain dosa (£3.50), masala dosa (£4.50), and chutney dosa (£4.60) – which has spices and chilli swirled into the dosa batter. Try the farari cutlets (£3.50); not cutlets at all, in fact, but very nice, well-flavoured dollops of sweet potato mash, deep-fried so that they have a crisp exterior. In fact, all the deep-fried items are perfectly cooked – very dry, with a very crisp shell, but still cooked through. A difficult feat to achieve. Also worth trying are the bhel puri (£3.30), the pani puri (£2.50), and the sev puri (£3.30) – amazingly crisp little taste bombs. Pop them in whole and the flavour explodes in your mouth.

Some say that the juices at Sakonis are the best in London, and while that may be hyperbole they certainly are very good indeed. Try madaf (£2.50), made from fresh coconut; melon juice (£2.25), which is only available in season; or the orange and carrot mix (£2.50), which is subtitled "health drink".

Further North

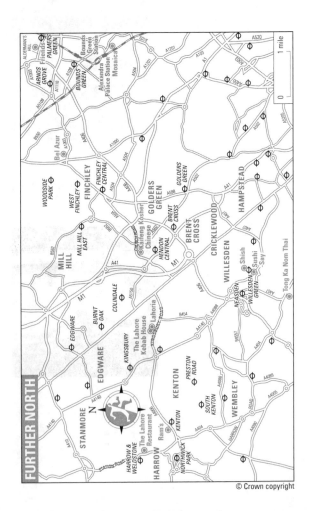

Bel Azur

Bel Azur is an unassuming little restaurant. The chairs are comfortable, the decor bland and the air conditioning strong enough to rattle the chandeliers. There is a short menu with a very limited choice. It is inexpensive. The food is fresh and presented simply. It all sounds good, but this is very much a couscous restaurant, and single-minded restaurants rarely do well in London. So Pasquale Barberio faces a tough time. Formerly head chef at Laurent (where before his retirement Laurent Ferrugia preached the gospel of couscous to North Londoners for over twenty years), Barberio opened his own place in October 2001, and called it Bel Azur.

Cost	£12–25

Address 189 Woodhouse Rd N12
℗ 020 8368 7989
Station Arnos Grove
Open Mon–Sat noon–2pm & 6–10.30pm
Accepts All major credit cards except AmEx

NORTH AFRICAN

If you adore couscous and live anywhere within range this will quickly become your favourite restaurant. There are two starters – oeuf en brique (£2.60) and oeuf en brique with tuna (£2.80) – and they are fine. The couscous, however, is amazing. It is light, shot through with cumin, and has a light granular texture. With this staple you get a choice of accompaniment: vegetable stew (£7); lamb and vegetable stew (£9); chicken and vegetable stew (£9); vegetable stew with a piece of halibut (£12); vegetable stew with "fruits de mer" (£14.50) – scallops, tiger prawns, mussels and calamari; and couscous Royale (£12.50), which adds skewers of grilled meats – merguez sausages, lamb chop and lamb fillet – as well as the vegetable and lamb stew. The stews are very well made. They are savoury and spicy (but not hot with chilli, there's a dish of harissa to see to that), and the meat has been slow cooked to melting point. Portions are huge – the couscous Royale is a formidable undertaking, and if you do look like clearing your plate someone is likely to offer you a little more couscous to mop up any stray gravy.

Bel Azur is a pleasant place that sells very good couscous in huge portions and at reasonable prices, but couscous is the only dish on the menu. In Paris this would be a winning strategy but it remains to be seen whether such a strangely monomaniacal establishment will ring the bell with the residents of Friern Barnet.

Friends

It is hard to think of a more unlikely place to find a chic, stylish and aspirational Indian restaurant than Palmers Green, N13. Here there are lots of detached houses, wide streets and smart cars, all is calm and perhaps a tad smug. As you drive along Alderman's Hill you come across a small parade of shops, and occupying a double frontage is Friends Indian Restaurant. It is a bright place with modern if slightly sparse decor. There's a good deal of bright minty-greeny-blue paint, an apricot-coloured dado and comfortable cane and bamboo chairs. The chef has a very deft touch – spicing is well balanced and flavours are rich and beguiling.

Cost	£18–40

Address 38 Alderman's Hill N13
℡ 020 8882 5002
Station Palmers Green
Open Tues–Sun noon–2.30pm & 6–11pm
Accepts MasterCard, Visa
⊛ www.friends.restaurant.com

Starters like chicken tikka kali mirch (£3.95) are delicious; it's a juicy chicken tikka with a pungent dusting of black pepper. Or there's a terrific interpretation of "crab pepper fry" (£4.95) – the white crab meat combined with the richer brown meat and classic Southern Indian spices such as curry leaves, fennel seeds and black pepper, with a squeeze of fresh lemon juice to balance the richness. Listed under mains, but an excellent choice as a starter, is adrak ke panji (£7.95) – a pair of thick cut, meltingly tender lamb chops heavily marinated and cooked in the tandoor; they taste vaguely gingery and go well with a roti. Other main course options include some sophisticated Southern Indian dishes like dhania nariyal ka murg (£6.50), which is a chicken curry with plenty of coconut, coriander, curry leaves and fennel. And there's lal mirch ka salan (£7.25), which is a lamb curry made with cinnamon, cardamom and cloves as well as an enticing belt of chilli. The breads are very good. Look out for the lacchi paratha (£1.95), which is as buttery and flaky as you could wish for. Amongst the veggie options, chole amchuri (£3.95) is a very simple and very good dish of chickpeas with sour mango powder.

This is accomplished cooking. Service is adept and not over pushy, and the dining room is comfortable. If this is the new face of middle-rank suburban Indian restaurants we should all be grateful.

Kaifeng Kosher Chinese

The Kaifeng Kosher Chinese restaurant is a one-off. This opulent Chinese restaurant – it was redecorated in 2002 – claims to be, and doubtless is, the only kosher Oriental establishment in Britain. According to the family tree on the wall, the most important family of Kaifeng's former Jewish community is named Chao Lunang-Ching. The inscription adds, rather enigmatically, that "Ezekiel is probably Chao Lunang-Ching Gwlyn Gym". So now you know. The long, narrow dining room is filled with affluent locals, happy to pay smart North London prices that have more in common with the West End than the suburbs. But you get a decent deal, friendly and excellent service that almost justifies the 15 percent surcharge, and fresh, well-cooked (if a trifle under-seasoned) dishes. If you're Orthodox Jewish, Kaifeng must make a welcome change; if you're not, then seeing how favourite dishes like sweet and sour pork, prawns kung po and so forth turn out kosher-style is a lot of fun.

Cost	£25–50

Address 51 Church Rd, NW4
℡ 020 8203 7888
Station Hendon Central
Open Mon–Thurs & Sun
12.30–2.30pm & 6–11pm
(also Sat from 1hr after sunset
to 11pm, Sept–April only)
Accepts All major credit cards
✆ www.kaifeng.co.uk

Start with the spare ribs (£7.50), which are absolutely delicious, made from lamb instead of pork and arguably even better for it. Hunan chicken with lettuce wrap (£12.50) is also fresh and good, while the usual prawn and sesame-seed toast becomes sesame chicken (£7.50). Of the main courses, the sweet and sour lamb (£12.95) is slightly less successful – the good, sharp sauce still makes no impression on fairly tough chunks of lamb. But there are some interesting and unfamiliar dishes like beef and straw mushrooms (£12.95), smoked shredded chicken (£12.50), and eggplant in garlic sauce (£6.50). Shellfish dishes, meanwhile, turn into fish, usually sole, which is served in a variety of familiar styles, including steamed with ginger and spring onion (£17.95), and drunken (£17.95) – which means sliced and served in kosher rice wine.

Given its unique status, the Kaifeng is a pretty popular place, and even early in the week it tends to fill quickly. So take the precaution of booking if you're travelling out here specially.

The Lahore Kebab House

This grill house was once a branch of the famous Lahore Kebab House in East London. Then, in 1994, Mr Hameed bought the business, and with it the right to use the name "Lahore Kebab House of East London" anywhere within a five-mile radius of Kingsbury. Although completely independent of the Umberstone Street establishment (see p.175), this unfussy restaurant remains faithful to the spirit of the original, despite a gentle refurbishment during 2002. Kebabs here are cheap, freshly cooked and spicy, while the karahi dishes are also worth delving into. This Lahore has the advantage of a drinks licence, so you can now purchase Tusker and Kingfisher beers without having to pop out to one of the neighbouring off licences.

Cost	£6–12
Address	248 Kingsbury Rd, NW9
	☎ 020 8905 0930
Station	Kingsbury
Open	Daily 1pm–midnight
Accepts	Cash or cheque only

There's not much point in coming to the Lahore unless you're after some kind of kebab. If you just want a starter bite, there's seekh kebab (75p each). Or, for more serious eating, there's a list of kebabs all with five pieces per skewer: mutton tikka (£2.20); chicken tikka (£3); jeera chicken (£4.20); chicken wings (£4.20); lamb chops (£5). Everyone is very helpful here, and they are happy to make you up a platter – with three pieces of each kebab, for example – and charge pro rata. Unusually, for such a stronghold of the carnivore, there's also a long list of vegetarian dishes, all served in the karahi. Include a couple with your order, perhaps karrai dhal (£3.50), or karrai sag aloo (£3.50), which is particularly rich and tasty. Back with the meats, karrai gosht (£4.70) is a rich lamb curry, while the Chef's Special (£6), a hand-chopped keema made with both chicken and lamb, is a revelation. It's very tasty, with recognisable, finely chopped meat – a far cry from the anonymous mince that forms the backbone of keema dishes in so many curry houses. It is thoroughly recommended, as are the breads – tandoori nan (90p) and tandoori roti (60p) – which are fresh and good.

The Lahore's weekend specials all appeal: karrai nehari (£7) brings slow-cooked lamb shanks; karrai bhindi (£4) is okra; and karrai karela (£4) is made from bitter melons.

The Lahore Restaurant

Are bring-your-own restos the next big thing? If so, with a BYO drinks policy and open kitchen the Lahore restaurant is well on its way towards being a groundbreaking sort of place. But that's where the trendiness stops. This homely and unpretentious Pakistani eatery serves grilled meats and karahi dishes. The service is friendly, the food fresh, and the prices are extremely reasonable. The only drawback is discovering that the off licence next door shuts at nine o'clock on weekday evenings. The room is plain, and a couple of ceiling fans struggle to disperse the fierce heat coming off the grills. When it is just a bit smoky it's not so bad, but sometimes the smoke comes with a chilli pungency that will reduce you to tears.

Cost	£6–16

Address 45 Station Rd, Harrow, Middlesex
ⓣ 020 8424 8422
Station Harrow & Wealdstone/ Harrow on the Hill
Open Daily 11.30am–11.30pm
Accepts Cash or cheque only
ⓦ www.clickwala.com

To start order a couple of rotis (60p) and some grilled meats. Chicken tikka (£3) is sound, a good portion; tandoori chicken wings (six for £4) are great – well marinated, perfectly cooked and spicy. Eat your heart out, Colonel. Tandoori lamb chops (six for £5) are outstanding – thick cut, heavy with spice, and juicy. Seek kebabs (two for £1.25) have a welcome belt of fresh chilli and green herbs. It would be quite feasible to make a decent meal of starters and bread, but the curries are very good, too, with simple dishes full of flavour like methi chicken (£4.50). When asked the question "Hot, medium, or mild?" it's worth noting that "hot" is not painfully so, and "medium" seems a bit tame. The star turn is the karahi karela gosht (£4.50); the tender, slow-cooked lamb has a rich sauce balanced by the addictive taste of bitter melon. The breads are very good indeed. For an interesting contrast, order a tawa paratha (£1.50) and an onion kulcha (£1.80). The paratha is wholemeal, thick, filling and fried until the outside is flaky crisp. The onion kulcha is doughy but stuffed with a rich onion mix that includes a good helping of fresh coriander.

There are no frills at the Lahore restaurant, and it can be a tad smoky, but the food is very honest, very good and very cheap, and that is a formula that will ensure success anywhere.

Lahoria

This guide used to go on a bit about the shabby, somewhat neglected decor of this Kingsbury stalwart. Then it was refurbished in pink. And now green. But even taking into account the refurbs, it's still true that nobody comes here for the ambience. There's plenty of competition, with half a dozen other Indian restaurants clustered on this stretch of road. No matter – this small place is still busy, particularly at the weekend. What makes the Lahoria stand out, what has kept it going from strength to strength, is the sheer quality of the food, which combines two admirable attributes – simplicity and goodness.

Cost	£12–25

Address 274 Kingsbury Rd, NW9
℡ 020 8206 1129
Station Kingsbury
Open Tues–Thurs 6–11.30pm, Fri & Sat 5.30pm–midnight, Sun 3pm–midnight
Accepts MasterCard, Visa

So, the food: it's fresh, not painfully hot (unless you want it to be) and well balanced. There are a lot of East African Asian specialities, and dishes come by either the plate or the karai. Start with a plate of jeera aloo (£4.95) – tasty, rich, soft, fried potatoes with cumin, a sort of Indian pommes Lyonnaises. Or have a plate of masala fish (£4.95) – two fat fillets of tilapia cooked in a fresh green masala. You must try the chilli chicken (£6.25), which is nine chicken wings in a dark green, almost black sludge that is rich with ginger, chillies, coriander and just a hint of tamarind sourness – triumphant but not so hot that it hurts. You can also try this sauce with potatoes (£4.95). Then there are the tandoori chops (£4.95), which are very good indeed. Also look out for the mari chicken (£6.25), which is chicken marinated in cracked black pepper. For a main course it is hard to give high enough praise to the karai spring lamb (£6.25), served on the bone. It is deliciously rich. Or try a simple classic like karai masala lamb methi (£6.25). The karai red kidney beans (£4.50) and karai bangan ka bartha (£5.25), based on aubergines and onions, are also good bets.

On Friday, Saturday and Sunday, Lahoria offers two notable specials: karai boozi ki goat (on the bone, £6.25) and karai undhiu (£5.50), which is a dish of mixed vegetables. They also have a magnificent chiller full of bottled beers, including Beck's, Holsten, Carlsberg, Budweiser and – best of all – Tusker from Kenya.

Mosaica

Up in the high pastures of Wood Green there is a large and hideous concrete "Shopping City" whose main claim to fame seems to be "secure parking". Around the corner is a straggle of large, run-down buildings called the Chocolate Factory that has been colonized by artists, potters, designers and anyone arty needing cheap, no-frills space. You'll find Mosaica hidden at the heart of Building C, and it is an amazing place – spacious, stylish and comfort-

Cost	£8–40

Address Building C, The Chocolate Factory, Clarendon Rd, off Coburg Rd, N22
℡ 020 8889 2400
Station BR Wood Green/ Alexander Park
Open Tues–Fri noon–3pm & 7–10pm, Sat 7–10pm, Sun noon–3.30pm
Accepts All major credit cards

able. There is a long bar made up of cinder blocks, topped with a twenty-foot sheet of glass. There's a terrace outside in the light well, which will be amazing should we ever get good weather. There's a huge open kitchen. And there are mismatched but comfortable straight-backed chairs. The atmosphere is dead right – stylish but informal, neighbourhood but sharp. The food is a complete surprise. It's terrific.

The two chef-proprietors, John Mountain and David Orlowski, have done time in various West End establishments, but here in N22 they are cooking with real passion. Genuine, unpretentious plating, well-handled fresh ingredients and accurate cooking: this is the difficult kind of simple stuff that looks simple until you try to do it. The menu at Mosaica is short and changes daily – at lunch the blackboard includes a cheap pasta dish for starving artists. In the evening, starters range from a well-made creamed fennel and celery soup (£3.95), to an old-fashioned, freshly made chicken liver parfait with toast and pickles (£5.95). Mains range from monkfish with charred radicchio and charlotte potatoes (£15.75), to rare rib-eye steak with garlic mash and spinach (£15.95) – the rib-eye sliced and meltingly tender, the mash rich and not over-gluey. Then there may be an epic dish like turbot fillet with mussels and whitebean broth (£17.95). The wine list is short and the service more enthusiastic than polished. But the food is great and the prices forgiving.

Puds are notable. How about a perfect chocolate mousse (£5.50), or panna cotta (£5.50)? And you have to warm to any place offering "Tart of some description" (£6).

Ram's

🍴 Anyone in downtown Mumbai will tell you that India's best vegetarian food comes from the state of Gujarat. And one of the leading contenders for the best of Gujarati food is the city of Surat. Much as European gourmets rate Castelnaudry for cassoulet, in India people go to Surat for the undhiu! Since the end of 2001, Londoners have had their very own

Cost	£6–18

Address 203 Kenton Rd, Harrow, Middlesex
☏ 020 8907 2022
Station Kenton
Open Tues–Sun noon–3pm & 5–10pm
Accepts MasterCard, Visa

Surti restaurant – Ram's. The staff rush around, eager and friendly; their pride in both the menu and their hometown of Surat is obvious and endearing. The menu is a long one with plenty of Surti specials, and the food is very good.

Gujarati snacks make great starters. Petis (£2.60) are small balls of peas and onions coated in potato and deep fried. Kachori (£2.60) are the same kind of thing but with mung daal inside a pastry coat. Patras (£2.60) are made by rolling vegetable leaves with a "glue" of chickpea flour batter; then the roll is sliced across, and each slice becomes a delicate and savoury pinwheel. Stuffed banana bhaji (£2.60) is a sweet and savoury combo. The rata ni puri (£3.50) is a Surti special – slices of purple potato in a savoury batter. Sev khamni (£3.50) is a sludge of well-spiced chickpeas with coconut, served topped with a layer of crisp sev. Flavours are clear and distinct, and some dishes have a welcome chilli heat. Mains do not disappoint. The famous undhiu (billed as a weekend special) is a complex dish of vegetables "stuffed" with a Surti spice paste. It combines aubergines with three kinds of potatoes (purple, sweet and white), as well as bananas and peas. The peas pilau (£1.95) is simple and good. The methi parathas (two for £1.50) are dry and tasty. The puris (£1.20) are fresh, hot and as self-indulgent as only fried bread can be. Drink the Surti lemon soda (£1.50) or the good salt lassi (£1.25), which has a lurking chilli sting.

When the elegantly rolled paan arrives alongside your bill, simply remove the clove holding the leaf shut, pop the whole thing into your mouth, and chew slowly.

Shish

Shish is pretty slick. A large, curved-glass pavement frontage displays a sinuous bar counter that snakes around the dining room, leaving grills, fridges and chefs' stations in the centre. Diners simply take a stool at the counter, for all the world like being at a modernist sushi bar, though there is also a private room upstairs. All is modern, just as current resto-design fashion dictates, with rough concrete here, polished concrete there, stainless steel everywhere... Towards the rear are a couple of further kitchens: one primarily for baking fresh flat breads, and the other for frying, preparation and so forth. This place owes a debt to Israeli roadside eateries, with its falafel and shish kebabs, but the "concept" (all fast food missions have to have a suitable "concept") is much more inclusive. As proclaimed at the top of the menu, the inspiration for Shish is the food of the Silk Road.

Cost £10–25

Address 2–6 Station Parade, NW2
☏ 020 8208 9290
Station Willesden Green
Open Mon–Fri 11.30am–midnight, Sat 10am–midnight, Sun 10am–11pm
Accepts All major credit cards except Diners

KEBAB

Starters are divided into lots of cold mezze and a shorter list of hot mezze. The tabbouleh (£1.95) needs a bit more coriander and parsley. The cucumber wasabi (£1.95) is pleasant pickled cucumber. The red and green falafel (£2.25) are well made – the red variety is engagingly spicy. The hot bread is as delicious as only good hot bread can be. Kebabs are served in two different ways: either plated with rice, couscous or French fries; or in a wrap. The shish kebabs are really rather good. Mediterranean lamb (£5.25) comes up very tender; apricot and ginger (£5.75) teams chicken with good tangy apricot flavour; the Persian chicken (£6.25) is flavoured with saffron, turmeric and citrus fruits. The portions all seem decent sized and there are fish and vegetarian options. Die-hard kebabbers can even insist on a satisfactorily fierce squelch of chilli sauce. This food benefits from being freshly cooked and eaten hot from the grill. It's relatively cheap, too. What's more, Shish is licensed, so there's a cold beer (£1.50) or a glass of wine (£2.50) to turn a quick feed into an enjoyable meal.

If this is the new face of fast food we should all be grateful.

Sushi-Say

Yuko Shimizu and her husband Katsuharu run this small but excellent Japanese restaurant and sushi bar. It has a very personal feel, with just ten seats at the bar and twenty in the restaurant, plus a private booth for five or six. Shimizu means pure water, and the cooking is pure delight. It's a tribute to how sophisticated Londoners' palates have become that a restaurant like this can do well so far out of town. The menu

Cost	£15–40

Address 33b Walm Lane, NW2

☎ 020 8459 2971

Station Willesden Green

Open Tues–Fri 6.30–10.30pm, Sat & Sun noon–2.30pm & 6.30–10.30pm

Accepts All major credit cards except Diners

offers a full classical Japanese selection, making it a difficult choice between limiting yourself to sushi or going for the cooked dishes. Perhaps adapting the European style, and having sushi or sashimi as a starter and then main courses with rice, brings you the best of both worlds, and will give you scope to enjoy this small establishment.

Sitting at the sushi bar allows you to watch Katsuharu at work. With a sumo-like stature and the widest grin this side of Cheshire, his fingers magic nigiri sushi of exquisite proportions onto your plate. It's an accomplished show and the sleight of hand will not fail to impress. In the lower price brackets you'll find omelette, mackerel, squid and octopus (£2.40). At the top end there's sea urchin, fatty tuna and yellow tail (£3.40). In between there is a wide enough range to delight even the experts. Nigiri yoku (£16.50) brings you eleven pieces of nigiri and seaweed-rolled sushi, and it's a bargain, heavy on the fish and light on the rice. Cooked dishes do not disappoint. Ebi tempura (£11.30) brings you crispy battered king prawns, the batter so light it's almost effervescent, and menchi katsu (£7) delivers a deep-fried oval shaped from minced beef and salad. There are set dinners for all tastes, priced from £18.50 to £28.50, and mixed sashimi for £16.50. It's worth trying the home-made puddings, such as goma (sesame) ice cream (£2.60). There's also a selection of special sakes, which are served chilled, and even a half-frozen sake (Akita Onigoroshi) at £6. Less a slush puppy than a slush mastiff.

The menu is in English and the staff are very helpful, so dining at Sushi-Say gives you a good chance to develop your knowledge of Japanese food by trying something new.

Tong Ka Nom Thai

At its best, Thai cuisine means intense and distinct flavours – a concept which nearly all of the hundreds of pubs selling Thai grub seem to have mislaid. However the good news is that fresh, cheap and authentic Thai food is alive and well and living on the Harlesden end of the Harrow Road. Tong Ka Nom Thai is a small and garish Thai restaurant with a wonderful view of the railway tracks. It is implausibly cheap. The food is very good, the service friendly, and this is a "Bring Your Own" place (although there is a wholly reasonable request on the menu that you buy any soft drinks on the premises).

Cost	£8–15

Address 833 Harrow Rd, NW10
℗ 020 8964 5373
Station Kensal Green
Open Mon–Fri noon–3pm & 6–10pm, Sat 6–10pm
Accepts Cash or cheque only

All the starters are priced at £4. For that, you get six well-spiced tod mun – delightfully chewy Thai fishcakes; or eight popia tod – well-made mini vegetarian spring rolls with a dark, mushroomy filling; or six goong hompha, which are prawns in filo – very nice but not as exciting as the other starters. But the star turn is gai bai toey – six morsels of chicken that are marinated, wrapped in pandan leaf and then fried; they are seriously delicious. The curries, all at £4, are splendid. Gaeng kheaw wan is a well-made green curry which comes with a choice of main ingredients. Other options are a red curry, a yellow curry and a "jungle curry". The House Speciality is called "boneless fish fillet" (£4.50), and you would be wise to order it. It's a large hunk of tilapia, and comes in a mesmerizing, light, elegant sauce with plenty of holy basil. The sauces here are good – not thickened to a sludge with cornflour but rich on their own account. You'll need some rice (£1.20) and you should have a noodle dish – perhaps the pad phrik (£4), which is rich and well balanced. The kitchens here are cramped, with room for only a couple of chefs, as you can see for yourself as you walk past the stoves to the toilet.

At Tong Ka Nom Thai they serve delicious and authentic Thai food. It is truly remarkable that they can do so at what are almost Thai prices.

South

Battersea

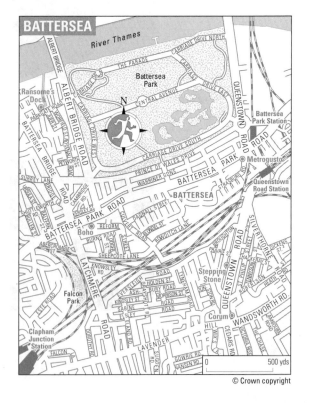

Boho

Let's be absolutely truthful about this. Boho is not the sort of place where gourmets trample each other in their headlong rush for a table. The grub here is ... Czechoslovakian. Boho has two ace cards to play: the atmosphere is agreeably loud and lively and there is truly wonderful beer to drink. The decor is rather stark (functional stark rather than Phillipe Starck) but the long tables with benches mix people up and give the place a cheerful ambience. Drinks are important here: there are various shots, a Czechoslovakian wine called Sekt Karistejn, and best of all there's beer. Kozel lager, which has won the World Beer Championships in Chicago five times in the last six years, is very good, particularly the Kozel Dark (500ml for £2.25), a chestnut-coloured brew as rich and delicious as you could wish for.

Cost	£5–25

Address 517–519 Battersea Park Rd, SW8
℡ 020 7228 4562
Station BR Clapham Junction
Open Daily noon–midnight
Accepts MasterCard, Switch, Visa

CZECHOSLOVAKIAN

The food is pleasantly informal, and there are good snacks – ordering karbanatek besi (£3) brings you two small hamburgers. Or there's Devil's Toast (£3), which is fried bread topped with spicy minced meat and melted Edam cheese. The goulash soup (£2.50) is the real deal and comes with a large hunk of bread. Mains are a similar ragbag. A Boho beefsteak goulash (£7) comes with Bohemian dumplings, which have had a bad press, but are much lighter in texture than you would suppose. As if to emphasize the point, they are dished up in slices which look very like pieces of bread. The roasted pork knuckle (£8) is an authentic dish – it's enormous. If you are in a serious eating mood, a few belts of Kozel dark and a pork knuckle will prove to be a very satisfactory outing. One thing is certain: you will probably need to take on board a good deal of Kozel and maybe some absinthe before the dessert special – strawberry dumplings (£3) – becomes a must-have dish. There is a floor-priced set lunch comprising soup, bread and a soft drink (£2.50).

Watch out for the see-through drinks. While an excess of beer will not kill you, melon schnapps, slivovice or becherovka (all £2.50) might.

Battersea

Corum

MODERN BRITISH

Corum opened towards the end of 2001, but still retains a new-ish "clean and keen" sort of feel. It is a perfect example of a gastro-bar. The bar part is a runaway success – locals have been known to "book" a particular sofa ahead of time, it is that crowded. Towards the rear the bar opens out into quite a large restaurant which looks as if it is a page torn from the design manual of modern London restaurants. Blond wood floor, check. Plain walls with modern art, check. Subtle lighting, check. Honey coloured leather chairs, chocolate leather banquettes, check. It looks great. Like a thousand other places, but great.

Cost	£15–35

Address 30–32 Queenstown Rd, SW8
℡ 020 7720 5445
Station Clapham Common/BR Queenstown Rd
Open Mon–Wed noon–3pm, Thurs & Fri noon–3pm & 5pm–1am, Sat & Sun noon–1am
Accepts All major credit cards except Diners
🌐 www.corumrestaurants.com

The menu at Corum is an essay in gastro-bar philosophy. Starters include a crab risotto with roasted peppers (£5.75), a Caesar salad (£4.95), egg Benedict with hash browns (£5.25), smoked duck salad (£5.75), and pan-fried scallops (£6.50). Nothing alarming there. The surprise is in the standard of cooking, which is very high. The scallops are perfectly cooked and markedly fresh, and they come in a decent portion with rocket and Tuscan bread salad. This dish works very well. The Caesar salad is very good, classical even to the point of omitting the anchovies now in vogue, with a great lemony dressing. The egg Benedict is comforting and made with kassler, or smoked pork loin. Main courses also tread the line between classic and dull: there are pork and leek sausages (£11.90), a Thai green fish curry (£12.90), rib-eye steak (£13.50), roast cod (£11.95), salmon fishcake (£11.50), char-grilled chicken salad (£11.50), and calf's liver and pancetta (£11.75). These dishes are grand when well made, and at Corum the chef knows his job. The fishcake is large, light and almost fluffy, and the perfectly cooked calf's liver sits on a cake of very decent bubble and squeak made with sage, and is topped with crisp pancetta.

Puds (all £5.50) are somewhat predictable, with enough sticky toffee and chocolate for the sweetest tooth. Gastro-bars serve the kind of food that everybody likes to eat, and when it is well executed it can be deeply satisfying.

Metrogusto

At Metrogusto describing the cuisine succinctly is something of a problem. "Progressive Italian" is one attempt, but it isn't perfect, and the in-vogue term Modern Italian, which would fit the bill nicely, has been hijacked by restos hell-bent on Haute Cuisine. Metrogusto aims for the simple food of the Italian locanda or trattoria, but with a few new and different combinations or techniques. Wherever you may pigeonhole it, this food is Italian, suitably unpretentious, and agreeably delicious.

Cost	£15–35
Address 153 Battersea Park Rd, SW8; with branches	
℡ 020 7720 0204	
Station BR Battersea Park	
Open Mon–Fri noon–3pm & 6.30–10.45pm, Sat noon–3.30pm & 6.30–10.45pm	
Accepts MasterCard, Switch, Visa	

The menu, which changes every month or so, is more extensive in the evening than at lunch. There is a bargain set lunch – paying £12.50 for two courses lets you choose from four starters, four mains and four puds. The cooking is good and the portions large. Starters range from the simple – buffalo mozzarella with tomato and fresh oregano (£6.50), or asparagus with crisp pancetta (£6.50); to the trendy – rucola salad with Parmesan and balsamic (£4.75); and the retro – chicken liver pâté with garlic toast (£6.50). There is always a pasta of the day (£8.50) and a pizza of the day (£8.50), plus one or two more interesting variants such as ravioli of funghi with hazelnut and thyme butter (£8.50). Commendably, the main courses include a fish and a meat special of the day (both £13.50), plus appealing combinations such as sea bream served with a baby squid stew (£13.50). Steadier options include Italian bangers with mashed potatoes (£9.50), rib-eye steak with crushed shallots and green beans (£13.50) and salmon fishcake with red pesto and wilted spinach (£10.50). The all-Italian wine list is long and well chosen, but has no explanations. Thankfully, the managers know it inside out and will advise something sensible.

Metrogusto has a relaxed, friendly atmosphere. The food is good, the pricing fair and the customers are a mixture of locals going out for a bite to eat, families celebrating and clubbers preparing for a night on the tiles. All look happy. No wonder.

BRITISH

Ransome's Dock

🍴 Ransome's Dock is the kind of restaurant you would like to have at the bottom of your street. It is formal enough for those little celebrations or occasions with friends, and informal enough to pop into for a single dish at the bar. The food is good, seasonal and made with carefully sourced ingredients. Dishes are well cooked, satisfying and unfussy, the wine list is encyclopedic, and service is friendly and efficient. All in

Cost	£20–60

Address 35–37 Parkgate Rd, SW11
☎ 020 7223 1611
Station BR Battersea Park
Open Mon–Fri 11.30am–11pm, Sat 11.30am–midnight, Sun 11.30am–3.30pm
Accepts All major credit cards
🌐 www.ransomesdock.co.uk

all, Martin Lam and his team have got it just right. Everything stems from the raw ingredients: they use a supplier in East Anglia for the smoked eels; they dicker with the Montgomerys over prime Cheddars. The menu changes monthly, but the philosophy behind it does not. Look out for the weekday set lunch – two courses at £14.25.

Before rampaging off through the main menu, make a pit stop at the daily specials; if nothing tempts you, turn to the seven or eight starters. If it's on, make a beeline for the grilled Norfolk smoked eel, Trevisse and ratte potatoes with horseradish sauce (£8.75). It's very rich, very good and very large. Or there may be Perroche goat's cheese crostini with grilled pears and winter leaves (£6.50). Or Morecambe Bay potted shrimps with wholemeal toast (£7.50). Main courses are well balanced – Dutch calves' liver (£15.50) may come with herb polenta, green beans and Cabernet Sauvignon onions. Or perhaps Trelough duck breast with Cumberland sauce and braised chicory (£17.50) tempts? Or boiled ham hock with steamed leek suet pudding (£11)? Or there may be a "shorthorn" sirloin steak (£20) with herb butter and chips – not just any old steak, but one from a well-hung, Shorthorn steer. Puddings run from the complicated – a hot prune and Armagnac soufflé with Armagnac custard (£7) – to the simple – Greek yoghurt with honey and toasted pistachio nuts (£5).

The wine list makes awesome reading. Long, complex, arcane – full of producers and regions you have never heard of – with fair prices. Advice is both freely available and helpful.

Stepping Stone

Although outwardly insignificant among the trendy shops in this recently fashionable part of Battersea, Stepping Stone seems to have engendered a fierce loyalty in its clientele. As you enter, there's little to distract the eye. The walls of the rather plain dining room are jollied up by block painting in lime and brick red, and there's a small bar at one end. Otherwise the restaurant is refreshingly unadorned. There's no question – you're here to eat. Thankfully, there's a chef who likes food and knows how to cook, and a host who intends that his guests enjoy themselves. A better formula for running a successful and ultimately satisfying restaurant has yet to be devised, and the restaurant deserves its strong local following.

Cost	£15–40

Address 123 Queenstown Rd, SW8
℡ 020 7622 0555
Station Clapham Common/ BR Queenstown Road
Open Mon noon–2.30pm & 7–10.30pm, Tues–Fri noon–2.30pm & 7–11pm, Sat 7–11pm
Accepts All major credit cards
ⓦ www.thesteppingstone.co.uk

The menu changes every service, allowing the kitchen to be truly market led. Though reasonably fashionable, the cooking stays well within the kitchen's capabilities. There are likely to be a few simple-sounding dishes, such as potted mackerel and toast (£4.75), and butternut squash soup (£4.25) – good examples of their type – but the menu ranges further for the more adventurous. A pork and duck liver terrine (£5.50) comes with pear chutney; or there may be a tomato and red onion tart Tatin (£5.25). Main courses may include solid, dependable options such as Gloucester Old Spot bacon chop with celeriac, apple and pine nuts (£13), or fillet of brill with herb gnocchi and braised fennel (£13). You can expect dishes to be generous, cooked with care and served with a friendly smile. Puddings – treacle tart and clotted cream (£4.75), or hot chocolate pudding with blood orange salad (£5) – are hearty rather than works of art. Commendably, the well-priced, well-planned and mostly European wine list features precious little that's much over £20.

Stepping Stone has taken the admirable decision to oppose the two sittings per table per night trend. This means that it's essential to book, especially at weekends. The weekday set lunch is a bargain at £13 for two courses.

Brixton & Herne Hill

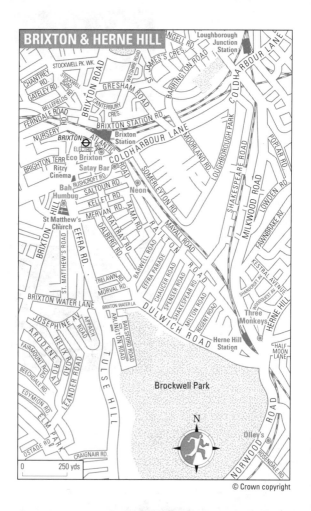

BRIXTON & HERNE HILL

STOCKWELL PK. WK.
CHANTREY RD
GATELEY RD
BELLEFIELDS RD
FERNDALE ROAD
NURSERY

GRESHAM ROAD

CANTERBURY CRES.

BRIXTON STATION RD

Brixton Station

BRIXTON ROAD

WILTSHIRE ROAD

JAMES'S CRES

ANGELL RD

Loughborough Junction Station

BARRINGTON ROAD

COLDHARBOUR LANE

BRIGHTON TERR

BRIXTON
ELECTRIC

COLDHARBOUR LANE

MOORLAND RD

SHAKESPEARE ROAD

LOUGHBOROUGH PARK

POPLAR RD

Eco Brixton

Ritzy
Cinema

Satay Bar

MILKWOOD ROAD

LOWDEN RD

Bah
Humbug

RUSHCROFT RD

SALTOUN RD

Neon

SOMERLEYTON RD

FAWNBRAKE AV.

KELLETT RD

MERVAN RD

TALMA RD

RATTRAY RD

St Matthew's
Church

BRIXTON HILL

ST. MATTHEW'S ROAD

EFRA RD

DALBERG RD

RAILTON ROAD

MAYALL ROAD

KESTRAL AVENUE

SHARDCROFT AV.

SHARCROSS AV.

Three
Monkeys

TRELAWN RD

MORVAL RD

BARWELL ROAD

EFRA PARADE

CHAUCER ROAD

SPENSER ROAD

SHAKESPEAR RD

MILTON ROAD

REGENT ROAD

HERNE HILL

BRIXTON WATER LANE

BRIXTON WATER LA.

DULWICH ROAD

HALF
MOON
LANE

JOSEPHINE AV.

HELIX ROAD

ARPACH ROAD

BALSORD ROAD

ARLINGTON ROAD

Herne Hill
Station

ARODENE RD

TULSE HILL

FAIRMOUNT ROAD

LEANDER ROAD

BEECHDALE RD

EDYMION RD

ELM PARK

Brockwell Park

OSTADE RD

CRAIGNAIR RD.

NORWOOD ROAD

ROSENDALE RD

Olley's

N

0   250 yds

© Crown copyright

Bug

Bug lurks in the crypt of a converted church. Hardened Presbyterians may feel a little peculiar eating, drinking and making merry in such circumstances, but the less puritanical may even enjoy the thought that it's a short step to the Bug Bar, the trendy club-bar in the neighbouring crypt, and scarcely any further to the nightclub upstairs. The restaurant's subterranean location makes it naturally atmospheric, and the large space, divided by low vaults, feels remarkably intimate. A recent refurb has brought in a slick new private dining room called the Cocoon Room. The atmosphere in the main area is considerably lighter than it used to be, and the service verges on jolly.

Cost	£18–30

Address The Crypt, St Matthews Church, Brixton Hill, SW2
℡ 020 7738 3184
Station Brixton
Open Mon–Sat 5pm–midnight, Sun 5–11.30pm
Accepts MasterCard, Switch, Visa
🌐 www.bahhumbug.co.uk

MODERN BRITISH

Traditionally, the menu has always been mostly vegetarian here, with a fish dish or two to vary the pace, but a new head chef arrived in summer 2002 and he intends to add some meat dishes by and by. On the old menu a favourite starter was the Middle Eastern couscous and pine nut fritter with beetroot and sour cream (£4.70), or perhaps sag aloo samosa with spicy coconut Puy lentils (£4.70) – which should be multicultural enough for anyone! Or how about organic salmon gravadlax (£4.70)? Main courses run from a Wellington en croute made from cashews, brazils, almonds and mushroom duxelles with a red wine and shallot gravy and a 20-minute wait (£9.20), to pan-fried scallops and ginger risotto cake (£12.50) or pistachio and green chilli kofta (£10.50). Puds are simple but good, leading with a warm chocolate tart with orange sorbet (£4.50), and finishing at moody ice creams and sorbets (£2.20–3.60).

For the discerning drinker wishing to stray from the wine list, Bah Humbug offers various classic liqueur coffees so you can get your sugar high with a mixture of coffee, Cointreau and cream. Very retro. Very tasty.

PIZZA

Eco Brixton

If you're in Brixton around noon, Eco is a must for your lunch break. Make your way to Brixton Market – London's first market with electric light – and don't be put off by the smell from the fishmonger's shop opposite. Once inside Eco, the whiff soon gives way to more appetizing wafts of cooked cheese and coffee from your neighbour's table. Peruse the menu while you queue among the trailing shoppers – be prepared to share your table – then sit down to one of

Cost	£8–20

Address 4 Market Row, Brixton Market, Electric Row, SW9
☎ 020 7738 3021
Station Brixton
Open Mon, Tues & Thurs–Sat 8am–5pm
Accepts All major credit cards except AmEx
⊛ www.ecorestaurant.com

the best pizzas are here in South London. Formerly Pizzeria Franco, now Eco Brixton, this place has the same menu as its sister, Eco on Clapham High Street, but the Brixton branch closes at 5pm. It's small and popular, so things can get hectic. Still, the service is friendly, the pizzas crisp and the salads mountainous. Plus there is an identically priced takeaway menu.

All the famous pizzas are here, including a pleasingly pungent Napoletana (£5.90) with the sacred trio of anchovies, olives and capers, and quattro stagioni (£6.90), packed full of goodies. But why not try something less familiar, such as coriander-topped roasted red pepper and aubergine (£6.50)? Or enjoy la dolce vita (£6.70), where rocket, mushrooms and dolcelatte all vie for attention? Or even the amore (£6.70), with its French beans, artichoke, pepper and aubergine? Or one of the calzone (all around £7)? It's a difficult choice. For a lighter meal – lighter only because of the absence of carbohydrate – try a salad. Tricolore (£6.20) is made with baby mozzarella, beef tomato, avocado and olives. Side orders like the melted cheese bread (£3.25) and mushroom bread (£3.75) are highly recommended. For sandwiches, Eco also impresses. Focaccia are stuffed with delights like Parma ham and rocket (£6.25) or asparagus and chicken (£5.90).

You could also go for starters, but at lunch they seem a little surplus to requirements. There are just eight options, ranging from avocado vinaigrette (£3.90) to mozzarella and asparagus (£4.90). Puddings are even scarcer – pecan pie (£3.40), or tiramisù (£3.90). Stick with the pizzas.

Neon

🍴 Marco Rebora is proprietor of Neon and since it opened in 1999 he has encouraged it to evolve. Neon seems to be swimming against the flow, and while all around the trend is to rely on bar trade, this place is making progress as a restaurant. Wander up Atlantic Road, past the debris left after the day's trading at Brixton Market, and look out for Neon on your left. Despite

Cost	£14–35

Address 71 Atlantic Rd, SW9
☎ 020 7738 6576
Station Brixton
Open Tues–Fri 6pm–midnight, Sat 11.30am–3pm & 6pm–midnight, Sun 1–10.30pm
Accepts MasterCard, Switch, Visa

the fashionably deep-red reception area and the minimalist dining space – all black and white, with a huge monochrome painting on one wall – this is a friendly and laid-back place which has obviously struck a chord with trendy Brixtonians. Perhaps they like sitting on black lacquer benches and eating at black lacquer tables?

The food is authentically Italian and the menu broadly seasonal. It leads you through starters to pastas and on to some grander main courses, sides and salads, before weighing in with a heavyweight array of focaccia and pizzas, and so to desserts. Starting at the back of the book, think bread. What about focaccia aromatica (£3.90), with cumin and fennel seeds? Or focaccia with garlic (£3.90)? Or with speck (£5.20)? Pizzas are bold and good. Pizza bietola e salsiccia (£7.20) is a successful marriage of Italian sausage with Swiss chard and mozzarella; while sfiunciuno pesco (£8.80) teams seafood mozzarella and tomato sauce. If you feel more formal there are serious soups, such as cotechino e lenticchie (£5.30/7.60), which is sausage and lentil; or zuppa di cavalo nero (£4.90/7.20), which is black cabbage. Onwards to pasta: orecchiette alla Pugliese (£4.40/6.40) is small pasta with turnip greens and anchovy. Mains range from classics like involtini di pollo alla speck (£11.50), to stufato di cinghiale con polenta grigliata (£12.50) – wild boar stew with grilled polenta. Puds are predictable, so best opt for torta di Merano (£3.50) – chocolate cake always appeals.

The wine list is short, carefully chosen and perfectly attuned to the food. There are some moody bins like Papiri from Sardinia (£17.80), and a splendid Cannonau (£15.70).

FISH AND CHIPS

Olley's

Olley's is a famous fish and chip shop. It is partly famous because it has won various awards, and partly because of proprietor Richard Niazi's tireless publicity offensive. Olley's takes up two shop fronts just across the road from Brockwell Park: one shop is the takeaway and the other is the sit-down restaurant. The restaurant decor revolves around unfinished brickwork and patchy terracotta plaster, reminding you of the Mexican ruin so ably defended by the Magnificent Seven. Even for an eccentric restaurant in SE24, Olley's looks very odd.

Cost	£8–35

Address 67–69 Norwood Rd, SE24
℡ 020 8671 8259
Station BR Herne Hill
Open Mon & Sun 5–10.30pm, Tues–Sat noon–10.30pm
Accepts All major credit cards except Diners
🌐 www.olleys.info

Start with the avocado with prawn (£3.85) – ripe avo, pink prawns, pinker sauce; or clench your teeth at the kitsch of "Neptune's Punchbowl, a planktonic delight" and try the creamy, home-made fish soup (£3.50), which is surprisingly good – smooth and well seasoned. On to more serious matters: the chips are good here. Niazi believes in pre-blanching, and when done well this technique guarantees chips that are fluffy inside and crisp outside. The mushy peas (£1.50) are commendable and so are the wallies (45p) – which translates as gherkins, for non-Londoners. The fish is a triumph, fresh, white and flaky inside, crisp and golden outside – obviously the fryer knows his craft. Each served with chips, the leader board reads as follows: cod (£7.65); plaice (£8.10); haddock (£8.15); salmon (£8.95); monkfish (£9.35); swordfish (£9.75); halibut (£10.50); and hake (£9.95). Then there is the seafood platter: three prawns, three scampi, three haddies, three plaice goujons, three calamari and chips (£9.95). If you have the temerity to ask for a fish and *large* chips, the plateful that arrives is so large that the staff must be taking the proverbial.

The only puzzle (apart from the Mexican decor and the menu whimsy) is why anyone should come out to a really good fish and chip restaurant and choose the "Wild mushrooms in brandy sauce – folded layers of puff pastry filled with fresh mushrooms, courgettes and brown rice, topped with brandy sauce and served with broccoli and new potatoes" (£6.90), a dish sadly bereft of either fish or chips.

Satay Bar

The Satay Bar, part of the regeneration of the heart of Brixton, is tucked away behind the Ritzy cinema. First impression of this lively restaurant and bar is one of fun, pure and simple; the term "laid back" could have been invented for it. The interior is dark and warm, and the non-stop party atmosphere is bolstered by the thumping beat of the background music. If you are old and grizzly it will certainly be too loud for you. If not, settle in, relax and take a look at the art. If you happen to like one of the many paintings adorning the walls, buy it – they are for sale.

Cost	£15–30

Address 450 Coldharbour Lane, SW9
℡ 020 7326 5001
Station Brixton
Open Mon–Fri noon–3pm & 6–11.30pm, Sat & Sun noon–midnight
Accepts All major credit cards
⊛ www.sataybar.co.uk

Dishes are Indonesian with the chilli factor toned down (for the most part) to accommodate European taste buds. The menu is a testing one – at least when it comes to pronouncing the names of the dishes – but the food is well cooked, service is friendly and efficient, and the prices are reasonable. Your waiter will smile benignly at your attempt to say udang goreng tepung (£6.25) – a starter of lightly battered, deep-fried king prawns served with a sweet chilli sauce. Obvious choices, such as the chicken or prawn satay (£5.75), are rated by some as the best in London. Otherwise try the chicken wings with garlic and green chilli (£5.25), which are no less appealing. The hottest dishes are to be found among the curries. The medium kari ikan (£6.95), a red snapper-based Javanese fish curry, packs a punch even though styled "medium", while the rendang ayam (£5.95), a spicy chicken dish, is only cooled by the addition of a coconut sauce. For something lighter, the mee hoon goreng (£5.25) is a satisfying dish of spicy egg noodles fried with seafood and vegetables; or there's gado-gado (£4.95), a side dish of bean curd and vegetables with spicy peanut sauce, which is almost a meal in itself.

If terminal indecision sets in and you find yourself pinned by the menu like a rabbit in the headlights, try the rijstafel (£13.95 per person, minimum order for two), a combination of six specially selected dishes. This also has a vegetarian option.

Three Monkeys

In the West End and the City, cool restaurateurs are forever buying up old banks, ripping the insides out, slapping on a coat of ultra-chic frosted glass and re-opening as the latest thing in slick designer restaurants. It's just a bit of a shock to see such an establishment – complete with a gangplank bridge over the basement bar – in sleepy old Herne Hill. And if that doesn't rock your imagination back on its heels, let's just add that Three Monkeys is an Indian restaurant, albeit an unusual one. The well-written menu steers firmly away from clichéd Indian food.

Cost	£20–40

Address 136–140 Herne Hill, SE24
℡ 020 7738 5500
Station BR Herne Hill
Open Daily 6–11pm
Accepts All major credit cards
⊛ www.3monkeys restaurant .com

Starters range from shammi kebab (£4.95) – minced lamb rissoles the size and shape of a hockey puck – to a brilliant, messy-looking dish, palak palodi chat (£4.75), which is small cubes of spinach mixture deep-fried until crisp and served with plenty of chunky raw veg and two sauces – sharp, sharp tamarind and creamy yoghurt. Very nice. As is the vogue, there is an open kitchen, and the grills and bread are all visibly well made. The main courses run from simple dishes like lamb rojangosh (£8.95) to dishes like chicken tikka makhani (£8.95), which many curryologists assert is the parent of chicken tikka masala. Look out for a range of good fish dishes, and do not be put off by the fact that most of the curries have names unfamiliar to British curry houses; they are authentic for all that. Try the mean colambo (£9.50), cod that has been given the fiery Chettiyar treatment. Prices are always steepest anywhere you find the words "large" and "prawn". Prawns masala (£10.50) is a laconic title for prawns simmered in a sauce made with vinegar and a spicy Goan masala. Also in the good-but-expensive category is bhindi Jaipuri (£4.50), a dish of okra cut very fine and deep-fried before being served with a seasoning of sour dried mango powder.

Three Monkeys flies the flag for culture in Herne Hill. On Sunday evenings there is live jazz, there are monthly wine-tasting dinners (plus a wine shop), and the restaurant is also pressed into service as an art gallery.

Clapham & Wandsworth

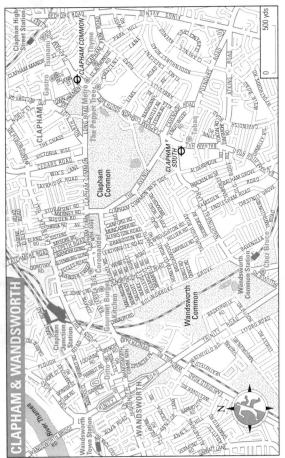

CLAPHAM & WANDSWORTH

© Crown copyright

Clapham & Wandsworth

SOUTH

Chez Bruce

Every year a nervous band of gastronomes spend valuable time worrying abut Chez Bruce. When a restaurant is so very good it is hard not to worry that it will slip; that the kitchen's Michelin star will mean menu changes; that the multiple awards for the wine list will mean fewer bargains; that chef-patron Bruce Poole will get bored. To put it simply the idea that Chez Bruce might "go off" is one of the worst gastro-nightmares you can have. Sleep easy. Chez Bruce is still delivering honest, unfussy, earthy, richly flavoured food. It is old-fashioned food that avoids the latest gastro-trend and often features the likes of pig's trotters, rabbit or mackerel. It is also a real bargain. Prix-fixe three-course menus offer lunch for £23.50 (Sun £25), and dinner for £30.

Cost	£27–60

Address 2 Bellevue Rd, SW17
℡ 020 8672 0114
Station BR Wandsworth Common
Open Mon–Thurs noon–2pm & 7–10.15pm, Fri & Sat 12.30 –2.30pm & 6.30–10.30pm, Sun 12.30–3pm
Accepts All major credit cards

FRENCH

The menu changes from season to season and day to day. Generally, the lunch menu is a shortened version of the dinner menu. The kind of starters you can expect are cream of watercress soup; stuffed pig's trotter and saddle of rabbit with endive and mustard salad; grilled organic salmon with ragout of cucumber, mussels and dill; deep-fried plaice with tartare sauce; or assiette of charcuterie with onion confit and toasted brioche. Or there might be a classic lurking, perhaps vitello tonnato. Main course dishes are deeply satisfying. You could well find persillade of pot-roast lamb with creamed potatoes and pearl barley; grilled turbot with wild mushrooms, beetroot and vermouth sauce; sauté of calf's kidneys and sweetbreads with caramelized apple, mustard and sage; or bourride of black bream with squid, cockles and green beans. This is one of those places where everything on the menu tempts, which is perhaps the reason why this restaurant is the favourite haunt of so many off-duty chefs.

The sweets here are well-executed classics: proper crème brûlée; clafoutis of plums with clotted cream; tarte Tatin aux poires. There's a stunning cheeseboard. No wonder Chez Bruce is booked every evening well in advance. Go for lunch instead – it'll make your day.

335

Coromandel

The Coromandel Coast (bottom of India, on the right) has lost out in the publicity war with the Malabar Coast (bottom of India, on the left). London has a good many Keralan restaurants (Malabar) and a good many Goan restaurants (Malabar-ish), but Tamil Nadu (Coromandel) isn't so readily front-of-mind. This restaurant hedges its bets quite suc-

Cost	£17–50

Address 2 Battersea Rise, SW11
℡ 020 7738 0038
Station BR Wandsworth Town
Open Daily 11am–3pm & 6.30–11pm
Accepts All major credit cards

cessfully, proclaiming itself a "Southern Indian" restaurant and offering a menu that runs all the way from South Indian vegetarian dishes – dosas and so forth – to Keralan dishes, chilli-rich Chettinad dishes from Tamil Nadu, and Sri Lankan specialities. Spread over two floors, the dining room is brightly painted, modern and busy. Prices are at about the same level as most of the other restaurants hereabouts, which ends up being somewhat higher than you'd expect in a run-of-the-mill curry house. Which is fair enough, as Coromandel is not run-of-the-mill.

On the menu you will find a small letter "s" beside some dishes, this means that they are only available on selected days. So, on one day starters might include fish cutlets (£4.95), which are a kind of Sri Lankan fish rissole, and on another occasion there may be devilled chicken (£4.95) – a chilli-hot Sri Lankan stir fry. Try the pakodas (£3.45), which are small vegetable fritters like chunky, spicy, tempura. Or consider starting in the tandoor section with the fish tikka (£4.95), which is a well-marinated kingfish, and very tasty indeed. Main course stars include the famous Chettinad chicken (£6.95), rich with small, infamous, dried red chillies. Or there's mutton poriyal (£7.95), which is a splendid, dry, almost musty curry. From the fish section try the fish kuzambu (£7.95) – kingfish again in subtle spicy gravy. The vegetable dishes are good – cadju curry (£6.95) is made with cashews and is rather surprising, if only because the nuts have been cooked until quite soft. Coromandel's breads are also worth investigating, as is their lemon rice (£2.50).

The service is solicitous here, but the staff are clearly concerned lest the food prove too hot for you. So remember to insist that your wonderful chicken Chettinad is authentically, painfully, blisteringly hot.

Ditto

Ditto is split down the middle: half is bar, half is restaurant. You are in Wandsworth, on the borders of Clapham, and this is a neighbourhood restaurant with a local clientele – hold those two images in your mind and you'll have a very clear idea of what this place is like. The bar is busy and loud, the restaurant is busy and loud. Don't even consider popping in at peak time without a booking. Most nights, at just after eight,

Cost	£12–45

Address 55–57 East Hill, SW18
℡ 020 8877 0110
Station BR Wandsworth Town
Open Mon–Thurs noon–3pm
& 7–11pm, Fri noon–3pm & 7–
11.30pm, Sat 10.30am–4.30pm
& 7–11.30pm, Sun noon–4pm;
bar food Sun 6–10pm
Accepts All major credit cards
ⓦ www.doditto.co.uk

a trampling herd of affluent nearly forty-somethings leave their au pairs watching over the infants and arrive for nosebag. The service is adroit, the menu is mainly French or Modern British and the food is good but not great. Thankfully the pricing keeps in perfect step with all of the above and delivers pretty good value.

The menu changes weekly and you can approach it two different ways. There's a set menu offering two courses for £14.50 and three courses for £18.50. There's a choice of three, three and three, and they are not "second best" dishes. Starters might include chicken liver parfait with Cumberland sauce, while mains range from confit duckling to pan-roast fillet of black bream. There is also an à la carte. From the starters, a smoked haddock fishcake on chive butter sauce (£5.50) is large and spherical; there's a risotto of smoked salmon and spring onions (£6.75); or perhaps a salad of black pudding with new potatoes and a soft poached egg (£5.75). Mains range from seared fillet of sea bass with chorizo mash and red wine vinaigrette (£12.25); to twice-cooked shank of lamb and basil mash (£12.50); and lasagne of Swiss chard and asparagus with melted cherry tomatoes (£11.95). Thankfully, the wine list won't make you dive for your wallet – it stretches across continents and from £11.50 to £30 a bottle.

Lunch is an excellent deal – on weekdays three courses with a glass of wine costs £10. Think about goat's cheese with sun-dried tomato crostini; cod fillet pan-roasted on clam Provençal; and sticky toffee pudding. Worth skiving for.

Gastro

Gastro was one of the pathfinders in the steady march to trendiness here in Cla'am, and it has changed accordingly. Where once all was favouritism for regulars, supported by a no-bookings policy, now you may need a reservation to get in. The big table you have to share with other diners is still there and the food is still unabashed about its Frenchness, but there are competing eateries up and down Venn Street, and Gastro is no longer streets ahead.

Cost	£18–32
Address	67 Venn St, SW4
℡	020 7627 0222
Station	Clapham Common
Open	Daily 8am–midnight
Accepts	Cash or cheque only

The staff are French and the menu lists all the Gallic favourites, which tend to be inexpensive and generously portioned. Think yourself back to your last French holiday and enjoy. Under hors d'oeuvre you'll find a pukka soupe de poisson (£4.85) with the classic trimmings. Ordering seafood is straightforward: oysters are sold in sixes (£8.45); mussels arrive à la marinière (£7.05); and crabe mayonnaise (£9.95) is exactly that – a whole crab and mayonnaise. No arguments there! Ordering a salade Norvegienne (£7.05) brings smoked salmon, poached egg, lemon cream and French beans. The mains will also cosset any Francophile tendencies you may have: jarret de porc aux lentilles de Puy (£12.50); andouillette frites sauce moutarde (£8.75) – that deadly French sausage made from pigs chitterlings, very much an acquired taste; or an authentically straightforward entrecôte grillé, sauce Béarnaise, frites (£12.85). And there is always boudin noir pommes purées (£9.95) – black pudding, apples and mash – which is as good and as simple as it sounds. Fish dishes are well represented: try bar roti farci au thym et romarin (£14.60). Or perhaps a fish choucroute (£11.60) tempts? Or half a lobster (£18.95)? For puds think patisserie, and good patisserie at that.

House wine is served by the glass, carafe and bottle. The red is better than the white, but not by much. If funds are sufficient, delve further into the short list, or do the sensible thing and order a bottle of top-class French cider (£6.25).

Gourmet Burger Kitchen

On the face of it, the words "gourmet burger kitchen" do not make easy bedfellows when strung together. "Gourmet" contradicts "burger", and "kitchen" has an unnervingly homely ring to it. But taken as a whole phrase you can see the intention. "There are burgers here", the proprietors seem to want us to know, "but not those thin, mass-produced ones. Our burgers have flair and originality, but they are not high falutin' burgers; everything is hand-made and good." Anyway, GBK will do for now. The room is cramped and dominated by a large counter behind which there seem to be serried ranks of waitresses and chefs. Everything is pretty casual – you go up to the bar, order and pay, and then your meal is brought to the table.

Cost	£14–22

Address 44 Northcote Rd, SW11; with branches
℡ 020 7228 3309
Station BR Clapham Junction
Open Mon–Fri noon–11pm, Sat 11am–11pm, Sun 11am–10pm
Accepts All major credit cards except Diners
ⓦ www.gbkinfo.co.uk

The menu starts at the "classic – 100 per cent Aberdeen Angus Scotch beef, salad and relish" (£4.95). It also offers the blue cheese burger (£6.60), which adds the tang of Stilton to the main event; the chilli burger (£5.90); the avocado and bacon burger (£6.90); the Jamaican (£6.80) – with mangoes and ginger sauce; the pesterella (£6.90) – with fresh pesto and mozzarella; lamb (£6.90); venison (£6.95); chicken, bacon and avocado (£6.95); or chorizo (£6.95). There is even a "burger" made from Portabella mushroom (£6.30); or the falafel (£5.90), for any bemused vegetarian who strays into this unashamedly carnivorous place. The fries are good and the side salad is excellent, with good fresh leaves and a perky dressing. The Gourmet Burger Kitchen has a good feel to it, and the food is top quality. Despite the dread word "gourmet", prices are not out of reach.

Consider the Kiwiburger (£6.70). This is made of Aberdeen Angus beef with beetroot, egg, pineapple, cheese, salad and relish. (What, no spatchcocked kiwi? No roundels of kiwi fruit?) This burger is 15cm tall, and to take a bite out of it you would need the gape of an anaconda. Simply sawing it in half scatters complex garnishes across the plate. But any dish so magnificently eclectic has to be tried. Bizarrely enough it tastes pretty good.

FUSION/MODERN BRITISH

Metro

🍴 As you emerge from the depths of the southern exit of Clapham Common tube station, Metro is facing you – which is presumably how the place came by its name. Until 2001, Metro was a wine bar where the raucous crowds were usually loud enough to muffle the ping of the microwave that dominated the cuisine. Then the business was taken

Cost	£16–30

Address 9 Clapham Common
South Side, SW4
☎ 020 7627 0632
Station Clapham Common
Open Mon & Tues 6–11pm,
Wed–Sun noon–11pm
Accepts All major credit cards
except AmEx

over by Fran Macmillan and it was all change. Macmillan has served time as the front of house in various West End establishments and understands that all the meeting and greeting stuff goes a lot better when underpinned by decent food.

The food is sophisticated but whole-hearted. Start with something simple, like a pea, mint and spinach soup (£4.50); or something more modern, such as balsamic baby octopus with wilted greens and Parmesan rice pie-crust (£5.25). Or perhaps char-grilled chorizo on creamy coconut spinach (£4.95)? Or easy-snap crab claws with warm lime and coriander couscous (£5.50)? Or maybe something a touch less spooky, such as seared harissa beef strips with char-grilled polenta and tomato yoghurt (£5.95). These are brave combinations of taste and texture that make for adventurous dining. Mains are in the same style: salsa verde and ostrich steak on rosemary-roasted new potatoes (£12.50); leek and Applewood envelope of pork with Portabella mushroom and creamed Madeira sauce (£10.50). Pan-fried marlin fillet is served on a pork and chicken paella, and drizzled with red pesto (£11.50); while fresh fettucine comes with wild mushroom broth and Parmesan shavings (£11). Puds (all £3.95) are sound if predictable: chocolate pecan pie; crème brûlée; white lemon cheese tart. The service is slick and friendly.

Metro has a very pretty secret garden with a profusion of candles, small terracotta braziers for chilly moments and the reviving green of plants. This is the perfect formula for relaxed dining and it is heavily booked by those in the know. And it is uncommonly thoughtful for any establishment to provide blankets for the dogs of Sunday brunchers lingering over the newspapers.

The Pepper Tree

Situated on the seemingly endless south side of the Common, just a stone's throw from the tube station, this open-fronted Thai eatery serves no-non-sense, short-order dishes. This kind of spicy Thai food is perfectly in tune with the clientele, which is predominantly made up of twenty-somethings, as will be instantly apparent from both the crowds and the hubbub. Thankfully, the food is well cooked in a pleasantly straightforward sort of way and prices are competitive. Look out for the weekly "chef's special" (£5.50) which depends on a telling combination of the chef's mood and just what ingredients are good each particular week.

Cost	£12–25

Address 19 Clapham Common South Side, SW4
℡ 020 7622 1758
Station Clapham Common
Open Mon noon–3pm & 6–10.30pm, Tues–Sat noon–3pm & 6–11pm, Sun noon–10.30pm
Accepts MasterCard, Visa

You can build your meal in stages, rather like you would a Greek meze. Vegetable rolls (£2.25) are made with vermicelli noodles, shaved carrots and Chinese mushrooms wrapped in filo pastry. Egg-fried rice (£1.75), is just that; and there's a stir-fry of mixed seafood (£4.50), which is tossed with fresh chillies, garlic and sweet basil. Green prawn curry (£3.95) is simmered in coconut milk with Thai aubergines, lime leaves and sweet basil, and comes medium-hot. Big tum chicken noodles (£4.75) are thick, yellow and fried with chillies and sweet basil. Among the salads, the Pepper Tree (£3.95) combines marinated grilled slices of beef with lemon juice, coriander, spring onions and chilli. Many dishes use the same ingredients but ring the changes in terms of balance and preparation techniques. Sweet things include stem-ginger ice cream (£1.95) and bananas in coconut milk (£2.50), sprinkled with sesame seeds. Sticky rice with mango (£2.50) is described on the menu as mango with sticky rice, which seems a model of accuracy.

The Pepper Tree churns out simple spicy food, which is distributed by cheerful staff and sold at affordable prices. Even the drinks are reasonable – you can get a mug of tea for under a quid and there are bottles of house reds and whites at £8.50. There's also an Argentine Norton Merlot (£11.95), which is a real bargain.

341

Tabaq

The owners of Tabaq used to drive up from the suburbs to work in a smart West End restaurant, and on the way they would travel along Balham Hill and past Clapham Common. They had set their sights on having a restaurant of their own, smarter than the usual curry house, somewhere they would serve traditional Pakistani specialities. So when signs went up outside 47 Balham Hill they took the plunge. They named their restaurant after the *tabaq* – a large serving dish – and set about dishing up authentic Lahori fare. Nearly a decade later they have a shelf full of awards and a restaurant full of loyal customers to show for it.

Cost	£14–25

Address **47 Balham Hill, SW12**
ⓣ 020 8673 7820
Station **Clapham South**
Open **Mon–Sat noon–2.45pm & 6pm–midnight**
Accepts **All major credit cards**
ⓦ www.tabaq.co.uk

The menu comes with a multitude of sections: starters, grills, seafood, chicken curries, specialities, rice, breads and natural vegetables. To start, go straight for the tandoor and grill section, which features some of the best dishes on the menu, and most commendably carries the boast "we do not add colour to our food". Seek kabab Lahori (£6.25) is made from well-seasoned minced lamb, and shish kabab lamb (£6.25) is delicious. Or try the masala machli Lahori (£6.25) – fish in a light and spicy batter. As an accompaniment, order raita (£1.95) – yoghurt with cucumber, herbs and spices, and maybe a naan-e-Punjabi (£2.50) of heavy, butter-rich bread from the tandoor, with kachomer (£1.95), a kind of coarse-cut Asian salsa. At this stage of your meal you may well be tempted to choose simply from the salan, or chicken curries. There's murgh taway ka makhani (£8.50) – this sauce is thought to be a buttery ancestor of chicken tikka masala – or murgh palak (£7.25), chicken and spinach. Maybe you'd like to try one of the dishes that won the Tabaq chef one of his many awards? Zaikadaar haandi gosht (£8.50) is a rich dish of lamb marinated in yoghurt and cooked in a traditional *haandi*, or cooking pot. And there are good biryanis, too.

Desserts include one item you do not immediately associate with Pakistani cuisine – baked Alaska (£12), which serves two and must be ordered in advance.

Thyme

This site used to be home to one of London's only neighbourhood fish restaurants, so regular customers waited nervously when it changed hands in autumn 2001. Out went the miserably uncomfortable chairs, in came softer seating and softer lighting; out went the hideous collage of sardine bones in salt and in came an equally ugly painting of a blue nude on the back wall. Then the restaurant re-opened as Thyme. The food is good, the prices are fair, the service is friendly ... this is an engaging little restaurant where the kitchen tries hard and succeeds more often than it fails.

Cost	£20–65

Address 14 Clapham Park Rd, SW4
☏ 020 7627 2468
Station Clapham Common
Open Tues–Sat 6.30–10.30pm, Sun 12.30–3pm
Accepts All major credit cards except Diners

The idea is that you approach dinner as a multi-course affair. Four-course (£24) and six-course (£33) meals are given as examples. The menu is written to support this strategy, with two soups and a salad at £4, then choices at £5, £6, £7 and £8 before three dishes at £9. Portions are good, and some of the dishes masquerading as starters are easily large enough to be sold as mains. Soup (£4), fish (£6) and a main (£9) makes an economical three-course dinner at £19. White onion and thyme velouté with white truffle oil (£4) is very smooth and creamy. Minestrone of mussels, saffron noodles and crème fraîche (£5) is equally good. The pressed foie gras and game with smoked ham hock (£7) comes with a hunk of warm raisin bread. Or perhaps confit of rabbit with chestnut noodles and buttered broad beans (£7) appeals? Or roast skate wing, shallot mash and herb-caper jus (£8)? By the time you hit £9 – cassoulet of lamb with cannellini beans and balsamic carrots; or braised shin of beef with pot-roast parsnips, port jus and horseradish Chantilly – you will certainly be won over. The food is well seasoned even if the descriptions tend to be a tad florid – calling the lamb dish a cassoulet will earn Thyme a writ from the mayor of Castelnaudary. Puds (all £5) include a white chocolate and yoghurt soup, and chestnut "Tiramisu" pears with clementine ice.

The wine list is unagressively priced, and there's an epic tasting menu available every day except Sunday – £55 to include four glasses of wine.

Tsunami

(icon) Tsunami opened towards the latter part of 2001, and within weeks the proprietors could have filled a scrapbook with glowing reviews. Which is not entirely unexpected, as the prime movers of this new venture include time served at Nobu on their CVs. The dining room is surprisingly large, and elegant in a minimalist, Japanesey sort of way. All the staff are outstandingly helpful and friendly and the kitchen bustles away in full view through a long serving hatch. The restaurant is at the end of Clapham High Street that is nearest to Brixton, and it is very much an area in transition. Scruffy shops have given way to trendy bars and these are just starting to be supplanted by ambitious restaurants, of which Tsunami is the perfect example.

Cost	£14–40

Address Unit 3, 1–7 Voltaire Rd, SW4
℡ 020 7978 1610
Station Clapham North
Open Mon–Fri 6–11pm & Sat 6–11.30pm
Accepts All major credit cards except Diners

The food is very good, the presentation on the plate is quite outstanding, and the bill is not over the top. For once all those pretty-as-a-picture arrangements seem to stem from a genuine love of the beautiful. Order a few starters to share. The butternut ebi with creamy spicy sauce (£5.95) is very good – plump prawns in crispy overcoats. Or there's the mint tea duck with plum and honey miso (£6.10) – slivers of tender duck breast served cold. Or the agedashi tofu (£4.25) – this is a strange one; cubes of melt-in-the-mouth tofu have been fried for a crisp exterior, and each square of tofu topped with a tiny pyramid of daikon radish – it's a fascinating exercise in multiple textures. Best of all is the tuna tataki (£6.95), which is a sashimi made with seared tuna and dressed with a sharp ponzu dressing. Each slice is raw in the middle and firm around the edge – very delicious indeed. The sushi here look good. The tempura is light and there are lots of interesting vegetable tempura (2 pieces £1–2.80). An old favourite like grilled marinated eel (£11.95) comes with rice and miso soup, and that strange, smooth, Japanese chicken curry, nami katsu (£8.95), is well done.

The food at Tsunami is worth a detour, and the style police will be happy here – yet another indicator of Clapham's new dawn.

Greenwich & Blackheath

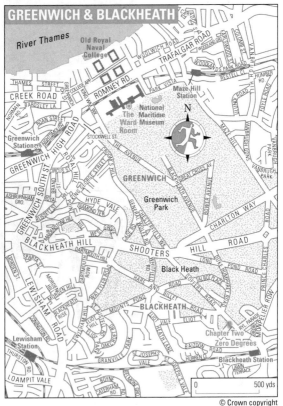

GREENWICH & BLACKHEATH

River Thames

Old Royal Naval College

WOOLWICH ROAD

TRAFALGAR ROAD

THAMES STREET

CREEK ROAD

ROMNEY RD

PARK VISTA

Maze Hill Station

NORMAN RD

ROAN STREET

BARDSLEY LA.

STOCKWELL ST.

The Ward Room

National Maritime Museum

N

Greenwich Station

GREENWICH HIGH ROAD

ROYAL HILL

CIRCUS ST

KING GEORGE STREET

THE AVENUE

GREENWICH

GREAT CROSS AV

ASHBURNHAM GRO

HYDE VALE

GENERAL WOLFE ROAD

Greenwich Park

BOWER AVENUE

CHARLTON WAY

GREENWICH SOUTH ST.

ROYAL HILL

DIAMOND TER.

MAIDENSTONE HILL

GRAVE

CROOMS HILL

BLACKHEATH HILL

DARTMOUTH HILL

DARTMOUTH ROW

SHOOTERS   HILL   ROAD

LONG POND ROAD

PRINCE CHARLES

SPARTA ST

MORDEN HILL

BLACKHEATH RISE

HARE AND BILLET ROAD

Black Heath

TALBOT PLACE

LEWISHAM

LEWISHAM ROAD

MOUNTS POND

BLACKHEATH

ELIOT

VALE

HEATH LANE

BAIZDON ROAD

Chapter Two
Zero Degrees

Lewisham Station

THURSTON RD

GRANVILLE

ST. JOSEPHS VALE

ST. JOSEPH'S VALE

Blackheath Station

LAWN TERRACE

MONPELIER ROW

RYL. PARADE

LOAMPIT VALE

BOYNE

CATERHAM RD

| 0 | 500 yds |

© Crown copyright

Chapter Two

Occupying a bright, sunny position (weather permitting) in a small smart parade of shops just off the heath, Chapter Two seems to promise good things even from the outside. Its clean, half-clear, half-frosted glass frontage allows you to glimpse the band of well-dressed diners enjoying themselves within. And when you enter you'll find yourself in a sleek, modern space, with light wood and metal complemented by richly coloured walls, all coming together to set off crisp linen and sparkling glassware. The whole place has a professionally-run air, exuding comfort and confidence.

Cost	£15–40

Address 43–45 Montpelier
Vale, Blackheath, SE3
℡ 020 8333 2666
Station BR Blackheath
Open Mon–Thurs noon–
2.30pm & 6–10pm, Fri & Sat
noon–2.30pm & 6–11pm, Sun
noon–3.30pm & 7–9.30pm
Accepts All major credit cards

This feeling of competence also embraces the menu. Dinner is a set price affair: £16.50 for two courses; £19.50 for three, from Sunday to Thursday, going up to £22.50 on Friday and Saturday evenings. There's nothing particularly unusual or showy on offer, but there's plenty of choice among the reasonably classic, well-thought-out dishes, and they use decent ingredients to good advantage. Among the first courses you may find pumpkin soup with a foie gras tortellini and confit ginger; or beetroot gravadlax. Main courses range from the likes of roast cod with spinach and shellfish chowder; or lamb rump with a wild mushroom and kidney faggot. Portions are generous and presentation is top class. The puds are mainly tried and tested favourites: warm chocolate fondant; warm blueberry Madeleine with strawberry ripple ice cream and a Florentine biscuit; baked almond cheesecake; home-made ice cream.

Chapter Two is a decent local restaurant, special enough for annual occasions but not so expensive as to prohibit more regular visits. Service is efficient and professional rather than pally, and someone has obviously given the wine list some thought – there's a wide range of wines from around the world, available at ungreedy prices, including a fair choice by the glass. If you've a nose for a bargain, visit for lunch, when the menu is much the same as the evening but prices fall to £14.50 for two courses and £18.50 for three (Sunday lunch, £13/16).

BRITISH

The Wardroom

Should a morning's sightseeing work up an appetite too serious for the fast food shacks and tourist restos of Greenwich, then The Wardroom (found within the magnificent buildings of the Old Royal Naval College) is the perfect place for lunch. It was the pensioners of the old Greenwich hospital who first caught on to the benefits of dining in the Undercroft – the room under the painted hall – there was the lack of stairs, the bright, airy feel, the vaulted ceilings and hopefully, then as today, the decent food. In 1939, the Royal Navy took over and they used the Wardroom continuously until 1998. Determined to continue this tradition, the Greenwich Foundation re-opened the restaurant to the public in late 2000. It still retains its airs and graces – a huge portrait of the Queen and the Duke of Edinburgh gazes down at you as you tuck into lunch, and the names of past Commanders of the College adorn the walls. The food is solid English, the sort of thing your Mum would make if she was a good plain cook.

Cost	£18–35

Address Old Royal Naval College, Romney Rd, SE10
☎ 020 8269 4797
Station DLR Cutty Sark Gardens
Open Mon–Fri & Sun noon–2.30pm
Accepts MasterCard, Visa

Menus are changed every two to three months and prices are fixed at £15.50 for two courses, £19.50 for three and £23.50 for three courses with cheese. On Sunday a traditional three-course lunch (£15.50) is available. For starters, there are old friends such as home-made soup – "chunky vegetable", with the emphasis on chunky – and egg and bacon salad with mayonnaise. Mr Addington's home-made pâté (named after the executive chef) is simple yet delicious. Tradition and reliability are also the themes of the main courses. Fillet of lamb with boulangère potatoes is particularly good, and the pan-fried sirloin is well worth a try. The deep-fried cod in beer batter, complete with mushy peas and the fattest chips in Greenwich, is a delight. As a nod to vegetarians, the blue cheese soufflé with watercress, orange and pine nut salad is a fine alternative.

And so to puddings, where comfort rules: rhubarb crumble; baked Alaska with a tangy raspberry sauce; and the must-have chocolate orange and Grand Marnier pudding in a fudge sauce. Anyone for seconds?

Zerodegrees

(icon) 0° – as the logotype, napkins, menus and so forth would have it – is a lively fun factory in the heart of sedate and respectable Blackheath. The proprietors have taken the idea of the microbrewery, a formula that has been honed to perfection in the West End, and put together a lively venue. It's a grand looking space, all aluminium cladding and stainless steel brewing equipment, with a large bar which dominates and a small area for seating and eating by the open kitchen.

Cost	£8–20

Address 29–31 Montpelier Vale, Blackheath SE3
⏺ 020 8852 5619
Station BR Blackheath
Open Daily noon–11.30pm
Accepts All major credit cards except Diners
ⓦ www.zerodegrees
-microbrewery.co.uk

ITALIAN/PIZZA

The menu is an obvious one. Other beer places do wood-fired pizzas – so does Zerodegrees. Other beer places do special sausages – so does Zerodegrees. Other beer places do mussels … you've guessed it, so does Zerodegrees. It's an engagingly simple idea, and given that this is a loud, happy place full of people keen to get blatted by some pretty decent beers, the food admirably fulfils its role as a solid counterweight. If you want starters, it's best to keep it simple: garlic bread (£2.50); dough balls (£1.95); a trio of crostini (£3.95); marinated artichokes (£3.95). Listed under salads there's a sound if uninspired Caesar salad (£6.95) – pity there are no anchovies. The moody sausages come with mash (£6.95), mussels come in a kilo pot with frites and mayo (£10.95) and there are eighteen different pizzas all tasting suitably smoky and ranging from traditional cheese to Peking duck by way of American hot and all the usual suspects (£5.25–7.25).

Five different beers are brewed on the premises: a Pilsner; a good, hoppy-tasting pale ale; a brown ale; a wheat ale; and a "special" which changes regularly to stop you getting bored. The pricing is simple: halves (£1.15); pints (£2.30); four-pint jugs (£8.25); and at happy hour, which is in force from 4–7pm Monday to Friday, all pints are £1.50. Beer and loud music – everything you need to get happy, and then a pepperoni pizza to follow. It may not be original, and it's certainly not for the middle aged, but it works.

Kennington & Vauxhall

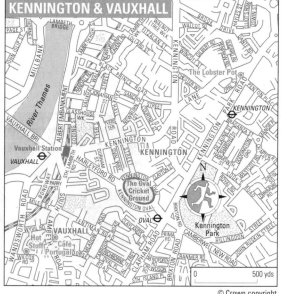

© Crown copyright

Café Portugal

Cost	£11–27

Address Victoria House,
South Lambeth Rd, SW8
℡ 020 7587 1962
Station Vauxhall
Open Mon–Sat 8am–11pm,
Sun 10am–10.30pm
Accepts All major credit cards
except Diners

When setting up a bar, café or restaurant, the first item on any proud new Portuguese owner's shopping list must be the telly. All the televisions in South Lambeth Road seem to be turned up loud, and the one in the bar of Café Portugal is no exception (thankfully the one in the restaurant half of the operation is not always switched on). Portuguese restaurateurs have all mastered the trick of integrating their establishments with the community and Café Portugal is a laid-back, easy-paced kind of eatery with distinctly dodgy mud-orange decor. The food is workmanlike and appears authentically Portuguese, as do some of the television programmes.

There is now a rather twee menu which comes complete with a small photo of the dish in question – rather like those models in the windows of Japanese restaurants. To start with you can opt for calamares (£3.70) and sopa do dia (£2.20), the soup of the day. Or more interesting dishes like ameijoas a Café Portugal (£3.80), which are clams and must be a step up on that trusty old Portuguese special, avocado with prawns (£3.30). The menu goes on to display a dozen fishy options: lobster, sea bass, Dover sole, three monkfish dishes and three ways with salt cod. Of the latter, the most adventurous sounding, bacalhau à Gomes de Sá (£9) turns out to be a stunning and gloriously simple dish of salt cod cooked in the oven with potatoes, onions and chunks of hard-boiled egg. For the meat-eater there's carne de porco à Alentejana (£9), another all-in-one, home-cooked kind of meal in which small chunks of pork are served with some clams, chorizo and chopped pickled vegetables, then small cubes of crisp-fried potato are scattered over the top. The resulting dish is a grand blend of tastes and textures. At Café Portugal, puddings are largely pastries and you are doomed if you don't like eggy confections.

The wine list here is a Portuguese affair, and reasonably priced, so look out for interesting little numbers from the Dão and the Douro. Café Portugal caters to its knowledgeable, mainly Portuguese, clientele.

INDIAN

Hot Stuff

This tiny restaurant, run by the Dawood family in south Lambeth, is something of an institution. It has only a few seats and offers simple and startlingly cheap food to an enthusiastic local following. The food is just what you would expect to get at home – assuming you were part of Nairobi's Asian community. Trade is good and has been the catalyst for a refurb – now all is soft blues and orange with an array of different coloured chairs.

Cost	£10–20

Address 19 Wilcox Rd, SW8
☎ 020 7720 1480
Station Vauxhall/Stockwell
Open Mon–Fri noon–10pm,
Sat 4–10pm
Accepts All major credit cards
🌐 www.eathotstuff.com

The starters are sound rather than glorious, so it's best to dive straight into the curries. There are a dozen chicken curries and a similar number of lamb dishes, all priced at between £3 and £5. It is hard to find any fault with a curry that costs just £3! The most expensive option is in the fish section – king prawn biryani, which costs £6.50, not much more than you would pay for a curried potato in the West End. The portions aren't monster-sized, and the spicing isn't subtle, but the welcome is genuine and the bill is tiny. Arrive before 9.30pm and you can sample the delights of the stuffed paratha (£1.30) – light and crispy with potato in the middle, they taste seriously delicious. Chickpea curry (£2.30), daal soup (£2.20) and mixed vegetable curry (£2) all hit the spot with vegetarians. For meat-eaters, the chicken Madras (£3.15) is hot and workmanlike, while the chicken bhuna (£3.15) is rich and very good. However, the jewel in the crown of the Hot Stuff menu is masala fish (£3.75), which is only available from Wednesdays to Saturdays; thick chunks of tilapia are marinated for 24 hours in salt and lemon juice before being cooked in a rich sauce with coriander, cumin and ginger.

Hot Stuff closes prudently before the local pubs turn out, and part of the fun here is to watch latecomers – say a party of three arriving at 9.50pm and seeking food. Promising to eat very simply and very quickly may do the trick, as this restaurant is driven by the principles of hospitality and puts many more pretentious establishments to shame. Bring your own alcohol, as no corkage is charged.

The Lobster Pot

You have to feel for Nathalie Régent. What must it be like to be married to – and working alongside – a man whose love of the bizarre verges on the obsessional? Britain is famed for breeding dangerously potty chefs, but The Lobster Pot's chef-patron, Hervé Régent, originally from Vannes in Brittany, is well ahead of the field. Walk down Kennington Lane towards the restaurant and it's even money as to whether you

Cost	£10–35

Address 3 Kennington Lane, SE11
℡ 020 7582 5556
Station Kennington
Open Tues–Sat noon–2.30pm & 7–11pm
Accepts All major credit cards
Ⓦ www.lobsterpotrestaurant .co.uk

are struck first by the life-size painted plywood cutout of Hervé dressed in oilskins, or the speakers relaying a soundtrack of seagulls and melancholy Breton foghorns.

These clues all point towards fish, and doubtless Hervé will appear to greet you in nautical garb, moustache bristling, and guide you towards his best catches of the day. The fish here is pricey but it is fresh and well chosen. Starters range from well-made, very thick, traditional fish soup (£6.50) to a really proper plateau de fruits de mer (small £11.50, large £22.50). The main course specials sometimes feature strange fish that Hervé has discovered on his early-morning wanderings at Billingsgate. There are good spicy dishes too, such as fillet de thon à la Créole (£14.50), which is tuna with a perky tomato sauce, and monkfish with Cajun spices and white butter sauce (£15.50). Simpler, and as good in its way, is la sélection de la mer à l'ail (£14.50), which is a range of fishy bits – some monkfish tail, an oyster, a bit of sole, tiny squid, and so on – all grilled and slathered in garlic butter. The accompanying bread is notable, a soft, doughy *pain rustique*, and for once le plateau de fromage à la Française (£6) doesn't disappoint.

The Lobster Pot's weekday set lunch (£10 for two courses, £13.50 for three) makes lots of sense. It could get you moules gratinées à l'ail followed by filet de merlan sauce Créole and crêpe sauce à la mangue. During 2002 the Régents introduced an eight-course surprise menu which has proved very popular – three fish dishes, one meat and so on, for £39.50 per person.

The Lobster Pot

Putney

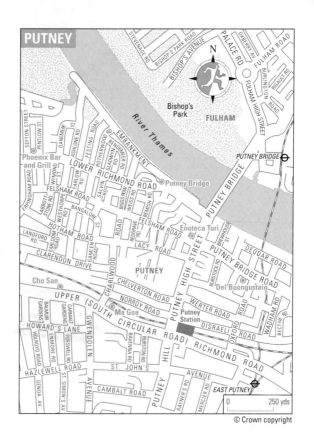

PUTNEY

© Crown copyright

Del Buongustaio

On the first day of each month it's all change at Del Buongustaio as they unleash a new menu on the appreciative residents of Putney. The menu here features well-cooked, authentic food with a sprinkling of less familiar dishes from Cinderella regions like Puglia and Piedmont, as well as some painstakingly researched gems that once graced tables in Renaissance Italy. The dining room is

Cost	£16–45

Address 283 Putney Bridge Rd, SW15
ⓣ 020 8780 9361
Station East Putney
Open Mon–Sat noon–3pm & 6.30–11pm, Sun noon–3.30pm
Accepts All major credit cards except Diners
ⓦ www.theitalianrestaurant.net

light, airy and pleasantly informal. The cooking is good too, with authentic dishes and friendly service. Take time to study the wine list, which is particularly strong on classy bottles from less familiar provinces.

Who knows what the next menu will bring? But you can hazard a guess that there will be interesting pasta dishes, such as a splendid spaghetti con melanzane e ricotta (£5.90/8.40) – spaghetti with cherry tomatoes, aubergine and ricotta. Or perhaps papardelle al sugo d'anatra (£6.45) – pasta served with a ragout of duck. Thoroughly delicious. The piatto pizzicarello (£7.50), described with disarming modesty as a "plate of savouries", is a regular starter option. And then there may be the torta rinascimentale di fave, ricotta e prosciutto (£6.25), an amazing multi-layered cake of broad beans, prosciutto, ricotta and Fontina cheese that comes with a rocket and egg sauce. Main course dishes may include lamb, sea bass, veal, pork, chicken, guinea fowl, cod or perhaps a Swiss chard and ricotta pudding. In season, there may be a pastello di caccia-gione (£15.50), which is a kind of medieval game pie containing a bit of everything. Look out for the rustic *dal campo* side dishes, particularly verdure al vapore (£2.95), which is mixed seasonal greens. The multi-choice set lunch deal brings three courses for £12.95.

It's worth saving space for a dessert if only for the eight splendid pudding wines, served by the glass, including Vin Santo (£3.80), the befuddlingly alcoholic Aleatico di Puglia (£3.80) and a 1995 Recioto della Valpolicella (£4.50). There is also a huge selection of merciless grappas...

JAPANESE

Cho-San

🍴 Too many Japanese restaurants use extremely high prices and ultra-swish West End premises to keep themselves to themselves. As a European adventurer basking in the impeccably polite and attentive service, it's hard not to feel a little anxious. What should you order? How do you eat it? Will it taste nice? How much does it cost? If you have ever been assailed by

Cost	£8–35

Address 292 Upper Richmond Rd, SW15
☎ 020 8788 9626
Station BR Putney
Open Tues–Fri 6.30–10.30pm, Sat & Sun noon–2.30pm & 6.30–10.30pm
Accepts All major credit cards

these worries you should pop along to Cho-San in Putney. This small, unpretentious, family-run restaurant opened in 1998 and has built up a steady trade. As well as a host of knowledgeable Japanese drawn by the good fresh food and sensible prices, there are interested Londoners tucking into sushi with gusto. On one occasion these devotees included a twelve-year-old girl, who, judging by her uniform, had dropped in for dinner on the way home from school.

The menu is a book. And one worth reading. This is your chance to try all those dishes you have never had, without wounding your pocket. The sushi is good. The sashimi is good. And a giant boat of assorted sushi and sashimi, with miso soup and dessert costs £19.90. But why not try some more obscure sushi? The prices of the fancy ones range from £2.50 to £5.90 for two pieces. Or, if you prefer your fish cooked, choose the perfect tempura cuttlefish (£7.90) – a stunning achievement, its batter light enough to levitate. And then there are always the kushiage dishes, where something is put onto a skewer, gets an egg and breadcrumb jacket and is treated to a turn around the deep fryer. Ordering tori kushiage (£5.60) gets you two skewers, each of which holds two large lumps of chicken and a chunk of sweet onion. Delicious. Or opt for tempura king prawn (£9.90). Then there are the meat dishes, the fish dishes, the rice dishes, the soba noodles, the udon noodles ... and the hot sakes, cold sakes and beers. You could eat your way to a good understanding of Japanese food here. Ask the charming, helpful staff and get stuck in.

Newcomers should take the easy option: a profusion of seven-course set meals costing between £17.90 and £19.90.

Enoteca Turi

If you like your Italian food a little more adventurous than the usual, then it is worth making the journey to Putney and Giuseppe Turi's newly refurbished restaurant. Everything is based on fresh ingredients and, like some other notable venues, Enoteca offers a very personal version of good Italian regional cooking. Turi himself hails from Apulia,

Cost £25–65

Address 28 Putney High St, SW15
℡ 020 8785 4449
Station Putney Bridge
Open Mon–Fri 12.30–2.30pm & 7–11pm, Sat 7–11pm
Accepts All major credit cards

ITALIAN

and many dishes are based on recipes from this area. Enoteca takes its name from the Italian term for a smart wine shop, so it's hardly surprising that wines are a prominent feature. There's a monumental list of more than ninety specialist Italian wines and a separate by-the-glass menu offering eleven Italian regional wines – an excellent way to educate the palate. Exploring the Italian wine regions is something of a hobby for Turi; he has bought widely and wisely and laid them down for future drinking.

As for the food, at lunch there is a shortened version of the dinner menu and dishes are a couple of pounds cheaper. In the evening you'd do well to start with charred artichoke hearts with Sardinian pecorino (£7.50); or perhaps a fresh crab salad with chickpea puree and spinach (£9.50). Pasta choices may include a scallop and asparagus risotto (£11 at lunch, £12.50 at dinner); garganelli with artichokes (£9/10.50); or fettucine al frutti di mare (£14.50). Main courses may include petto d'anatra (£14.50) – duck breast served with lentils and baked fresh ricotta. There is always a fresh fish of the day and a dish of the day. Desserts will test your mettle – go for the torta di cioccolata con nocciole (£5.50), a blockbusting chocolate and hazelnut cake, or perhaps the particularly good, authentic tiramisù (£5).

Though there are many good restaurants in this area, Enoteca has a loyal following and, except for Monday and Tuesday nights, it is essential to book. If you're more of a wine bluff than a wine buff you'll be grateful for the discreet numbers printed beside each dish on the menu – they represent the recommended wines, all of which are available by the glass.

Ma Goa

Despite the stylish ochre interior, complete with fans and blond wooden floor, despite the café-style chairs and tables, and the computer system to handle bills and orders, the overwhelming impression you are left with when you visit Ma Goa is of eating in somebody's home. This place is as far as you can possibly get from the chuck-it-in-a-frying-pan-and-heat-it-through

Cost	£14–30

Address 244 Upper Richmond Rd, SW15
℡ 020 8780 1767
Station BR Putney/East Putney
Open Tues–Sat 6.30–11pm, Sun 12.30–3pm & 6–10pm
Accepts All major credit cards
ⓦ www.magoa.co.uk

school of curry cookery. The food is deceptively simple, slow-cooked and awesomely tasty. And it is authentically Goan into the bargain.

The menu is fairly compact: half a dozen starters are followed by a dozen mains, while a blackboard adds a couple of dishes of the day. Shrimp balchao (£4) is a starter made from shrimps cooked in pickling spices and curry leaves. Sorpotel (£4/7) is made from lamb's liver, kidney and pork in a sauce rich with roast spices, lime and coriander. The Ma Goa's sausage (£4) is rich too, with palm vinegar, cinnamon and green chillies. Main courses are amazing. The spices are properly cooked out by slow cooking, which makes lifting the lids of the heavy clay serving pots a voyage of discovery. Porco vindaloo (£8.65), sharp with palm vinegar, is enriched with lumps of pork complete with rind. Gallina kodi (£7.95) is a gentle guinea fowl curry made with rose water. Ma's fish caldin (£8.75) is kind of fish stew with large chunks of fish in a coconut-based sauce. Or there's kata masala (£7.65), a chicken dish served on the bone (hooray) and heavy with cinnamon, black pepper, ginger and lime. Vegetarians are equally well served. Bund gobi (£3.50/6.50) is stir fried, shredded cabbage with carrots, ginger and cumin, while beringella (£3.50/6.50) is an aubergine dish made with pickling spices. The rice here is excellent.

On the specials board you might be lucky enough to find lamb kodi (£8), described as "lamb with cloves, garlic and chilli". On the electronic message winging its way to the kitchen this is altered to "Bella's lamb" – dishes here really are made from family recipes.

Phoenix Bar and Grill

This restaurant is a member of London's leading family of neighbourhood restaurants, and is related both to Sonny's (see p.403) and the Parade (see p.418). Anyone fancying their chances in what is a cut-throat marketplace would do well to study these establishments. They are all just trendy enough, the service is just slick enough and the cooking is marginally better than you would expect, with competitive pricing. In the spring of 2002, the Phoenix unveiled a new secret weapon, having lured Franco Taruschio (of Walnut Tree fame) out of retirement to re-write the menu and oversee one of his protegés in the kitchen. There's a large, white-painted room inside and a large, white-painted courtyard out front where you can eat alfresco.

Cost	£15–45
Address	162–164 Lower Richmond Rd, SW15
☎	020 8780 3131
Station	BR Putney
Open	Mon–Sat 12.30–2.30pm & 7–11pm, Sun 12.30–3pm & 7–10pm
Accepts	All major credit cards

Signor Taruschio's ever-changing menus draw on his heritage (the Marche in Italy) and that of his family (Thai influences), and the menu here includes some of the famous dishes that made the Walnut Tree a place of foodie pilgrimage. Chief among them is the epic eighteenth-century truffled lasagne, or vinicsgrassi maceratesi (£12.50). This is ambrosial stuff, and you can also order it as a starter (£7.50). Other starters may include baked cockle and mussel pie with bacon and leeks (£6.50); home-cured bresaola (£7.50); and goujonettes of cod with Thai dipping sauce (£6.50). Mains range from wild mushroom risotto with Parmesan and black truffle (£10.50); to roast chump of lamb with polenta cumedada (£14.50); lamb's sweetbreads with wild mushrooms and Marsala (£12.50); and mixed seafood brodetto (£14.50) – a stunning Adriatic fish stew. Puds range from pannacotta with orange salad (£5.75); to spume Amaretto (£5.95); and semifreddo of ricotta with candied fruit and nuts (£5.75).

The set lunch and "early bird" dinner (order by 7.45pm and go home by 8.45pm) are grand value at £12 for two courses and £15 for three. Try Jerusalem artichoke soup, then roast cod with mussels and parsley mash, culminating in affogato al caffe. This would be good value even without the imprimateur of Franco Taruschio, and it's worthy of the attentions of any early bird.

Putney Bridge

FRENCH

Putney Bridge occupies a purpose-built modern building that has deservedly won plaudits from the great and the good in the world of architecture. The chef, Anthony Demetre, favours a full-on approach, with amuse-gueules and pre-desserts, accomplished presentation and a wine list that leads you gently through the expensive classics. And it is an approach that has

Cost	£25–100

Address The Embankment, SW15
☎ 020 8780 1811
Station Putney Bridge
Open Tues–Sat noon–2.30pm & 7–10.30pm, Sun 12.30–3pm
Accepts All major credit cards
🌐 www.putneybridgerestaurant .com

already found favour with Mr Michelin and his band of inspectors. The food is good. Flavours are well balanced, everything looks attractive and there is plenty of inspiration. Then you pay, and this is not a bargain bite. Entry level is a three-course set lunch at £22.50 (£25 on Sunday), thereafter the price increases to £45 for three courses (with occasional swingeing supplements) and £55 for a six-course Menu Dégustation.

The menus change to reflect what produce is available. A typical set lunch might start with fresh spaghetti with fricasée of morels and garlic leaves; then a piece of skate roast on the bone with caramelized root vegetables; followed by a baked rhubarb "Alaska" and orange-flower scented sorbet. Very nice too. Venturing on to the à la Carte (at £45) you might start with scallops (roast, daube and mi-cuit) with artichoke and vanilla cream and caramelized endive. This is fanciful stuff. Or a platter of duck – foie gras ballotine, rillettes and tartare. Or roast young squid with warm salt cod brandade. For mains there are four fish and five meat options, all elegant. What about a roast Dover sole with étuvée of vegetables and truffles? Or squab pigeon with warm spiced Bulghur "risotto"? Or roast côte de veau glazed with truffle honey, macaroni, peas and fèves? All ingredients are top-quality and the sauces very well made. The wine list must be taken seriously by both you and your wallet.

Even if you can avoid the allure of a very good Francophile cheese-board (supplement £3), you won't be able to dodge the iced peanut butter parfait with chocolate cromesquis. Or how about gariguette strawberries and rhubarb, scented with lemon balm?

Tooting

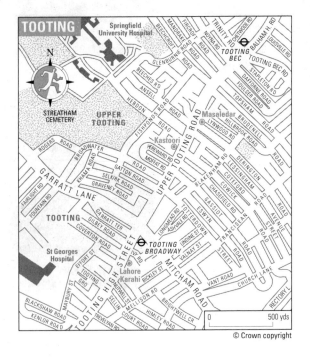

© Crown copyright

Kastoori

Anyone who is genuinely puzzled that people can cope on – and indeed enjoy – a diet of vegetables alone should try eating at Kastoori. Located in a rather unpromising-looking bit of Balham, Kastoori is a Gujarati "Pure Vegetarian Restaurant". The food they serve is leavened with East African influences, and so delicious that you could invite even the most hardened carnivore and

Cost   £12–20

Address 188 Upper Tooting Rd, SW17
☎ 020 8767 7027
Station Tooting Broadway
Open Mon & Tues 6–10.30pm, Wed–Sun 12.30–2.30pm & 6–10.30pm
Accepts MasterCard, Visa

be pretty sure that they would be as entranced as everybody else. The large and cavernous restaurant is run by the admirably helpful Thanki family – do be sure to ask their advice, and act on it. Kastoori's most recent facelift has changed the decor from pink to blue and yellow, but thankfully the quality of the food has stayed the same.

First onto the waiter's pad (and indeed first into the mouth, as they go soggy and collapse if made to wait) must be dahi puri (£2.75) – tiny crispy flying saucers filled with a sweet and sour yoghurty sauce, and potatoes, onions, chickpeas and so forth. You pop them in whole; the marriage of taste and texture is a revelation. Samosas (three for £1.95) are excellent, but also in the revelation category are the onion bhajis (five for £2.25) – bite-sized and delicious, a far cry from the ball-of-knitting variety served in most high-street curry emporia. Then make sure that someone orders the vegetable curry of the day (£4.50), and others the outstanding cauliflower with cream curry (£4.50) and special tomato curry (£4.50) – a hot and spicy classic from Katia Wahd. Leave room for the chilli banana (£4.75), bananas stuffed with mild chillies – an East African recipe – and mop everything up with generous helpings of puris and chapatis (both at £1.30 for two).

The smart move is to ask what's in season, as the menu is littered with oddities that come and go. For example, you might find rotlo – millet loaf (£2.75, served only on Sunday), or the dish called, rather enigmatically, "beans curry" (£4.50). Another interesting and esoteric dish is drumstick curry (£4.75). Drumsticks are thin, green Asian vegetables about eighteen inches long and twice as thick as a pencil. You chew the flesh from the stalk. This is a place where it pays to experiment.

Lahore Karahi

Though the bright neon spilling onto the pavement beckons you from Tooting High Street, spiritually speaking, the Lahore Karahi is in the curry gulch of Upper Tooting Road. It's a busy place, which has been refurbished – in 2001 they invested in new tables and chairs to cope with the ever-growing

Cost	£9–22
Address	1 Tooting High St, SW17
☎	020 8767 2477
Station	Tooting Broadway
Open	Daily noon–midnight
Accepts	Cash or cheque only

swell of customers. Behind a counter equipped with numerous bains-marie stand rows of cooks, distinguishable by their natty Lahore Karahi baseball caps, turning out a daily twelve-hour marathon of dishes. Prices are low, food is chilli-hot and service is speedy. Don't be intimidated: simply seat yourself, don't worry if you have to share a table, and start ordering. Regulars bring their own drinks or stick to the exotic fruit juices – mango, guava or passion, all at just £1.

Unusually for what is, at bottom, an unreconstructed grill house, there is a wide range of vegetarian dishes "prepared under strict precautions". Karahi karela (£2.95) is a curry of bitter gourds; karahi saag paneer (£3.50) teams spinach and cheese; and karahi methi aloo (£2.95) brings potatoes flavoured with fenugreek. Meat-eaters can plunge in joyfully – the chicken tikka (£2.25), seekh kabab (£1.20 for two), and tandoori chicken (£1.75) are all good and all spicy-hot, the only fault being a good deal of artificial red colouring. There are also a dozen chicken curries and a dozen lamb curries (from £3.95 to £4.25), along with a dozen specialities (from £3.95 to £7.50 for king prawn karahi). Those with a strong constitution can try the dishes of the day, like nihari (£4.95), which is lamb shank on the bone in an incendiary broth, or paya (£3.95), which is sheep's feet cooked until gluey. Breads are good here: try the jeera nan (70p) or the tandoori roti (60p).

The Lahore Karahi comes into its own as a takeaway, and there's usually a queue at the counter as people collect their considerable banquets – not just chicken tikka in a naan, or portions of curry, but large and elaborate biryanis as well – meat (£3.50), chicken (£3.50), prawn (£4.95) or vegetable (£2.95). For wholesome, fast-ish food, the cooking and the prices here are hard to beat.

Masaledar

What can you say about a place that has two huge standard lamps, each made from an upturned, highly ornate Victorian drainpipe, topped with a large karahi? When it comes to interior design, Masaledar provides plenty of surprises, and a feeling of spaciousness that's the very opposite of most of the bustling Indian restaurants in Tooting and

Balham. This establishment is run by East African Asian Muslims, so no alcohol is allowed on the premises, but that doesn't deter a loyal clientele, who are packing the place out. Along with several other restaurants in Tooting Road, Maseladar has had to expand, and has added another 25 covers. The food is fresh, well spiced and cheap – there are vegetable curries at £3.25 and meat curries for under £5 – and, to cap it all, you eat it in an elegant designer dining room.

As starters, the samosas are sound – two meat (£1.95) or two vegetable (£1.95). Or try the chicken wings from the tandoor (five pieces £2.25), or the very tasty lamb chops (four pieces £3.75). You might move on to a tasty, rich chicken or lamb biryani (£4.50). Or perhaps try a classic dish like methi gosht (£4.60) – this is strongly flavoured and delicious, guaranteed to leave you with fenugreek seeping from your pores for days to come. Then there's the rich and satisfying lamb Masaledar (£4.75), which is disarmingly described as "our house dish cooked to tantalize your taste buds". The breads, however, are terrific, especially the wonderful thin rotis (60p). Look out for the various deals that range from "free naan and popadom with every main course Monday to Thursday" to "birthdays, parties, conferences ... private parties of up to 120".

Sometimes the brisk takeaway trade and the fact that all dishes are made to order conspire to make service a bit slow. And despite, or because of, the absence of alcohol, you can have an interesting evening's drinking. Mango shake (£1.75) is rich, very fruity and not too sweet; order one before your meal, however, and greed will ensure that you have finished it by the time your food comes. Both the sweet and salty lassi (£1.75) are very refreshing, as is the "fresh passion juice".

Tower Bridge & Bermondsey

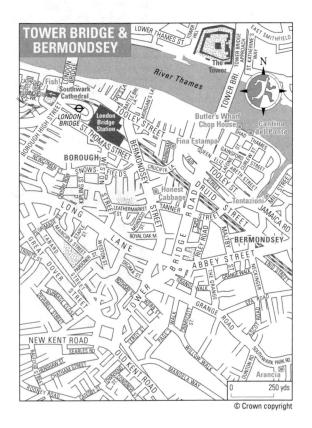

Arancia

Gentrification is spreading through this part of town, where the neat rows of rather nice old terraced houses have been spotted by people toiling in the City of London. Arancia is a product of these changing times. Ten years ago this patch was all pie and mash and car chases. Now sensible and authentic Italian food is quite acceptable – and the proprietors of Arancia are to be congratu-lated on keeping the food cheap enough to attract the long-term residents, while at the same time good enough to ensnare newcomers. Success on all fronts. This is an old-fashioned, regularly changing, sea-sonally inspired menu. At Arancia they manage to offer a two-course set meal for £7.50, and three courses for £10.50 – a bargain whether you are bourgeois or Bermondsey.

Cost	£10–20

Address 52 Southwark Park Rd, SE16
℗ 020 7394 1751
Station BR Bermondsey
Open Mon & Tues 7–11pm, Wed–Sun 12.30–2.30pm & 7–11pm
Accepts MasterCard, Visa

Starters might include minestra con cannellini (£3), a soup made from spring greens, cannellini beans and pesto. Or you might find cannelloni di ricotta (£4.20), made with roast onion, ricotta and pine nuts (£4.20). Sarde arosto (£4.30) is a dish of fresh sardines baked with caperberries and lemon. For main course there may be pollo ripieno (£9.30) – chicken stuffed with goat's cheese and served with an aubergine and onion salad. You can also bank on dishes like salsicce and puree (£9.20), which is bangers and mash, Italian style. Or there may be stufato di agnello (£9.40), a lamb stew served on buttered pappardelle with a lemon gremolata. Vegetarians are catered for with dishes like polpette di patate (£9) – a potato rosti topped with roast field mushrooms. The puddings are adventurous: perhaps a rather good chocolate semifreddo (£3.30); or pear and almond tart (£3.50); or that quintessentially Italian finishing touch – Vin Santo and biscotti (£4).

The pursuit of bargain prices is also the theme when you look at the all-Italian wine list. There are certainly inexpensive wines, and they are all drinkable, but if you're after something really splendid you'll be out of luck. The proprietors of Arancia also run an outside catering business. With food as simple and as good as this, it should be worth investigating.

Butler's Wharf Chop House

Butler's Wharf Chop House – another Conran creation – really deserves everyone's support. For this is a restaurant that makes a genuine attempt to showcase the best of British produce. There's superb British meat, splendid fish, and simply epic British and Irish cheeses. What's more, the Chop House wisely caters for all, whether you want a simple dish at the bar, a well-priced set lunch or an extravagant dinner. The dining room is spacious and bright, and the view of Tower Bridge a delight, especially from a terrace table on a warm summer's evening.

Cost	£15–40
Address	36e Shad Thames, SE1
☎	020 7403 3403
Station	Tower Hill/London Bridge
Open	Restaurant Mon–Fri & Sun noon–3pm & 6–11pm, Sat 6–11pm; bar Mon–Sat noon–3pm & 6–11pm, Sun noon–3pm
Accepts	All major credit cards
🌐	www.conran.com

Lunch in the restaurant is priced at £19.75 for two courses and £23.75 for three. The menu changes regularly but tends to feature starters such as veal, pork and mushroom terrine; or Loch Fyne smoked salmon; or a lambs lettuce, Stilton and pear salad. Mains will include dishes like fish and chips, and slow-roast belly pork with prunes, as well as the house speciality of spit roasts and grills. They do a flawless roast rib of beef with Yorkshire pudding and gravy, and excellent braised lamb shank with mashed potato and red wine. After that you just might be able to find room for a pud like rhubarb crumble tart with vanilla ice cream, even if the jam roly-poly pudding is a dish too far. Dinner follows the same principles but is priced à la carte and adds a few dishes to the choice. Thus, there may be starters like venison and wild boar faggot served with black pudding and sage (£8), or hot-smoked eel served with horseradish and bacon (£7.50). Mains may include steak, kidney and oyster pudding (£15), or smoked haddock fish pie (£14.50). There's also steak and chips, priced by size – from £16.50 for an 8oz sirloin to £25 for a 12oz fillet. Butler's Wharf is also one of the few places in London where you can have a savoury to end the meal – Welsh rarebit (£3.50).

The bar menu is appealing: two courses for £8, three for £10. You might choose crab soup, roast lamb and lemon tart – a pretty good tenner's worth.

Cantina del Ponte

ITALIAN

Jostling for attention with the Pont de la Tour, its more renowned and considerably pricier Conran neighbour, the Cantina del Ponte does not try to keep up, but instead offers a different package. Here you are greeted with the best earthy Italian fare, presented in smart Conran style. The floors are warm terracotta, the food is strong on flavour and colour, the service is refined, and the views are superior London dockside.

Cost	£10–35

Address Butler's Wharf, Shad Thames, SE1
℡ 020 7403 5403
Station Tower Hill/London Bridge
Open Mon–Sat noon–3pm & 6–11pm, Sun noon–3pm & 6–10pm
Accepts All major credit cards
ⓦ www.conran.com

Book ahead and bag a table by the window or, better still, brave the elements in summer and sit under the canopy watching the boats go by. Inside is OK but less memorable, and the low ceilings are a bit claustrophobic if you're seated at the back.

The seasonal menu is a meander through all things good, Italian-style, with a tempting array of first courses, and mains that include pizza, pasta and risotto, not to mention side orders, puddings and cheeses. Simple, classic combos like mozzarella di bufala wrapped in prosciutto with olives and herbs (£6.75) always appeal. Or grilled squid with chilli and rocket (£5.95). Veggie dishes like polenta with field mushrooms and mascarpone (£9.50) are good, or how about wild mushroom lasagne with girolles and broad beans (£11.95)? Pizzas are equally filling, and feature all the old favourites, like quattro formaggi (£7.95), Margherita (£7.25), and Napoli (£7.50). Main courses range from fillet of sea bass with Jerusalem artichoke mash and lemon olive oil (£14.50); to veal escalope saltimbocca (£14.95); and braised lamb shank with baked fennel, cream and Parmesan (£14.50). Puds veer from tiramisù (£4.95), through torta di cioccolata and noci (£4.50), to pannacotta with rhubarb (£5.25).

As well as competitive set menus (lunch and pre-theatre), priced at £10 for two courses and £12.50 for three, Cantina does a mean line in takeaway pizzas – always presuming that you live near enough to fetch it yourself, or perhaps that you like a serious snack when you get home after dinner out.

Fina Estampa

PERUVIAN

(⚑) While London is awash with ethnic
eateries, Fina Estampa's proud
boast is that it is the capital's only Peruvian restaurant. Gastronomy may not be
the first thing that springs to mind when
one thinks of Peru, but the husband-and-
wife team running the place certainly tries
hard to enlighten the customers, and
bring a little downtown Lima to London

Cost	**£15–30**
Address	150 Tooley St, SE1
℡	020 7403 1342
Station	London Bridge
Open	Mon–Fri noon–2.30pm
	& 6.30–10.30pm, Sat
	6.30–10.30pm
Accepts	All major credit cards

Bridge. Following a refurb in 2001, all is now cream, gold and coffee, and
there's also a new bar, which opens at 5.30pm. With its fresh interior, Fina
Estampa has a warm and bright ambience, and the attentive, friendly
staff add greatly to the upbeat feel of the music.

The menu is traditional Peruvian, which means there's a great
emphasis placed upon seafood. This is reflected in the starters, with such
offerings as chupe de camarones (£6.95), a succulent shrimp-based
soup; cebiche (£5.95), a dish of marinated white fish served with sweet
potatoes; and jalea (£9.50), a vast plate of fried seafood. Ask for the salsa
criolla – its hot oiliness is a perfect accompaniment. There is also causa
rellena (£5.50), described as a "potato surprise" and it is exactly that:
layers of cold mashed potato, avocado and tuna fish served with salsa –
the surprise being how something so straightforward can taste so good.
Main courses – the fragrant chicken seco (£10.95), chicken cooked in a
coriander sauce; or the superb lomo saltado (£12.95), tender strips of
rump steak stir fried with red onions and tomatoes – are worthy ambas-
sadors for this simple yet distinctive cuisine. Perhaps most distinctive of
all is the carapulca (£10.95), a spicy dish made of dried potatoes, pork,
chicken and cassava – top choice for anyone seeking a new culinary
adventure.

One particularly fine, and decidedly Peruvian, speciality is the unfortunately named Pisco sour (£3.50). Pisco is a white grape spirit and the
Peruvian national drink, not dissimilar in taste and effect to tequila. Here
they mix Pisco with lemon, lime and cinnamon, then sweeten it with
honey, add egg white, and whip it into a frothy white cocktail, which is
really rather good.

Fish!

You feel like a fish at Fish! The restaurant's huge windows and glass ceiling contribute to a tank-like feeling. They also contribute to high noise levels and a general party ambience. The restaurant is large and there's a courtyard for alfresco eating, plus bar seating for armchair chefs who like to watch the real ones at work.

Cost   £20–50

Address Cathedral St, SE1;
with branches
☏ 020 7234 3333
Station London Bridge
Open Mon–Sat 11.30am–11pm,
Sun noon–10pm
Accepts All major credit cards
🖰 www.fishdiner.co.uk

FISH

The menu comes on the place mat, so you can get sat down and immediately start reading. On one side there are Fish! homilies that explain the restaurant's ethic: kids' menus and games, highchairs, GM-free fish(!), takeaway, a website and a nutrition section. The real menu is on the reverse, which is certainly innovative. On the one card is a smallish selection of dishes, wines and accompaniments, but the main justification for Fish! is the self-selection menu. From a printed list of 22 contenders there is a daily choice of nine kinds of fresh fish, depending on what the market has come up with. You select your favourite, choose whether you want it steamed or grilled, and then choose salsa, Hollandaise, herb butter, olive oil dressing or red wine fish gravy to go with it. Create your own combo. Prices range from £8.50 for mullet to £14.50 for sea bass. Portions are huge and the fish is as good and fresh as you'd expect. The traditional menu also offers starters like prawn cocktail (£5.95), while main dishes include fishcake (£8.95); spaghetti tuna Bolognaise (£5.50/9.50), with fresh tomatoes and minced tuna; or fish and chips with mushy peas (£11.80). And for poor lost carnivores who have rather missed the point there is even a grilled free-range chicken breast (£11.50). If you like a traditional approach to fish, Fish! won't disappoint. Puddings include stalwarts like chocolate fondant (£3.95), and bread-and-butter pudding (£3.95), the latter rich with double cream. The house white, a Sauvignon (£9.90), is light, crisp and a bargain.

Fish!'s menu adds interest to eating, with information that makes sense. There's also a Fish! shop next door for wet fish and sauces, and a touch-screen recipe machine.

Honest Cabbage

The Honest Cabbage is heralded by a beguiling picture of a cabbage crowned with a halo, which sticks out into Bermondsey Street like an inn sign. Without the sign, the restaurant would be difficult to spot, as the Cabbage, for all its honesty, seems to lurk shyly away from the limelight. Once found, the place is a welcome lesson in simplicity. Dark wooden tables and chairs are dotted around a medium-sized, plain room. At the far end is a small bar and counter, but the whole of the shopfront is sheet glass, giving a spacious and well-lit feel. Decoration is provided by glass jars of pulses along the windowsills.

Cost	£12–35

Address 99 Bermondsey St, SE1
☎ 020 7234 0080
Station London Bridge
Open Mon–Wed noon–3pm & 6.30–10.30pm, Thurs–Sat noon–3pm & 6.30–11pm, Sun noon–4pm
Accepts MasterCard, Visa
🌐 www.thehonestcabbage .co.uk

The menu is chalked up on a blackboard, though if you can't quite see it they have a printed version as well. There is a choice of ten or eleven dishes, with no division between first and main courses. It follows a simple formula of a soup, a sandwich, a salad, a pasta, a pie, a pot, a vegetarian dish, and so forth. The menu changes every day broadly in line with the seasons and what the markets have to offer. So you might choose red kidney bean soup with guacamole (£4) or a BLT (£5), either of which would make a satisfying light lunch. Or the pot might be lamb shank with raisin and pine nut caponata (£12); the pasta garganelli, cockles and saffron cream (£5/8); the pie, steak and kidney (£10). There's always a vegetarian option – along the lines of pumpkin and orange cannelloni with vegetables (£10). And then on to the fresh meat and fresh fish options (these cost £14), which might be a large portion of calves' liver with sage butter, spinach and caramelized onions, plus mash or chips. Or a whole grilled sea bass with orange and ginger Hollandaise. Puddings are straightforward – like a good lemon-meringue pie (£4).

A short but considered drinks list not only provides a couple of organic wines but also a succession of bottled and draught beers. The Cabbage's strengths lie in its attitude and pricing, so, as you would expect, it is consistently busy. There's a serious brunch on Sunday morning.

Tentazioni

This small, busy and rather good Italian restaurant has crept up behind Sir Terence Conran's Thameside flotilla of eateries and is giving them a terrific run for their money. The food is simple, high-quality peasant Italian, with strong, rich flavours. The pasta dishes are good here, as are the stews, and the wine list is interesting. As well as a

Cost	£10–20

Address 2 Mill St, SE1
℡ 020 7237 1100
Station Bermondsey/Tower Hill
Open Mon–Fri noon–2.30pm & 7–10.45pm, Sat 7–10.45pm
Accepts All major credit cards
🖳 www.tentazioni.co.uk

ITALIAN

splendid four-course Regional Menu (£26) that changes on a monthly basis, there is a daily changing set lunch – two courses for £15, three for £19. They also offer a Menu Degustazione, which gets you five courses for £36.

All the starters can be turned into main courses, and the menu changes to reflect the seasons and the markets. You may find choices such as gnocchetti di ceci con polipi piccanti e funghi porcini (£8/12) – chickpea gnocchi with spicy octopus; or tortino di riso allo zafferano in guazzetto di pesce (£10/14) – a cake of saffron rice served with a light fish broth; or mozzarella di bufala gratinata con funghi misti trifolata (£9/13) – buffalo mozzarella with wild mushrooms. Main courses offer hammer blows of flavour. Bocconcini di coniglio impanati con carcofini (£15) is described as a breaded navarin of rabbit with artichokes; while triglie con cicoria, fave e pecorino (£14.50) is pan-fried red mullet with chicory, broad beans and pecorino. Or how about an unusual dish, like filetto di manzo al vapore con verdurine, salsa verde e mostarda (£16.50), which is steamed fillet of beef given vibrant colour from the salsa verde and a hit of flavour from the mustard-pickled fruits? For pudding it is hard to better the torta alle prugne e pere con gelato alla vaniglia (£6), a delicious plum and pear tart with vanilla ice cream.

The "Degustazione" provides an interesting and very tempting option. How does this sound? First, vitello tonnato; then agnolotti di patate e menta con peperoni; then the red mullet mentioned above; then a rabbit dish; and finally pannacotta alla grappa con arance caramellate. Pretty convincing.

Wimbledon & Southfields

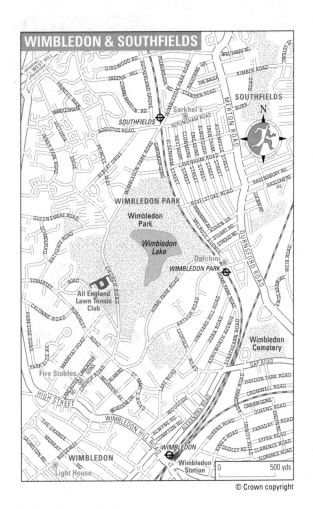

WIMBLEDON & SOUTHFIELDS

SOUTHFIELDS

N

WEST HILL
GIRDWOOD RD
BRATHWAY RD
KIMBER ROAD
SKEENA HILL
PRINCES WAY
WANDLESHAM
SUTHERLAND GROVE
FURDROUGE RD
WIMBLEDON PARK ROAD
THE BAILY
STANDEN ROAD
Sarkhel's
SOUTHFIELDS
REPUNGHAM ROAD
BURR
MERTON ROAD
VICTORIA DRIVE
AUGUSTUS ROAD
ASTOWELL RD
ELSENHAM STREET
TRENTHAM STREET
HEYTHORP ST
ALBERT DRIVE
PRINCES WAY
WIMBLEDON PARK ROAD
PRINCES WAY
LAVENHAM ROAD
STREET
RAVENSBURY RD
QUEENSMERE ROAD
WIMBLEDON PARK ROAD
WIMBLEDON PARK
REVELSTOKE ROAD
HASLEMERE AV
ARTHUR ROAD
SOUTHBRIGHT ROAD
BATHGATE ROAD
Wimbledon
Park
MELROSE AVENUE
ASHEN GR.
STUART RD
DURNSFORD ROAD
Wimbledon
Lake
Dalchini
WIMBLEDON PARK
SOMERSET
ROAD
CHURCHFIELD
HOME PARK ROAD
VINEYARD HILL ROAD
DORA ROAD
All England
Lawn Tennis
Club
CALONNE ROAD
BUSHEY ROAD
ARTHUR ROAD
COPSE
HILL ROAD
KENILWORTH AVENUE
STRATHEARN ROAD
Wimbledon
Cemetery
PARKSIDE GDNS
MARSHALL ROAD
GAP ROAD
PARK ROAD
LANCASTER RD.
CHURCH GDNS
HAYDON PARK ROAD
Fire Stables
MELBURY RD
LAKE ROAD
CROMWELL ROAD
HIGH STREET
WOODSIDE
CRAVEN GDNS
QUEENS ROAD
BELVEDERE RD
WIMBLEDON HILL ROAD
WIMBLEDON PARK ROAD
ALWYNE RD.
COMPTON RD.
WIMBLEDON
ALEXANDRA ROAD
FARADAY ROAD
EFFRA ROAD
THE GRANGE
QUEENS ROAD
CLARENCE ROAD
MURRAY
RIDGWAY
LING DUDLEY RD.
FLORENCE ROAD
WIMBLEDON
WIMBLEDON
Light House
Wimbledon
Station
0   500 yds

© Crown copyright

Dalchini

Dalchini is an Indian word for the cinnamon-like spice cassia, made by combining the words dal, meaning bark, and chini, meaning China. Which makes it a jolly appropriate name for this small and friendly family restaurant, as Dalchini serves the kind of Chinese food that has emigrated to Bombay. This is Chinese with a pronounced Indian accent – lots of spice and a good deal of chilli. The restaurant was opened in early 2001 by Udit Sarkhel's (see p.386) wife Veronica, who is Hakka Chinese and comes from a long line of Chinese restaurateurs based in Bombay.

Cost	£12–30

Address 147 Arthur Rd, Wimbledon Park, SW19
☏ 020 8947 5966
Station Wimbledon Park
Open Tues–Thurs & Sun noon–2.30pm & 6–10.30pm, Fri & Sat noon–2.30pm & 6–11pm
Accepts All major credit cards except Diners

INDIAN-CHINESE

Upstairs, Dalchini is a coffee bar and deli, serving everything from coffee, cakes and pastries to lunchboxes and Indian dishes. Downstairs, the restaurant is pleasantly unpretentious. Toy with a few starters and then turn to the specials list for the classic Indo-Chinese dishes. Start with the chicken lollipops (£3.95); or the pepper garlic fish (£3.95) – cod that has been given an Indo-Chinese twist. Team these with the vegetables pickled in sweet vinegar (£1.50). Or perhaps the red pumpkin fritters (£3.75) appeal? The corn cream (£3.75) is that rarity – a vegetarian dish that really shines. Whether you are keen on Indian or Chinese food, the Dalchini main courses are great fun. There is chilli chicken (£6.25), a big seller in Bombay, sweet and chilli hot; or "American chicken chop suey" (£7) – the story goes that chop suey was a dish first devised by Chinese coolies working on the American railroads. Or stewed lamb and tofu with yellow bean sauce (£6.25) – slow cooked with chilli and a few water chestnuts. Or the house signature dish, which is ginger chicken (£6.25). Or show off with the standing pomfret (£9.95), a cunningly de-boned fried pomfret that is presented upright as if swimming. As an accompaniment to all this, vegetable Hakka noodles (£4.25) fit the bill.

You also deserve to try one very different dish: goat meat curry (£6.25), a simple Calcutta-style curry with potato. Or for pudding, how about honey noodles with ice cream (£4.25)? These are egg noodles as you've never seen them before!

The Fire Stables

The Fire Stables opened in 2001 and before it was a year old it had already secured a shortlisting in the gastro-pub section of the annual awards. But there must be a problem deciding just what the Fire Stables represents. It certainly has a busy bar, and there is bar food available, but there is a formal restaurant as well. But, by any measure, the "gastro" side has the pub on the back foot; as modern restaurants go, this is a pretty good example. The chairs are comfortable and the tables big enough, the high ceiling and large windows give a spacious feel, the floor is made of painted floorboards, and the music will be familiar to forty- and fifty-somethings, as Brubeck's "Take Five" segues into The Average White Band.

Cost	£12–40
Address	27–29 Church Rd, SW19
☎	020 8946 3197
Station	Wimbledon
Open	Mon–Fri noon–3pm & 6–10.30pm, Sat noon–4pm & 6–10.30pm, Sun noon–4pm & 6–10pm
Accepts	All major credit cards

The menu changes daily and the food is well presented and reasonably priced. Starters range from mixed bean, minestrone soup w pesto (£4.50) to a chicken liver parfait w red onion marmalade (£5.75). You may already have spotted the typographical idiosyncrasy, which wears pretty thin pretty quickly. They don't write "with" at the Fire Stables, what they put is w. So you get carpaccio of tuna w wasabi and soy dressing (£6) – this could get irritating by the time you get to cheese w Bath Olivers. A starter of Portobella mushrooms w gremolata and mozzarella on bruschetta (£6) is much more successful – good mushies, very tasty. Or perhaps grilled smoked ricotta and leeks w crouton (£5.50)? Main courses include slow-roast pork belly w braised red cabbage and mash (£9.50); roast cod w prawns and chickpea broth (£11.50); linguine w clams, squid, chilli garlic and parsley (£10.50); chicken supreme wrapped in Bayonne ham w fondant potato and braised Savoy (£12); and rack of lamb w ratatouille and basil mash (£13.50). With a spinach and ricotta risotto (£9.50) pressed into service for vegetarians (no w for them!).

Puds (all £5) are desirable if predictable numbers such as panettone bread-and-butter pudding; chocolate torte w espresso ice cream; passion fruit tart w coconut and Malibu sorbet; and chocolate tart w pistachio ice cream.

Light House

Light House is a strange restaurant to find marooned in leafy suburbia – you would think that its modern, very eclectic menu and clean style would be more at home in a city centre than in a smart, quiet, respectable neighbourhood. Nevertheless it seems to be doing well. The restaurant, which opened in late 1999, has found its feet and the local clientele quite obviously enjoy it and keep coming back for more. First impressions always count and a light, bright interior – cream walls and blond wood – plus genuinely friendly staff make both arriving and eating at Light House a pleasure.

Cost	£20–50

Address 75–77 The Ridgway, SW19
℗ 020 8944 6338
Station Wimbledon
Open Tues–Sat noon–2.45pm & 6–10.30pm, Sun 12.30–3pm
Accepts All major credit cards except Diners

MODERN EUROPEAN

At first glance, the menu is set out conventionally enough in the Italian style: antipasti, primi, secondi, contorni and dolci. But that's as far as the Italian formality goes – the influences on the kitchen here are truly global. Starters may range from a bocconcini, tomato, pine nut and caper cresenta with rocket and anchovy salsa (£6.90), to wild mushroom tagliatelle with white truffle oil (£8.50), or deep-fried prawn ravioli on sautéed porcini and oyster mushrooms with grilled nori (£7.20). It would be very easy to get this sort of cooking wrong, but in fact Light House does remarkably well. Among the "secondi", dishes like rack of lamb with char-grilled vine plum tomatoes and herbed couscous salad (£15.50) jostle with complex combinations like cod with bok choy, chilli and ginger on cucumber and green papaya salad with mango salsa (£16.50), or even Gorgonzola and pecan tortellini with pepperonata and deep-fried crispy herbs (£10). Perhaps the cooking is a little over-complicated, but it's well executed and certainly intriguing. Puddings take us back towards Italy (ish!) with dishes like cherry yoghurt ripple semifreddo with fonseca Victoria plums (£4.90).

Someone has had a lot of fun choosing the wine list – a selection of about twenty each of whites and reds which crosses as many frontiers as possible. If you want a bargain, go for lunch – the "midday menu" is a steal at £12.50 for two courses.

Sarkhel's

(YI) Before opening his own place in SW18, Udit Sarkhel was heading the kitchens of the famous Bombay Brasserie in the West End, where he had all the latest kit and a large brigade of chefs. Moving to Sarkhel's in Southfields must have been like resigning as conductor of an orchestra and setting up a one-man band, but it is certainly a huge asset to South London. And South London has certainly responded – the dining room seems to be enlarged at least once a year. Today Sarkhel's is a large, elegant restaurant, serving well-spiced food with a number of adventurous dishes scattered through the menu – the hot, fresh Chettinad dishes are particularly fine. Moreover, it's a pleasant, friendly, family-run place offering good cooking at prices, which, though not cheap, certainly represent good value (particularly on Friday, Saturday and Sunday lunchtimes, when you can get a bargain set lunch for £9.95). Booking is recommended.

Cost	£11–35

Address 199 Replingham Rd, Southfields, SW18
☎ 020 8870 1483
Station Southfields
Open Tues–Thurs 6–10.30pm, Fri & Sat 6–11pm, Sun noon–2.30pm
Accepts All major credit cards except Diners
✪ www.sarkhels.com

Start by asking Udit or his wife if there are any "specials" on. These are dishes which change according to what is available at the markets. You might be offered a starter of macchli Koliwada (£4.25) – fish cooked in a spicy batter, a famous Bombay dish. Or vagatore bangde (£5.95) this is a mackerel boned-out and stuffed with shrimp balchao, and it's pleasantly chilli-hot. The khass seekh kebab (£4.25) is as good as you'll find anywhere. For main-course dishes, check the specials again – it might be something wonderful like a kolmi nu Patia (£8.50), a spicy Parsee prawn dish. On the main menu, try the chicken reszala (£7.25), a rich dish that is the speciality of Calcutta Muslims; or the achar gosht (£7.25), which is lamb cooked slowly in a sealed pot "dum phukt" style; or perhaps the jardaloo ma gosht (£7.25), a sweet and sour lamb dish made with apricots. All are delicious, without even a hint of surface oil slick.

Be sure to add some vegetable dishes. Perhaps the baigan patiala (£5.95), which is a dish of cubed aubergines and cashew nuts stewed with a touch of ginger and chilli.

Further South

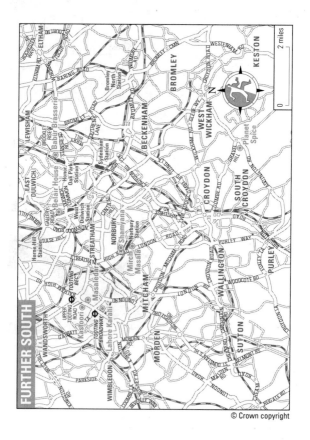

FURTHER SOUTH

© Crown copyright

Babur Brasserie

The Babur Brasserie is a stylish and friendly restaurant serving elaborate and interesting dishes which bear no resemblance to ordinary curry house fare – an unexpected find in SE23. The food is both subtle and elegantly presented and, while it does cost a touch more than most suburban Indian restaurants, you are still paying a great deal less than you would in a French or Italian place of similar quality. There is a buffet lunch on Sunday (£8.95) at which children eat free if they are less than seven years old.

Cost	£10–25

Address 119 Brockley Rise, SE23
℡ 020 8291 2400
Station BR Honor Oak Park
Open Daily noon–2.30pm & 6–11.30pm
Accepts All major credit cards
🌐 www.babur-brasserie.com

INDIAN

How nice to be faced with a list of appetizers and see so few familiar dishes. Patra (£3.25) is a Catherine wheel sliced off the end of a roll of avial leaves that have been glued together with chickpea paste and deep fried. The result is crispy and very tasty. Ragda pattice (£3.75) is a grown-up potato croquette with a dried pea curry. Càlamari balchao (£3.95) is a Goan-style squid dish, agreeably hot, while harrey murgh tikka (£3.95) gets you a plate of chunks of chicken which have been marinated in green spices, then cooked in a tandoor – delightfully juicy inside. Main courses are just as good. Try jalfrezi (£7.25) – lamb with onions, ginger and capsicums. Or the green fish curry from Goa (£8.95) – salmon in a typical Goan hot and sour sauce. Duck xacutti (£8.75) is a complex curry made from a smoked duck breast and an awesomely long list of spices. Then there are ten fresh vegetable dishes – vegetarians will applaud the thali option (£11.75) of picking three from the list with raita, rice and a naan bread. On the subject of bread, try the lacha paratha (£1.95), a flaky paratha made with ghee. The dessert menu is more extensive and elaborate than usual, too, running the gamut from rasmalai with summer berries (£3.75) to kulfi (£3.75), that dense and tasty Indian ice cream.

Hing, or asafoetida, is a spice that has not only a distinctive flavour but also a rude name. In oonbhariu (£4.95) – a dish from the vegetables section – it is blended with lovage and cumin to accompany bananas, sweet potato, baby aubergines and shallots. Particularly delicious, and not stinky at all.

Belair House

Belair House is a large, pale Georgian establishment standing alone in Belair Park. A Grade Two listed building, it was sensitively and painstakingly restored in 1998 by the actor Gary Cady and his wife Jayne. In summer the two terraces do sterling service, one filled with diners and the other with drinkers. This establishment is already justly popular with locals, and Sunday lunch in particular is booked up well ahead. With its head start of tall, well-proportioned rooms and a sweeping staircase, the decor is both elegant and surprisingly bright. Research shows that when it was built the interior of the building would have been painted in the lurid colours fashionable at the time. The kitchen makes use of whatever is best from the markets to produce a regularly changing seasonal menu.

Cost	£20–60

Address Gallery Rd, Dulwich Village, SE21
℡ 020 8299 9788
Station BR West Dulwich
Open Tues–Sat noon–2.30pm & 7–10.30pm, Sun noon–2.30pm
Accepts All major credit cards
⊛ www.belairhouse.co.uk

The deals work like this: the set lunch (available from Tues to Sunday) costs £18 for two courses and £22 for three. Dinner costs £32 for three courses. The set lunches offer a selection of the dishes on the dinner menu. So there you have it. The cooking is ambitious and dishes have a classical French feel to them, so starters may include white truffle and quail consommé; a cep and snail fricassée with garlic and parsley; or foie gras served three ways – terrine, parfait and roulade served with grapes and Sauternes jelly. Some dishes attract a supplement, among them the ravioli of langoustines with coral and langoustine coulis, which ups the bill by £5. Mains are appetizing, seasonal and rich: spiced slow-roast shoulder of lamb with courgettes and aubergine; roast Châlon duck with sardalaise potatoes, winter vegetables and morels; braised pig's trotter with chicory; or baked black cod with fennel chicory and sweet pepper sauce. Puddings are a more sober and self-indulgent affair. Pear tarte Tatin comes with vanilla ice cream; chestnut and raspberry pancake gets chestnut ice cream; and the mascarpone tartlet is served with a balsamic sorbet.

Look carefully in the toilets downstairs and you will spot vestiges of a former incarnation of Belair House – it used to act as a changing room for teams using the surrounding playing fields.

Mirch Masala

INDIAN

You'll find Mirch Masala just up London Road from Norbury station. It may not look much from the outside, but it deserves a place on any list of London's top Indian restaurants – something South London's Asian community appears to have cottoned on to. As befits such a culinary temple, the chefs take centre stage. The kitchen is in full view and you can watch the whole cooking process, which culminates, as likely as not, in a chef bringing the food to table. They are certainly prone to wandering out while you are enjoying the last of your starters to ask if you're ready for your main course. What's more, at the end of the meal they are also happy to pack up anything you don't finish so that you can take it home. Take advantage, and over-order! This is a very friendly and unpretentious place serving spectacular food at low prices, which makes for very contented diners indeed.

Cost	£6–16

Address 1416 London Rd, SW16
☎ 020 8679 1828
Station BR Norbury
Open Daily noon–midnight
Accepts All major credit cards
🖳 www.mirchmasalarestaurant
.co.uk

Start with a stick each of chicken tikka (£2.50) and lamb tikka (£2.50), crusted with pepper and spices on the outside, juicy with marinade on the inside. Very good indeed. Or try the butter chicken wings (£3), cooked in a light, ungreasy sauce laden with flavour from fresh spices and herbs. Then move on to the karahi dishes, which are presented in a kind of thick aluminium hubcap. The vegetable karahis are exceptional, so go for the butter beans and methi (£3.50) – an inspired and delicious combination of flavours – or karahi valpapdi baigan (£4), which is aubergines cooked with small rich beans. Among the best meat dishes are the deigi lamb chops (£4.50), and the deigi saag gosht (£5) – spinach, lamb and a rich sauce. Even something simple like karahi ginger chicken (£5) proves how good and fresh-tasting Indian food can be. Rice (£1.50) comes in a glass butter dish complete with lid. Breads include a good naan (70p) and an indulgent deep-fried bhatura (60p) that will provoke greed in anyone who has ever hankered after fried bread.

A meal at Mirch Masala will be a memorable one. As they say on the menu, "Food extraordinaire. You wish it – we cook it".

Planet Spice

Planet Spice is a fish out of water. Even the presence of the latest transport innovation, the much vaunted tramway, cannot prepare you for the surprise you get when you arrive here. The restaurant (a sister establishment to the Babur Brasserie, see p.389) is located at the junction of two major roads and in premises that have been used for everything from a Greek restaurant to a dance school. Today the building houses an Indian restaurant of a very high order indeed. If Planet Spice were in the West End it would be showered with critical acclaim.

Cost	£15–32

Address 88 Selsdon Park Rd, Addington, South Croydon
☏ 020 8651 3300
Station Croydon Tramway
Open Mon–Sat noon–2.30pm & 6.30–11.30pm, Sun 12.30–3.30pm & 6–11.30pm
Accepts All major credit cards
🌐 www.planet-spice.com

The chefs have had to make certain compromises. The takeaway side of things is still dominated by old-style dishes – korma, Madras, chicken tikka masala – and any sit-down customers perplexed by the main menu can opt for these. The main menu, however, is agreeably sophisticated and really is the one you should work from. Start with the Mysore chilli prawns (£4.50), good and hot; or ros-tos-crab (£4.95), a kind of crab gratin served in the shell; or malai murgh tikka (£3.95), which combines chicken with yoghurt and cashew nuts; or calmari balchao (£3.85) – squid given the spicy South Indian treatment. Main courses are distinguished by accurate and well-balanced spicing and unusually careful cooking. Try the Kerala Syrian sea bass (£11.25), a fairly hot masala from the Syrian Christian community. Team it with the lime and cashew nut rice (£2.25). Or there's Bangalore duck (£8.85). Otherwise try a simple dish like kadhai lamb (£13.25, serves two), which is essentially tandoori lamb chops; salmon moilee (£10.95), a mild Keralan fish dish; or chicken Chettinad (£7.25), a South Indian dish famous for its fieriness – although it is somewhat tamed here. If all this sounds a bit fierce then there is always the murgh mumtaj (£7.95), which is chicken stuffed with herbs and spices.

These are ambitious dishes, handled well. It is undoubtedly due to the able chefs in the kitchen. Not what you'd expect of a curry house in Addington.

Shamyana

The rather good Indian food that you'll find in Tooting is gradually making its way south. At the forefront of this diaspora was the peerless Mirch Masala (see p.391), then Shamyana followed suit and opened a few hundred yards up the road. What these successful restaurants seem to have in common is well-made, unfussy, spicy food. In 2001 Shamyana changed hands, and a new chef-proprietor took over. Dishes became

Cost	£7–20

Address 437–439 Streatham
High Rd, SW16
℡ 020 8679 6162
Station BR Norbury
Open Daily noon–midnight
Accepts All major credit cards
except Diners
🌐 www.shamyana-restaurant
.co.uk

INDIAN

simpler and if anything even better value. And the menu breaks new ground too: it lists the calories and grams of fat involved in each particular dish. Trouble is, this often fiercely spicy Punjabi food is so good to eat that you may prefer not to be burdened with such information!

Start with chilli chicken wings (£2.50), chicken tikka (£2.55), or lamb chops (£3.70) – or maybe something different such as zeera chicken wings (£2.50) spiced with cumin. These tandoori dishes are all well spiced and well cooked. They're not at all dried-out, so the man on the marinades knows his stuff. A sound option is the Shamyana mixed grill (£4.15), which includes everything from lamb chops to masala fish. As you move on to main courses there is an imposing array of vegetarian dishes – over a dozen to choose from (between £3.45 and £3.75) – tarka dal, karahi bhindi and zeera aloo stand out. Then there is an assortment of Punjabi favourites: ginger chicken (£4.50) or chicken jalfrezi (£4.95), rich with onions and capsicums. Another very good dish is the masala karella gosht (£4.50); the pundits will tell you that the flesh of the karella, or bitter melon, is very good for the blood and has a cleansing effect. But, medicinal or not, this is certainly an addictively good flavour – this lamb and karella curry is a real winner. Other stars are karahi gosht (£4.50) and karahi fish (£5.90). The "specials" are good, too, so look out for them.

The rotis are grand here. And there's an intriguing side dish you must order: mixed fried ginger, chilli and onion (£1) lives up to its description exactly, and is very handy for adding to rice or eating on its own with bread.

West

Barnes & Sheen

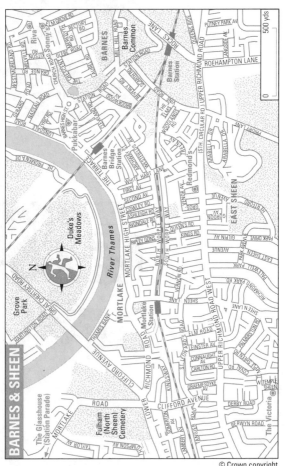

BARNES & SHEEN

© Crown copyright

The Glasshouse

In 2002 The Glasshouse picked up a well-deserved star in the yearly Michelin extravaganza. Chef Anthony Boyd honed his craft at the Michelin-bedecked Square (see p.85) and Chez Bruce (see p.335), and at The Glasshouse he has made a good job of combining the rich flavours of Chez Bruce with the sophistication of The Square. What's more, the restaurant is on the doorstep of

Cost	£20–50

Address 14 Station Parade, Kew Gardens, Surrey
⑦ 020 8940 6777
Station Kew Gardens
Open Mon–Sat noon–2.30pm & 7–10.30pm, Sun 12.30–3pm
Accepts All major credit cards except Diners

FRENCH

Kew Gardens underground station, which makes it easy for anyone who can get onto the District line. The interior has a clean-cut, modern feel to it and the chairs are worthy of lavish praise – they are blissfully comfortable, an aspect of dining which is all too often overlooked. The food is good. Very good.

The menu is a simple one which changes daily and usually gives you the choice of eight starters, nine mains and nine puds in the evening with slightly fewer options at lunch, when two courses cost £17.50 and three £19.50; for dinner the price is £27.50 for three courses. This is a snatch-their-hand-off bargain. The imaginative and straightforward cooking owes much to French cuisine. Starters range from foie gras with quail and pickled vegetable terrine; through crisp mackerel with watercress, capers, Charlotte potatoes and grain mustard; and cauliflower and smoked haddock soup; to warm salad of wood pigeon with deep-fried truffled egg. Main courses vary from a classical Chateaubriand with all the trimmings (including a small supplement to the bill), to roast sea bass with butternut squash broth, Provençal vegetables and sage beurre noisette. The ravioli of calf's tongue and sweetbreads with spiced red cabbage will appeal to offal-fanciers. Puddings have a deft touch and include old favourites like hot chocolate fondant and steamed golden syrup sponge pudding. The wine list is short and thoughtfully drawn up, with one or two unusual selections.

Service at Glasshouse is masterful, and will leave you feeling thoroughly cosseted. However, it's just as well to note their warning: "Please order taxis at least 25 minutes before they are required" – you are in the wilds of Kew.

Pukkabar

Pukkabar, or "The Pukkabar and Curry Hall", to spell out its more fulsome title, started life in Sydenham. It was the brainchild of Trevor Gulliver, the mastermind behind that headquarters of nose-to-tail cuisine, St John in Clerkenwell (see p.198). Mr Gulliver's quaint theory was that curry is a very British dish, and that this British perspective is the one from which it is best approached. The Pukkabar offers well-made, well-spiced, good-value food in clean surroundings and with the minimum pretension and fuss. Curries are batch-cooked and the rest of the menu is made up of fresh food from the tandoor and, for starters, a range of tasty Indian street food. As with so many kinds of food, when it comes to curry, simple is good, and despite its English antecedents, the Pukkabar has ended up having a good deal more in common with clear flavours than most high-street curry houses.

Cost	£10–30

Address 21 Barnes High St, SW13
ⓣ 020 8878 7012
Station BR Barnes Bridge
Open Mon–Fri 6.30–11pm, Sat 12.30–11pm, Sun 12.30–10.30pm
Accepts All major credit cards
ⓦ www.pukkabars.com

The menu changes regularly, but you can expect to find about eight starters listed, several of which are suitable for vegetarians. From the tandoor there's malai tikka (£3.95) – well-cooked and tender chicken; or gulabi kebab (£4.25) – minced lamb kebabs; or salmon suslik (£5.65). The presentation is accomplished here. As well as old favourites like onion bhaji (£3.95), there are moodier items such as crab cakes (£4.95) and tandoori quail (£4.95). In addition to the mixed tandoori (£8.95) of chicken, lamb and salmon, the main courses are curries. There's chilli chicken (£6.95); Goan prawn curry (£8.75); masaledar fish (£7.25); a lamb xacutti (£7.50); and even that all-British favourite, chicken tikka masala (£6.95). Rice dishes and breads are good – check out the garlic naan (£2). For pud there are Hill Station ice creams (£3) – better a reputable bought-in ice cream than a poorly made one from the kitchen.

There is a sensible Pukka lunch for £6.95 which comprises a couple of tasters from the main menu and rice. The Pukkabar delivery service now includes a "fleet" of small and steady Piaggio vans, but it only operates if you live within a mile of the restaurant.

Redmond's

When Redmond and Pippa Hayward opened this small neighbourhood restaurant towards the end of the 1990s, it was head and shoulders above anything else the locale had to offer. A few years down the line and "Barnes & Sheen" may not quite be a match for Soho, but there are a good many very decent places to eat. Redmond's is one of the best, propelled by a telling combo of very good cooking and reasonable prices. They tweak the menu on a daily basis, so it reflects the best of what the season and the markets have to offer. The dinner menu is not particularly short – about six or seven starters and mains – and proves astonishing value at £23 for two courses and £27 for three. There is also a competitive lunch menu: £16.50 for two courses and £19.50 for three. What's even more astonishing is that the list is not splattered with supplements or cover charges. And the food here really is very good indeed: well seasoned, precisely cooked, immaculately presented.

Cost £18–45

Address 170 Upper Richmond Rd West, SW14
℡ 020 8878 1922
Station BR Mortlake
Open Mon–Fri noon–2pm & 7–10.30pm, Sat 7–10.30pm, Sun noon–2.30pm
Accepts Delta, MasterCard, Switch, Visa

If the terrine of duck confit and foie gras with roast shallots and aged balsamic is available when you visit, pounce. It's multi-layered, multi-textured and superlative-inducing in every way. There may also be a mussel, leek and smoked haddock chowder; or perhaps roast marinated pigeon breast with creamed celeriac and Puy lentils. Main courses combine dominant flavours with elegant presentation. Roast brill on the bone with saffron mash, spinach and grain mushroom sauce; open ravioli of Jerusalem artichokes and wild mushrooms with Parmesan, gremolata and truffle oil; roast duck breast with a foie gras risotto; roast, crispy, spiced belly pork with crushed new potatoes. A fennel compote with tapenade and crab sauce partners roast red mullet fillets. The puddings are wonderful, too: passion fruit pannacotta with blackberry sauce and hazelnut tuille; steamed banana pudding with butterscotch sauce and mango sorbet.

The short wine list is littered with interesting bottles at accessible prices. There are halves, magnums, pudding wines and just plain bargains.

ITALIAN

Riva

Andrea Riva has always been something of a darling of the media, and his sophisticated little restaurant exerts a powerful pull. Strong enough to convince even the snootiest of fashionable folk to make the dangerous journey into the unknown territory on the south bank of the Thames. When they get there they find a rather conservative-looking restaurant, with a narrow dining room decorated in a sombre blend of dull greens and faded parchment, and chairs which have clearly seen service in church. As far as the cuisine goes, Riva provides the genuine article, so most customers are either delighted or disappointed, depending on how well they know their Italian food. The menu changes regularly with the seasons.

Cost	£25–45

Address 169 Church Rd, SW13
℡ 020 8748 0434
Station BR Barnes
Open Mon–Fri noon–2.30pm & 7–11pm, Sat 7–11.30pm, Sun noon–2.30pm & 7–9.30pm
Accepts All major credit cards except Diners

Starters are good but not cheap. The frittelle (£9) is a tempura-like dish of deep-fried Mediterranean prawn, salt cod cakes, calamari, sag and basil, with a balsamic dip. If it is on the menu, you must try bocconcini di bufala – buffalo mozzarella with baby spinach, cherry tomatoes and chiodini mushrooms (£7), vibrant and deliciously oily. The brodetto "Mare Nostrum", a chunky, saffron-flavoured fish soup (£7), is also superb, a delicate alternative to its robust French cousin. Serious Italian food fans, however, will find it hard to resist the sapori Mediterranei (£19 for two), which gets you grilled scallop and langoustines; baccalà mantecato and polenta; eel and lentils; mussels in tomato pesto; and grilled oysters. Among the main courses, rombo al rucola (£18.50) is a splendid combination of tastes and textures – a fillet of brill with a rocket sauce and mashed potato. Fegato and polenta unta (£14) – calves' liver served with garlic polenta and wild mushrooms – delivers a finely balanced blend of flavours.

If there's anybody out there who still thinks that pizza and pasta are the Italians' staple diet, Riva's uncompromising regional menu proves otherwise. The house wines are all priced at a very accessible £11.50. Of the whites, the pale-coloured Tocai is crisp, light and refreshing.

Sonny's

(🍴) If the scientists are to be believed, we must evolve or die, and if they're looking for corroborating evidence they'll find it at Sonny's. This is one of those restaurants people describe as a "neighbourhood stalwart" but it has grown into something more polished. Barnes-ites have been supporting Sonny's since modern British cuisine was just a twinkle in a telly chef's eye. The interior is modern but gratifyingly unthreatening and there is a busy, casual feel about the place. Sonny's shop next door sells a good many of those little delicacies that you would otherwise have to make the dangerous journey to the West End to procure. Leigh Diggins is chef here and he has a good grasp of just what his customers want. The menu is modern but not aggressively so, dishes are interesting but not frightening, and you will find the occasional flash of innovation.

Cost	£18–38

Address 94 Church Rd, SW13
℡ 020 8748 0393
Station BR Barnes Bridge
Open Mon–Sat 12.30–2.30pm
& 7.30–11pm, Sun 12.30–3pm
Accepts All major credit cards

MODERN BRITISH

The menu changes on a regular basis to reflect the seasons, so you might find starters like watercress soup with Jersey Royals and truffle oil (£4.25), or chicken and sweetbread terrine with mixed leaves and sweet pickle (£6.50), or even, on a more whimsical note, boudin of foie gras with caramelized apricots, organic leaves and Poilane toast (£8). Main courses may take a classic combination like pan-fried calves' liver with Alsace bacon, and then add spätzle, pumpkin puree and sherry vinegar reduction (£11.50). There tend to be some attractive fish dishes, too: steamed fillet of halibut with beetroot chutney, smoked eel and apple ravioli, and crisped pancetta (£14.50), say, or fillet of red mullet with grilled fennel and pak choi in a shrimp vinaigrette (£14). Or you could go much heartier with the slow honey-roast duck (£13), which comes with garlic mash, braised red cabbage and a red wine jus. The service is welcoming and the wine list provides some sound bottles at sound prices.

Puddings are comfortable: sorbets, jellies, baked Alaska with griottines (£5.25). If Barnes is your neighbourhood, you will be glad of Sonny's Café menu, which slips effortlessly from BLT (£3.95) to smoked haddock, saffron and chive risotto (£6). If Barnes isn't your neighbourhood, you could always move.

Barnes & Sheen

The Victoria

It would be nice to live in West Temple Sheen. The name has a good ring to it. The houses are palatial and pricey, both Sheen Common and Richmond Park are close at hand, and then there's The Victoria, a truly outstanding gastro-pub. The Victoria made the transition from pub to gastro-pub in late 2000. It emerged with a conservatory, squashy sofas and painted floorboards – very smart. And now there are seven bedrooms as well (which are described as simple but stylish), so now it should probably be called a hotel. Just when you thought that you had mastered the distinction between restaurants and gastro-pubs... The Victoria just about hangs onto gastro-pub status by virtue of its accessible prices. What you're getting is restaurant cooking, a restaurant wine list and restaurant service, and you're getting it on the cheap.

The menu is blessedly short and changes daily – or even more frequently than that, should items run out. There are a handful of starters such as endive au gratin (£5.50); caponata with creamed goat's cheese and focaccia (£5.50); potted salmon (£6); pork, game and green peppercorn terrine with onion chutney (£6.50). Or perhaps the plate of charcuterie with pickles (£7) appeals? Or how about a duck confit and lentil soup (£4.50)? Mains are also pretty triumphant. Roast and confit pheasant with red cabbage and chestnuts (£10.50) is excellent – the cabbage and chestnuts hearty enough to make a dish by themselves. Then there's a shellfish tagine (£12.50); or Toulouse sausages and mash with onion gravy (£8); or Gorgonzola, white wine and sage risotto (£8). Or cassoulet (£12). These are all examples of those special, simple-sounding dishes that are hard to get right. Desserts are top stuff. It's a pleasure to watch punters savouring a baked ricotta cheesecake with pine nuts and raisins (£4.50), or taunting chocoholics with chocolate nemesis and crème fraîche (£5).

Turning the outbuildings into a hotel has brought an added bonus. The Victoria is now open for breakfast from 8.30am; it's best to book.

Cost £12–30

Address 10 West Temple Sheen, SW14
℡020 8876 4238
Station BR Mortlake
Open Mon–Fri noon–2.30pm & 7–10pm, Sat & Sun noon–3pm & 7–10pm
Accepts All major credit cards
🖰www.thevictoria.net

Chelsea

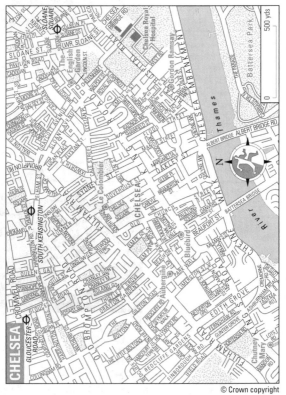

© Crown copyright

Aubergine

Aubergine deserves a prolonged burst of applause. It's hard to imagine it, but a decade or so ago this neck of the woods was a bleak-ish place to eat out. Aubergine changed all that, and it now merits the accolade "old-established". In 2001 they re-decorated and re-organized the reception arrangements and it is now light and airy enough

Cost	£28–100
Address	11 Park Walk, SW10
☎	020 7352 3449
Station	South Kensington/ Earl's Court
Open	Mon–Fri noon–2.15pm & 7–10.15pm, Sat 7–10.15pm
Accepts	All major credit cards

for even the most discerning of ladies who lunch. The menu changes with the seasons and is driven by an emphasis on quality ingredients. The best of everything in season and a talented kitchen make for a busy place, so booking is a must. The set lunch at £20 for two courses and £25 for three is an outrageous bargain.

A lunch that comprises tortellini of lobster with braised fennel, followed by boudin of pheasant with creamed cabbage and roasted carrots, doesn't read, look or taste like twenty pounds' worth. Even at full throttle the main dinner menu offers three courses for £48, which is not so very fierce for cooking of this calibre (although supplements hang on the coat tails of lobster, turbot, cheeses and the like). Starters may include sauté of foie gras with a cassoulet of white beans, onions and bacon; or roast scallops with a velouté of salsify. Main courses include dishes such as pan-fried sea bass with roasted artichokes, confit tomatoes, sweet pepper purée and basil oil; best end of lamb with confit turnips and a thyme-scented jus; breast of wild mallard with Madeira jus; and fillet of turbot poached in cider with a tagliatelle of celeriac, mussels, apples and chives. These are well-conceived and well-executed dishes, beautifully presented. It would be hard to suggest improvements. The Menu Gourmand at £65 will spin the experience out by presenting seven pixie portions and so allow you to make the kitchen brigade jump through a few extra hoops. Desserts are equally accomplished – assiette of orange; tarte Tatin with vanilla ice cream; banana parfait with banana toffee. The service is accomplished and unobtrusive.

The only cautionary note relates to the wine list, where the prices bolt swiftly out of reach for all but the most special of special occasions.

Bluebird

Bluebird is Sir Terence Conran's vision of a corner shop for the wealthy Chelsea set. Downstairs, in what was the largest motor garage in Europe, you'll find a rather grand food hall with a real butcher and fishmonger, top quality vegetables and dry goods. In the old forecourt there's a popular, bustling café and to the side there's both a flower stall and a kitchen shop. Everything that's for sale is beautifully prepared, good-looking and reassuringly expensive.

Cost	£22–70

Address 350 King's Rd, SW3
☎ 020 7559 1000
Station Sloane Square
Open Mon–Fri noon–3pm &
6–11pm, Sat 11am–3.30pm &
6–11pm, Sun 6–10pm; brunch
Sun 11am–3.30pm
Accepts All major credit cards
🌐 www.conran.com

Above this temple to good food is Bluebird Restaurant. Even if you haven't wandered around the shops below, a feeling of well-being emanates from the whole building, and as you arrive at the restaurant you cannot help but feel kindly towards it. The room itself takes advantage of natural light and space, with plenty of blond wood and acres of crisp white linen. It's functional, comfortable and very familiar. The menu offers a mixture of traditional English and Mediterranean dishes. Among the starters, pressed ham and parsley terrine with piccalilli (£6.50) rubs shoulders with vegetable bruschetta and salsa verde (£6.75), and marinated chicken and herb salad (£7.95). Main courses range from steamed halibut with baby leeks, mussels and saffron broth (£19.95) to fillet of beef Rossini (£21.95), covering a lot of territory in between. The menu is long and well balanced and the cooking, though not the finest in the land, is perfectly sound. However, in the unlikely event that there's nothing on the menu that takes your fancy and you're in the mood for shellfish, you're really in luck. Bluebird is shellfish heaven. The crushed ice and marble altar to crustacea is an unmissable feature; prices and availability vary by season.

Bluebird is a well-designed and reliable restaurant, willingly and ably staffed, which has a decent local following and proves very popular with local families for weekend brunches. If you're not wary, prices can escalate, but there's a steal of a set-price menu (£17 for three courses) for weekday lunchtimes and early or late dinners.

Chutney Mary

In the spring of 2002 Chutney Mary shut down for a thorough refurbishment and the locals held their breath, worried that the restaurant they had grown fond of since the mid 1990s would be changed out of all recognition. Good news! A sensitive design job has meant that everything looks new and chic it is still as comfortable as ever. The lighting designer (seduced from his day job as a theatrical lighting expert) has done a particularly fine job and it is hard to tell that the moonlight – which plays over the tree in the conservatory as night falls – is not the real thing. This is not a cheap restaurant but it is a good one. The men in the kitchen know their job and turn out refined Indian food. These are the complicated dishes that were developed for Maharajahs: sauces are silky textured; flavours are subtle; the spicing authentic. The refurb has also added a modern wine "cave" and there's a long and interesting new list of bottles to fill it.

Cost	£30–90

Address 535 King's Rd, SW10
℡ 020 7351 3113
Station Fulham Broadway
Open Mon–Fri 6.30–11.30pm,
Sat noon–3pm &
6.30–11.30pm, Sun
noon–3pm & 6.30–10.30pm
Accepts All major credit cards
🖰 www.chutneymary.com

Start with the crab cake (£9.50) – spankingly fresh crab, loosely bound and top-and-tailed with a potato rosti. Delicious. Or there's the tokri chaat (£6), which is an edible basket filled with various street-food treats and topped with yoghurt and chutney. Or the crab claws with black pepper and garlic (£9.50) – huge tender claws swimming in a sea of garlic butter. Vegetarians will enjoy the platter of mixed tikki (£6.50) – different crisp-coated patties served with excellent chutneys. Mains are equally impressive. Mangalore prawns (£17.50) are giant prawns, chilli hot and tamarind tangy. Nalli gosht (£15) is a splendid lamb curry, served on the bone, with intense flavours. Or there's duck with apricots (£16.50) – pink duck breast and a Parsee masala. From the side dishes, the sarson ka saag (£4.50) – mustard leaves cooked with lotus root – stands out; as does the butter beans methi malai (£3.50).

The dessert menu (all at £5) is also inspired. There is a strawberry brûlée with garam masala; a dark chocolate fondant served with orange-blossom lassi; and small eclairs stuffed with Srikhand (a sweetened cottage cheese/yoghurt) and served with chocolate sauce.

Le Colombier

(🍴) Viewed from the pavement outside on Dovehouse Street, you can see that Le Colombier was once a classic, English, street-corner pub. But now it's a pub that has a small, glassed-in area in front, covered with tables and chairs. How very Parisian, you might think, and you would be right. This is a French place. It is run by Monsieur Garnier, who has spent most of his career in the slicker reaches of London's restaurant business. With his own place he has reverted to type and everything is very, very French.

Cost	£15–30

Address 145 Dovehouse St,
Chelsea Square, SW3
℡020 7351 1155
Station South Kensington
Open Mon–Sat noon–3pm &
6.30–11pm, Sun noon–3.30pm
& 6.30–10.30pm
Accepts All major credit cards

The menu is French, the cooking is French, the service is French and the decor is French. When the bill comes, you tend to be surprised – first that it is no larger and secondly that they ask for pounds not francs. The cooking is about as good as you would have found in a smart Routiers in rural France during the 1970s – before such places became hard to find. Starters include such bistro classics as oeufs pochés meurette (£5.80), soupe de poissons (£5.30), and feuilleté d'escargots à la crème d'ail (£6.80). And there are oysters, goat's cheese salad, duck liver terrine, and tomato and basil salad. Listed under "les poissons" there is filet de loup de mer roti au thym (£16.90); and coquilles St Jacques aux champignons sauvages (£14.80), which is scallops with wild mushrooms. Under "les viandes" there is steak tartare pommes frites (£14.80) and lapin à la moutarde (£13.50). Under "les grillades" are the steaks and chops. Puddings include crêpes Suzette (£4.90) and omelette Norvégienne pour deux (£12), which is also described as "baked Alaska" – something of a geographical conundrum.

Service is as French as the menu itself, but Le Colombier is not some trendy retro caricature. None of the atmosphere is posed. If this seems like a provincial French eatery, it's because that's what it is. The fact that it is located in Chelsea makes the set menu for lunch and early dinners (two courses for £13; on Sunday £15) very good value indeed.

The English Garden

Searcy Corrigan Restaurants took over this Chelsea stalwart during the autumn of 1999, and after a steady start, The English Garden has grown into its new persona. There's a maple-wood bar, lashings of soft, creamy and biscuity tones, and a judicious use of grey British slate. The new kitchen is headed up by Malcolm Starmer, who worked with

Cost	£22–50
Address 10 Lincoln St, SW3	
☎ 020 7584 7272	
Station Sloane Square	
Open Mon 6–11pm, Tues–Sat noon–3pm & 6–11pm, Sun noon–3pm & 6.30–10.30pm	
Accepts All major credit cards	

MODERN BRITISH

Richard Corrigan for five years at The Lindsay House, and before that in The Barbican. The service is slick, the room is comfortable, and Starmer's food is good. There are echoes of The Lindsay House, but only faint ones; this is well-conceived Modern British food which relies on good combinations of strong flavours.

The menu changes twice a day. For lunch there is a three-course set lunch at the modest price of £19.50. Less than £20 for smoked eel and scrambled egg, with bacon and red wine jus, followed by grilled leg of rabbit, black pudding, carrots, mustard and thyme, and then chocolate pot with caramelized oranges and chocolate ice cream? This is a stellar bargain. Or perhaps crab ravioli with marinated fennel, followed by rib-eye with pommes frites, and finishing with roast bananas with spice bread and banana ice cream? In the evening these dishes would be bolstered by one or two more serious numbers. Starters might include terrine of foie gras, or oxtail tortelloni with celeriac mash and marjoram. Mains might be dishes such as "daube" of organic farmed pork with apricots and Savoy cabbage; pigeon in puff pastry with Madeira jus; poached haddock with leek, brow shrimp and chive butter; and seared scallops with linguini, and chanterelle and cep velouté. At dinner the price moves up to £27.50 for three courses, with supplements kept to a minimum. Puds are indulgent: try ginger madeleines with poached pear.

Elsewhere in the Garden are two elegant private rooms that can be joined together, creating space for parties of ten, twenty or thirty. There is an irresistible temptation to say that everything in the garden is rosy.

Chelsea

Gordon Ramsay

Gordon Ramsay is on a roll. His new-ish resto within Claridges (see p.80) continues to delight the critics, and in 2002 he added the dining room at the Connaught to his increasingly large sphere of influence. At Chelsea, his restaurant continues to be packed. Thankfully, the prices are not as high as you might fear. There are two fixed-price à la carte menus at both lunch and dinner

Cost	£35–130

Address 68–69 Royal Hospital Rd, SW3
ⓣ 020 7352 4441
Station Sloane Square
Open Mon–Fri noon–2pm & 6.45–11pm
Accepts All major credit cards
ⓦ www.gordonramsay.com

(£65 for three courses, £80 for seven), and a steal of a set lunch (£35 for three courses). Even if you add £5 for a glass of good house wine, this offers the more accessible face of truly great cooking – as long as you can get a booking.

The menu here is constantly evolving and changing. On the main menus, look out for a ravioli of lobster and langoustine poached in a lobster bisque and served with a tomato and herb velouté; or a carpaccio of pigeon from Bresse with shavings of confit foie gras, baby artichokes and a Parmesan salad – this is a stunning dish of unusual delicacy; or a warm salad of caramelized calf's sweetbreads with sautéed Jerusalem artichokes, grilled asparagus and mustard and honey vinaigrette, which is as robust and delicious as you could wish for. And those are just starters! Mains intrigue: braised fillet of turbot on a bed of tagliatelle finished with roquette, asparagus, sautéed mushrooms and a cep velouté; poulet de Bresse poached then grilled with braised Savoy cabbage and seasoned with marjoram, with confit shallots, asparagus and foie gras sauce; and sautéed loin of Scottish venison with confit cabbage and bitter chocolate sauce finished with raspberries. Even the puds fascinate – coffee soufflé with whisky-scented milk ice cream. To order successfully here, just pick a dish or even an ingredient you like and see how it arrives; you won't be disappointed. This restaurant is a class act through and through.

You will have to book at Gordon Ramsay, but, sensibly enough, reservations are taken only a month in advance, avoiding a potentially huge backlog. Book now, and count the days.

Ealing & Acton

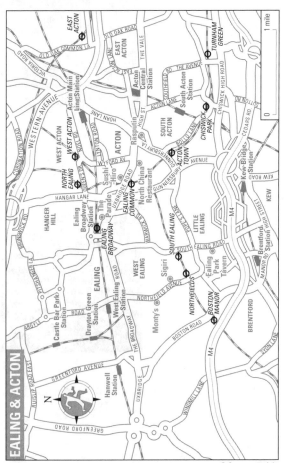

EALING & ACTON

© Crown copyright

Ealing Park Tavern

In 2001, when it was transformed from a lager and football hovel into a tidy pub and eatery, this establishment reverted to its original name – the Ealing Park Tavern. The new owners were the people behind another fine gastro-pub, St John's (see p.264), so it is no surprise that they have made a decent fist of it. It is a handsome place and, like its North London sibling, is founded on the simple premise that hospitality is important. The bar has two or three decent real ales and a blackboard featuring decent bar snacks like proper pork pies. The wine list is short but gives a fair choice around the £15 a bottle mark, topping out at £35. The dining room has a tall counter separating it from an open kitchen and the menu is chalked up on a blackboard. What makes the Park Tavern so popular is the food.

Cost	£12–40

Address 222 South Ealing Rd, W5
☎ 020 8758 1879
Station South Ealing
Open Mon 6–10.30pm, Tues–Fri noon–3pm & 6–10.30pm, Sat noon–4pm & 6–10.30pm, Sun noon–9pm
Accepts All major credit cards except Diners

The menu is a short one – seven or eight starters and half a dozen mains – but it is thoughtfully written, changes daily and there is something for everybody. Starters may include a rich potato and cabbage soup (£4.50), which is just eclipsed by the very rich crab and mussel soup with cheese croutons (£5.50), or an accomplished smoked haddock and chive terrine with potato and egg (£5.50), which is very good eating. Main courses are well presented, substantial and seem implausibly good value. A Scotch rib-eye with serious chips, sun-dried tomatoes and horseradish cream weighs in at £10.50. A chicken, leek and saffron pudding (£9.50) is a mighty thing, rich and satisfying winter food. Or there's a lamb Wellington with a cep potato cake and beans (£9.75). This is all good stuff, but one dish stands out – roast hake with boulangère potatoes, French beans and pastis cream (£9.50), which is a very large piece of perfectly cooked, ultra-fresh fish (the credit for this goes to overnight deliveries from the Tavern's fishmonger in Brixham).

The food is good at the Ealing Park Tavern, prices are reasonable, the atmosphere is informal and the service is friendly. We could all do with a local like this one.

Monty's

🍴 Once upon a time, the now defunct
Ealing Tandoori held West London
curry lovers in thrall – it was the undis-
puted first choice. Then, in the late 1970s,
the three main chefs left to open their
own place, which they called Monty's, on
South Ealing Road. As business boomed,
two of the chefs moved on to set up inde-
pendently. But as all three co-owned the
name Monty's, they all use it, and that is
why there are now three different Monty's, all fiercely independent but
each with the same name and logo. Unlike many small Indian restaurants,
these are "chef-led", which is a key factor in making Monty's in Northfield
Avenue an almost perfect neighbourhood curry house. You won't find
banks of flowers or majestic staircases, the tables are too close together
and you may be crowded by people waiting for a takeaway. But the
cooking is classy, the portions are good and prices are fair. This is a
restaurant which has a fine grasp of what its customers want.

Cost	£12–24

Address 54 Northfield Ave,
Ealing, W13; with branches
ⓣ 020 8567 6281
Station Northfields
Open Daily noon–2.30pm &
6–11.30pm
Accepts All major credit cards
🌐 www.montys.uk.com

A complimentary plate of salady crudités arrives with any chutneys
and popadoms ordered, but starters are the exception rather than the
rule here – perhaps because of the well-sized main course portions. Trad
tandoori dishes are good, like the tandoori chicken (£4.75 for two
pieces). Or there is hasina (£6.50), lamb marinated in yogurt and served
as a sizzler. The boss here remembers introducing the iron-plate sizzlers
at the Ealing Tandoori years ago and claims that his were the first in
Britain. Breads are delicious – pick between nan (£1.75) and Peshwari
nan (£2.50). But the kitchen really gets to shine with simple curry
dishes like methi ghosht (£7.25) – tender lamb (and plenty of it) in a
delicious sauce rich with fenugreek; and chicken jalfriji (£7.25), which
is all that the dish should be. Vegetable dishes also shine – both brinjal
bhaji (£3.80) and sag paneer (£3.80) are delicious.

Monty's is one of very few local curry houses to serve perfectly
cooked, genuine basmati rice. So the plain boiled rice (£2.10) – nutty,
almost smoky, with grains perfectly separate – is worth tasting on its
own.

North China Restaurant

The special Peking duck, which always used to require 24 hours advance notice, is now so popular that the restaurant cooks a few ducks every day regardless. So you don't always have to pre-order. But then you do, because it is *so* popular that they cannot guarantee that you'll get one unless you order it. The North China has a 24-carat local reputation, it is the kind of place people refer to as "being as good as Chinatown", which in this case is spot-on, and the star turn on the menu doesn't disappoint.

Cost	£14–25

Address 305 Uxbridge Rd, Ealing Common, W3
☏ 020 8992 9183
Station Ealing Common
Open Mon–Thurs & Sun noon–2.30pm & 6–11.30pm, Fri & Sat noon–2.30pm & 6pm–midnight
Accepts All major credit cards
🌐 www.northchina.co.uk

Unlike most other – upstart, deep fried – crispy ducks, the crispy Peking duck here comes as three separate courses. Firstly there is the skin and breast meat, served with pancakes, shreds of cucumber and spring onion, and hoisin sauce. Then there is a fresh stir-fry of the duck meat with beansprouts, and finally the meal ends with a giant tureen of rich duck soup with lumps of the carcass to pick at. It is awesome. And the price, £42, is very reasonable, working out at just over £3 per person per course. If you're dull and just want the duck with pancakes the price drops to £32. So what goes well with duck? At the North China the familiar dishes are well cooked and well presented. You might start with barbecued pork spare ribs (£4.90), or the whimsically named lettuce puffs (£3.40 per person, minimum two), which turn out to be our old friend "mince wrapped in lettuce leaves". For a supplementary main course, prawns in chilli sauce (£7.25), although not very chilli, is teamed with fresh water-chestnuts and tastes very good. Singapore fried noodles (£4.10) is powered by curry powder rather than fresh chilli, but fills a gap.

The genuinely friendly service at the North China stems from the fact that it is a family restaurant. If the genuine Peking duck does not appeal perhaps you should consider the North China's other high-ticket item. When lobsters are good at market they go onto the menu at a seasonal price of about £22.50 per lobster.

Parade

People who live in the better parts of Ealing drive Jaguars and live in million-pound houses. These are the sophisticated and leafy suburbs, but until the arrival of Parade in 1999 there was not a single proper restaurant to while away those evenings when the television disappoints. So when Parade opened (on a site that formerly hosted a rather arch Indian restaurant) you could hear the

Cost	£15–50

Address 18–19 The Mall, Ealing, W5
℡ 020 8810 0202
Station Ealing Broadway
Open Mon–Sat 12.30–2.30pm & 7–11pm, Sun 12.30–3pm
Accepts All major credit cards except Diners

sighs of relief echoing around the neighbourhood. A sister restaurant to Sonny's in Barnes (see p.403), this is a modern, clean, keen sort of place, where neither the food nor the service will let you down. If you plonked this eatery down in the West End it would be run-of-the-mill, but here it deserves star billing. Which is why it is so amazingly busy every night of the week. Nowadays locals bemoan the fact that they cannot get in without booking.

At lunchtime, when the restaurant is under a lot less pressure, there's a very decent set lunch, which costs £12 for two courses and £15 for three. In the evening everything goes à la carte. The menu changes regularly and is seasonally based. Starters are eclectic but well conceived, as the kitchen understands what the customer wants. Perhaps cream of cauliflower soup with Stilton wonton (£5.50); ballotine of salmon with avocado puree and lemon oil (£7); or oxtail and foie gras ravioli with winter greens and white bean velouté (£7.50). Mains are grown-up versions of the starters, with dishes like braised shoulder of lamb with root vegetables and rosemary (£13.50); grilled sea bass with saffron polenta, tomato fondue, olive and herb relish (£14.50); or assiette of pork with prunes and mustard mash (£13.50). The cooking is sound and the dishes are well presented. Service is generally slick, but has been known to creak under the intense pressure.

Parade's puddings are good: try the Bramley apple bavarois with blackberry sauce (£5.50); the warm chocolate pudding with malt ice cream (£5.50); or pears poached in red wine with Greek yoghurt and sesame tuille (£5.50).

Rasputin

You'll find the "Rasputin Russian Restaurant and Wine Bar" up at the Ealing end of Acton High Street. In 2001 the restaurant underwent a refurbishment and is now, in the words of the proprietors, "modern". It's still a jolly place, and the Russian specialities are homely and delicious, with an authentic

Cost	£14–30

Address 265 High St, Acton, W3
⊤ 020 8993 5802
Station Acton Town
Open Daily 6–11.30pm
Accepts MasterCard, Visa

emphasis on game in season. All this must be noted before you have made any inroads into the twenty different vodkas, which come both as single shots and – take care here – "by the carafe".

With the menu comes a plate of cucumber, cabbage, green tomatoes and peppers, all markedly salty and with a good vinegary tang. For a starter, try pierogi – rich little dumplings that come stuffed with a choice of potato and cheese, meat, or sauerkraut and mushrooms; they are all priced at £3.95 a portion. The blinis – small buckwheat pancakes – are also good; try them with smoked trout (£5.50) or, if you enjoy the special thrill of finding a bargain, with Sevruga caviar (£24.95). The Moscovite fish platter (£8.95) is also delicious. At Rasputin they are constantly tinkering with the menu and there usually seem to be several versions extant at once. Hold out for the golubtsy (£9.95), which is permanently under threat of banishment from the menu and is now called "cabbage parcels" – this is a simple but satisfying dish of cabbage leaves stuffed with meat and rice. Very wholesome and very good. Or there's a chicken Kiev made with tarragon butter (£9.90). Fish fans may want to try the salmon fillets in dill sauce (£10.95). Desserts are rather staid – crème brûlée (£3.50) or pancakes filled with a choice of chocolate, walnuts or fruit preserve (£3.50). Also interesting is the Russian tea served in a glass and holder. It is made with tea, lemon and a splash of vodka (£2.50), with a small bowl of honey alongside for sweetening.

If you are of fearless disposition (or possibly if you are a Russian exile) then the formidable game mixed grill is for you: wild boar chop, venison steak, pigeon breast, pheasant sausage and so forth, all for £14.95.

Sushi-Hiro

Sushi-Hiro is a very self-effacing sort of restaurant. The sign outside says "Sushi-Hiro, Japanese Gourmet Foods", and if it were not for the constant stream of Japanese people calling for sushi boxes to go, the blanked out windows would make it look a bit like one of those very discreet "specialist" shops. When you push open the door you find

Cost	£15–40

Address 1 Station Parade,
Uxbridge Rd, W5
☎ 020 8896 3175
Station Ealing Common
Open Tues–Sun
11am–1.30pm & 4.30–9pm
Accepts Cash only

that half the room is given over to a waiting area for takeaway customers, there is a sushi counter with stools and a handful of tables and that's about it. The ceiling is high, the lighting bright, and all is spotlessly clean. It can be bit intimidating, but take heart; all the experts agree that Sushi-Hiro serves some of the best sushi in London.

The menu offers sushi in various guises. You are given a miniature clipboard with a small form to fill in your order and that's when it all gets tricky, as there are fifty or so boxes to tick. The best strategy is to start with the chef's selection of superior nigiri (£12), which brings ten pieces of sushi – tuna, salmon, herring roe, turbot, bass, red clam, scallop, salmon roe, red bream and sweet shrimp. Try them all and then repeat the ones you like the most. The sushi here is very good: the rice is soft and almost warm, the balance between the amount of rice and amount of topping is just about perfect, and the fish is squeakily fresh and very delicious. When you've taken the sting out of your appetite with the chef's choice, consider trying a piece of eel (£1.80) – very rich; mackerel (90p) – a revelation, light and not oily at all; pickled plum roll (£2.20 for four) – made with rice, pickled plum and shiso leaves, an addictive flavour; or salmon roe (£1.50) - salty, and sticky. Then round things off with a small bowl of rather splendid miso soup (£1), which comes with a couple of little clams lurking in the depths. These are all sophisticated flavours and textures.

This establishment works to Japanese rules, so beware of the opening times, which are "early" by European standards, and the cash only rule which means they do not even take cheques.

Earl's Court

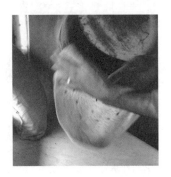

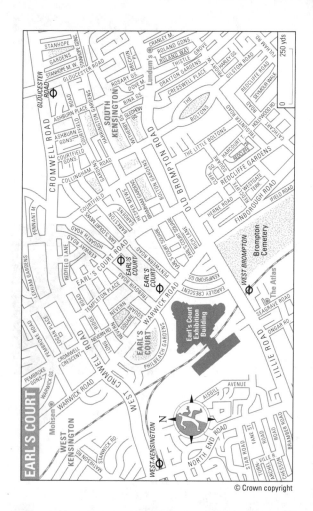

© Crown copyright

The Atlas

Once upon a time, pubs were for boozing. You got sarnies maybe, and pickled onions if you were lucky. The Atlas is as far away from that kind of place as it is possible to get. In a lively and informal atmosphere, brothers Richard and George Manners serve the kind of innovative, Mediterranean-inspired food that many full-blown restaurants would be proud of. George is the chef – he trained at gastro-pub head-

Cost	£15–30
Address	16 Seagrave Rd, Fulham, SW6
☎	020 7385 9129
Station	Earl's Court
Open	Mon–Sat 12.30–3pm & 7–10.30pm, Sun 12.30–3pm & 7–10pm
Accepts	MasterCard, Switch, Visa

quarters, The Eagle in Farringdon (see p.196). The flavours come mainly from Spain, Italy and North Africa, and huge strings of dried peppers and bundles of cinnamon sticks vie for attention in the kitchen. But there are no concessions. The menu is chalked on the board at lunch and becomes a tad more formal in the evening; both depend on what's in supply and what has inspired George.

Starters may include pappa al pomodoro (£3.50), a rich Tuscan tomato and bread soup; verdura misto (£6.50), a salad made from grilled vegetables; or a saffron and wild rocket risotto with cherry vine tomatoes and Parmesan (£6.50). Main courses range from grilled Italian sausages, smashed parsnips with chilli and oregano, and roast red onions with red wine and balsamic (£8); to grilled whole sea bass with spiced black beans and choricero peppers, and tomato and chilli jam (£11.50). Or there's Catalan beef casserole (£9.50), which has an intriguing combination of flavours – chocolate, cinnamon, garlic, bay and marjoram. Or even poached smoked haddock, grilled new potato and green bean salad with shaved shallots and rocket, with tarragon aioli (£8). The dessert selection is short and to the point, with dishes such as baked quince with maple syrup, cinnamon and cream (£4), or Donald's chocolate and almond cake with ice cream (£4).

The wine selection is also chalked up, and there are some unusual offerings served by the glass, which makes The Atlas a good venue for wine-lovers in search of a bit of impromptu tasting. Everyone else will be pleased to have found an eatery where you can get a decent pint. The Atlas is busy, noisy, friendly and young, and the food is good into the bargain. You're likely to end up sharing a table, so get there early.

Earl's Court

Lundum's

This is a genuine family restaurant – four Lundums work in the business. They took this site on the Old Brompton Road and set about turning it into London's premier Danish restaurant. The Lundums would be the first to admit that there is not a lot of competition; in fact this may well be London's only Danish restaurant, which gives them something of a head start. There's nothing particularly Danish about the room, which is pleasantly light and airy with huge mirrors and a skylight, much the same as in previous incarnations. But the staff proudly produce interesting (and delicious) dill-flavoured aquavit, which they import specially. They also import the Danish sausages and all manner of other delicacies. The food is elegantly presented, competently handled and ... Danish. At lunchtime it's trad Danish, in the evening modern Danish. You cannot help but be swept along by the tidal wave of commitment and charm – remember, there is a whole family working on you.

Cost	£25–65
Address	119 Old Brompton Rd, SW7
☎	020 7373 7774
Station	Gloucester Road/South Kensington
Open	Mon–Sat 10am–11pm; brunch Sun 10am–4pm
Accepts	All major credit cards

At dinner (£17.25 for two courses, £21.50 for three) the menu, which changes seasonally, reads like a lot of other menus – smoked salmon gravadlax, roast lamb, pan-fried cod. Best, then, to visit at lunch (£12.50 for two courses, £15.50 for three), when there are more Danish dishes on offer. Go à la carte and try the shoal of herrings (£4.25/5.75) – simply marinated, or spicy, or lightly curried, or sour with dill. You can also choose a smorrebrod (£5.75 to £6) of fiske-frikadeller (fish meatballs) or frikadeller (meat meatballs). There are also platters: The Danish (£14.50) contains herrings, meatballs, plaice and salad; there's an all fish platter (£15.50); or Munck's platter (£14.75), which features all manner of sausages and meaty delicacies. Or try the Medisterpolse (£7.25) – Danish sausage with red cabbage. Desserts are indulgent and the aquavit deadly.

"Gammel Ole – Danish Old cheese (18 months) served on rye bread and lard with onions, aspic and rum dripping" (£4.50). At first glance this dish, on the lunch menu, doesn't read well. But persevere, because it is really good, with tasty strong cheese and a seductive combination of tastes.

Mohsen

Just suppose that you are visiting Homebase on the Warwick Road. As the traffic thunders past, spare a thought for the people who still live here. For indeed, across the road you will see signs of habitation – two pubs, one a Young's house, the other selling Fuller's beer, and between them Mohsen, a small, busy Persian restaurant. This

Cost	£8–25
Address	152 Warwick Rd, W14
☎	020 7602 9888
Station	Earl's Court
Open	Daily noon–midnight
Accepts	Cash and cheques only

shouldn't come as a complete surprise, as you are not so very far from the nest of Iranian shops on Kensington High Street, but for somewhere so hidden Mohsen tends to be gratifyingly busy. There is nothing better than a loyal core of knowledgeable Middle Eastern customers to keep up standards in a Middle Eastern restaurant.

In the window is the oven, where the bread man works to keep everyone supplied with fresh-from-the-oven sheets of bread. This bread is terrific – wholemeal, large and flat, but not too flat, with a perforated surface and a sprinkling of sesame seeds that gives a nutty crunch. The waiters conspire to see that it arrives in a steady stream and never has a chance to get cold. The pricing structure changed in 2001 and now "starters" and a main are banded together and will cost between £15 and £17. The starters list is largely made up of things to go with the bread. You must have sabzi, which is one of the most delicious and health-oriented starters in the world. It is a basket containing a bunch of fresh green herbs – tarragon, flat parsley and mint – plus a chunk of Feta. Eat it with your bread. Or there's koo koo sabzi, which is rather like an under-egged Spanish omelette made with a bumper helping of parsley, dill, coriander, barberries and walnuts. Very tasty. Hummus is good. The main courses tend to revolve around grilled meat – joojeh kabab, for example, is a poussin, jointed, marinated, grilled and served on rice. Then there is chellow kabab-e-barg, which is outstanding – a tender fillet of lamb flattened and grilled. It is traditionally accompanied by an egg yolk.

Look out for the dish of the day. On Wednesday it is kharesh badenjan (£6), a stew of lamb and aubergines. And always be sure to finish with a pot of aromatic Iranian tea (£2.50), which is served in tiny, elegant, gilded glasses.

Fulham

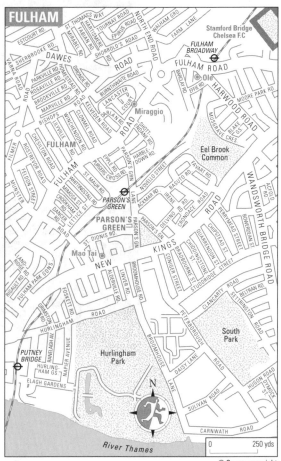

FULHAM

Stamford Bridge
Chelsea F.C.

FULHAM
BROADWAY

FULHAM ROAD

ST. THOMAS'S WAY
MARTIGNETE
FABIAN RD.
MIRABEL RD.
TOURNAY ROAD
EPIRUS ROAD
WALHAM GRO.
FARM LANE

ESTCOURT RD.
SHORROLD'S ROAD
NORTH END ROAD

SHERBROOKE RD.
DAWES ROAD
Olé

VARNA ROAD
PARKVILLE RD.
HOMESTEAD RD.
GRONDGE RD.
BURNTHWAITE ROAD
BARCLAY RD.
EFFIE RD.
MOORE PARK RD.

ROSAVILLE RD.
BROOKVILLE RD.
MARVILLE RD.
BISHOPS
DAGLAN RD.
KELVEDON RD.
LANCASTER COURT
Miraggio
HARWOOD ROAD
BLAKE GDS.
MUSGRAVE CRES.

CHESILTON ROAD
LILLVILLE
WINCHENDON RD.
CLONMEL ROAD
SHOTTENDANE RD.
Eel Brook
Common

FILMER
FULHAM ROAD
RESTORAN RD.
FELDON STREET
WHITINGSTALL RD.
ST. MAUR RD.
PURSERS CROSS RD.
PARSON'S GRN.
EPPLE RD.
HARBLEDOWN RD.
NOVELLO STREET
FAVART RD.
BASUTO RD.
WANDSWORTH BRIDGE ROAD

MUNSTER
MIMOSA ST.
CROOKHAM RD.
DANCER RD.
LETTICE ST.
PARSON'S
GREEN
ACKMAR RD.
IRENE RD.
DELVINO RD.
CRONDACE ROAD
PERRYMEAD STREET
ROAD
ASHCLO
ARTHUR

LAND-RIDGE RD.
RISAULT RD.
PARSON'S
GREEN
ST. DIONIS RD.
PARSON'S GRN.
PARSON'S DELVINO
QUARRENDON ST.
CHIPSTEAD ST.
BOWERMAN ST.

Mao Tai
KINGS ROAD
CONIGER STREET
CHIDDINGSTONE ST.
BRADBOURNE ST.
STUDDRIDGE ST.
FARMEAD STREET
BELTRAN RD.
SETTRINGTON ROAD

FULHAM PARK GDNS.
FORSETT RD.
GRIMSTON RD.
NEW
ALDERVILLE RD.
LINVER RD.
BROOMHOUSE RD.
PETERBOROUGH
CLANCARTY ROAD
HUGON ROAD
DYMOCK ST.

HURLINGHAM ROAD
RANELAGH AV.
NAPIER AVENUE
BROOMHOUSE
DAISY LANE
South
Park

PUTNEY
BRIDGE
HURLING-
HAM GDS.
Hurlingham
Park
LANE

ELAGH GARDENS
N
SULIVAN ROAD

River Thames
CARNWATH ROAD

0   250 yds

© Crown copyright

Mao Tai

Mao Tai is much more Chelsea than Chinatown, both in appearance and in the kind of food it serves. It's a pretty restaurant, cleverly lit, well decorated and with brisk, efficient service. The food is Szechuan – sophisticated, but with a satisfactory chilli burn and a nice scattering of old favourites. The clientele is just what you would expect from an area that is the very apple of any estate agent's eye. Such surroundings – and, to be fair, such food – do not come cheap. Still, you'll leave well fed and well looked after, as both the cooking and service are slick and chic.

Cost	£20–45

Address 58 New King's Rd, SW6; with branches
☎ 020 7731 2520
Station Parsons Green
Open Mon–Fri noon–3pm & 7–11.30pm, Sat 12.30–3pm & 7–11.30pm, Sun 12.30–3pm & 7–11pm
Accepts All major credit cards
🌐 www.maotai.co.uk

Start with steamed scallops (£7.85 for two). These are usually a pretty good indication of things to come, and at Mao Tai they are well cooked – just firm without having become rubbery. Salt and pepper prawns (£7.85 for six) are very fresh but somewhat disconcertingly fried in their shells, so the lovely crispy bits end up on the side of the plate. Firecracker dumplings with Chinese chives (£6.40) are terrific – innocent-looking Shanghai-style dumplings with a reassuring belt of chilli lurking to surprise the unwary. Also good in the starters section are the salt and pepper soft-shell crabs (£6.50 each). For main courses, you have a choice of more than fifty dishes. Do not be too daunted: order Szechuan squid in a hot bean sauce (£9.50) – tender squid with, as it says, a hot, beany sauce. No disappointments here. Also good is the tangerine peel chicken (£8.50), a delightful and delicate dish. Or General Tseng's chicken (£8.50), which is diced chicken and peppers in Ma La sauce. "Mao Tai" duck (£11.50) is a variant of duck in plum sauce – this one is boneless and very tasty indeed, the ubiquitous chilli making only a small guest appearance.

In the vegetable section there's a choice of braised lettuce or broccoli in oyster sauce (£5.85) – opt for the lettuce. The still-crisp furls of cos are nicely wilted and make the perfect match for oyster sauce. Very good indeed. Alternatively, you can opt out of the decisions and order the Mao Tai feast – £24.70 per person for a minimum of two.

Fulham

Miraggio

Bright café-style gingham table-cloths and a simple rustic air belie the quality behind this family-run establishment, which underwent something of a refurbishment in spring 2002. Your first sign of this is the appetizing display of antipasti in the window. There are mouth-watering wafer-thin strips of char-grilled courgette and aubergine, nutty little boiled potatoes with virgin olive oil and roughly chopped flat-leaf parsley, strips of grilled peppers, small and large mushrooms and an aubergine and tomato bake with tiny melted mozzarella cheeses. It's enough to stop even the most jaded foodie in their tracks.

Cost	£15–40

Address 510 Fulham Rd, SW6
℡ 020 7384 3142
Station Fulham Broadway
Open Tues–Thurs 12.30–3pm
& 7.30–11pm, Fri 12.30–4pm
& 7.30–11pm, Sat 12.30–4pm
& 7.30–10.30pm, Sun
12.30–4pm
Accepts All major credit cards
except Diners

For starters, choose the antipasti misti della casa (£8.50) and you'll get the window dishes. Otherwise, try sauté vongole (£10), sweet little clams sautéed until they are just open, or carpaccio di manzo (£8), a paper-thin raw beef fillet. Pastas include the usual suspects, with some less familiar dishes like rigatoni funghi e salsiccia (£8), which is rigatoni with sausages and mushrooms, or gnocchi crema scampi (£8.50). There are plenty of meat and fish choices, too, including spigola al forno con patate (£18), which is oven-baked sea bass with potatoes; calamari fritti (£15), a dish of perfectly cooked deep-fried squid; abbacchio scottadito (£9), simple grilled lamb; and filetto spinaci e patate (£15), a carefully cooked fillet steak with spinach and potatoes. If you're not already having spinach with your main course, try a side order of spinaci burro e Parmigiano (£4). Popeye would faint with pleasure. Puddings include what is claimed to be the best tiramisù in the area (£4), and zocolette (£4.00), a home-made profiterole with a Nutella filling. The kitchen is open to the dining room, so you can see your food being cooked, which makes for great entertainment.

Also remarkable is that Miraggio is currently a bring-your-own-bottle establishment, so your choice of wine is very wide indeed. This is a delightfully straightforward place, and a grand place to enjoy good home-style Italian cooking in Fulham.

Olé

(icon) You can't miss Olé. It's bright and modern with blond wood everywhere, and right opposite Fulham Broadway tube. Olé is a combination bar and restaurant. The bar is open for drinks if you're not hungry and there's the restaurant at the back if you are. This is the sort of place where you may start by going for a drink, and end up eating and being pleasantly surprised by the food.

Cost	£15–40

Address Broadway
Chambers, Fulham Broadway,
SW6
☎ 020 7610 2010
Station Fulham Broadway
Open Mon–Sat noon–11pm,
Sun noon–10.30pm
Accepts All major credit cards

The menu, which changes monthly, is modern Spanish and geared to tapas-style sharing. Larger main courses are confined to the daily specials board, and the reasonably priced wine list, which changes every three months, is exclusively Spanish.

The menu is divided into Frias (cold dishes), Calientes (hot dishes) and Ensalades (salads). For the conventional there are favourites like jamón Serrano (£5.75), boquerones (£3.90), patatas bravas (£3.20), chorizo al vino blanco (£4.50) and gambas al ajillo (£4.95). The gambas are sweet and hot, with garlic, chilli and olive oil. For the more adventurous there are dishes like calabacin relleno de jamón y queso con almendros y crema de queso (£3.95). This translates as "layers of courgette stuffed with ham and cheese, topped with cream of almonds and cheese sauce". It is delicious, and incredibly rich. Tortillas abound here. Instead of just tortilla española (£4.10), there are four more: with pimentos (£4.50), with chorizo (£4.50), with tuna (£4.50) and with a spinach cream filling (£4.20). All are freshly made. Meat eaters can enjoy tapas like solomillo de cerdo con verduras al vapor, a la esencia de mostaza (£4.80) – fillet of pork with steamed vegetables and mustard essence; carne de buey a la plancha con verduras y salsa de tomate y datiles (£4.50) – beef fillet with vegetables and date sauce, or pollo a la plancha con surtido de pimientos y crema de ajo (£4.50) – grilled chicken with peppers and cream of garlic. For the sweet of tooth there are eight puddings (all under £4).

Olé also features two notable Spanish beers: Estrella Galicia (£2.55), from northern Spain, and Damm (£2.65), from Barcelona.

Hammersmith & Chiswick

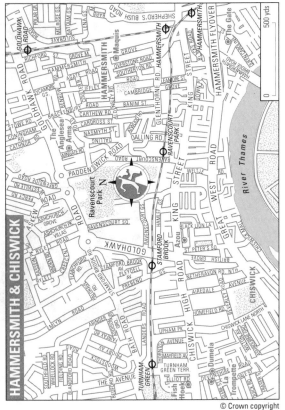
© Crown copyright

The Anglesea Arms

Do not make the mistake of thinking that this establishment is merely a pub. The Anglesea serves very good food indeed. The chef-proprietor is Dan Evans, a seasoned campaigner who was head chef at several of the brightest eateries of the 1990s. At the Anglesea, Dan runs the kitchen while his wife Fiona runs the bar and front of house. The

Cost   £11–27

Address 35 Wingate Rd, W6
℡020 8749 1291
Station Ravenscourt Park
Open Mon–Sat 12.30–2.45pm
& 7.30–10.45pm, Sun
1–3.30pm & 7.30–10pm
Accepts MasterCard, Visa

MODERN BRITISH/PUB

menu changes at least twice a day, dishes are crossed out as they run out, and when you've achieved "favoured local" status, you can ask for something simple that's not even on the board. If they have the ingredients you can have the dish. Pitch up early, claim a seat, and not only will you dine well but you'll leave feeling good about the bill.

Who knows what Dan will have chalked up on the blackboard when you visit? The menu is both eclectic and attractive, and prices have an upper limit of about £6 for starters and £10 for mains. In the spring you might have to choose between a warm salad with rabbit, chorizo, dandelion and beans, and spinach and bean soup. Or between a Provençal fish soup and a pissaladière. Main courses may include venison and sage faggots, or honest, market-fresh fish dishes like skate, or cod in butter. You may find diver-caught scallops with pak choi, or something simple like Gloucester Old Spot ham with egg and chips, or saddle of lamb. To round things off, there is always one British cheese in perfect condition – like St Andrew's, a cow's milk cheese served with black grapes. Dan Evans has a very sure touch, and this cooking is about as far from the kind of grub you'll be offered in a thousand chain pubs as you can get.

As befits food such as this, there's a wine list to match. A dozen wines are on offer by the glass, and the choice is thoughtful. Not very many restaurants, and very few pubs, offer a range of pudding wines by the bottle, half-bottle and glass. Among them is a delicious pudding wine called Le Pacherence from southwest France (£16.50 a bottle, £4.50 a glass) – a far cry from the builders' overalls and pints of Guinness that once ruled the roost here.

Azou

Azou opened at the very end of 1999, so by London restaurant standards it can now claim to be old-established. It is a small, comfortable, informal North African restaurant where you can enter into the spirit and end up sitting on the floor on a cushion. This is a family business and you will be sure of a warm welcome and attentive service. The kitchen knows its business and the classics – tagines and couscous – are presented with some panache.

Cost	£10–30

Address 35 King Street, W6
☎020 8563 7266
Station Stamford Brook/
Ravenscourt Park
Open Mon–Fri noon–2.30pm
& 6–11pm, Sat & Sun 6–11pm
Accepts All major credit cards

The menu is split into four sections. First there is a list of kemia, by way of starters. These are the North African equivalent of tapas and include all the favourites, from dips like hummos (£3.20) and baba ganoush (£3.95) to bourek (£4) – those little pastries filled with cheese or mince – and "briks" from Tunisia (£4.20), which are deep-fried filo parcels of potato, tuna and egg. The main courses are mostly billed by country of origin. Couscous is included under "Algerian", and it comes as vegetarian (£8.50), fish (£12) or royale (£14.50), which brings lamb shank, chicken breast and Merguez sausage. Under Moroccan you'll find a mixed grill (£11) and a selection of tagines, among which the Casablanca (£9.75) is made with lamb shank, artichoke hearts and peas. Tunisia is the heading under which you'll find a dish of king prawns which are pan fried in garlic butter (£9.95), and a sirloin steak which is marinated in chermoula (£8.95). From the "Azou Specials", the tagine Romanne (£8.95) appeals – chicken in sweet and tangy pomegranate sauce with almonds, raisins and caramelized onions. The menu layout may be a touch arbitrary in terms of geography but the dishes are well made and fairly priced. There's a sound Morrocan wine for a reasonable £13.50 a bottle and an interesting beer from Casablanca (£2.90).

The ultimate dish at Azou is only available if ordered in advance. "Mechoul" is laconically described as a whole lamb, marinated, spiced and roasted. It is served with starters as a buffet for up to twelve people – a snip at £280.

Dumela

With the advent and the runaway success of his new venture, Fish Hoek (p.438), Pete Gottgens has re-thought his original establishment. Thus the Springbok Grill has become a restaurant called Dumela and the menu has adopted some of the principles of its fishy neighbour. Most dishes come in

Cost	£15–35
Address	42 Devonshire Rd, W4
☎	020 8742 3149
Station	Turnham Green
Open	Mon–Sat 6.30–11pm
Accepts	All major credit cards

whole or half portions, and which you choose as a starter and which as a main is down to you. The restaurant has been given a makeover, but it is still small, busy and friendly.

The menu starts gently with Portuguese sardines and peri-peri mayonaise (£5.50/10) or asparagus and morago mielie risotto (£7/14), before getting more ambitious. Pan-seared yellowfin tuna with new potatoes and San Manzano tomatoes (£7/14); pan-fried guinea fowl with crushed potatoes, sugarsnap peas and vanilla chilli sauce (£7/13.50); and Mozambique pink queen prawns with peri-peri and rice (£12.75/23) all seem straightforward and appealing. Then it hits its stride with dishes such as char-grilled ostrich sosatie with butternut squash and parsley mash (£16.50); grilled warthog with garlic mash and roast shallots (£9/18.50); zebra fillet with butternut squash and grilled asparagus (£9.75/19.50); char-grilled crocodile and lamb soastie with garlic mash (£16.50); marinated kudu steak and thick cut chips (£9.75/19.50); and grilled blesbok with spring vegetables (£10/19.50). There are some vegetable side dishes but the ghost of the Springbok Grill hovers approvingly over the rather good grilled meats, and this is a good place to take a carnivore out to dinner. For the sweet-toothed, desserts are grand. Chocolate mielie-meal cake (£6.50), Bourbon vanilla ice cream (£5.50) or Amarula Dom Pedro (£4.50) are suitably self-indulgent.

Hidden amongst the sensible sauces (all £3) such as whisky and cracked black pepper, creamy mushroom and brandy, and garlic butter, you'll find that genuine South African delicacy, monkey gland. Take heart, no monkey (or bit of monkey) gets anywhere near it. It is a rich, sweet, savoury creation about which legend has it that the vital "secret ingredient" is Coca Cola.

Fish Hoek

Cost   £16–45

Address 6–8 Elliot Street, W4
℡ 020 8742 3374
Station Turnham Green
Open Tues–Sat noon–2.30pm
& 6.30–11pm
Accepts All major credit cards
except AmEx

At the end of 2001, Pete Gottgens of the Springbok Grill (see p.437) carried through his plan to dominate the neighbourhood and opened a restaurant dedicated to South African fish. Which would not be surprising were it not that he has chosen to do so in leafy Chiswick, which is some way from the abundant waters of the Cape. But due to the efficiency of the air-freight industry, fish can be landed and iced in South Africa and then pitch up in W4 in about the same time as they would take to get from Aberdeen. The restaurant is a light and airy place with those glassed-in super-bay window areas that Parisians are so fond of jutting out onto the pavement.

The menu changes daily and features an impressive array of South African fish – twenty-five or so choices, and most of them can be had as half or full portions. Try out three half portions and live a bit! Crispy-fried ribbon snoek with fresh chilli, coriander and roquette mayonnaise (£6.25/12.25) is commendably simply cooked, as is pan-seared East Coast blue shad (£6.25/12.50), which comes with pak choi and a ginger-lime sauce. Fish is an ingredient that responds well when treated simply, and that rule seems to apply even when you are eating something that is completely unfamiliar, such as pan-seared Kabeljou fillet teamed with roast red peppers, mange tout and seared lemon (£7.25/14.75); or Atlantic Hottentot fillet with sugarsnaps and roast Zuma tomatoes (£7/14). Some non-South African fishes stray onto the list – there may be Cuban mahi mahi (£7.25/14.75), South Coast plaice or Cornish mackerel – but the stuff from S.A. is well worth trying, as are the monster prawns from Mozambique (£12/22). Fish Hoek is a pleasant and informal restaurant where they take a good deal of trouble over simple fish cookery.

The walls are lined with Hemingway-esque black-and-white photos of big game fishing. These are from the Gottgens' family albums, and if you look at the shot to the right of the door to the toilets, you can see the proprietor of Fish Hoek – he's the small boy trotting along beside his father and that enormous fish.

The Gate

The extraordinary thing about The Gate, which is tucked away behind the Hammersmith Apollo, is that you hardly notice that it's a vegetarian restaurant. This is enjoyable dining without the meat. It's not wholefood, it's not even healthy, indeed, it's as rich, colourful, calorific and naughty as anywhere in town. The clientele is a quiet and appreciative bunch of locals and pilgrims – it's unlikely that anyone could just stumble across this hidden-away, former artists' studio, which Adrian and Michael Daniel have leased from the nearby church since 1990. The airy decor and the high ceiling give it a serene, lofty feel, which may be The Gate's only nod to veggie solemnities. Basically this place is about good food and has been so successful that there is now a Gate 2 in Belsize Park (see p.244).

Cost	£16–35

Address 51 Queen Caroline St, W6
☎ 020 8748 6932
Station Hammersmith
Open Mon–Fri noon–2.45pm & 6–10.45pm, Sat 6–11pm
Accepts All major credit cards
🖰 www.gateveg.co.uk

The short menu changes monthly, but starters are always great. There's usually a tart, like the three onion tart baked with crème fraîche (£5.75) which elsewhere, with its sophisticated salad, would be served as a main course. Also excellent are the couscous and feta cheese fritters (£5.50), which are served with harissa and coriander oil. Portions are invariably hearty, so it's a good idea to share starters in order to pace yourself and sample all the courses. The mains are generally well executed. Mezzelune (£9.50) is a pasta crescent filled with goat's cheese and rocket, pan fried in a light chive and leek sauce (£9.50). Or there's a laksa (£9.50), which has an interminable list of ingredients and is founded on a lemongrass, galangal and coconut broth. Puddings are splendid: there may be rhubarb and plum crumble (£5.50), or the pressed chocolate torte (£5.50), which is a thinking person's death-by-chocolate. Those without a sweet tooth should go for the cheese platter (£5.50) – it comes with nut biscotti, prunes in port and fresh fruit.

The drinks list is extensive, with all manner of freshly squeezed juices (£2.25), herbal teas (£1.50–3) and coffees (£1.35–1.75), while the wine list tops out at £24 (except for champagne) and has something for everyone – vegan, vegetarian, organic-only and carnivore alike.

FRENCH

Maquis

(icon) Maquis burst onto the London restaurant scene late in 2001, and is the brainchild of the people who run Moro (see p.197) – Mr Sam Clark and Ms Sam Clark. One Sam Clark has upped sticks from the feted Moorish establishment in Exmouth Market to open Maquis in Hammersmith. In many ways the new place defies simple classification, as the food doesn't seem to fit any of the current trendy pigeonholes. The menu has French elements and retro elements, the chief of which has been grabbed gleefully by the reviewers – this is a place where you can get a cheese fondue.

Cost	£15–50

Address 111 Hammersmith Grove, W6
℡ 020 8846 3850
Station Hammersmith
Open Mon–Fri 12.30–3pm & 7–10.30pm, Sat 7–10.30pm, Sun 12.30–3pm
Accepts All major credit cards

The menu changes from day to day, but there may be a pumpkin soup (£4.50), or a tart filled with pork rillettes and served with cornichons (£5) which manages to be opulent, taste of pork, and combine three elements that at first seem like bitter enemies – clammy, solid, shredded pork, a creamy sauce and crisp pastry. Pine for "retro" and there's pear, Roquefort, endive and walnut salad (£4.50); or frogs' legs braised with white wine, parsley and garlic (£6). Main courses also appeal – how about roast rack of lamb with salsify and pumpkin gratin (£12.50)? A perfectly cooked charcoal-grilled chunk of turbot comes with tapenade and fennel purée (£12.50), and is a dish with complimentary textures and contrasting flavours. Or there may be a slow-cooked veal shank with morilles and tarragon (£12.50) – silky-rich and almost gluey, very good indeed. Puds range from oeufs à la neige with apple purée (£4) to a simple and satisfying combo such as pruneaux d'Agen with crème fraîche (£3.50). The dining room is spacious and airy, service is relaxed but efficient, and prices are commendably restrained. As at Moro, there are some stunning sherries by the glass and an unrapacious wine list.

This place sells as many as a dozen pots of fondue (£11 as a starter to share, or £12.50 as a main course with salad) each and every midweek lunch session. It is certainly very good fondue, made with cider and Gruyère, but how can anyone enjoy the afternoon after ingesting a vat of molten cheese at lunchtime?

La Trompette

Cost	£20–50

Address 5–7 Devonshire Rd,
W4
☎020 8747 1836
Station Turnham Green
Open Mon–Sat noon–2.30pm
& 6.30–10.30pm, Sun
12.30–3pm & 6.30–10.30pm
Accepts All major credit cards

FRENCH

La Trompette opened in 2001, and it did not take more than six months before the restaurant had settled in, won the hearts and minds of Chiswickians and accumulated a lengthy waiting list for tables. This state of affairs wasn't a great surprise as Trompette is a thoroughbred from the same stable as Chez Bruce (see p.335), The Glasshouse (see p.399) and The Square (see p.85). It's a pleasant dining room with a good deal of light oak and chocolate leather on show. The food is very good, the wine list is comprehensive, the pricing is restrained and the service is on the ball.

The prix-fixe arrangements are straightforward: lunch is £17.50 for two courses, and £19.50 for three (rising to £23.50 on Sunday); dinner is £27.50 for three courses. The head chef is Ollie Couillard, who served time at both Chez Bruce and The Square. He is a very good cook. Dishes tend to have French roots and to be dependent on fresh, seasonal produce. The menu changes on a day-to-day basis. Presentation is simple but elegant. Starters may include such delights as a persillade of snails and duck hearts with green beans, croutons, garlic and thyme; or a tarte fine of wood pigeon, onion and mushroom; or warm smoked eel with celeriac, egg-yolk ravioli and grain mustard Hollandaise; or deep-fried lemon sole with tartare sauce. Mains are rich and satisfying. In the appropriate season you might be offered soupe paysanne with foie gras, duck confit, ham hock, white beans and pistou; or loin of venison with chestnut purée, Jerusalem artichokes, port and redcurrant sauce; or roast cod with olive oil, mashed potatoes and aged balsamic vinegar. Or two people may consider forking out the extra £10 supplement and having the côte de boeuf with chips and Béarnaise sauce. This is a very good restaurant indeed.

Puds range from classics such as lemon tart, or gateaux Basque with rhubarb and orange compote, to ultra-trad blasts from the past, like Baked Alaska (for two people), or chocolate profiteroles. Enjoy!

Notting Hill

© Crown copyright

Alastair Little Lancaster Road

Alastair Little is a name that commands respect among restaurant-goers in London. Back in the 1980s, he was one of the main pioneers of the Anglo-Italian movement, a man without a professional catering background who wanted to serve real food – clean, fresh cooking, with home-made pastas and terrines – of the style and type that we all wish we could serve at home. Following the success of his clean-cut site in Frith Street (see p.117), he opened this much less expensive sibling in 1996. Notting Hill trendies rushed in hordes to try it out, but they have since moved on, returning Alastair Little to the foodies. Forget the trends. This is a top-class place and one that, even after a modest refurb and repaint, feels extremely comfortable.

Cost	£16–50

Address 136a Lancaster Rd, W11
℡ 020 7243 2220
Station Ladbroke Grove
Open Mon–Fri noon–2.30pm & 6.30–11pm, Sat noon–3pm & 6.30–11pm, Sun 12.30–3.30pm
Accepts All major credit cards

MODERN EUROPEAN

The daily-changing menu is short and sweet at lunchtime, and middle-sized and sweet for dinner. At lunch, the price is fixed at £12 for two courses and £16 for three – extraordinarily inexpensive for this quality. In the evening the same dishes are priced à la carte. Starters might be the likes of spinach soup with dal rava dosa and raita (£7); or unorthodox chopped liver with chopped egg and onion, and poppy seed biscuits (£6.50) – this kitchen cannot resist a little joke; or papardelle with a Tuscan game sauce (£7.50). Move on to no less exotic mains like wild mushroom risotto and salad (£12.75); grilled Torbay sole, parsley salad, tapenade dressing and fried potatoes (£12.75); calves' liver, bubble 'n' squeak and onion gravy (£14); or "two stage roast spring chicken (breast with tarragon with mash, legs with a mesclun salad)" (£14.50). But it is the apparently simple Italianate dishes that are Alastair Little's real strength, dishes like the soups, pastas and risottos that are fixtures on the menu. Don't miss out on them.

Desserts are the kind of rich, indulgent things that are so good that you almost feel embarrassed to be seen choosing them. Italian chocolate brownie, vanilla ice cream and hot fudge sauce (£5.50); rhubarb trifle (£4.50); and that wonderful indulgence, affogato al caffè (£4.50), which teams espresso with vanilla ice cream.

Assaggi

(🍴) Assaggi is a small, ochre-painted room above The Chepstow pub. It's generally full at lunch and booked well in advance in the evenings. The prices are unforgiving and, on the face of it, paying so much for such straightforward dishes could raise the hackles of any sensible diner. But the reason Assaggi is such a gem, and also the reason it is always full, is that selfsame straightforwardness. The menu may appear simple but it is littered with authentic and luxury ingredients, and the cooking is very accomplished indeed. Prepare yourself for a meal to be remembered.

Cost	£32–70

Address 39 Chepstow Place, W2
ⓣ 020 7792 5501
Station Notting Hill Gate
Open Mon–Fri 12.30–2.30pm & 7.30–11pm, Sat 1–2.30pm & 7.30–11pm
Accepts All major credit cards

You'll find a dozen starters – with the option to have the pastas as main courses – and half a dozen main courses. Start with pasta, maybe tagliolini con ragu di pesce (£8.95/10.95), a dish of perfectly cooked pasta with a fishy sauce. Or a plate of sensational bufala mozzarella (£8.25). Or grilled vegetables with olive oil and herbs (£8.75). Or bresaola punta d'Anca (£8.25). Or there may be a dish like capesante con salsa alla Zafferano (£10.95) – a simple plate of perfectly cooked, splendidly fresh scallops. Main courses are even more pared down: calves' liver (£15.95); a plainly grilled veal chop with rosemary (£18.95); branzino alla griglia (£18.25) – grilled sea bass; or fritto misto di pesce (£18.95). All are memorable, while the side salad of tomato, rucola e basilico (£4.75) is everything you would wish for. Puddings change daily and cost £5.75. Look out for pannacotta – a perfect texture – and the beautifully simple dish made from ultra-fresh buffalo ricotta served with "cooked" honey. To accompany, the short wine list features splendid and unfamiliar Italian regional specialities.

Assaggi is known for its bread. This is the famous Sardinian carta di musica – very thin, very crisp and very delicious. It's like a kind of Italian popadom, only better. The name came about because, when well made, the papery texture is reminiscent of the sheets of vellum on which music was first written.

Black & Blue

🍴 Say the words "steak house" to a
Londoner and they immediately
conjure up a very 1960s image – lots of
tartan and red plush, with hapless
tourists reaffirming their worst misgivings
about British food. The time is right for a
decent chain of steak houses. And Black
& Blue may just be the first of a new
breed. For a start, this establishment,
which opened towards the end of 2000,
has the very best provenance for its meat. All the steak here comes from
Donald Russell of Inverurie – the company which is king of the Aberdeen
Angus beef trade.

Cost	£12–40

Address 215–217 Kensington
Church St, W8
☎ 020 7727 0004
Station Notting Hill Gate
Open Mon–Thurs & Sun
noon–11pm, Fri & Sat
noon–11.30pm
Accepts MasterCard, Visa

Black & Blue certainly looks like a smart modern restaurant. There are
banquettes, a good deal of wood panelling, a stylish bar and some rather
nice vintage Bovril posters – a restaurant designer has been hard at work
here. Starters are predictable. There's a prawn cocktail (£5) – half a
dozen large prawns in pink stuff. Or you could have butterfly prawns
with a sweet chilli dip (£5). Or there's that American abomination, a
whole deep-fried onion (£5). Thereafter there are burgers, salads,
baguettes, two chicken dishes and tuna – ignore them in favour of the
steaks. The steaks are good. Aberdeen Angus is well-flavoured meat and,
commendably enough, when you say rare you get rare. Each steak
comes with a very decent mixed salad of watercress, flat parsley and
rocket – steer clear of the proffered dressings – and tolerable fries. There
are four kinds of steak: sirloin, rib-eye, fillet and T-bone. Everywhere else
in town, fillet is the most expensive, then sirloin, followed by rib-eye.
But not here, where a 6oz sirloin costs £11 and a 10oz costs £15, while
an 8oz rib-eye costs £14. Why does the sirloin work out cheaper than
the rib-eye here? Go for the 10oz sirloin! 6oz fillet costs £15, 8oz £18;
and a 14oz T-bone steak costs £19. There's a small choice of simple
desserts: chocolate mousse and lemon tart (both £5) are served with
clotted cream.

The wine list is not long but is agreeably ungrasping. It makes a
pleasant change to see simple reds priced at around £10 on a restaurant
wine list.

The Churchill Arms

In the ever-expanding field of pub restaurants, the Churchill is something of an old stager. It was possibly one of the first in London to offer Thai food. Do you wonder why we see so few pubs selling Indian food, incidentally? Or Chinese food? Could it be because of the grand profit margins on Thai cuisine? Well, whatever the motivation behind it, the Churchill has nurtured its clientele (who are largely students and bargain hunters) over the years by the simple expedient of serving some of the tastiest and most reasonably priced Thai food in London. The main dining area is in a back room featuring acres of green foliage, but don't despair if you find it full (it fills up very quickly) – meals are served throughout the pub. Service is friendly, but as the food is cooked to order, be prepared to wait – it's worth it. If you really can't wait, pre-cooked dishes such as chicken with chillies (along with that other well-known Thai delicacy, Stilton ploughman's) are also available.

Cost	£7–20

Address 119 Kensington Church St, W8
℡ 020 7792 1246
Station Notting Hill Gate
Open Mon–Sat 12.30–2.30pm & 6–9.30pm, Sun noon–2.30pm
Accepts MasterCard, Visa

Dishes are unpronounceable, and have thoughtfully been numbered to assist everybody. The pad gai med ma muang hin-maparn (no.15 – £5.50) is a deliciously spicy dish of chicken, cashew nuts and chilli served with a generous helping of fluffy boiled rice. Kwaitiew pad kee mao (no.16 – £5.25) is pork, chicken or beef cooked with flat Thai noodles heated with red and green chillies – hot, but not unbearably so. The same cannot be said for khao rad na ga prao (no.5 – £5.50), which is described as very hot. Not an understatement. This prawn dish with fresh chillies and Thai basil is guaranteed to bring sweat to the brow of even the most ardent chilliholic. For something milder, try the pad neau nahm man hoi (no.17 – £5.25), or beef with oyster sauce and mushrooms, or the khao rad na (no.3 – £5.25), a rice dish topped with prawns, vegetables and gravy. Both are good. Puddings are limited in choice and ambition, but for something sweet to temper the heat, try apple pie (£2.50) – a strange accompaniment to Thai food, but surprisingly welcome.

One of the refreshing things about the Churchill is you get restaurant-standard food with drinks at pub prices, and they even do takeaways in traditional foil trays.

Cow Dining Room

The Cow is something of a conundrum. On the one hand it is a genuine pub – a proper pub, with beer and locals – and on the other it has become something of a meeting place for Notting Hill's smarter residents. Downstairs all is fierce drinking and cigarette smoke, while upstairs you'll find an oasis of calm and, at its centre, a small dining room. It is a good place to eat. The atmosphere is informal but the food is accomplished. The chef here is James Rix who formerly served time in Alastair Little's Frith Street establishment. The menu changes on a daily basis and delivers fresh, unfussy, seasonal food, and if anything dishes are slightly cheaper than they were in the last edition of this guide – quite an unusual occurrence but one that we should encourage!

Cost	£18–48

Address 89 Westbourne Park Rd, W2
☎ 020 7221 5400
Station Westbourne Park
Open Mon–Fri 7–11pm, Sat 12.30–2.30pm & 7–11pm, Sun 12.30–3.30pm & 7.30–10.30pm
Accepts All major credit cards except Diners

Starters put together tried and tested combinations of prime ingredients such as fresh potato and fennel soup (£4.50); baked buffalo mozzarella, roasted tomato and red pepper sauce (£7); warm salad of wood pigeon with French beans, pancetta and a soft-boiled egg (£7); or griled sardines with chermoula (£7). Main courses cover most of the bases, from aubergine and ricotta ravioli with sage butter sauce (£13.50); through grilled mackerel with ratatouille (£13); to fillet of sea bream wih lentils and salsa verde (£14). The menu finishes triumphantly with roast leg of lamb with Dauphinoise potatoes, spinach and rosemary jus (£15). Puddings are a suitable mix of the comfortable and the desirable: crème brûlée (£4.50); chocolate and coffee tart (£4.50); poached champagne rhubarb with custard (£4.50). Or you could go for cheese, which comes with the imprimatur that signifies well-chosen and well-kept cheeses – "Neal's Yard" cheeses with oatcakes (£5.25).

The menu encourages diners to commence proceedings with a glass of Black Velvet (£4.50) or Prosecco di Conegliano e Valdobbiadene (£4). But the staff will happily fetch you some of the excellent De Koninck beer from downstairs if these more exotic fizzies don't tempt.

E&O

(icon) E&O (it stands for Eastern & Oriental) is geared to non-traditional eating. You're encouraged to abandon the starter and main course convention, and order a mix of small and large dishes to share. Cooking is based on Japanese with added eponymous influences. The venue itself is modern Japanese in feel and is relaxed at the same time as being stylish. Forks, knives, spoons and chopsticks sit in stone pots on the table, and cloth napkins are piled high. It's no-rules eating and your fingers are as useful as anything else. Staff are knowledgeable and take trouble to explain if you're unfamiliar with dishes or the spirit of the place. But even more than the taste, it is the presentation of the food that makes it exceptional.

Cost	£25–50

Address 14 Blenheim
Crescent, W11
(T) 020 7229 5454
Station Notting Hill Gate/
Ladbroke Grove
Open Mon–Sat noon–midnight, Sun noon–10.30pm
Accepts All major credit cards
(W) www.eando.nu

The menu divides into soups, dim sum, salads, tempura, curries, futo maki rolls/sashimi, barbecue/roasts, specials, sides and desserts. Edamame, soy and mirin (£3.00) is a dish of soy beans in the pod to pop and suck out. Fun and delicious. Steamed gyoza dumplings (£6.00) are rich with chunks of pork inside rather than the usual mush; chilli-salt squid (£5.50) is well-seasoned crispy squid served in a Japanese newspaper cone; baby pork spare ribs (£5.00) come with a sauce good enough to eat with a spoon. Avocado and sweet potato tempura (£6.00) proves you can deep-fry avocado. In the barbecue/roasts section, black cod with sweet miso (£19.50) is as good as this fish gets. Green chicken curry (£10.50) tastes authentic, with sharp and bitter Thai vegetables, and daikon salad (£10.75) is a mix of Japanese radish, mixed leaves and herbs in rice-paper rolls. Home-made sorbets (£5.00) are green apple, mango, guava and lychee. Lemongrass and vanilla brûlée (£5.00) is lemony and creamy, and the exotic fruit plate (£6.50) contains fruits you won't find in a greengrocers. Wines are well chosen and reasonably priced, and there's a selection of six teas (£2.50) served in large Chinese pots.

E&O is deservedly popular, and it has two sittings for dinner. It is both essential to book and difficult to get a table. An option is the separate bar, which has a dim sum menu.

Galicia

As you walk up the Portobello Road it would be only too easy to amble straight past Galicia. It has that strange Continental quality of looking shut even when it's open. Only make it through the forbidding entrance, however, and Galicia opens out into a bar (which is in all probability crowded), which in turn opens into a small, forty-seat restaurant (which is in all probability full). The tapas at the bar are straightforward and good, so it is no surprise that quite a lot of customers get no further than here. One regular once confided that some of the best Spanish dishes he had ever sampled were given to him as tapas in the bar while he was waiting for a seat, and that when he finally got the elusive table, he had eaten so much that he was forced to surrender it to someone in greater need. So, first secure your table...

Cost	£14–35
Address	323 Portobello Rd, W10
☎	020 8969 3539
Station	Ladbroke Grove/ Westbourne Park
Open	Tues–Sat noon–3pm & 7–11.30pm, Sun noon–3pm & 7–10.30pm
Accepts	All major credit cards

SPANISH

...then cut a swathe through the starters. Jamón (£4.50) is a large plate of sweet, air-dried ham; gambas a la plancha (£6.25) are giant prawns plainly grilled; and pulpo a la Gallega (£5.50) is a revelation – slices of octopus grilled until bafflingly tender and powdered with smoky pimenton. Galicia does straightforward grilled fish and meat very well indeed. Look for the chuleto de cordera a la plancha (£8.40), which are perfect lamb chops, or lomo de cerdo (£7.75), which are very thin slices of pork fillet in a sauce with pimenton. Or there's the suitably stolid Spanish omelette, tortilla (£5.25). And you should have some chips, which are very good here – thick and yet chewy, they taste just like those superior chips you get in Spain. The wine list is short but also full of opportunities for exploration – you may find yourself the proud possessor of a Vega Grand Riserva for just £18.90. Or then again that bin may have run out.

Galicia is a pleasant place without pretension. The waiters are all old school – quiet and efficient to the point of near grumpiness. The overall feel is of a certain stilted formality. The clientele is an agreeable mix of Notting Hill-ites and homesick Iberians, both of which groups stand between you and that table reservation, so book early.

Ginger

🍴 Given that nearly every curry house on nearly every High Street in the land is owned and manned by Bangladeshi businessmen, you might think that Ginger, which opened in the spring of 2001, would be pretty run of the mill. Until you eat there. This is a restaurant that offers genuine Bangladeshi home cooking. Not the sweet and toma-

Cost	£16–35

Address 115 Westbourne Grove, W2
☎ 020 7908 1990
Station Notting Hill Gate/ Bayswater
Open Daily 6–11pm
Accepts All major credit cards

toey dishes worked up to suit the British palate, but the real deal. The restaurant is modern, and turquoise (*very* turquoise – if you don't like turquoise, don't go). There is attentive service, a thoughtful wine list, and some slick cocktails. Most important of all, the men in the kitchen really know their stuff. Genuine Bangladeshi cooking has long deserved a decent showcase, and at Ginger it has finally got one.

There are some stunning dishes. Start with the maach paturi (£3.95) – a fillet of pomfret, spiced, seasoned, then wrapped in a banana leaf and steamed. That's it. Fresh tasting fish, a citrus twang, heat from some mustard seeds. From the other end of the spectrum, try the shingara (£2.95) – imagine a solid vegetable samosa that has been made with shortcrust pastry, like a deep-fried pasty. The boti kebab (£3.95) is also good – lamb kebabs with a chilli bite. The difficult choices continue among the main courses. Katta macher jhol (£8.95) is epic – chunks of imported river fish in a spicy broth. Bangladeshis are besotted with fish – try the very traditional chingri chichinga (£9.95), which teams huge king prawns with a green Bengali vegetable called chichinga. Carry on to the shatkora murgh (£6.95), which is spicy and good, the sharpness of the Bangladeshi vegetable contrasting well with the chicken. The kashimangsho bhuna (£7.95) is a thick, dark, satisfying goat curry with a good belt of heat to it. Tok dal (£3.95) is a revelation: the creaminess of yellow split peas with balancing sharpness from green mango. The parathas (£1.95) are very good – flaky and suitably self-indulgent.

Puddings are sweet. If you think you're up to it, just attempt the mishti doi (£3.50), which is a lurid set yoghurt. Toothkind it is not.

Kensington Place

The first thing to know about Kensington Place is that it is noisy. The dining room is large, echoing, glass-fronted and just plain noisy. It's the racket of hordes of people having a good time. Rather than background music, there's the busy hum of confidences, shrieks of merriment, and the clamour of parties. The service is crisp, the food is good and the prices are fair. The menu changes from session to session to reflect whatever the market has to offer, and there is a set lunch which offers a limited choice of three good courses for £16 during the week and £18.50 on Sunday. By way of example: you might have razor clams with parsley and garlic, followed by fricassée of wild rabbit with prunes and bacon, and then a chocolate and coffee Japonaise with cocoa sorbet. This is fine value for money. Regulars claim that the set lunch menu is the key to knowing just when head chef Rowley Leigh is cooking in person – apparently his handwriting is very distinctive!

Cost	£18–60

Address 201–207 Kensington Church St, W8
☎ 020 7727 3184
Station Notting Hill Gate
Open Mon–Sat noon–3pm & 6.30–11.45pm, Sun noon–3pm & 6.30–10.15pm
Accepts All major credit cards

Rowley Leigh's food is eclectic in the best possible way. The kitchen starts with the laudable premise that there is nothing better than what is in season, and goes on to combine Mediterranean inspirations with classic French and English dishes. Thus you may find, in due season, starters like fish soup with croutons and rouille (£6.50), escarole salad with pears and Roquefort (£6.50), wild mushroom risotto (£7.50), or omelette fines herbes (£5.50). These are sophisticated dishes, and well-chosen combinations of flavours. Main courses might be cod with lentils and salsa verde (£15), wild boar chop with red cabbage and chestnuts (£16.50), roast leg of lamb with grilled red onion salad (£16), or goujons of sole with tartare sauce (£10).

The dessert section of the menu offers what may be one of London's finest lemon tarts (£6) and some well-made ice creams (£5). There are also traditional favourites with a twist: bread-and-butter pudding made with pannetone (£6.50), or hot bitter chocolate mousse (£6.50). And for hardened pudding addicts there is the ultimate challenge – the grand selection (£12.50). Indulge yourself (or share) and take a glass of Tokaji Aszu 5 Puttonyos (£5.50) alongside.

Lucky Seven

Following the success of the Cow (see p.449), Tom Conran has shifted his attention a few hundred yards up the road to a site which was previously a shabby and agreeably seedy little Portuguese café-restaurant-drinking den. Just before Christmas 2001 it re-opened as Lucky Seven, an American diner freshly transplanted to Notting Hill. The kitchen runs across the back behind a high counter and the tiny dining area accommodates 36 people in two sets of booths. There are engraved mirrors. A Pepsi clock. Sally didn't meet Harry here, but doubtless she will soon.

Cost	£8–24

Address 127 Westbourne Park Rd, W2
℗ 020 7727 6771
Station Westbourne Park
Open Mon–Sat 6am–11pm, Sun 6am–10.30pm
Accepts Cash and cheques only

The menu is on a peg-board over the kitchen and it opens with breakfast dishes: 2 eggs any style (£2.75); with sausage (£3.75); with bacon (£3.50); with hash browns (£3.50) – wending its way through omelettes (£3.25) and eggs Benedict (£5.95) to buttermilk pancakes (£3.75). Then there's a section of "soups, stews and salads" and then "hamburgers and sandwiches" before it moves towards "sides". In the evening there's a blue-plate special dish (£6.50 to £8), which ranges from club sandwich to gammon and eggs. The range of chips (all £2) is formidable. You can have fries, fat chips, or home fries – the fat chips are best, well crisped and chunky. The fries are a little on the dry side (perhaps a tad too thin?), and the home fries are made from peel-left-on segments of fried potato that are so large as to seem claggy. The burgers are well made, although on the small side for serious trenchers – but as they start at just £3.95 for the "Classic hamburger", perhaps that is best resolved by ordering two Classics. In the stews section you will come across such delights as New England clam chowder, chicken noodle soup, and a Cuban black bean chilli (all £2.50 a cup, £3.95 a bowl).

Lucky Seven is a small, agreeably informal place serving sound enough food at sound enough prices. It is full of vaguely trendy customers who seem to approve whole-heartedly of both grub and prices. And the fat chips are very good, needing no more than a hint of Mr Heinz's red elixir to attain perfection.

The Mandola

The food at The Mandola is described as "urban Sudanese", and as that means forgoing the doubtful pleasures of some of the more traditional Sudanese delicacies – strips of raw liver marinated in lime juice, chilli and peanut butter springs to mind – it seems like a pretty good bet. This would be a small, seriously informal, neighbourhood restaurant, but for the fact that it attracts people from all over town with its sensible pricing and often strikingly delicious dishes. They have not only had to expand into the shop next door, but also to institute two sittings a night. Despite such minor irritations there's much to praise. The staff are so laid-back as to make worriers self-destruct on the spot. The restaurant is unlicensed, so everything from fine wine to exotic beer is available – if you choose to bring it with you.

Cost	£12–22

Address 139–141 Westbourne Grove, W11
℗ 020 7229 4734
Station Notting Hill Gate
Open Mon 6–11pm, Tues–Sun noon–11pm
Accepts All major credit cards
Ⓦ www.mandolacafe.co.uk

SUDANESE

To start there is a combo of dips and salads, rather prosaically listed as "mixed salad bar" for two (£10.50). There are a few Middle Eastern favourites here, given a twist, and all of them are strongly and interestingly flavoured. Salata tomatim bel gibna (£3.50) is made from tomatoes, Feta and parsley; salata tahina (£3.25) is a good tangy tahini; salata aswad (£4.20) is a less oily version of the Turkish aubergine dish iman bayeldi; salata daqua (£3.50) is white cabbage in peanut sauce; and tamiya (£4.75) is Sudanese falafel. All are accompanied by hot pitta bread. As for main courses, samak magli (£10.50) shows just how good simple things can be – fillets of tilapia are served crisp and spicy on the outside, fresh on the inside, with a squeeze of lime juice. Chicken halla (£9.50) is cooked in a rich, well-reduced tomato sauce that would be equally at home in a smart Italian eatery. Lovers of the exotic can finish with the Sudanese spiced coffee, scented with cardamom, cinnamon, cloves and ginger – your own flask and coffee set, enough for nine tiny cupfuls, for £4.

It is lucky that the bowl for the crushed green chilli with lime, onions and garlic (£1.75) is stainless steel, as the contents must be one of the hottest things in the known universe.

Osteria Basilico

Long before Kensington Park Road became the borough's hottest spot for outdoor dining, there was always a restaurant on this corner. When Duveen closed, the restaurant cat stayed on to have the next establishment named in its honour – Monsieur Thompson. Then, in its turn, Monsieur T became Pizza by Numbers. Finally, in 1992 came Osteria, which has flourished ever since. Daytime stargazing is enlivened by arguments between parking wardens, clampers and

Cost	£12–45

Address 29 Kensington Park Rd, W11
℡ 020 7727 9372
Station Ladbroke Grove/ Notting Hill Gate
Open Mon–Fri 12.30–3pm & 6.30–11pm, Sat 12.30–4pm & 6.30–11pm, Sun 12.30–3.15pm & 6.30–10.30pm
Accepts All major credit cards except Diners

their victims, while the traffic comes to a standstill for the unloading of lorries and for a constant stream of mini-cabs dropping off at the street's numerous restaurants. At dusk you get more of the same, with the street-lights struggling to make the heart of Portobello look like the Via Veneto.

Inside, pizza and pasta are speedily delivered with typical chirpy Italian panache to cramped, scrubbed tables. Go easy on the baskets of warm pizza bread, as the antipasti (£6) – various grilled and preserved tit-bits arranged on the antique dresser – are a tempting self-service affair. Of the other starters, frittura di calamari e gamberoni (£6.80) and carpaccio di manzo con pesto, rucola e Parmigiano (£7.50) are both delicious. Specials change daily and have no particular regional influence. Old favourites include branzino al forno con pomodoro, mozzarella e salsa al funghi porcini (£16); or perhaps fettucine con tartufo bianco, Parmigiano e salsa al rosmarino (£13.50) – classic, well-prepared dishes. Among the permanent fixtures, spigola alla griglia con olio aromatizzato (£14.50) is a simply grilled sea bass; while costolette d'agnello con pomodori freschi e melanzane (£12) is char-grilled lamb cutlets with fresh tomato and aubergine. Pizzas vary in size depending on who is in the kitchen – perhaps staff with shorter arms throw the dough higher, resulting in a wider, thinner base – but all are on the largish size. Pizza Diavolo (£7.50) comes with mozzarella and a good, spicy pepperoni sausage.

There's a house Chianti at £9.50, but it's much better to opt for the Montepulciano d'Abruzzo (£13), a pretty decent wine at a pretty decent price.

Rodizio Rico

If you're a lover of smoky grilled meat, Rodizio Rico will come as a godsend. In the south of Brazil this restaurant would be pretty run-of-the-mill stuff, but in W11 *churrascarias* are the exception rather than the rule. Rodizio can be a puzzling experience for first-timers. There's no menu and no prices – but no problem. "Rodizio" means "rotating", and refers to the carvers who wander about the room with huge

Cost £18–25

Address 111 Westbourne Grove, W2
☎ 020 7792 4035
Station Notting Hill Gate/Bayswater
Open Mon–Fri 6.30pm–midnight, Sat 12.30–4.30pm & 6.30pm–midnight, Sun 1–11pm
Accepts All major credit cards except Diners

skewers of freshly grilled meat from which they lop off chunks on demand – rather like the trolleys of roast beef at Simpson's in the Strand. You start by ordering and then help yourself from the salad bar and hot buffet. As the carvers circulate they dispense bonhomie as they cut you chunks, slivers and slices from whichever skewer they are holding. You eat as much as you like of whatever you like, and then pay the absurdly reasonable price of £17.70 a head.

When you're up helping yourself to the basics, look out for the tiny rolls, no bigger than a button mushroom, called pão de queijo – a rich cheese bread from the south of Brazil. Also bobo, a delicious kind of bubble and squeak made from cassava and spring greens. Return to your seat and await the carvers – they come in random order, but they keep on coming. There's lamb, and ham, and pork, and spare ribs, and chicken, and silverside beef (grilled in a piece and called lagarto after a similarly shaped iguana!). Then for offal aficionados there are grilled chicken hearts. But the star of the show is picanha – the heart of the rump, skewered and grilled in huge chunks. Taste it and the arguments over the relative merits of rump and fillet are over forever – the "rumpers" would win by a landslide. Brazilians seem to revere the crispy bits, but if you want your meat rare you only have to ask.

South Americans rate the impossibly sweet soft drink Antarctica Guarrana (£2) very highly. "Just like the guarana powder you can get in the chemist's shop," they insist. If the lure of alternative rainforest stimulants doesn't appeal, house wines start at a reasonable £10.90 a bottle. And, as you would expect of a Brazilian establishment, the coffee is very good indeed.

Richmond & Twickenham

RICHMOND & TWICKENHAM

N

Drainage Works

© Crown copyright

0   500 yds

Old Deer Park

RICHMOND

Richmond Green

Richmond Station

North Sheen Station

Origin Asia

Chez Maria

The White Horse

Kozachok

Chez Lindsay

A Cena

Brula Bistrot

Marble Hill Park

TWICKENHAM

Twickenham Station

St Margaret's Station

Twickenham R.U. Football Ground

Rugby Road

Richmond Park

Richmond Park

River Thames

PETERSHAM ROAD

RICHMOND ROAD

ST. MARGARETS ROAD

TWICKENHAM ROAD

TWICKENHAM ROAD

LONDON ROAD

CHERTSEY ROAD

SHEEN ROAD

LOWER RICHMOND ROAD

UPPER RICHMOND ROAD

MANOR ROAD

RICHMOND HILL

STAR AND GARTER

LAWYER'S HILL

Pallavi

A Cena

If you stumble over Richmond bridge towards Twickenham, A Cena is the first restaurant on the right. It opened at Christmas 2001 and from the start seemed an ambitious sort of place. The chef is a lady who was previously behind the stoves at Emporio Armani, which seems appropriate as the decor and style of the place is more Knightsbridge than Richmond. This restaurant has definite aspirations. The lighting is

Cost	£20–50

Address 418 Richmond Rd, Twickenham, Middlesex
☎ 020 8288 0108
Station Richmond/BR St Margarets
Open Tues–Sat noon–2.30pm & 7–10.30pm, Sun noon–2.30pm
Accepts All major credit cards except AmEx

stylish; there is a bar area to the front which aims to tempt streetwise locals with modish cocktails; there are large displays of lemons; all is trendy, all is modern. The menu changes to suit the seasons and the markets, and the food is good – simple in the best kind of way, with clever combinations of flavour and texture. These are straightforward Italian dishes and all the better for that. The only caveat is that portions are on the small side, especially when viewed in conjunction with their price tags.

Dishes are admirably seasonal – start with walnut and ricotta ravioli (£7), or pan-fried sweetbreads with Marsala and artichokes (£7.50). Simple dishes like a Savoy cabbage salad with Parmigiano and balsamic (£5.50) always appeal. The pasta of the day and the risotto are well made; the pancetta and rosemary risotto (£6.50/11) is perfect – perfectly cooked, perfectly seasoned, perfect textures. The gnocchi alla Romana with Portobello mushrooms (£5/9) is a solid, satisfying dish. Main courses read and eat well: baked sea bream with green olives, cima di rapa and lemon (£14); breaded pork belly with tomato, pancetta and sage cannellini beans (£13.50). The puds are good – the home-made espresso ice cream (£5) is truly awesome, and the chocolate tartufo (£5) is seriously rich, and so it should be.

Some pundit somewhere once defined the differences between French and Italian food by saying that while French cuisine uses skill and artifice to hide the shortcomings of poor ingredients, in an Italian kitchen the aim is to do as little as possible and allow truly wonderful ingredients to speak for themselves. Whoever it was hit the nail on the head. A Cena may just convince you it is true.

Brula Bistrot

In 1999, two friends who worked in smart central London restaurants decided that the time had come to open their own place. They chose St Margarets as a locale and, as they were called Bruce Duckett and Lawrence Hartley, they called their restaurant Brula. It had a tiny, yellow-painted dining room about as wide as a railway carriage and an equally modest kitchen. It was very much a family affair.

Cost	£10–20

Address 43 Crown Rd, St Margarets, Surrey
℡ 020 8892 0602
Station BR St Margarets
Open Mon–Fri 12.30–2pm & 7–10.30pm, Sat 12.30–2pm & 7–10.30pm
Accepts Delta, Electron, Solo, Switch

Within 18 months Brula had become so successful that they had to move across Crown Road into larger premises. Now the Brula Bistrot (the name was enlarged in keeping with the new premises) is no longer a cramped affair. There are large windows with a profusion of rather elegant stained glass. Thankfully, the food and philosophy have endured – well-cooked French bistro food, limited choice, low, low prices.

You have to admire anyone who has the good sense not to mess with something that works really well. Lunch at Brula Bistrot will cost you £8 for one or two courses and £10 for three. Extra veg (should you want any) costs a further £2.50; an espresso to finish is £1.50. The menu changes on a weekly basis, so you might face a choice of celeriac remoulade, soft egg and chives; duck rillette with onion marmalade; or rustic fish soup with rouille. Then on to beef meatballs with thyme dumplings; fish of the day with soy and ginger dressing; or spinach and mushroom tart. Finally your pick of the puds. All very French, and all rather nostalgic, evoking that dimly remembered rural France when you could pitch up at any bistro de gare and be sure of a good, cheap, satisfying meal. In the evenings they go à la carte (starters between £4.50 and £6; mains £9.50 to £11; puds £4) and add an extra dish to make four choices for each course – perhaps nine escargots de Bourgogne to start with, and venison steak with creamed endives and a red wine sauce to add gravitas to the main courses.

The Frenchness even extends to the list of suggested apéritifs at the top of the evening menu: kir (£3.50), Pilsener (£3), or kir royale (£4.50). And, should you spurn these blandishments, the wine list is short and agreeably priced – a Chablis Premier Cru Fourchaume was sighted at £25.

Chez Lindsay

At first glance, Chez Lindsay looks rather like Chicago in the 1920s – all around you people are drinking alcohol out of large earthenware teacups. The cups are in fact traditional Breton drinking vessels known as *bolées*, the drink is cider, and Chez Lindsay lists a trio of them, ranging from Breton brut traditionnel to Norman cidre bouché. This small, bright restaurant has had a loyal local following for a good many

Cost	£7–27

Address 11 Hill Rise, Richmond, Surrey
☎ 020 8948 7473
Station Richmond
Open Mon–Sat 11am–11pm, Sun noon–10pm
Accepts MasterCard, Visa

VERY FRENCH

years. Most people are attracted by the galettes and crêpes, though the menu also includes a regularly changing list of hearty Breton dishes – especially fish. It's a place for Francophiles: both the kitchen and the front of house seem to be staffed entirely by Gauls, which in this instance means good service and tasty food.

Start with palourdes farcies (£5.95), where nine small clams are given the "snail butter" treatment – lots of garlic. Or the moules à la St Malo (£5.75), which are cooked with shallots, cream and thyme. Then you must decide between the galettes or more formal main courses. The galettes are huge buckwheat pancakes, large and lacy, thin but satisfying. They come with an array of fillings: egg, cheese and ham (£6.25); scallops and leeks (£8.75); Roquefort cheese, celery and walnuts (£6.50); and "Chez Lindsay" (£6.50) – cheese, ham and spinach. The other half of the menu is very Breton, featuring a good steak frites (£12.75) and lots of fish and shellfish. The "gratin de Camembert, rouget Grondin et crevettes" (£11.75) is an interesting dish – a gratin containing red snapper, prawns and Camembert. Or there is the bar grillé (£15.75) – a whole grilled sea bass with salad and new potatoes. Ask the amiable staff about off-menu goodies, which, depending on the market and the season, might be anything from exotic fish to roast grouse.

At lunch, the menu de midi delivers two courses – a salad and a galette – for just £5.99, and there is always a three-course prix fixe at £14.99. Real pud enthusiasts will save themselves for the chocolate and banana crêpe (£4.50), topped with a scoop of gin and lavender ice cream (£1.30), a bizarre-sounding combination that ends up tasting strangely delicious.

Richmond & Twickenham

Chez Maria

(Y) Michel de Ville has won his share of battle honours in his forty years in the catering industry, and his certificates and medals adorn the walls of this tiny restaurant he runs with Maria, his wife. The insignia of the Chevaliers de Tastevin is on one side and the gold medal he won as executive chef of the Playboy Club of America is on the other.

Cost	£20–24
Address	5a Princes St, Richmond Market, Surrey; with branches
☎	020 8948 1475
Station	Richmond
Open	Mon–Sat 6–10pm
Accepts	MasterCard, Visa

This place is a *bistro du marché* of the kind that you would find in France. Michel sees to the cooking; Maria, the service. You fetch your own wine from a nearby off-licence or wine merchant – Chez Maria is strictly BYO. There's also a sensibly simple pricing structure: £16.50 for two courses and £17.50 for three, with no charge for corkage. As there are only thirty seats you would be wise to book, especially at the weekend.

Maria is Portuguese and the menu claims that the restaurant offers "French and Portuguese Specialities", but the French side seems to have the upper hand. Michel cooks the kind of food that he is completely at home with, a sort of frozen-in-time bistro-favourites selection, but one where the dishes have been chosen to make the most sense of a single-handed kitchen. The pastrywork is good – try the tian des crevettes à la sauce Aurore et basilic, a sort of mini-quiche with prawns and a classic cream and tomato sauce. Fish of the day "façon du chef" is generally reliable. Or there might be a roast duck breast on a bed of braised cabbage. Recipes are traditional: lamb might be paired with a rich haricot bean dish. Good, honest, very unpretentious French food. Puddings continue the theme: tarte au citron, terrine au chocolat, and crème brûlée. Modernist gastronomes will not approve, but people who fondly remember cheap eats in France will feel pleasantly nostalgic. And here you can enjoy something very rare indeed in a world of lattes, Americanos and tall, skinny, cappuccinos – a good cup of ordinary coffee for £1.50.

Michel is not above the occasional gastro-jest. To celebrate Burns night, you might be offered "Champignons farcis au Haggis et herbes fraîches", which somewhat gives the lie to the philosophical observation that life is too short to stuff a mushroom.

Kozachok

Tourists will know Richmond as that funny little town on the Thames that cannot quite make up its mind whether it is in London or not. What is less immediately obvious is that it is also a good place to go and eat Ukrainian food. This is a significantly eccentric restaurant. Everything within is painted – bowls, decorative cruets, even the walls have naive cartoon murals. And bunches of twigs have been used to decorate the ceiling. You will feel as if you have strayed onto a set during the filming of "Smiley's People". Service is more akin to treacle than quicksilver, and the food is limited in choice and stolid in demeanour. "Why bother?", you will probably be asking. You should eat at Kozachok because you will enjoy yourself. The service is genuinely welcoming, the food is unfussed-about-with and the vodka (along with the excellent Obolon Ukrainian beer), will leave you giggling irresponsibly while the charm of the place and the people get to work.

Cost	£18–40

Address 10 Red Lion St, Richmond, Surrey
℡ 020 8948 2366
Station Richmond
Open Tues–Thurs 6.30–11pm, Fri & Sat 6.30–11.15pm, Sun 6.30–10pm
Accepts All major credit cards except Diners

UKRAINIAN

There are half a dozen starters. Far and away the best is the blini. This is a large and fluffy creation, about 2cm deep and 8cm across, crisp outside, and very delicious – probably "best ever" when topped with aubergine ikra (£4.95), smoked salmon (£5.50), salmon caviar (£7.50), or – best of all – marinated herring (£5.75). Drunken salmon is also good (£6.95) – home-salted, vodka-cured salmon. Or there is ruletka (£4.75), which is sliced aubergine rolled around cheese. Mains include a Ukrainian speciality called varenki (£8.75), which is like grandparent ravioli filled with potato and cheese. From Siberia there are pelmeni (£8.75) – thick dumplings stuffed with mince and served with sour cream, not for the faint hearted. Or there's shashlik (£8.95), a pork kebab which will seem a bit tame if you're drinking properly. Pud means mind-numbing and artery-clogging pancakes, as light as sandbags.

Vodka comes in a wide variety of guises here. And you will be fine right up to the moment when someone suggests beer chasers and you agree. Kozachok is further laid back than most of us can manage without a bed handy, but it is a charming place, run by genuine people who have a real grasp of hospitality.

Origin Asia

(①) The section of Kew Road that runs
up to Richmond has always been
something of a restaurant gulch. So it
was no surprise when, in March 2002,
Origin Asia opened its doors. This is an
aggressively modern, markedly stylish,
somewhat over-the-top Indian restaurant
– all of which would count heavily against
it if the food were not very good indeed.

Cost	£18–38

Address 100 Kew Rd,
Richmond, Surrey
☎ 020 8948 0509
Station Richmond
Open Daily 11.30am–2.30pm
& 6–11.30pm
Accepts MasterCard, Visa

The large restaurant is divided into four sections, the most attractive of
which is the one at the back with a grand view of the open kitchen. In the
front section the "goldfish bowl" feeling is just about mitigated by a rather
splendid Indian glass chandelier; the middle sections are agreeable; but
the back is the place to be.

Starters like chaman-ki-chat (£3.25) are most intriguing; this is made
from fresh sharp fruits – apple, strawberry, kiwi fruit – cubed and made
into a salad with chunks of boiled potato, cubes of salty home-made
paneer (Indian cheese) and a tangy, spicy dressing. An original dish that
works well. Or how about something from the tandoor? Phir wohi moti
(£6.25) are mushrooms that have been stuffed with a paneer and herb
paste before being cooked on a skewer. From the meatier tandoor offerings, go for adrak-ke-panje (£10.25) – five top-class tandoori lamb
chops, with well-seasoned, tender meat. Like the surroundings, some of
the dishes are a little over the top. Methi-ke-scallops (£12.50) is one of
them – the scallops are perfectly cooked, soft and sweet, and the methi
sauce is a belter, strongly flavoured and well balanced. But together? Try
the gosht saagwala (£8.50) instead. This is an epic dish – a simple spinach
and lamb curry, but the fresh spinach is still green and perky, the lamb is
tender, and the sauce rich. A well-flavoured, traditional combination.
There are also plenty of vegetarian dishes that tempt – the Punjabi-di-dal
(£5.95) is a good, buttery-rich dal. The breads are outstanding: lacchedar
Kerala paratha (£2.25) is flaky and delicious, and there are rotis (£1.75).
The simple jeera rice (£2.95) is also wholly successful.

There are a few tables outside, which will have a powerful appeal if
and when there is weather clement enough to use them.

Pallavi

This is a small outpost of an Indian restaurant empire which also includes Malabar Junction (see p.13) – an impressive pedigree. Pallavi, the simplest and the cheapest, started its days as a large takeaway counter with just a few seats, then moved over the road from the original site to these smart new premises. The cooking has travelled well, and still deserves the ultimate compliment – it is genuinely home-style, with unpretentious dishes and unpretentious prices. True to its South Indian roots, there is an impressive list of vegetarian specialities, but the menu features just enough meat and fish dishes to woo any kind of diner.

Cost	£10–23

Address 1st Floor, 3 Cross Deep Court, Heath Rd, Twickenham, Middlesex
℡020 8892 2345
Station BR Twickenham
Open Daily noon–3pm & 6–11pm
Accepts All major credit cards
ⓦ www.mcdosa.com

INDIAN

Start with that South Indian veggie favourite, the Malabar masala dosa (£3.50). This huge, crisp pancake is made with a mixture of ground rice and lentil flour, and is a perfect match for the savoury potato mixture and chutney. There's also a meat masala dosa (£4.95), described on the menu as a "non-vegetarian pancake delicacy" – full marks for accuracy there. Or try the delightfully named iddly (£3.50), a steamed rice cake made with black gram which is eaten as a breakfast dish in India. Whatever you open with, have some cashew nut pakoda (£2.95), a kind of savoury peanut brittle made with cashew nuts, which is wholly delicious. The main dishes are simple and tasty, and are served without fuss. For unrepentant carnivores, chicken Malabar (£3.95), keema methi (£3.95) or kozhi varutha curry (£3.95) all hit the spot. But there are also some interesting fish dishes, including the fish moilee (£5.95). Veggies are good too: try parippu curry (£2.15) – split lentils with cumin, turmeric, garlic, chillies and onions; kalan (£2.50) – a traditional sweet and sour dish of mango, yam, coconut and spices; or cabbage thoran (£2.50) – sliced cabbage with carrots, green chillies and curry leaves. The pilau rice, lemon rice and coconut rice (all £2.20) are tasty, and parathas are even better – try a green chilli or a sweet coconut paratha (both £2.50).

In this posh new incarnation, Pallavi is fully licensed, so you are no longer obliged to bring your own carryout. Thankfully, the lassi (£1) is still just as good.

Richmond & Twickenham

The White Horse

🍴 All over town, brave entrepreneurs are taking pubs away from the traditional breweries and transforming them into gold mines, but in this instance Fuller's brewery can be congratulated for encouraging quality themselves. The White Horse is a dark, spartan bar-restaurant with good, large tables that are well spread out – no sitting in your neighbour's pocket here. The food and pricing

Cost	£12–30

Address Worple Way, Richmond, Surrey
☎ 020 8940 2418
Station Richmond
Open Mon–Sat noon–3pm & 6.30–10pm, Sun noon–4pm
Accepts All major credit cards except Diners

are also spot-on, as is confirmed by a steady trade and a note on the menu saying "we are now taking bookings for both lunch and early evening meals".

The menu is a short one, and all the better for it. Half a dozen starters and five main courses change twice a day to accommodate whatever is best from the market. There might be grilled chicken livers with Parma ham and a poached egg (£5). Or a chicken velouté soup (£3.75); or smoked salmon mousse with a coriander dressing (£5.50); or pan-fried Brie, Cumberland sausage and wild rocket (£5.50). Main courses are also simple and well executed, like the devilled pork chop with French beans and Lyonnaise potatoes (£9.50); or the parrot-fish fillet, with tomato and chicory salad and an aubergine salsa (£10) – fresh fish, well cooked and well presented. Or fettucine with pine nuts, sun-dried tomatoes, spinach and Parmesan (£7). The wide-ranging wine list tops out at £30 for a bottle of the Kiwi classic Coudy Bay. What's more, there is the intelligent option of a 250ml glassful of any one of seven different wines (£4). Puds are also seasonal, so you might be tempted by cinnamon bread pudding with stewed plums (£4.50), or prune and Armagnac tart (£4.50). And if they don't get you, then the dark chocolate pot (£4.50) probably will.

The last item in The White Horse's dessert section is Vivian's cheeses with wheat wafers and chutney (£5.50). The cheese in question has made the short journey from Vivian's, the superb delicatessen a few doors down the road – call in there for all manner of goodies. The White Horse cheeseboard proves how much more satisfying it is to sample two or three cheeses in perfect condition than to be faced with a huge selection of the unripe and overripe.

Shepherd's Bush & Olympia

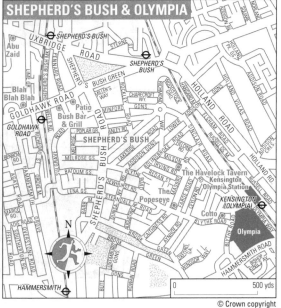

Abu Zaad

To reach the dining room here you must first wend your way through lots of tables full of happy people, some grazing by the pastries (£4.30 per lb), some gossiping in front of the counter filled with the numerous meze, some at the coffee-making area. Then turn left at the open kitchen, where there's a char-

Cost	£12–20

Address 29 Uxbridge Rd, W12
℡ 020 8749 5107
Station Shepherd's Bush
Open Daily 11am–11pm
Accepts All major credit cards
except AmEx

SYRIAN

coal grill, stews ready for re-heating, and a full-sized bread oven. Abu Zaad is a busy place and a friendly one – the food is good and awesomely cheap. Finally you go up a few steps to a raised area where the rich green walls look as if they are decorated with metal panels. Very Damascene.

This may be the cheapest place in London to experiment with meze, as whether hot or cold they all cost about £2. Here £2 will buy you a large portion of makanic – meaty, chipolata-sized sausages; baba ganouj – delicious aubergine mush; or foul medames – boiled fava beans with chick peas, tomato and lemon juice; or hummos. A stunning haystack of tabbouleh is more expensive at £2.50, but comes with spankingly fresh chopped parsley and mint. Ordering a dish called falafi (£1.50) brings four crisp and nutty falafel. You must try the fattoush (£2), a fresh, well-dressed salad with croutons of deep-fried flatbread. In fact, all meze you order will arrive with a basket of delicious fresh flatbread. The food is described on the menu as "Damascene Cuisine" but most of these dishes are claimed by every Middle Eastern chef. Drink a glass of carrot and apple juice (£1.50) and feel healthy. The menu goes on to list dozens of main courses, from rich casseroles to charcoal grills, and they are all priced at about £4.90. There's a good case for not bothering with a main course here, simply order seven or eight meze between two.

On the menu at Abu Zaad there is a two-stage cartoon of a man with a donkey cart making collections and deliveries; the caption runs as follows: "Mr Abu Zaad used to collect meals from traders' wives and deliver them to traders in the souk". Things are different in the Uxbridge Road, but it's easy to imagine that the food is just as good.

Blah Blah Blah

Following a cruel comment in the last edition of this guide (something along the lines of "looks a bit like a funeral parlour"), Blah has repainted outside and now faces the world in deep maroon with gold lettering. Inside the status is still quo. The floors, tables and chairs are wooden, there are blinds rather than curtains, and the only decorations of note are driftwood and old iron lamps. Add wallpaper music and the echoing noise levels become formidable. It is alleged that this is the restaurant where Paul McCartney asked for the music to be turned down.

Cost	£16–25

Address 78 Goldhawk Rd, W12
☏ 020 8746 1337
Station Goldhawk Road
Open Mon–Sat 12.30–2.30pm & 7–11pm Sun 7–11pm
Accepts Cash or cheque only

The menu casts its net widely and you can expect dishes with all manner of influences. Among the starters there may be an avocado, citrus and Mexican salad (£4.95) – the Mexican interest being represented by tortilla chips; a Greek salad (£4.50); and an aubergine, chickpea and spinach puri (£4.95) – pepped up with a pathia sauce and a brinjal pickle. Dodging over to Italy, there's a tortino made with sweet potatoes (£4.95) – roast sweet potatoes and leeks in the Italian answer to a soufflé. Main courses are similarly eclectic. Saffron fazzoletti (£9.50) is handkerchief pasta layered with mozzarella and Jerusalem artichokes. And there may be a Thai-style noodle laksa (£9.95) of wheat flour noodles in a hot coconut curry sauce; or a simple roast fennel tart (£9.95) – puff pastry, the fennel cooked with cream and white wine. Or roast pumpkin tyropizza (£9.50), with feta and filo adding the Greek elements to this dish. Puds (all £4.95) are rewarding: chocolate and pear tart with ice cream; white chocolate muffin; or banana and toffee profiteroles with butterscotch sauce to keep the local dentists prosperous.

Blah Blah Blah offers well-prepared food that just happens to be vegetarian, rather than the kind of heavy, wholemeal and meaningful fare you would expect from a more in-your-face vegetarian restaurant. It is unlicensed, so bring your own. There is a very reasonable corkage charge of £1.25 per person.

Bush Bar & Grill

The rise and rise of Shepherd's Bush seemed to culminate in the arrival, in late 2000, of the Bush Bar & Grill. The Bush end of the Goldhawk Road was once the preserve of curry houses, cafés, the street market and a pie-and-mash shop. Now they are joined by the Bush Bar, full of renegade stylistas who have travelled west from Notting Hill. This is a serious bar, complete with serried ranks of bottles, smart raised booths and smartly dressed punters. The large dining area is busy and the whole place has an agreeable buzz to it.

Cost	£12–45

Address 45a Goldhawk Rd, W12
℗ 020 8746 2111
Station Goldhawk Road
Open Mon–Sat noon–3pm & 6.30–11.30pm, Sun noon–4pm & 7–11pm
Accepts MasterCard, Visa
ⓦ www.bushbar.co.uk

MODERN BRITISH

The Bush Bar & Grill captures the informal, pacey bustle of a classic brasserie rather well. Service is brisk and with attitude, and the food comes flying out over the pass from an open kitchen that runs the length of the room. The menu changes on a monthly basis and is written in a way that encourages casual meals – starters lead on to salads, grills, roasts and "other" mains. Starters may include watercress soup (£4) – served hot or cold; grilled asparagus with poached egg and tarragon butter (£6.50); and warm tart of Blue Brie, spinach and spring onion (£4.50). Salads range from celeriac remoulade (£4.50) to a smoked chicken and avocado salad (£5.50/8.50). From the grill there's seared blue-fin tuna salad Niçoise (£12.50); and Aberdeen Angus rib-eye steak and chips (£14.75) – all the beef here is from Donald Russell of Inverurie. Puddings are a tad predictable: bread-and-butter pudding (£4); tarte Tatin (£4.50); crème brûlée (£4). This restaurant has the measure of its customers, serves admirably unfussy food, and has prices that are grounded in reality. The wine list at the Bush Bar & Grill is also extremely encouraging. In such a chic establishment, a reliable house wine (Armit's French Red or White) priced at £11 deserves a warm welcome, and even a top bottle like Chateau La Lagune 1995 has an agreeably ungrasping price tag of £50.

There's a good-value set lunch here: £10.50 for two courses and £12 for three. Moules marinières; chicken breast with pancetta and asparagus; then chocolate pudding – that should tempt them away from the nearby BBC canteen.

MODERN BRITISH

Cotto

From the outside, Cotto, which stands on a corner site in a residential neighbourhood behind Olympia, is nothing special. Acres of plate glass frontage reveal a sprinkling of tables around a large central bar area. Once you have taken in the clean white walls, the dark ribbed carpet and the collection of

Cost	£17–60

Address 44 Blythe Rd, W14
℗020 7602 9333
Station Kensington Olympia
Open Mon–Fri noon–2.30pm
& 7–10.30pm, Sat 7–10.30pm
Accepts All major credit cards

primary-coloured abstract paintings on the walls, there is precious little decoration. And therefore minimal distraction from the real purpose of this restaurant, which is to provide good grub for discerning local residents.

The balance of the menu will strike a chord with foodies. Though the restaurant has an Italian name (*cotto* means "cooked"), its menu draws from both English and French traditions. It seems that the cooking is firmly rooted in the best of all approaches: treating ingredients with respect and striving to get the most out of each of them. The menu – which changes regularly to follow the seasons – is not long, but there's plenty of variety, and the deal is a simple one: two courses for £20 and three for £25. The six starters might include a cavolo nero soup with Gorgonzola tortellini; or a soft-boiled duck with shrimp mayonnaise and celeriac remoulade. Main courses usually include a proper vegetarian choice, such as a Pithivier made with Jerusalem artichokes, wild mushroom and goats' cheese, as well as a couple of fish options, like baked salmon with endive marmalade and samphire; or John Dory with courgette and basil lasagne, white beans and foie gras butter. Meat dishes may include a pot-roast rump of veal with root vegetables, anchovy and caper sauce; and roast chicken with thyme and soft polenta. Puddings, such as baked rhubarb Alaska, or chocolate and griottines terrine, will please any sugar addict.

Eating at Cotto is a satisfying experience, and the food is served with good manners and grace. You should be aware, though, that the bill has a tendency to escalate, especially if you give the wine list full play. But a visit for lunch is much more affordable: two courses are offered at £15.50, and three at £18. The dishes may not be as complex, but the same philosophy applies as at dinner.

The Havelock Tavern

The Havelock is one of those pubs marooned within a sea of houses; in this instance it's the sea of houses just behind Olympia. It's a real pub, with a solid range of beers as well as an extensive wine list. What is most attractive, though, is the attitude that lies behind the menu, which is chalked up daily on the blackboard. As the chef half of the pro-

Cost	£8–25

Address 57 Masbro Rd, W14
℡ 020 7603 5374
Station Shepherd's Bush
Open Mon–Sat 12.30–2.30pm & 7–10pm, Sun 12.30–3pm & 7–9.30pm
Accepts Cash or cheque only

MODERN BRITISH/PUB

prietorial partnership says, "We're in the business of feeding people." And that's just what they do, serving up seasonal, unfussy food – the kind of fresh, interesting, wholesome stuff you wish that you could get around to cooking for yourself. The bar seats 75 and during the summer there's a terrific garden complete with vines and a pergola. Service involves stepping up to the bar and ordering what you want, so there's no service charge to bump up what are very reasonable prices indeed.

The menu is different every session, with more "one-hit" dishes served at lunch, when most customers are pressed for time. Starters might be deep-fried monkfish cheeks, red chilli and garlic mayonnaise (£5.50); Jerusalem artichoke soup (£4); chorizo, chickpea, snail and tomato stew with crostini (£5.50); or deep-fried mozzarella with red pepper, spring onion, caper and basil salad (£6). Main courses range from fillet of cod with olive-oil mash, rocket, grilled artichoke, caper, chilli and tomato relish (£10); to roast duck breast, salsify and potato gratin with green peppercorn sauce (£10.50). Or a classic like veal saltimbocca with soft polenta, spinach, garlic and rosemary sauce (£10.50). Puddings are equally reliable – try the warm apple, honey and polenta cake with vanilla ice cream (£4), or the chocolate and almond terrine with crème fraîche (£4).

A great deal of effort goes into selecting slightly unusual wines for the blackboard wine list. Many of them are offered at bargain prices, but the biggest seller is still a glass of the house red. Popular rumour has it that the Havelock is one of Simon Hopkinson's favourite eateries. No wonder.

POLISH

Patio

The ebullient Eva Michalik (a former opera singer) and her husband Kaz have been running this Shepherd's Bush institution for more than a decade, and it's not hard to see why the show is still on the road. At Patio you get good, solid Polish food in a friendly, comfortable atmosphere, and for a relatively small amount of money. And this little restaurant is a people-pleaser – you can just as easily come here for an intimate tête-à-tête as for a raucous birthday dinner. The food is always reliable and sometimes it's really excellent. There are two floors; downstairs feels a little cosier and more secluded.

Cost	£13–26

Address 5 Goldhawk Rd, W12
℡ 020 8743 5194
Station Goldhawk Road/
Shepherd's Bush
Open Mon–Fri noon–3pm &
6pm–midnight, Sat & Sun
6pm–midnight
Accepts All major credit cards

The set menu (available at lunch and dinner) is Patio's trump card. For £11.90 you get a starter, main course, dessert, petits fours ... and a vodka. The menu changes daily – ask Eva to tell you what's new in the kitchen and you could get something that's not yet listed. Starters may include plump and tasty blinis with smoked salmon; wild mushroom soup; Polish ham with beetroot horseradish; and herrings with soured cream. Everything is fresh and carefully prepared. For mains, there's a good selection of meat, fish and chicken dishes – the scallops in dill sauce, when available, are outstanding. Or you might try a Polish speciality such as golabki (cabbage stuffed with rice and meat), which is also available as a vegetarian dish; or chicken Walewska (chicken breast in fresh red pepper sauce); or sausages à la Zamoyski (grilled with sautéed mushrooms and onions). Main dishes come with a hearty selection of vegetables such as roast potatoes, broccoli and red cabbage. Be prepared, too, for high-octane puds, such as the Polish pancakes with cheese, vanilla and rum – the fumes alone are enough to send you reeling. Also good is the hot apple charlotka with cream. For those after more variety, including a scattering of non-Polish dishes, the à la carte offers further choice, and for not a great deal more money.

Patio is a good night out. The piano crammed in near the entrance is often put to use by a regular customer, and there are frequent sightings of a roving gypsy quartet.

The Popeseye

🍴 Just suppose you fancy a steak. A good steak, and perhaps a glass (or bottle) of red wine to go with it. You're interested enough to want the best, probably Aberdeen Angus, and you want it cooked simply. The Popeseye is for you. This quirky restaurant is named after the Scottish word for rump steak, and every week the proprietor buys his meat not from Smithfield or a catering butcher, but from the small butcher his family uses in the north of Scotland. The meat, of course, is Aberdeen Angus and the restaurant is a member of the Aberdeen Angus Society. The dining room is small, things tend to be chaotic, and the atmosphere is occasionally pretty smoky. As to the food, there is no choice: just various kinds of steak and good chips, with home-made puddings to follow. Oh, and the menu starts with the wine list. You choose your drink, and only when that's settled do you choose your steak – specifying, of course, the cut and the size (and they come very big here), and how you want it cooked.

Cost	£18–60

Address 108 Blythe Rd, W14; with branches
☎ 020 7610 4578
Station Hammersmith
Open Mon-Sat 7–10.30pm
Accepts Cash or cheque only

STEAK

There are those times when, for nearly everyone, only a large piece of meat will do. You may have curry days, fish days, or pasta days, but for red meat days the Popeseye really hits the spot. Now – about these steaks. Popeseye comes in 6oz, 8oz, 12oz and 20oz (at £9.45, £11.95, £16.45 and £21.45), as does sirloin (£11.95, £14.95, £19.45 and £24.95), and fillet (£13.45, £17.95, £22.45 and £30.95). All prices include excellent chips, and a side salad is an extra £3.45. Puddings are priced at £4.25 and come from the home-made school of patisserie – such delights as apple crumble, sticky toffee pudding and lemon tart.

The wine list is an ever-changing reflection of what can be picked up at the sales and represents good value. There are eighteen clarets and half a dozen wines from Burgundy, plus others picked from the Rhône, Spain and Argentina – and there are also two white wines on offer for people who have lost the plot. Ask advice. People have been seen here happily drinking Château La Lagune 1986 for £75 a bottle; despite being a tidy sum, this is also a bargain.

Southall

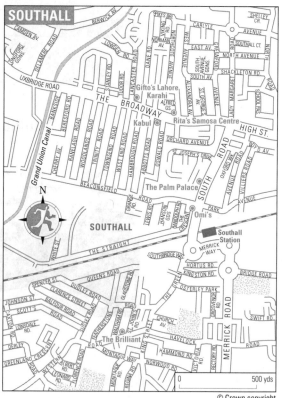

SOUTHALL

© Crown copyright

The Brilliant

The Brilliant is a Southall institution. For more than twenty years the Anand family business has been a non-stop success and it is now a bustling 250-seater. For twenty-five years before that, the family's first restaurant, also called The Brilliant, was the toast of Kenya. The food at The Brilliant is East African-Asian, and very good indeed. D.K. Anand (known as Gulu) rules the kitchen with a rod of iron and, to quote him, "there's no frying-pan cookery here". A relatively small number of dishes are freshly cooked in bulk, and if a curry needs to be simmered for three hours then that's what happens. The resulting sauces are incredibly rich and satisfying – and yet Gulu won't countenance any cream, yoghurt, nuts or dried fruit.

Cost	£15–30

Address 72–76 Western Rd, Southall, Middlesex
☎ 020 8574 1928
Station BR Southall
Open Tues–Fri noon–2.30pm & 6pm–midnight, Sat & Sun 6–11.30pm; closed Aug
Accepts All major credit cards
🌐 www.brilliantrestaurant.com

INDIAN

To start with, you must try the butter chicken (£8 half, £16 full). A half-portion will do for two people as a starter. This dish is an enigma: somehow it manages to taste more buttery than butter itself – really delicious. There's also jeera chicken (£8/16), rich with cumin and black pepper. And chilli chicken (£9/18), which is hot, but not quite as hot as it used to be! If you're in a party, move on to the special meals section – these come in two portion sizes, suggested for three people and five people. Methi chicken (£17.50/32), masaladar lamb (£17.50/32) and palak chicken (£17.50/32) are all winners. Alternatively, choose from among the single-portion curries, which include masala talapia (£9), a fish curry of unimaginable richness with good firm chunks of boneless fish. Well-cooked basmati rice costs £3.50 and, as well as good rotis (£1), the breads list hides a secret weapon, the kulchay (£1). This is a fried, white-dough bread, for all the world like a very flat doughnut. Hot from the kitchen they are amazing – it's best to order a succession so that they don't go cold.

Ask to try Gulu's pickles – carrot, sharp mango and hot lime. They are splendid. Also try the Kenyan beer Tusker (£2.50), with its label rather engagingly designed like a bank note.

Gifto's Lahore Karahi

In Southall they know a good thing when they taste it. Gifto's Lahore Karahi specializes in freshly grilled, well-spiced meats and exceptionally good breads, backed up by a few curries and one or two odd dishes from Lahore. They do these superbly well and consistently. It is a sign of the towering success that 2001 saw a major renovation and refurb but the emphasis is still on a no-frills operation. A row of grinning chefs seem to juggle with the three-foot skewers as meat goes into the tandoor caked in a secret marinade and comes out perfectly cooked and delicious. Despite having a hundred seats downstairs and the same again upstairs, there is a still a queue outside at the weekend.

Cost	£9–17

Address 162–164 The Broadway, Southall, Middlesex
⌖020 8813 8669
Station BR Southall
Open Mon–Thurs noon–11.30pm, Fri–Sun noon–midnight
Accepts All major credit cards
⊕www.gifto.com

Whatever else you order, you need some bread. Peshwari nan (£1.80) is a triumph, hot from the oven, flavoured with garlic and fresh herbs, and liberally slathered with ghee and sesame seeds. It's hard to imagine it bettered. To accompany it, you might start with an order of chicken tikka (£3.80), which is juicy and strongly spiced. Or go straight for a portion of five lamb chops (£5.50), encrusted in tandoori paste and grilled until crisp. Or try pomfret fish (£8.90) from the tandoor, a worthwhile extravagance. Curries include sag gosht (£6.20), which is chunks of lamb in a dark green, velvety spinach base; Nihari lamb (£6.20), cooked slowly on the bone in a rich gravy; and, more unusually, batera – quail – curry (£6.20). The menu describes paya (£6.20) as "lamb trotters in thick gravy" – a gravy created by three hours' cooking in a pot with ginger, onions and garlic. For specialists only, perhaps. Very delicious, and supposed to "purify the blood", is the karela gosht (£6.20), a telling combination of bitter melon and lamb. The side dishes will tempt all comers, especially the tarka dhal (£4.20), which is rich and buttery.

You can specify your seasonings for all the Lahore's dishes – mild, medium or hot. Hot is very hot and will have you calling for a large mango shake (£2). All drinks at the Lahore are soft, though you can bring your own beer or wine (no corkage is charged).

Kabul

(🍽) Find the Himalaya Shopping Centre and wend your way past the silk merchants and the shops selling exotic CDs. Head up the escalator and to the left you'll find the Kabul, which has taken over the space allocated to an entire shop. It's a spacious restaurant with comfortable chairs, dark blue tablecloths and a series of banquettes running along the wall. At one end of the room there's an open kitchen where the chefs work quietly and without fuss. The menu splits into two sections: Afghan food and Indian food. Curiosity should compel you to try some Afghan dishes but the cooking seems to be of a high standard whatever you order. Portions are very large and prices very competitive.

Cost	£5–15

Address 1st Floor, Himalaya Shopping Centre, Southall, Middlesex
☎ 020 8571 6878
Station BR Southall
Open Daily noon–midnight
Accepts MasterCard, Visa

Start with dumplings – ordering the Afghan starter called mantu gosht (£5.99) brings a dinner plate covered in large savoury dumplings filled with spiced lamb. Ashak are also dumplings and come in meat and non-meat versions – the vegetarian ones (£4.99) are amazingly good, light dumplings with dough so thin that you can see the green leaves of the filling through the skins. Also notable is the showr-na-kath (£1.99), a bowl full of chickpeas in a thin, green, herby, chilli-warmed liquid. You eat them with a spoon, or more sensibly with some of the excellent Afghan nan bread (£1.20). For mains, the quabuli murgh (£5.99) is a large plate of delicious rice pillau made with plenty of sultanas and garnished with shreds of carrot; on top of it is a tender chicken drumstick, and it comes with a bowl of curry with a large minced lamb cake hidden in its depths. Another winner is the karahi tukham (£2.50), which is a small karahi full of light, buttery, rich and spicy scrambled eggs. Stray onto the Indian side and you will not be disappointed: karela gosht (£5.40) is well seasoned and the striking taste of the bitter melon acts as a perfect foil for the richness of the other dishes on the table. The food is good here, and large portions make it very good value as well.

On your way out, stop and shop – there's an intriguing poster on the stairs singing the praises of tooth jewellery.

Omi's

Omi's is a small, no-frills eatery
with a kitchen that seems at least
as spacious as the dining area. The
explanation for this lies down the street,
where you'll find one of Southall's larger
banqueting and wedding halls. Omi's is a
thriving outside-catering operation and
has never been purely a restaurant – until
some years ago the food shared a

Cost	£5–12

Address 1 Beaconsfield Rd,
Southall, Middlesex
☎ 020 8571 4831
Station BR Southall
Open Mon–Thurs 11am–9pm,
Fri & Sat 11am–9.30pm
Accepts All major credit cards

counter with a van-rental business. 2002 was a busy year for Omi's as
they fulfilled a long-held dream and expanded into the next door prop-
erty, doubling their capacity to eighty seats. But you'll still find tasty,
Punjabi/Kenyan-Asian dishes, lots of rich flavours and great value. The
idea of opening for a bit longer each day and even on Sunday is often
discussed – best ring and check.

The food is cooked by a formidable line-up of chefs in the back,
doubtless knocking up dishes for diners with one hand while master-
minding the next Indian wedding for eight hundred with the other.
There's a constant stream of people picking up their takeaways. The
starters are behind the counter: chicken tikka (£3) is good and spicy,
while aloo tikki (50p) is a large, savoury potato cake, delightfully crisp
on the outside. Or try the masala fish (£2.75), a large slab of cod thickly
encrusted with spices. Go on to sample a couple of the specials. Aloo
methi (£3.50) – potatoes cooked with fenugreek – is very moreish
indeed. All the curries are commendably oil-free and thrive on the
cook-and-reheat system in operation here. They are best eaten with
breads – parathas (70p), rotis (40p) and the mega-indulgent, puffy fried
bhaturas (50p) are all fresh and good.

Don't miss out on a bottle of Ambari (£3.25), a Goan beer which
sports an intriguing injunction on the back label: "For real fun drink
chilled". If you feel a sudden tightening of your fist, you'll warm to the
multi-course set meal on offer here – it costs a miserly £4, either vegetarian or non-vegetarian. West End emporia please note these prices!

Palm Palace

The Palm Palace may be short on palms, and it is not palatial by any manner of means, but the food is great. This is the only Sri Lankan restaurant among the restaurant turmoil that is Southall, and the menu features a great many delicious and interesting dishes. As is so often the case with Sri Lankan food, the "drier" dishes are particularly

Cost	£9–18

Address 80 South Rd, Southall, Middlesex
☏ 020 8574 9209
Station BR Southall
Open Daily noon–3pm & 6–11.30pm
Accepts All major credit cards

appealing, and there is a good deal of uncompromising chilli heat. The dining room is clean and comfortable in a sparse sort of way, and service is friendly and attentive.

Starters are very good here. Try the mutton rolls (£1.50) – long pancake rolls filled with meat and potatoes. Or there's the fish cutlets (£1.50), which are in fact spherical fish cakes very much in the same style as those you find in smart West End eateries, but better spiced and a tenth of the price. Move on to a "devilled" dish: mutton (£4.50), chicken (£4.50) or, best of all, squid (£4.95). With a dark tangy-sweet sauce with chilli bite, these dishes combine spices with richness very well. There was a time when every curry house in the land featured Ceylon chicken, usually just a standard chicken curry with an additional dollop of coconut milk. Here you'll find a short list of real "Ceylon" curries including mutton (£3.95) – they're good, if straightforward. Try the chicken 65 (£4.50), whose name is said to refer to the age of the chicken in days; any younger and it would fall apart during cooking, any older and it would be tough. Whatever the provenance, it is a name worth noting, as it gets you delicious chunks of chicken with a rich and spicy coating. The hoppers (Sri Lankan pancakes) are good fun – string hopper (£2.50); egg hopper (£1.25); milk hopper (£1). Try a simple vegetable dish as well – saag aloo (£2.50) brings fresh spinach and thoughtfully seasoned, well-cooked potato.

Beer-lovers must order a big bottle of Lion Stout (£3.50), which is dark, dangerous and delicious. As well as being 8% alcohol, it brings with it a ringing endorsement from Michael Jackson, the "beer hunter" himself. Look at the back label and you will find not only his portrait, but also a short eulogy – "chocolatey, mocha, liqueur-like" and so forth. This beer is surprisingly good with spicy food.

INDIAN

Rita's Samosa Centre

Those diners with an artistic bent will be disappointed by the refurb at Rita's, which has meant the loss of the garish, other-worldly murals (and also the little paan shop by the doorway). This place is now light and bright and has a good many more seats, but business continues much as before. It is still noisy,

Cost	£3–12

Address 112 The Broadway, Southall, Middlesex
℡ 020 8571 2100
Station BR Southall
Open Daily 11am–10.30pm
Accepts Cash or cheque only

busy and bustling, and if you are a shy, retiring type, this isn't a place for you – indeed, you probably won't get served. To eat here you must go up to the counter where all the dishes are set out in giant trays, choose your meal, pay, and then seat yourself. The food will eventually arrive. There's no sign of a system but everything seems to turn up in the end. And when it does, it is simple, tasty and cheap. Who could ask for more? Perhaps a few bright murals?

The dishes are divided into sections: curries, bread and rice, chaats (street food) and snacks. Snacks make good starters, as do chaats. Try an onion bhaji (£1) – huge, and opened out flat so that it's all the crisper. Bhel puri (£2.25), alu tikki (£2) and dahi puri (£2.50) are all street-food items, tasty and good value. Or how about half a pound of chicken tikka (£3.50)? Or a superb, half-pound fish tikka (£3.50)? They both eclipse the samosas (40p each) after which this diner is named. Main course curries are rich and simple: try lamb (£4.50), lamb saag (£4.50) or a deadly chilli lamb or chilli chicken (£5.50), both of which arrive scatter-bombed with halved fresh green chillies. And despite the demise of the paan shop, there is still the kebab roll section by the door. This place offers really good, freshly cooked, delicious, reasonably priced fast food.

You can take your own beer or wine to Rita's, but it is much more fun exploring the (non-alcoholic) drinks section. A pint of salty lassi (£2) is wonderfully cold and pleasantly sharp, with a savoury dusting of fine-ground cumin seed. And then there's faluda. Faluda is very thin, very soft vermicelli which comes in a glass of milkshake. The sensation of these "worms" slithering up the straw and into your mouth is most disconcerting. Furthermore, you can have faluda with a scoop of ice cream in it (£2). What a way to end a meal.

Further West

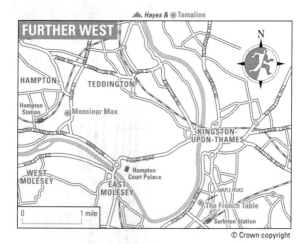

FURTHER WEST

▲ Hayes & ◉ Tamaline

N

HAMPTON

TEDDINGTON

Hampton Station

◉ Monsieur Max

PARK RD

HAMPTON RD

HIGH ST

BROAD ST

UPPER SUNBURY ROAD

HAMPTON

KINGSTON-UPON-THAMES

COOMBE LANE

COURT ROAD

■ Hampton Court Palace

WEST MOLESEY

EAST MOLESEY

HURST ROAD

MAPLE ROAD

◉ The French Table

◉ Surbiton Station

0   1 mile

The French Table

The French Table serves well-cooked, modern French/Mediterranean food. The restaurant is owned by Eric and Sarah Guignard; he cooks and she runs the front of house. Things have gone from strength to strength for this small, elegant, modern restaurant and it seems to have bedded in well. The menu is an interesting one because despite a good many modern influences, Guignard's food is rooted in the French classics – as befits a cook who has served time in various Michelin-starred establishments.

Cost	£15–45

Address 85 Maple Rd, Surbiton, Surrey
☏ 020 8399 2365
Station BR Surbiton
Open Tues 7–10.30pm, Wed–Fri noon–2.30pm & 7–10.30pm, Sat 7–10.30pm, Sun noon–3pm
Accepts MasterCard, Visa

MODERN EUROPEAN

Flavours are upfront and the seasoning spot on. There is a deft handling of different textures and presentation is commendably unfussy. Things change regularly, but starters may include dishes like deep-fried scallops with an asparagus and lime leaf risotto (£6.80); or terrine of marinated salmon, potato and dill (£5.50). The kitchen's classical approach shows in starters like the duo of foie gras (£8.50) – a ballotine with trad "quatre épices" and a tranche pan fried with warm mozzarella. Main course dishes are robust and delicious. Caramelized pork belly with creamy white beans and a croustillant of confit tomato (£12.80) is a grand dish – the pork is cooked to melting point. Or there's pan-fried cod with a courgette purée and watercress sauce (£12.50). Or rump of lamb served with cannelloni of sweetbreads, spinach and garlic confit (£13.80). Simple dishes are also well handled – try deep-fried vegetables in a light tempura batter with garlic mayonnaise (£9.80). Puds are good. The wine list here is largely French and gently priced, the service is friendly and everybody seems to be trying very hard indeed – as befits an "owner driver" establishment.

The set lunch is a bargain at £12.50 for two courses and £15.50 for three. Parmentier of oxtail with red wine; followed by pan-fried marinated carp with a julienne of vegetables; and then praline mousse with hot chocolate moelleux for just £15.50 would make a grand lunch anywhere – but in Surbiton it is downright miraculous.

Monsieur Max

You know those tabloid stories about people being trapped in the wrong bodies? Well, Max Renzland is a Frenchman trapped inside an Englishman. Monsieur Max embodies all the best bits of those legendary small French restaurants. At the head of the menu you'll find two subheads, "Cuisine Bourgeoise" and "bienvenue à Hampton Hill" – both statements are true. Service is cheerful and unashamedly biased towards regulars. The short menu changes every day. Dishes range from stunningly simple to French classics. And, joy of joys, Monsieur Max is in London – well, nearly.

Cost	£24–45

Address 133 High St, Hampton, Middlesex
℡ 020 8979 5546
Station BR Fulwell
Open Mon–Fri & Sun noon–2.30pm & 7–9.30pm, Sat 7–9.30pm
Accepts All major credit cards

Prices everywhere tend to creep upwards, and M. Max is no exception, but it still remains something of a bargain. Dinner (or Sunday lunch) is £37.50 for three courses; the midweek lunch is £20 for two courses or £25 for three, but supplements may apply to the more fanciful choices. Starters range from the simple – nine Irish oysters from County Louth – to more complex dishes such as gâteau of smoked salmon with smoked eel, watercress and fromage blanc; or terrine of foie gras and coq au vin, with haricot vert salad and Monbazillac jelly. For a main course, you can expect classic and balanced cooking – dishes like roast Anjou squab pigeon with consommé, foie gras, black pudding and bone marrow "en farce". Max is very picky about his pigeons, and once you taste one you'll see what all the fuss is about. His duck, pork, Scotch beef and fish suppliers are equally impressive – try the fillet of dorade royal roasted on a bed of rosemary; or the roast rack of Welsh lamb basted with herbs and served with sweetbreads and glazed endives. Puddings are of the order of rum baba, or an old-fashioned rice pudding with Madagascan vanilla, Agen prunes and cognac caramel. Push them aside and go for the cheeseboard – twenty French farmhouse cheeses in perfect condition. As for wine, there are about 250 bins – enough for the choosiest oenophile.

If you are a West London Francophile, you're probably already a regular here and will be unfazed by the minor eccentricities of the menu and service.

Tamaline

Since it opened in the late 1980s, this scruffy little restaurant in Hayes (along the Uxbridge Road, just west of the Southall strip) has had a well-deserved reputation for Sri Lankan seafood dishes. The only confusing factor is the name – for most of its life this place was called Thamoulinee, and that is still what it says on the menu covers. Whatever it may be called, this is a friendly, informal place. Food is made with care – which can mean slowly – presented without frills, and is very delicious. Relax and take your time – there is always the television banging out Tamil TV to keep you amused.

Cost	£8–20

Address 128 Uxbridge Rd, Hayes, Middlesex
℡ 020 8813 6170
Station BR Southall
Open Wed–Sun 6pm–midnight
Accepts All major credit cards except Amex

Start with the mutton rolls (2 for £1.50) – these are short, crisp and chewy spring rolls with a hearty mutton filling. Bonda (four for £2) are also good – savoury spheres of fried mash. Fried crab claws (four for £2.25) is an interesting dish of minced crab formed into lumps and fried crisply – like a vastly improved crabstick. The devilled squid (£4.50) is truly wonderful – tiny squidlets stuffed and cooked until meltingly tender. Very rich. The sambols are well done – these are a sort of condiment like chutney which you use to add flavour to rice or bread. Try the coconut sambol with Maldive fish (£2) – the rich, sweet coconut contrasts well with the salty, savoury fish. The flat, flaky, buttery breads are sensational; the plain gotthamba roti (£1.10) is only eclipsed by the egg roti (£2), which has an egg cooked between the layers. The food is good and spicy here (although dishes can be made as mild as you wish), the bill is a gentle one, and you get two names for the price of one.

One of the most famous Sri Lankan specialities is the hopper. These are dish-shaped, crisp-ish, bready sorts of things which can be made plain, with milk, or with an egg. If you yearn to try them do not visit Tamaline on Friday, Saturday or Sunday as the lady who does the hoppers doesn't like to come out at the weekend, and so they are off the menu. You have to admire such an explanation.

Index

Index of restaurants with branches

Index of restaurants by cuisine

Categories below are pretty self-explanatory, though note that "Indian" includes Bangladeshi, Indian and Pakistani restaurants.

Fusion

Georgian

Greek

Hungarian

Indian

See also Sri Lankan.

Index

INDEX OF RESTAURANTS BY CUISINE

Index

Index of restaurants by name

A-Z INDEX OF RESTAURANTS BY NAME

Index

Index